IMPROVING INSTRUCTIONAL PRODUCTIVITY IN HIGHER EDUCATION

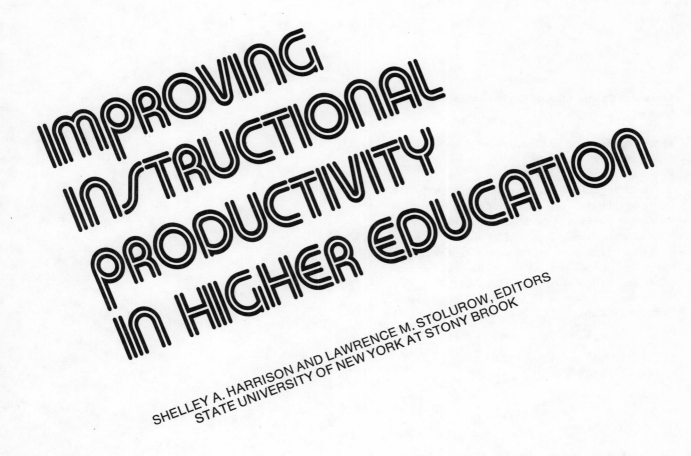

IMPROVING INSTRUCTIONAL PRODUCTIVITY IN HIGHER EDUCATION

SHELLEY A. HARRISON AND LAWRENCE M. STOLUROW, EDITORS
STATE UNIVERSITY OF NEW YORK AT STONY BROOK

Educational Technology Publications
Englewood Cliffs, New Jersey 07632

Library of Congress Cataloging in Publication Data
Main entry under title:

Improving instructional productivity in higher
  education.

  Proceedings of a symposium sponsored by the U.S.
Office of Education and the National Institute of
Education, and held at the State University of New
York at Stony Brook, Sept. 1973.
  1. College teaching—Congresses. 2. Educational
technology—Congresses. 3. Individualized instruction
—Congresses. I. Harrison, Shelley A., ed.
II. Stolurow, Lawrence M., ed. III. United States.
Office of Education. IV. National Institute of
Education.

LB2301.I53   378.1'2   74-23506
ISBN 0-87778-079-X

This work was produced by The Research Foundation of the State University of New York with
support from the National Institute of Education
under Contract No. OEC-0-73-6812. However, its
contents are the responsibility solely of the Research
Foundation of the State University of New York and
are in no way the responsibility of the National
Institute of Education.

Library of Congress Catalog Card Number: 74-23506.

International Standard Book Number:
0-87778-079-X.

Printed in the United States of America.

First Printing: January, 1975.

PREFACE

Symposium

The United States Office of Education and the National Institute of Education jointly sponsored a three-day Symposium, in September of 1973, on technology-based systems for improving productivity in Higher Education. The Symposium was hosted by the State University of New York at Stony Brook under the joint supervision of Professor Shelley A. Harrison of the School of Engineering and Professor Lawrence M. Stolurow, Chairman of the Department of Education.

Higher Education faces increasing demands for more and varied educational experience by the consumer (students and parents) and diminishing fiscal resources available to support this educational enterprise. Technological systems offer the potential for meeting a number of these needs including an increase in productivity. This Symposium examines a range of critical issues relating to the successful use of educational technology directed toward increasing productivity in both traditional and nontraditional settings. Equal concern is given both fiscal and quality of life variables as are gains in cognitive skills, critical thinking, and improved attitudes of all involved with education: students, faculty, administrators, parents, and the community.

Technology-based educational systems are best studied in the context of specific *learning environments.* This approach places primary emphasis on real learning needs and sets the stage for discussing potential technology-based solutions. The essential premise of this Symposium is that a thoughtful marriage of an engineering "systems approach" and behavioral objectivism may well offer the support necessary for wider access to better, more individualized learning at improved costs.

In Institutions of Higher Education and Institutions of Continuing Education, today's society is confronted with *three learning environments:*

1. Grouped and Bounded Learning Environments

2. Individualized, Bounded Learning Environments

3. Personalized, Open Learning Environments

Each of these three learning environments is, in turn, a day-theme for our three-day Symposium. Space-time *bounded* environments refer to institutionalized educational systems exhibiting definite learning requirements, entrance requirements, physical locations, and definite space, time, and resource constraints on the teaching/learning process. Technology support of both conventional and individualized learning in bounded environments occupies the discussions on day-one, and day-two, respectively. The third day addresses *open,* more personalized environments free of many requirements and constraints of institutionalized education. These include home study, continuing education, and cultural activities.

Each expert speaker addresses a technology-based system supportive of a specific learning environment. Speakers discuss *mode and media, management,* and *measurement* as addressed by their systems.

> *Mode and Media:* What procedures are utilized to define educational goals and institutional objectives? How are mode and media treatments decided upon? What are major considerations in production, delivery, maintenance, and revision of system components?

v

Management: Who takes part in the learning environment? How does personal management proceed? What form does personal management take? What form does program and institutional management take? How are resources (people, materials, space, time) managed?

Measurement: How does the system provide for measurement and adaptive feedback on personal achievement, effectiveness of environment (people, things), learning (cognitive, skill, affective), costs (capital, development, recurrent, revision)?

Discussants and reactants at each session analyze:

. . . effectiveness of system in supporting the learning objectives

. . . effectiveness of system in measurement and management of resource allocation and costs

. . . effectiveness of system in gaining acceptance, validation, and providing adequate teacher training

. . . comparative relationship to other demonstrated systems operating in common learning environments

Early in the Symposium it became obvious that the issue is not whether educational technology can work and indeed improve productivity but whether institutions of higher education are, in fact, prepared to use it. Clearly, in order for educational technologies to be used effectively, an institution must have a well-defined sense of purpose, direction, and commitment. Campuses where technology has been and continues to be successful surely prove this point.

It is our hope that the information in this report will lead to the organization of study groups on campuses which will develop plans for action and policies to foster the growth and development of the most suitable and cost-effective technologies to meet local needs.

Productivity

"There is little confusion about the definition of productivity: outputs of a process are related to inputs and the relationship is taken to indicate productivity. The difficulties arise in making the concept operational and applying it."[*]

Unlike the commercial sector where profitability provides a pervading production criterion, the higher Education enterprise as yet possesses no useful set of measurement and interpretation procedures. A theory of teaching is long overdue. Without it we can only continue to be unsatisfyingly descriptive in our use of intrinsically limited productivity ratios such as FTE's, cost per student hour, etc.

Bound up in these questions of output/input measures of efficiency is the perhaps more fundamental question of effectiveness. But this requires the precise definition of instructional goals and learning objectives bearing in mind relevance to learners' present and future life and job environments. The production of intelligent, capable citizens is the charge and responsibility of institutions of higher education. Until the goals (benefits) of this process are clearly enunciated we cannot even begin to develop useful cost/benefit analysis. Productivity analysis should be a dynamic, evolutionary process of setting educational goals, continually estimating and monitoring goal production costs, and improving production and output for the changing inputs.

Application of technology concepts and techniques to the general problem of resource allocation and program planning and budgeting is still in its infancy. This Symposium treats these matters in only rather general terms placing its major emphasis on the instructional process and supportive technology-based development and presentation systems.

---

[*]Productivity: Burden of Success, by William Toombs, ERIC/Higher Education Research Report, No.2, 1973.

Educational Technology

The Symposium addresses mainly the instructional aspects of educational technologies as these are of central priority and have received the majority of attention. Technology promotes a true systems approach in the adaptive development of curriculum, instructional delivery, performance, measurement, and evaluation. Course curricula are defined behaviorally in terms of their cognitive and affective instruction objectives—an imperative process enabling unambiguous communication and thus enhancing transferability of materials and measurability of performance. Instructional objectives are organized into small logical sets or modules amenable to instructional delivery support in one or another appropriate mode and medium combination. The speakers of this Symposium investigate the many ways in which technology supports the numerous strategies of instruction from the group-paced through the various self-paced, individualized environments that accommodate natural variations in learner preparedness, aptitude, and interest. The talks are by no means exhaustive in their coverage (that being well beyond the intended scope of the Symposium). They do, however, treat in depth most of the major successful technology endeavors in instructional learner-teacher organization and delivery in Higher Education today. The report reveals the status of several promising experiments currently in progress around the nation, as well as extensively documenting the development and delivery successes of England's Open University.

Issues and Problems

Open and frank discourse over a full spectrum of educational issues and problem areas pervaded the sessions and numerous informal gatherings. Discussions were vigorous and often argumentative. The air was one of deep concern for the issues and noticeable dedication to improving the quality of learning and reducing the cost of instructional delivery. Below, are highlighted several of the areas of major concern:

- Lack of adequately researched models of learning sufficient for higher education.

- Inadequate models and procedures for (a) curriculum and materials development, (b) formative evaluation, (c) faculty training, and (d) productivity analysis.

- Existence of major traditional foci of resistance to instructional innovation and development within institutions of higher education.

- Lack of legitimacy afforded research in learning and instructional system development.

- Inadequate professional and financial incentives.

- Lack of coordinated methods and agencies for transport and dissemination of R & D results in educational technology projects and applications.

The State University of New York campus at Stony Brook is happy to have been selected as the site for this forum on Higher Education. The School of Engineering and Department of Education at Stony Brook are actively engaged in numerous experimental and developmental projects involving technology-based learning systems. We hope that there will be free and rapid communication and dissemination of experiences and materials in educational technology efforts across the nation. The need and opportunity for innovation and change are at hand. It is our common responsibility to make thoughtful and effective use of available communication technologies.

The editors of this report acknowledge Ms. Fern Singer's tireless organizational and administrative efforts. We also thank Mr. Charles Miller for taping the Symposium Sessions and editing them onto individual cassettes, and Ms. Newilda LaGrandier for her tireless assistance in preparing copy and typeset.

Shelley A. Harrison
Lawrence M. Stolurow

CONTENTS

IV.   PERSONALIZED, OPEN LEARNING ENVIRONMENTS

V.   GENERAL SUMMARY AND RECOMMENDATIONS

IMPROVING INSTRUCTIONAL PRODUCTIVITY IN HIGHER EDUCATION

Part One

KEYNOTES

TECHNOLOGICAL INNOVATION IN A HOSTILE ENVIRONMENT:

PROBLEMS OF INCREASING PRODUCTIVITY IN HIGHER EDUCATION

Keith Lumsden
Professor of Economics
Graduate Business School, Stanford University

INTRODUCTION

This paper is concerned with the problems of introducing and evaluating technological innovations in the higher education industry. Given the incentive systems existing within established universities the paper argues that significant increases in educational productivity occurring through the adoption of technological innovations will be possible only if there is a massive research effort. Such a research effort is likely to prove invaluable even if it is mainly new institutions, unfettered by vested interests, which take advantage of the research results. The paper is in four parts. In the first, the various possible functions of the university are discussed together with the problems encountered when differences in perceived functions cause conflict. In the second part, the major obstacles to change are noted, given the existing structure of most of our major institutions of higher learning. The third portion is concerned with the inadequacy of much of past research on the economics of higher education. Finally a proposed research scheme is spelled out, which does not constitute an attempt to solve all of the problems raised earlier, but which is designed to yield the type of information on different pedagogies required by university decision-makers wishing to increase productivity in higher education.

COMPLEXITY OF THE UNIVERSITY

Economists have not been particularly helpful in providing a theory of the university which is both realistic and useful for policy implementation. Traditional theories of optimizing behavior, of equating marginal social benefits with marginal social costs are theoretically valid but of little practical significance for the university administrators. Indeed, many of the economists concerned with efficiency problems and armed with the tools of their trade, have avoided efficiency studies in the higher educational industry since that which is to be maximized cannot be agreed upon by a majority of the diverse interested parties.

The functions of the university are several, the interest groups the university serves are many, the output choices of the university for all practical purposes are infinite, the prices of many of the output elements are not readily available, the underlying engineering production functions have seldom been identified, and, finally, current institutional arrangements discourage actions which could lead to less inefficiency.

While many of the above points are obvious, identification of each may be necessary if universities are to be forced to move towards the existing efficiency frontier or if universities will be compelled to adopt technological innovations which shift out of that frontier.

Perhaps the most widely held view of the function of the university is that of capital creation. Each year the university's intake is a crop of freshmen, eager and anxious to increase their net worth. (It is important to note that with few exceptions, freshmen about to enter university are not chosen randomly by a university from the "college age" population or even randomly from all applying.) Does this imply that universities believe that the greatest value added is attainable by admitting the brightest students as measured by scholastic aptitude tests? Two main paths, which may travel several miles as one, can be followed. The first provides the student with a general education; he does not learn any specific skills but his analytical abilities and sensibilities are sharpened; his potential productivity is enhanced and he may utilize few resources in the future finding out where his true occupational interests lie. The other path is for the student who knows, or learns quickly, where he is going. He wants to build bridges and the engineering and technology faculties show him how to build them, the social sciences teach him (or should teach him) where, when and if to build them. But the question must then arise, do we need the institution of the university, as we now know it, to achieve these aims? Why not utilize videotapes, correspondence materials, etc., and test the student by national examination; why must we construct expensive buildings and bring students together for several years on a campus? From the point of view of the university as a producer of human capital, the answer must be that students learn enough from each other by being together or in close contact with the faculty to justify such costs. If we modify the pure capital formation approach and allow consumption benefits to be added, a case can be made for the campus university if these consumption benefits (plus the possible investment benefits mentioned above) outweigh the costs.

A second function of the university is to provide to prospective employers information about job candidates of different abilities who attend the university and to these job candidates information about their relative abilities to perform different tasks. One extreme hypothesis asserts that a university education adds nothing whatsoever to the abilities or capacities of an individual, but provides a set of filters and a set of obstacle courses through which and over which an individual must pass if he wishes to receive the official stamp that he is ably suited for society's better jobs. While, in this view, no increase in any one individual's productive capacity occurs through university attendance and graduation, the whole process by providing useful information to employers and graduates is extremely valuable to them. Given that the filter is effective, an employer no longer bears the risk of hiring unsuitable job candidates and can more efficiently allocate different types of labor to different job categories. Output is increased, employers are better off and support the filtering institution as do students who expect to graduate.

Treating the university as a filter yields some startling results. First, since more able individuals benefit by being officially classified as superior, even if no consumption or investment benefits accrued from attending a university, they would be willing to pay for an "education" if the expected lifetime earnings, appropriately discounted, exceeded the real costs. One outcome, in this circumstance, at odds with the traditional assumption about higher education, is that the private return from higher education may exceed the social return, i.e., the return to graduating students can exceed the productivity increase resulting from their "education," the difference being a decrease in incomes to the unfiltered workers.

Second, if the filtering system were ineffective, i.e., if unsuitable job candidates managed to be admitted to and graduated from universities (for example, through zero entrance requirements and watered down course and examination standards), the university would no longer serve any useful filtering function; everyone having a degree prevents a university education from being a distinguishing employee characteristic.

Third, if the chief filter is being *admitted* to the university, i.e., everyone admitted eventually graduates, then the university as it exists should be abolished with the exception of the admissions committee and the admitting office. When admitted, students are awarded a degree and the employer has the information he requires for efficient labor allocation among different jobs.

A third function of the university, claimed in both word and deed by many faculty members to be the main function of the university, is the production of research and repository of information and data. How much research and which research should be undertaken are not easily answered equations from the viewpoint of maximizing society's welfare. What is agreed upon is the fact that most of the research output is a public good and can be used by any individual in society without excluding others. It is this nature of the good that dictates that it be financed out of public funds, if indeed it is worth producing.

The university not only produces its own research output but also stores that output and copies of the output of similar institutions in libraries and computer centers. In addition, information and knowledge is embodied in the academic human capital within the university, i.e., in the community of academic scholars. This stock of capital, both non-human and human, that is stored in the university is available to pass on knowledge to future generations (education) and to make further additions to society's fund of knowledge (research).

One could hypothesize other functions of a university, such as serving local or national pride or providing a "baby-sitting," perhaps more accurately "adolescent-sitting," service to parents and so forth, but such functions are less seriously claimed than the three discussed above. The importance of being aware of the several possible functions of the university is that many actions of individuals or groups associated with the university are directly related to what they perceive the function of this institution to be and very often differences in these perceptions lead to significant conflict within the university. Such conflict poses significant constraints on the ability of the university to achieve efficiency in the short-run, i.e., with existing faculty and facilities. But perhaps of even greater significance, they limit the pace by which technological progress can proceed in the university.

Obstacles to Change

Within most universities there are five distinct "interest" groups: students, faculty, administration, library and computer personnel and other service staff. Some students—especially advanced graduate students—become part-time faculty members and some faculty members in turn become part-time administrators. For the sake of simplicity we shall ignore the internal conflicts of those who wear two hats.

Outside groups with interests in the university include government, foundations and private donors, professional associations, business firms, parents and potential students.

Essentially, outside interest groups determine the budget constraints within which all modern universities must operate. The government and parents finance the bulk of teaching and the government, foundations, private donors and businesses support most of the research. The government is under political pressure from households with children to provide college and university education at low cost. Foundations and private donors may be concerned with the general welfare of society and believe that money spent in higher education furthers this aim. Or they may have a narrower objective and specify that their donations be spent on "neglected" research or "critical" teaching programs. The private donor may also be concerned about leaving a monument to his or some relative's memory. Unfortunately the monument is often more grand and less efficient from the teaching/research viewpoint than it need be; in this respect what the church in bygone days obtained, the university now receives. Business firms, like the government, are concerned with both the graduates of the university and its research output and in some instances with the social image attached to the support of "worthwhile" activities. Parents undoubtedly differ in their perceived function of the university. Some view it from the value-added side (consumption, investment or both), others favor the filter hypothesis and still others see the university as the institution within which their children become adults. Finally, prospective students may see the university in any one or in some combination of its many possible roles.

Without belaboring the point there is ample evidence that when resources are not being allocated in the university in a manner which meets the approval of an outside group, pressures are often exerted to "rectify" the situation. When the outside group approves, appreciation can take the form of increased support, both financial and political. The retention of "communist" professors and the build-up of the successful football team are often quoted examples.

Perhaps even greater conflicts of interest lie within the university itself. Once admitted, students tend to demand (besides subsidized housing, subsidized food, recreational facilities, etc.) "academic power." Agitation exists for "relevant" courses, black studies, reduced or no course requirements and the abolition of grading. A significant portion of administration and faculty believe that students should have no, or few, consumer sovereignty rights. The students have not been around long enough to appreciate the importance of prerequisites, they can be manipulated by the charismatic but incompetent professor in the contentless course, and once admitted they have an incentive to "water-down" courses and erode grading standards. The administrators who want to preserve the integrity of the filter and the faculty who are concerned with academic prestige have a desire to maintain high standards. Part of the conflict arises because of the different perceptions the various interest groups have in the main function of the university. For example, those students who want a degree as a certification that they have passed through the university filter undoubtedly want to maximize the probability that they will get a degree and also want their stay at the university to have as high a consumption value as possible. From this standpoint it is quite rational to oppose any restrictions imposed by the administration or faculty.

Whether students believe the value added or the filter theory, once a student is admitted to the university many goods and services are provided, or are expected to be provided, at zero incremental financial cost to the student. Faculty time is one such commodity where conflicts arise. Since students are not charged tuition by the amount of faculty time they consume, there is no explicit reason why the student should not consume a faculty member's time until marginal benefits equal marginal (zero?) costs to the student. The opportunity cost of all (most?) faculty members' time is significantly greater than zero, and every hour spent with a student is an hour less of research, administration or leisure. Since the payoff to a professor in spending more time with a student than that "dictated" by the administration is, to all intents and purposes, zero, professors will not only make themselves scarce but also avoid where possible the fiats laid down by the administration. Those faculty who are readily available to students seldom receive the plaudits of their colleagues because they make their colleagues appear as shirkers and also by just being there are liable to inherit their absent colleagues' share of problems and students. Since there is no rationing device for determining optimal student-faculty contact, this will remain an area of conflict between students and faculty. The absence of incentives to resolve this conflict efficiently is apparent; in those few institutions where students are given a choice of attending live lectures or live television (or videotaped) instruction. Assuming the same quality of instruction, there is little incentive for the student to give up the spontaneity and intimacy of the live lecture when there is no difference in cost to him. The fact that production costs are substantially different for the two outputs does not affect the student because he is charged a flat tuition fee no matter which pedagogy he elects.

This is not to argue that technological innovations within the existing framework could not benefit enrolled students. If, for example, students were shown that the resources saved from videotaping say 5 to 6 required courses were to be allocated to additional course offerings, small seminars or whatever, the benefits would be obvious. If however the choice is between the live versus the non-live lecture, for example, *ceteris paribus* the latter will almost consistently prove to be less appealing, especially if it is an isolated case. What makes sound economic sense within the flat tuition fee system of most universities would be a tuition refund to those students economizing on scarce university resources. In such a case the students, administrators and faculty could all be better off and no one need be worse off.

The faculty can be separated with respect to their opinions regarding the relative importance of the research, teaching and filtering functions of the university. Since, for most universities, appointments and promotions are based on research output the major apportionment of faculty members' resources will be biased against teaching. Since many outside interest groups demand a minimum of teaching inputs, there is a lower limit of resource commitment to teaching which the faculty collectively cannot hope to evade in the long-run. There is no incentive for the faculty to maximize value-added to the student body; the alleged fact that better students are easier to teach and demand fewer contact hours* are adequate selfish reasons for faculty insisting that only the best students are admitted despite the fact that maximizing value-added might dictate that relatively few contact hours be devoted to the highly motivated "bright" students and relatively many hours to the poorly motivated "dull" students. Admission to the university of minority students, on paper underqualified, is often opposed by faculty

---

*In the United Kingdom, for example, faculty members of polytechnics who on average have lower calibre students than the universities maintain that students' demands and problems are such that no time is available for research; similar arguments are heard from junior colleges' faculty who have research aspirations.

members not because they do not believe in egalitarianism but because of potential encroachment on research time. Since many students, who play a passive role throughout their university lives, could well be "educated" through non-labor intensive pedagogies—videotaped lectures, packaged materials, programmed instruction, computer assisted instruction plus some faculty or teaching assistant inputs, the question arises why such innovations, which have proven to be, in many instances, equally effective as live instruction, are not enthusiastically endorsed by the faculty. The principal reason is that, under the present university *modus operandi,* resources saved by adopting technological advances cannot be readily appropriated by the innovative faculty member. To take an extreme example, the professor who videotaped all of last year's lectures and whose current students learn just as much by using these videotapes and are just as happy with their course (additional non-human, low marginal cost inputs may be added) without any actual student-faculty contact, is unlikely to receive full teaching salary from the dean or department head. Note that this is not because the output was not forthcoming, e.g., students learned less, rather it is because the standard inputs, especially live teaching time, were not employed. The lack of incentives for innovation exists for the department as well as the individual instructor. If the department can maintain output but reduce costs, the departmental budget is liable to be reduced and the efficiency gain cannot be captured by the department collectively. Thus, there is little incentive for the department to be efficient or to adopt new pedagogies which reduce costs while maintaining output.

Because of substantial economics of scale it is possible that the full potential of certain pedagogies will be realized only in either the largest of universities or in the combined efforts of several institutions. With minor exceptions there has been essentially no effort on the part of institutions of higher learning to attempt to allocate resources more efficiently on an industry-wide basis. Again the main reason is that the gains from such efforts are unlikely to be enjoyed by one of the principal interest groups in higher education, i.e., the faculty. The history of craft unionism yields many examples where technological innovations are embraced only when sufficient incentives exist for the principal actors to accept change or when the alternative of maintaining the *status quo* forebodes a greater loss in well being. Without a system for efficiently reconciling competing interests of different groups with a stake in the university, the actions of administrators in seeking local and national stature, tranquility on campus, "efficient and equitable" budgetary allocations, academic freedom, relatively magnificent offices, air conditioning and efficient secretaries for presidents and deans, and impressive buildings pleasantly landscaped, will often be vociferously opposed by students and faculty. Similarly the interests of the librarian in maximizing the number of titles, preserving rare books from anxious little hands and housing the collection in an expensive building are not necessarily in accord with student and faculty interests. Finally, other employees of the university, such as maintenance staff, desiring higher wages and union representation, pre-school and child-care centers, admission privileges for their children to the university and so forth are competing for resources sought by other interest groups.

Does the existence of competing interests and the lack of an efficient allocation mechanism dictate that we shall continue to bungle through? The answer need not be negative; for example, it is highly likely that the recent cutback in university financing has forced many institutions to reduce costs, without any appreciable reduction in output. But such savings are obviously limited without the adoption of technological change, i.e., the cutback may have forced many universities to move closer to the production frontier without shifting that frontier outward. In order to shift the frontier outward under present institutional arrangements it will be necessary to motivate faculty to become innovators through research rewards. Once more efficient teaching pedagogies have been validated as cost-effective, university administrations under pressure to cut costs can force these new practices on the faculty. The most fruitful research is likely to emerge only if agencies such as the National Science Foundation, the National Institute of Education and private foundations make a substantial commitment to the type of large-scale research which will provide information on the costs and effectiveness of pedagogies with different characteristics for students with different characteristics.

The Shortcomings of Past Research

Much of the research supported in the past has not been concerned with providing academic decision-makers with the information required for them to increase educational productivity. The economist's approach

9

to higher education has been largely confined to the following question: What is the proper allocation of resources between higher education and alternative uses? This question has been approached from several points of view, each of which provides at best an ambiguous answer and none of which begins to address the problems relating to the internal efficiency of the higher education system.

The most widely adopted research approach has been to estimate from data on differences in individuals' incomes and educational attainments the rate of return to investment in additional years of higher education. Whether society would make better use of its resources by allocating more or less of them to higher education exceeded or fell short of that on alternative investment opportunities.

A second approach has been to measure the aggregate cumulated educational investment embodied in the labor force for different years and to infer from time series data on aggregate output, labor, physical capital and the stock of educational capital the contribution that a marginal addition to the stock of educational capital would make to the production of national output. Again, given the costs of adding to educational capital, it is possible to calculate a rate of return to educational investment to be compared to the rates of return on alternative forms of investment with obvious implications for resource allocation.

A third approach has been to calculate average educational attainments of employees in different skill and occupational categories and, on the basis of forecasts in manpower requirements, to determine what resources must be devoted to higher education if the required numbers of employees with different qualifications are to be forthcoming. Clearly, if the resources available to higher education fall short of the needs calculated in this way, then according to the model it would pay to eliminate the gap.

Each of these three lines of inquiry has been marked by serious limitations resulting from inadequacies in the available data and untested restrictive assumptions in the theory. This paper will not attempt to summarize such shortcomings since they have been well documented in other publications. However, even if the research objectives could be fully attained, they would provide only a limited basis for educational policy, since they fail to suggest how resources allocated to higher education can be most effectively used. The full complexity of what is involved in the rational planning of higher education is only apparent when the problems in allocating resources between higher education and other economic activities are considered jointly with those relating to internal efficiency. It seems to be an unwise research strategy, past research efforts notwithstanding, to consider the first set of problems and ignore the second, when the elimination of substantial internal misallocations would have profound influence on the optimum share of resources to be devoted to higher education.

The inadequacy of the results of past research was made painfully evident by the crises that rocked higher education during the past decade. Hit by the dissatisfaction of taxpayers and the antagonism of students, together with rising costs and dwindling resources, educational decision-makers found themselves having to carry on with business as usual in the absence of a model of higher education which could form a basis for rational planning. It is in this context, that academics, dissatisfied with their own accomplishments and more acutely aware of the problems of colleges and universities, have begun to take a new look at the economics of education.

One theme that pervades much of the new effort in the field is that economics research on higher education must find a way to deal with the fact that the output produced by the contemporary university includes numerous and diverse components, whose quantities and prices are difficult to measure. The present lack of meaningful quantitative information creates serious difficulties for educational decision-makers, both within and outside universities. Unless techniques for measuring these variables can be found or methods of rational decision-making that do not depend on this information can be devised, the prospects for significant increases in efficiency will remain poor.

The fact that university output is multidimensional is not in itself the source of the analytical difficulty. If the components of university output were like other goods, it would be a relatively straightforward matter to apply the calculus of optimizing behavior to the allocation problem and find a reasonably efficient solution. As every elementary economics student knows, in order for an educational planner to determine the optimal amount of the different components of university output, it would be necessary for him to have information about both technology and preferences. Technology can be described in terms of production relations which indicate the amounts of each good that can be obtained from different combinations of inputs. Given the costs of acquiring various inputs, technology determines the cost of producing an extra unit of each good. Preferences, on the other hand, indicate the terms on which consumers would be willing to exchange one good for another. Given total income, preferences determine the price consumers would be willing to pay for an extra unit of each good. Clearly, as long as consumers value an extra unit of any component of university output more highly than it costs to be produced, then the university should expand production of that component.

In order to apply this simple model, it is necessary to obtain detailed information on the production relations which constrain the choices of university decision-makers. This will require large-scale research efforts which produce data on the costs and effectiveness of different pedagogical techniques for different types of students. Once this information is available it will be possible for a university administration to find the least-cost way of producing a given bundle of university outputs. What is being suggested is that the innovations which will bring about substantial increases in educational productivity will take place only through the combination of reliable cost-effectiveness research and the application of its results through administrative fiat.*

Suggested Research Approach

To assess reliably the efficacy of different pedagogies in any subject for students of varying characteristics requires a large-scale experiment financed with public funds to evaluate all promising pedagogies in many and diverse colleges and universities. A Massive effort is required, not only because of the large number of variables involved, but also because there is insufficient variation in existing methods of instruction in higher education to permit accurate evaluating of alternatives. Public funding is essential, apart from reasons already discussed, because institutions may be unwilling to allocate resources to explore the effectiveness of new technologies when the private costs to any one institution outweigh its expected private gains.

The number of universities to actively participate in the proposed experiment must be sufficiently large to

  i)   provide a broad spectrum of student, faculty and other institutional input characteristics

  ii)   allocate the different pedagogies to be evaluated over the ranges of characteristics above

  iii) assess different media and instructional mixes and

  iv)   provide a sufficient data base on input mixes and various outputs for statistical analysis.

The exact number of universities required therefore will be a function of the range of the input characteristics to be treated and the number of different pedagogies to be evaluated. Marginal costs incurred by potential participating institutions will have to be recompensed to reduce search costs, to ensure adequate numbers and to enlist the cooperation within each institution of the course organizer.

In order to obtain economies of scale in disseminating procedural information, cross fertilization of ideas and identification with the research team by the participating institutions, an initial conference with all parties concerned would be desirable. It is essential that unanimity of opinion on course objectives and procedures be achieved at such a conference. The most appropriate time for the conference would be approximately one full year before the actual experiment took place.

---

*While the resistance to change in established institutions of higher learning may be too strong to permit sufficient change to increase efficiency significantly, new institutions without vested interests may well be where the technological progress will occur.

It would be the responsibility of the principal researchers and consultants to design and prepare measuring instruments of output. Cost data, both average and marginal, would be required for each pedagogy analyzed. The total experiment, if the results are to be definitive and accepted, will have to be carried out under rigorous experimental procedures. To the extent that learning by doing may occur with new technologies certain portions of the experiment may be repeated during a second year in selected institutions. After the experimental period the data would be collected and analyzed and the results disseminated through publications and conferences to as large an audience as possible.

One of the major problems associated with designing and carrying out such a project concerns the defining and measuring of educational output. The failure to deal adequately with this problem is one reason why most research on cost-effectiveness has not convinced the skeptical educator to change his teaching practices. Typically, for the sake of simplicity, experimenters take account of only one or two dimensions of output which are regarded by many to be among the less important. Educational outputs can be put into at least three categories: increases in students' cognitive skills; changes in students' affective characteristics; and the enjoyment or consumption students obtain from the educational experience. Thus, any major research effort must take into account the range of outputs that fall into all three categories.

The first category contains numerous elements, many of which involve the learning of subject matter. One of the first steps that would need to be taken by the researcher is to define the body of material to be included in the courses under study which must be common to all pedagogies being evaluated. At the same time, what constitutes mastery of the subject should be clearly enunciated. In economics, for example, this would include the following:

(i)   a capacity to follow and sustain an economic argument and to make logical inferences from given information;

(ii)   the ability to set out and communicate to others a logical argument in economics;

(iii)   the ability to be aware of assumptions made implicitly in the use of an economic model to assist a process of reasoning and to perceive how a modification of the assumptions might affect the conclusions;

(iv)   the ability to understand the mutual interrelations and interdependencies of the various elements in an economic system and to take account of them in handling economic problems;

(v)   the ability to understand and explain the economic effects of important economic institutions on economic policies;

(vi)   the ability to make appropriate inferences from quantitative data;

(vii)   the ability to apply to an economic problem the models of economic analysis that are most appropriate to it.

Cognitive learning, however, is not limited to mastery of course subject matter. It includes as well the acquisition of general intellectual skills such as the ability to reason logically, to communicate effectively, assimilate information rapidly, etc. While any good measure of student performance on subject matter will reflect these general skills, it is important that the researcher explicitly define how the learning of general skills enter into aggregate educational output.

Adequate measurement of the various components in the cognitive category may require a battery of tests, ranging from standard objective examinations to written essays to the working of complex problems. An additional reason, invariably neglected by researchers, for a variety of measuring instruments is that students with different characteristics perform in a significantly different fashion in different types of tests. For example, in economics, recent preliminary research findings have shown that students performing well in objective tests do not necessarily perform well on essay examination and case analyses and that certain student characteristics are reliable predictors of how well certain classifications of students will perform on different types of test instruments.

If such research findings are substantiated it may be impossible to construct a single valued measure of output which would be universally appealing. Such an index would require a consensus on the weighting of each of the test instruments and this may be unattainable. The fact that a research proposal raises such an issue is no reason for substituting an incomplete measure of output; the issue can be, at least partially resolved, either by accepting the weight of experts in the field or allowing potential users of the results to choose their own weights.

Further information about course output may be obtained from the students themselves. While the validity of student opinion on courses and teachers has been seriously questioned as a basis for rewards to faculty, their considerable potential for research purposes has been essentially ignored. If the producers of educational output were subject to the same forces as are the suppliers of most commodities in our economy they could not afford to ignore the opinions of consumers. While faculty and administrators might remain relatively immune to the force of student sovereignty, it may well be that students' opinions of what they obtain from courses and faculty are more accurate measures of educational output in the cognitive category than all conventional tests combined. Consequently, a carefully defined student questionnaire is a critical element in a study of this kind.

In attempting to measure the efficacy of different pedagogies, proponents of increased productivity in higher education need to go beyond just the measure of output relating to changes in cognitive skills and assess what may be just as important to human capital formation, namely changes in affective characteristics. For example, students' feelings about and attitudes towards intellectual endeavor and the relevance of subject areas will affect their career choices. (Anecdotal tales abound about how famous men chose their fields; Max Planck, the famous German physicist, opted out of economics because he felt it too difficult a subject for him.) The manner in which a course is presented, given the subject matter, by influencing students' emotional outlook, will help determine time spent on a subject, opinion of courses and faculty, choice of undergraduate and graduate study and ultimately career choice. Since such factors could have far-reaching implications for both individuals and society in general, sound reasons appear to exist for attempting to assess changes in affective characteristics in the suggested research approach. Thus the student questionnaires should include questions designed to provide information on changes in affective characteristics.

The problems associated with defining and measuring inputs and accurately costing out different pedagogies, while much less difficult than those that arise in connection with educational output, are nevertheless real and substantial. How should different pedagogies be characterized? What are the differences between average and marginal costs and between short- and long-run costs? How can differences in the quality, as opposed to the type, of input be taken into account? While answers to these questions will not be attempted here, they are an essential element in any good research proposal on the cost-effectiveness of different techniques of educational production.

The above research proposal has implicitly assumed that universities, to some degree, create value-added in their teaching function. Earlier in the paper we advanced the hypothesis that another function of the university is filtering students. If one considers the university purely as a filtering institution, much of the proposed research is irrelevant. To achieve efficient resource allocation in such a situation requires only an analysis of relative costs and effective filtering potential of different courses and testing instruments. Since almost no one believes that zero value-added occurs in teaching in the university system, the research herein advocated should provide the type of information necessary to evaluate technological innovations and increase efficiency in higher education.

LEARNING, TECHNOLOGY, AND THE POTENTIAL INCREASE OF

PRODUCTIVITY IN HIGHER EDUCATION

Robert T. Filep
Associate Commissioner for Educational Technology
Director, National Center for Educational Technology,
U.S. Office of Education

— Congratulations to the organizers of the meeting!

— The group of participants assembled is indeed impressive.

— Educational technology and productivity, they sound like they should go together like love and marriage, horse and carriage and so forth!

Today I would like to share some thoughts with you in three areas:

1. Briefly, how do we define this new approach: Educational technology!

2. Any endeavors exploring ways for increasing productivity in higher education must take into consideration the changing nature of the learner as well as having a viewpoint which considers the faculty and administrators also as learners.

3. Quality and quantity of productivity that we seek must be reviewed in the context of the goals of higher education — yesterday, today and tomorrow.

Educational Technology

In trying to define educational technology, I am reminded of Justice Potter Stewart's opinion in Jacobellis vs. Ohio; I shall not attempt to define pornography, but I know it when I see it.

Almost everyone is looking for a definition of educational technology, some say it's the parts of instruction — aids and hardware, some say it's the process of instruction — determining needs and strategies — selecting and designing materials — using them with students — evaluating the results. Some claim it's the people of instruction — the students and the teachers. Most of us would probably agree a definition of educational technology includes all of those in a synthesis of the parts — the process — and the people, and perhaps most of us would agree that beyond the jargon and the buzz words, the term "Educational Technology" means simply the application of modern instructional systems and media to the learning process. As such, it *can be a total approach and* not just a bandage effort. Certainly, the process is not exclusively centered around the learner, it *must* include faculty, learners, administrators, and support staff. In short, all those involved in making teaching decisions. Clearly then, process success cannot be predicated entirely on successful machine- or text-related programs. Rather, it will depend in great part on the number of decision-makers who have been effectively introduced into the process of choosing teaching means and teaching ends.

The approach to the subject of the symposium could be along three lines; these three lines can be clearly separated, although they are intertwined for all practical purposes. During the symposium primarily the approach that I associate with monism was followed. I believe that the other two approaches are equally important, and I would like to draw attention to them here.

The three approaches to utilizing educational technology that I distinguish are:

A.   *Pragmatic Approach*

The pragmatic approach would be to look at what we have in educational technology that has been tested and what has proven to be useful for specific situations. This inventory and evaluation procedure should of course be nationwide. The second step of the pragmatic approach would be to identify situations in which the successful experiments — which have been selected out in the first inventory step — can be repeated with a large probability of equal success. The third step would be the implementation of step two.

B.   *The Pluralist Approach*

One way to think about the use of educational technology is to ask: What can it do to aid in solving the present *AD HOC* problems we are facing in education, or in another form the question is: How does educational technology relate to the present needs for the education system? More in *concerto* one could consider only

—Whether educational technology can be an alternative to on-campus instruction

— Of what use is educational technology in reducing student unrest, dropouts, etc.

and concentrate on those types of *AD HOC* needs.

I call this a pluralist approach for two reasons:

— The *AD HOC* needs could be fulfilled by means which are detrimental to other elements of the system and may create new problems (Classical Example: the creation of the nation-wide freeway network was considered an *AD HOC* need in the fifties to solve the military and civilian transport problems; it created the present *AD HOC* problem of pollution by combustion engines). Consequently, any utilization of educational technology must consider second order effects.

C.   *The Monist Approach*

While I recognize the importance of the last approach, the other two approaches should be pursued in parallel. However, we cannot lose sight of the fact that educational technology provided us with tools and techniques whereby productivity questions can be examined. The productivity theme was sounded very early in the history of educational technology when B. F. Skinner announced his "Twice as much learning in half the time." You recall that he, Holland, and Arnstein were trying to consider a science course for non-science majors. Students were utilizing self-paced instructional devices to garner the profane dimension of a psychology course (terminology, laws, etc.) which would allow them to then sit with Skinner, et al., to explore and interact "with great minds" exploring the sacred dimensions and theories of psychology.

The lecture or seminar was not discarded as a mode of teaching, nor is its demise advocated by the high priests of educational technology; it is one mode of learning and should be clearly linked to specific outcomes. *If conveying information is the main objective for utilizing a lecture*, then, it must be on the defensive. Almost everything we would like students to know we can place in their hands via paperback. Plays, too, can be read faster than when we sit through an evening at the theater, but reading doesn't take the place of the performance. Moreover, lectures provide the opportunity for trying out ideas while they are in the process of formation. They are thus part of the teachers' laboratory. The listener is not presented with a finished treatise, but rather observes a living mind at work, gaining an insight into strategies, not to mention the energy flow in exchange that takes place. This dimension of interaction between teacher and learner hasn't even begun to be measured. Let's take a moment and examine this learner.

Changing Nature of the Learner

Most of us grew up in an audio-age where the prime mode of communication was audio—the radio, via lecture, and the pulpit. In contrast, the average child today spends 16,000 hours viewing a TV set during the same years he spends 11,000 hours learning in elementary and secondary schools. He is a multi-image learner accustomed to learning from both audio and visual presentations. He has also come to expect effectively sequenced presentations with a rich use of color, graphics, and commercial television quality.

The students on our campuses today have a greater expectation for new and modern approaches that are technology based, effective, and relevant. Educational technology provides both the process and products to meet such needs.

The explosive increase in the volume of communication directed to the individual creates the need for resolving this concern. Thus, we might expect learners to deal with an increasing number of receptors — media for receiving communication, tape recorders, copying equipment, etc.

The growth of a differentiated communication system is part of a larger process by which our society has been producing a differentiated culture.

Richard Maisel, in the summer issue of the *Public Opinion Quarterly,* provides considerable data to support the thesis that mass media are shrinking in size relative to the total economy, and that the specialized media are becoming increasingly important.[1]

Educational technology is *in harmony with* this change, and suggests that one start out by thinking in terms of promoting learning, rather than providing instruction. To do this one needs a flexibility of approach that will accommodate the individual differences existent in all of us. I continue to be intrigued by the potential of the cognitive mapping activity of Joe Hill and Derek Nunney at Oakland Community College. Their idea of diagnosing students for most effective modes of learning (lecture, seminar, audio-tutorial, programmed text, individual study, etc.) based upon prior successes is that learning holds great potential. In this approach there is a dimension related to the schema suggested by Keith Lumsden where he outlined a method whereby students would be "billed accordingly" for each mode of instruction selected in relation to its cost (i.e., lecture, seminar, audio-tutorial, etc.), the mechanisms would be very easy. Think for one moment about a recent visit to Disneyland whereby a book of tickets marked A, B, C, D was purchased. Certain rides were selected based upon cost—others, because they were potentially more enjoyable.

Included in this booklet should be tickets that provide for "dropping out" for a semester or two, to participate in the world of work. The tickets should be designed, first, to make campus instruction more relevant, and secondly, to enable the student to make decisions relating to curricula that will provide some saleable skills upon graduation. A life-long learning, career education approach in higher education is long overdue.

The quality of education is not based on required courses; it is based on the interaction between teacher and student; in essence, we are giving much more freedom to both, but we are holding them more accountable for performance. We have not reduced rigor through flexibility; we have increased it, and need to *increase* it more if productivity is to be meaningful.

---

[1] Maisel, Professor Richard, "The Decline of the Mass Media," pp. 159-170, *Public Opinion Quarterly,* summer 1973, Columbia University, Journalism department, New York, N.Y.

Although appropriate reinforcers need to be implemented in faculty promotion considerations (i.e., developing an audio-visual course is equal to publishing one book, etc.), more important considerations are necessary, the majority of today's faculty did not learn, nor experience multi-image learning. For most of us, we were linear, print learners, and orbited and continue to orbit in what McLuhan so aptly describes as "The Gutenberg Galaxy."[2] Add to this fact that the body of knowledge in any field is increasing so rapidly that a faculty member may shun any new ideas for involvement in the process of the university to keep his head above water in his own field.

Consequently, educational technology must enter as a reinforcement, which the faculty member can utilize and also develop. However, time must be provided, as for research, to allow updating and media development activities; in fact, I would suggest that in today's world the sabbatical is obsolete and a "Cinq-Annee" for at least a half-year should be instituted to enable the faculty member to participate as a learner, as he evolves technology-based instruction. Residuals and royalties might accrue from the production and broad-scale use of television productions, media materials, etc. for both the university and the faculty member.

Paramount among our concerns for the success of such a project is that adequate faculty time be made available for intensive planning, production, and evaluation. A level of support for participating faculty must be provided which will, in effect, remove them almost completely from the many claims upon their time from university administrators and housekeeping groups. Faculty should also be retained at a level of support throughout the entire course development period (for instance, three years) to permit full participation in evaluation and resulting course modifications.

Further study should be given to encouraging participation in, and acceptance of, new forms of instruction by faculty who have not assisted directly with such preparation. Presumably they will become involved with a project of importance to the institution and to higher education, and their attitudes as well as those of their students should be evaluated.

Any discussion of the creative use of educational technology to increase productivity in higher education should take into consideration that the number of 18-year-olds graduating from high school in 1981 will be over 3 million, up 10% from 1971, and that the anticipated percent of high school graduates going on to college will increase about 6%. The current expenditure for institutions of higher education, public and non-public, for 1971-72 was $29.9 billion. Based upon constant 1971-72 dollars, which we know will not be true, we can anticipate almost a 50% increase by 1981 to $46 billion. Enrollments only up slightly—but expenditures increasing greatly.[3]

The contributions of the faculty, of course, are only one source of productivity growth. Other major sources include technological change, increased capital intensity, improved operating methods and work practices, economies of scale, advances in knowledge and shifting work to customers (the learners).

Evidence indicates that the bulk of the increases in productivity stem from sources that have little or nothing to do with the direct contributions of the faculty themselves.

For example, if 100 men moving a mound of dirt with hand shovels are replaced by one worker using a power shovel, the output per man-hour will go up tremendously.

The source of the increase, however, is not in harder work but the one remaining employee.

Rather, the source of gain comes from the advance in knowledge that permitted the power shovel to be invented, technological change in the invention of the power shovel itself, an increase in capital intensity embodied in the power shovel, and the better education and training that permitted a worker who was using a hand shovel to learn how to operate a power shovel.

[2] McLuhan, Marshall, *The Gutenberg Galaxy*, University of Toronto Press, Toronto, Canada, 1962.

[3] *Statistics of Trends in Education, 1961-62 to 1981-82*, National Center for Educational Statistics, U.S. Office of Education, Washington, D.C., January 1973.

Only the last of these — higher skill — might warrant an increase tied to his increased output per man-hour.

Taking another example, an important source of increased productivity in many industries in recent years has involved a shift of work from a company's employees to its customers.

Two outstanding illustrations are the trend toward self-service in retail stores and the switch to customer dialing of long-distance telephone calls.

Evaluation for Excellence

Institutions of higher education utilizing educational technology need courage but should not fear evaluation. For the very *essence of evaluation is to encourage the evolution of escalating levels of excellence.* Learning systems should undergo considerable development testing and revision with potential target audiences before they are used for larger audiences.

Careful examination of training to actual on-the-job requirements should be considerable. Faculty and student representatives should be encouraged to participate in the formulation of goals and objectives and pre- and post-evaluation.

We should be willing to examine very carefully the efforts of, for example, Britain's Open University, Empire State, S-U-N, and other forms of non-traditional instruction in higher education. By insisting on these formative and summative evaluations a great deal of information can be obtained without investing in the high set-up costs that have been "sunk" into activities. However, evaluations that are sensitive and innovative will need to be developed. Utilization of adaptations of market research will be required and, in some instances, development of new instruments and approaches to assessment; we must indeed beware of taking the approach in the anecdote about Mr. Green and his canary.

Challenges Ahead

University personnel utilizing educational technology need to be courageous and offer advice and counsel as to how to best proceed in the days ahead — particularly as they attempt to respond to the new clients, the new demands of the learning society, and the use of new approaches.

All I can say as a final item of guidance is "hold your hanky in a handy position." The early implementation of another technology, aviation, provided some caveats, and thanks to an olden 1920 pilot's manual from United Airlines[4] I would like to share these with you since they bear some analogous relationships with educational technology.

1.   Don't take the machine into the air unless you are satisfied it will fly.

2.   Pilots should carry hankies in a handy position to wipe off goggles.

3.   In case the engine fails on take-off, land straight ahead regardless of obstacles.

4.   No machine must taxi faster than man can walk.

5.   If you see another machine near you, get out of its way.

6.   Do not trust altitude instruments.

---

[4] Red Carpet Newsletter, United Airlines, October 1970.

7. Pilots will not wear spurs while flying.

8. If an emergency occurs while flying, land as soon as you can.

Think of the accomplishments the last 15 years have provided in educational technology — imagine what the next 15 could bring in higher education.

NEEDED: A COLLABORATIVE OPEN UNIVERSITY NETWORK

Joseph I. Lipson
Associate Vice Chancellor for Academic Affairs
University of Illinois at Chicago Circle

INTRODUCTION

There is a need for an educational system which transcends the limitations of the campus model. The documentation of this need is extensive. A general point to make is the following: Unprecedented numbers of people have and will have some post-secondary education and aspirations. These people will tend to be continuing consumers of education for the rest of their lives. They will have a higher probability of seeking additional education. Further, they will be somewhat more knowledgeable about what constitutes good education. As they look for programs to advance their interests, it is my contention that individuals with previous higher education will require advanced programs which in the past have been among the most expensive programs; i.e., training in the laboratory sciences, professional and pre-professional programs. It is not yet clear where the investment capital will come from for the new organizations which are needed. Also needed are new methods of marketing and financing education from the standpoint of the new class of student. It is the contention of the author that one way to deal with the problem (the only way which I have been able to think of) is through a coordinated collaborative effort *utilizing advanced educational technology,* among the states and with the aid of the federal government. The collaborative organization would have the objectives of developing *instructional* materials for systems of educational technology, *proficiency tests* to facilitate credit for knowledge acquired, systems of *student access* to reach those who cannot attend campus based institutions, and an effective information system to guide potential students with regard to the alternative opportunities.

Instructional Materials

The results of SESAME STREET, THE ELECTRIC COMPANY, and the courses of the British Open University have suggested that the way to truly effective mass use of educational technology is through increased investment in development of instructional materials. Materials which are "home made" have neither the qualities of craftsmanship, artistry, nor the proper incorporation of what is known about effective instructional design to be widely used. Thus the attempt to produce courses on a shoestring has resulted in giving educational technology a bad reputation.

The author's hypothesis is that poor instructional design is acceptable to the students so long as it is coupled to a social network which embeds the student's efforts in interpersonal situations which sustain his learning efforts; i.e., the campus system works in spite of the quality of teaching because the complex set of human expectations keeps the student working even in periods of discouragement, disinterest or contact with poor teaching. In systems which involve various degrees of teaching at a distance, these social supports are missing and, according to the hypothesis, this accounts for the high dropout rates of extension programs.

One of the remarkable achievements of the British Open University is their relatively low dropout rate (approximately 20% by one method of calculation). While it is true that the British system uses an extensive course tutor network to support the students' efforts, they also give credit to the high quality and excellent instructional design of the course materials. Thus the second hypothesis is that as the human network is weakened, the quality of the instructional materials must increase in order to hold the students' attention and to keep them actively involved.

20

Estimate of Magnitude and Cost

Let us estimate that for an effective Open University, approximately 300 courses will be needed. These need not be developed instantaneously, but should be developed over a five-year period. This would mean approximately 60 courses per year should be prepared to an extremely high standard of quality. Let us further estimate that each course will cost about $1,000,000 to produce. This estimate comes from both the British experience and other curriculum development projects. Thus an investment of approximately $60,000,000 per year is needed. Even after the first five-year period is completed, courses will need to be updated and new courses prepared. While $60,000,000 per year is a small fraction of the cost of higher education, at present there is no method of financing such efforts.

If each state were to take a portion of the task, the financing becomes much more reasonable. For example, Illinois with about 1/15th of the population of the United States would contribute 1/15th of the courses. Thus we would prepare four courses per year at a cost of $4,000,000 per year. This would not be too great an amount if the effort was recognized and endorsed by a suitable range of national organizations. It is also conceivable that the federal government would support either matching grants or a large-scale demonstration in one or two states. Some support is obviously behind some of the work which is taking place here and in other states. It is simply my contention that the scale and comprehensiveness is not yet sufficient to do the job which needs to be done. We are struggling along at subcritical mass.

Note: The estimate of 300 courses arose from the number of offerings in typical colleges and the need to provide an adequate range of options. It is not intended to be a precise number, but only the basis of rough estimates of effort and cost. Another point to be made is that some organization will be needed to monitor and manage the course production network. This will be returned to later. In any case, for the system to work, some assurance must exist that each course which is approved (by some procedure) will be used by large numbers of participating states.

Proficiency Tests

Adequate, widely accepted proficiency tests are an essential part of the design of an Open University network. They can provide for transferability of credit which is earned in a variety of institutions. They can certify learning which has taken place independently, outside of the formal system. Proficiency tests can also serve as placement tests, and diagnostic tests, for various degrees of individualized instruction. There are serious problems in developing proficiency tests in some areas of the curriculum and for some kinds of students who have learned much outside of traditional course structures. Nevertheless, the cost of developing such tests is much, much less, by my information, than course development. We should not allow the chain of the network to be weakened by a weak link in the testing component.

Much work is being done in developing reliable and valid proficiency tests. It is my intuitive judgment that there is a better match between talent and the task in this area than in any other component required for an Open University network.

System of Student Access

A wide variety of ways of enabling students to obtain instruction are being experimented with. These include courses by television, computer based education, independent study, modernized correspondence courses, individual student contracts, courses available through YMCAs and library networks — and various combinations of these. Different motivational and instructional arrangements are needed. Students who are handicapped have problems which will require thought in the design of methods of instruction.

The exact format of this component is probably least obvious at this time. The futures of videotape, computer assisted instruction, cable TV, are not clear; and their development and growth will be important considerations in the design of an Open University system. With adequate support and planning such approaches as open broadcast by TV and radio, broadcasting with on-site recording, educational newspapers, and other forms of media could change the design equations. I do not mean to imply that technological development can make or break the system. The educational and psychological dimensions are much more difficult and less well understood. It is true, however, that the state of uncertainty in technology makes it difficult to zero in on a particular format.

Further, some decision regarding media and technology should be made so that the courses which are produced will have a sufficient number of students using them to justify the investment. Whatever system is adopted will have to provide for maximum access by those who need an open system. Thus, while experimentation and development should continue, a format which offers maximum access and flexibility without excess cost should be agreed upon. While the author has some preferences and ideas, the decision should be based upon the best engineering and educational expertise that can be applied.

While aware of the difficulties, the analysis made by the British and by Dr. David Miller indicates that the cost (per student per course) of a system of student access can be brought well within the present conventional instructional costs. The importance of this analysis is that (except for development costs of the particular format) the cost can be treated on a per student basis and need not be sought as a capital expenditure.

In summary on this point, the system of student access should be established taking into account the current state of art in educational technology. Flexibility which is not so great that it drives up the cost of instruction is a desirable objective. Standardization of the media format which allows us to reach most of the potential students is another desirable factor. There is a tradeoff between flexibility and standardization of format which must be worked out.

Information System

Students need to know what educational programs are available to meet their personal objectives. They may also need to know something about their goals. If they are interested in preparing for a career, they need understandable descriptions of what a given career entails, what kind of life it offers. People need much better information about job prospects in various lines of work. Once they are certain that they want to seriously explore a given career, the system should provide the client with information about what kinds of preparation can be obtained, how long it will take, how much it will cost, what the entrance requirements to the various programs are, what the attrition rates are, etc.

Much work has been done along this line. The most advanced work which I am familiar with has been carried out in Oregon with a computerized career education information system. The system should inform of all appropriate programs: public schools, private schools, proprietary schools, on the job training programs, programs of the armed forces and the federal government, learning exchange programs and other nontraditional and open programs.

The most difficult part of keeping such a system is that of keeping the information complete and up to date. New programs are constantly being initiated while others are closing. Vital courses may be oversubscribed and credential requirements may be overly subscribed and credential requirements may suddenly be changed in certain professional programs. Because of this problem, it seems that a computer based system which feeds a network of terminals is the most effective model.

An additional consideration is the role of guidance counselors. It is my judgment that some human guidance is needed, but I am concerned about the past history of professionalizing guidance to the point that it becomes very expensive and the counselors become more and more remote from the people whom they should serve. It is my personal conclusion that the emphasis should always be on education. The individual should learn about the sources of information and how to interpret the information.

The cost of such an information system can be kept surprisingly low. The Oregon System operates at a cost of a few dollars per user per year.

An obvious possibility is to couple the information system with a testing service. The tests could be a wide variety ranging from aptitude and vocational interest tests to proficiency tests which can serve to obtain actual course credit. The services provided by such a network of information centers could be financed in a variety of ways. Probably some arrangement in which fees are adjusted to avoid some trivial use while not inhibiting serious clients would be ideal. Some subsidy of the overall operation of the information system and some way to forgive the fee for poor individuals would seem to be in the best interests of society.

Organization

An administration and coordination office is needed. Tasks, responsibilities and deadlines will need to be agreed upon. Schedule adherence will need to be monitored. Tests and instructional materials will need to be reviewed and tested for effectiveness. Completed products will need to be disseminated. Thus there will need to be an administrative officer and staff for each of the major components: instructional materials, proficiency tests, student access system, and information system.

In order to keep the network responsible to the needs of the higher education community and the states, some appropriate body with representation from the entire country will have to be selected or named to set policy. Perhaps, an elected Board of Directors of reasonable size could be practical policy setting group.

Such an arrangement immediately raises, in my mind, questions of autonomy and bureaucracy. I would hope for knowledge of organizations and organizational theory to avoid some of the dangers. In any case, my logic goes something like this: We need an open university system. An effective system needs a large investment of effort and capital. No individual institution or even individual state is likely to allocate the resources needed to do the job. Therefore, some means must be found to unify the strength of the higher education community.

The possible difficulties are the following:

It will be difficult to get a sizeable number of states to agree on a common formula for allocating resources and a common format for administering these resources.

The federal government will be reluctant to set up a national Open University effort of this magnitude because they would be charged with the interference in what are basically state operations. Even if they only fund and do not attempt to administer, they will be open to charges of unfairness in the allocation formula unless the funds are given in some relation to the size of the states.

It will be impossible to effectively administer such a confederation. The British Open University, it can be argued, works precisely because it is unified and focused.

In answer to the above difficulties, the following point can be made. The individuals who are attempting to set up an Open University are aware of the needs which have been outlined. The individuals I have spoken to have been uniformly enthusiastic about the basic idea which has been proposed. While it is not clear that enthusiasm for a far off idea will be translatable into action, it has been enough for me to continue to work on more detailed planning at our institution and our state.

SCENARIO

It may help make the concept more concrete if a brief sketch of the way the system would work is given.

Mrs. Jane Gurolski married when she was a junior in college. She had average to good grades. Her major was in history. When she married, she quit school to work to support her husband who was in graduate school. Now, Mrs. Gurolski has been out of school for 10 years. She has young children in school, but she wants to continue her education with a view of forming a career with more satisfaction and potential advancement than any she could manage with her present level of training.

Mrs. Gurolski noticed an ad in the daily paper encouraging people to make use of the career education information system. The ad promised that for a charge of two dollars one could explore career possibilities and find the educational programs to prepare one for a chosen career. Since one of the information offices was located in a nearby high school, Mrs. Gurolski stopped in one evening. (The information center kept hours until 10 p.m. each day and was open on weekends to encourage use by people who work.)

The information office was being manned by a young man who was earning money for his education by working at the center. In order to man the center, he had been given a three-week orientation and training program. A highly trained professional was in charge of ten of these offices and the professional had responsibilities to both the people who manned the offices and individuals who needed special forms of assistance.

The young man asked Mrs. Gurolski if he could help her. Somewhat awkwardly, she said that she wanted some way of establishing a career and possibly to find out how she could complete her education. The office aide asked her to sit down at a computer terminal and to type in the word, START. The computer program alterrately asked some questions, gave Mrs. Gurolski the chance to ask some questions, and offered lists of alternatives. Explorations of interests, limitations, past preparations, financial considerations, etc., gradually narrowed the number of desirable job targets and feasible educational programs suitable for Mrs. Gurolski.

Mrs. Gurolski became convinced that she should obtain her Bachelor's Degree in order to maximize her job chances. By taking each term for one year, one course at a local junior college, one Open University course which was available for home study, and one other Open University course which required her to come to a local learning center once a week, she could obtain her degree so that she would have several options upon completion of her undergraduate work. The courses included criminal sociology, general administrative theory, technical writing, and urban political science.

The forms which were needed were all available at the information center. Upon completion of the forms, they were immediately reviewed by the professional guidance person who was available to scan them by picture-phone, even though he was in an office about thirty miles away.

Mrs. Gurolski was assigned a personal tutor from the Open University whom she could call for assistance and who would monitor her progress and call her if trouble signals arose. In addition, she was given the names of people who were practicing in the careers that she was most interested in and showed the most aptitude for.

In each of the courses she signed up for, she was given a printout of five people who were taking the same course who lived nearby. Her name was also given to the other five. A letter encouraged the six students to meet and form a self-help group. She was also given the names of individuals who had completed the course who had indicated they would be willing to help students in the course.

Mrs. Gurolski was notified of acceptance into the courses by mail at her home. Thus, through the information center, she was able to renew her academic program by a single visit to a single office. She was able to establish a program which fitted her schedule limitations and her financial constraints. She elected to obtain her B.A. degree through the external degree granting authority of the Open University in her state.

In each of the courses she took, she was initially given a placement diagnostic test. This test informed her of weak elements in her background and how these could be remedied. They also identified her strong points which she should use to make her program more efficient and useful for her. If she had done extremely well on the tests, she could have tested out of the course and either taken a lighter load or taken other courses.

During her year of study, she made appointments with people working in her fields of interest so that by the time she completed her degree, she had a clear strategy for her next step.

CONCLUSION

In the author's judgment, an Open University network is urgently needed as we move toward the year 2000. Behind each of the points raised there is an extensive literature which can give detail and structure to the oversimplified version presented here. If the program begins, there will be a tremendous number of practical problems which will require planning, analysis, and accommodation. Without minimizing the problems, the opportunity is such that we have the technology, the knowledge, the talent and resources to produce this new alternative in higher education.

COURSE MATERIALS FOR ALTERNATIVE INSTRUCTIONAL SYSTEMS

SYNOPSIS

The institutions will plan for a long term cooperation in the a) production of course materials, b) systems of student access, c) proficiency tests, and d) evaluation of the system. The intention is to serve large numbers of unserved potential students in the greater Chicago area through the use of media and educational technology. In this proposal we seek support for planning and for the preparation of one course of high quality. The institutions will seek additional support from other agencies and will build a major cooperative effort for alternative instructional systems.

Justification of Proposal

There is a large number of potential students in the greater Chicago area who need and desire educational experience but who cannot become part of the campus system. On the other hand, there is outstanding talent and experience in alternative educational systems in the cooperating institutions. For example, the Chicago Television College has been a pioneer in televised instruction. What is needed is a way to coordinate the extensive talent which is present and to involve a sufficiently large number of students to justify the required investment in instructional materials of high quality. This proposal is a vital step in the development of an open university system for the Chicago area, and hopefully, the State of Illinois.

Televised instruction, extension courses, open universities, and other nontraditional forms of higher education have been struggling to become a major, respected component of the educational system. One difficulty has been that the instructional materials have not been of sufficiently high quality to attract use by institutions outside the one that originally produced them. As a result, the number of students involved has not been sufficient to justify the investment costs which would insure high quality. Sesame Street and the British Open University have demonstrated that important progress can be made if the circle can be broken with improvements in quality and through innovations in the way that students can gain access to educational experience.

In the decentralized world of American higher education, the innovation required is a system of collaboration and coordination in order to avoid duplication which forces mediocrity on each duplicated effort and which limits the size of the audience for each course. An important step can be taken by cooperation in the Chicago Metropolitan area among the public institutions of higher education. Among us, we have the combined resources to

25

develop outstanding course teams of subject experts, instructional designers, and educational system technologists. If we work together so that each institution uses the course developed, we will be dealing with numbers which will result in an excellent cost/benefit ratio.

Eventually, by starting at the local level in an area of high population density, we hope to develop a *model of collaboration* which will serve for expansion to the state and national levels. Several schools around the country have expressed interest in this concept.

Project or Program Director

The program will be guided by a representative from each of the cooperating institutions. The representatives presently are:

Dr. Ted F. Andrews, Dean
College of Environmental and
    Applied Sciences
Governors State University
Park Forest South, Illinois 60466
(312) 563-2211, Ext. 300

Dr. Anthony LaDuca
Project Director
Office of the Dean of Education
Chicago State University
Ninety-Fifth Street at King Drive
Chicago, Illinois 60628
(312) 996-4433

Dr. James Zigerell, Dean, TV College
Chicago City Colleges
3525 W. Peterson
Suite 17, Terrace Level
Chicago, Illinois 60659
(312) 588-2000

Dr. Frank Vogel
Associate Professor of Elementary
    Education
Northeastern Illinois University
Bryn Mawr and St. Louis Avenue
Chicago, Illinois 60625
(312) 583-4050

Dr. Joseph I. Lipson
Associate Vice Chancellor
    for Academic Affairs
University of Illinois at Chicago Circle
P.O. Box 4348
Chicago, Illinois 60680
(312) 996-4433

Under this proposal, a project coordinator will be hired. The proposal was prepared by Dr. Joseph Lipson.

Period of the Program

January 1, 1974 – December 31, 1974

Objectives of the Program

1. *To develop a plan for cooperative action in:*

   (a) the development of course materials for systems of instructional technology,

   (b) the development of systems of student access to accommodate people who cannot easily avail themselves of the campus-based system.

(c) the development of proficiency tests which will permit students to demonstrate competence without taking the course and which will serve other purposes in the instructional system, and

(d) the development of a system of continuous and overall evaluation of the cooperative effort.

2. *To develop a single course as a* practical exercise of the system. This course will be produced by a course team with members from each institution. The decision regarding the course to be produced will be made by the policy council of representatives from each institution. The course development project will be administered by the project coordinator who is to be hired.

3. *To develop a model of collaboration for an alternative education system.*

4. *To prepare proposals to other agencies* to enlarge the cooperative effort. With our central and pivotal location in a major state with a mixture of a large urban nucleus and rural areas, we could develop a major industry of course development in the state.

5. *To have an impact upon the effectiveness and efficiency of campus instruction through the developments of the project.* Many of our students work, and this reduces the flexibility of their scheduling. For these students, we hope to be able to blur the boundary between the campus system and the open university type of system. By offering a wide range of alternatives to all students, each student could find an educational program best suited to him.

Detailed Description of Program

1. *Development of Plan for Collaboration.*

(a) *Course Development.* Typically, educational technology has failed because the course materials did not match the hardware either in needed quality or supply of useful courses. It does little good to have sophisticated and expensive hardware systems (dial access, closed circuit TV, etc.) if there are no good materials to use with the system. Thus an important part of the project will involve planning for extensive, excellent course development.

We shall *identify the subject experts* who have the capability and the will to become deeply involved in course development for open university systems. We shall identify the courses which can most benefit from interaction with concepts of instructional design and the application of instructional technology. For example, all of our institutions have the need for individualized programs in basic learning skills: reading, writing, mathematics, and logical analysis. In other cases, certain large enrollment courses are vital to a number of career patterns. Many of these large enrollment courses could be made more effective through the systems we have in mind.

We shall explore and feed into the planning the probable *acceptance of courses* by students (both on and off campus) and faculties. We shall also explore appropriate methods for dissemination to other institutions of the courses developed.

(b) *Systems of Student Access.* We have among our institutions many of the pieces of extensive outreach systems of student access: open broadcast television, closed circuit television, videotapes in libraries and YMCAs, community and community college learning centers, extension systems, courses by newspaper, PLATO computer based education, independent study, CLEP credit and other proficiency and placement testing systems. None of these efforts has reached critical mass either in number of students who can be accommodated, in the range of courses available, or in adequate cost control. We must plan for cooperative use of certain facilities in order to make them feasible for present development. For example, if we can set up learning centers with computer learning terminals, audio and videotape units, counselors, and tutors which students from *any* cooperating institution can use, we may get levels of usage which would make this model extremely attractive. If we can improve the quality of open broadcast instructional materials in certain basic courses, we may attract greater course enrollments.

There is a large number of specific issues to be worked out in the planning. Standardization and trends in the hardware must be estimated. Acceptable initial and maintenance costs must be established and the organization of counselors and tutors must be carefully worked out. Overall unit costs of instruction for different models of access must be developed. Specific sites must be found and co-operative agreements for use of facilities must be prepared and agreed upon.

Schedules of development, funding requirements, and implementation will be prepared. The individuals responsible for different elements and new staff needed in different models will be listed.

(c) *Proficiency Tests.* Proficiency tests are important to the concept of alternative education. It is important to the philosophy of the open university that a student who has learned something should be able to receive credit without having to go through unneeded instruction. This requires proficiency tests which meet standards of the faculties of participating institutions.

Well designed proficiency tests can serve other important purposes. They can be used as placement tests, final examination tests, and diagnostic tests for individualized instruction. In general, they can make the entire educational process more efficient and less frustrating to the student.

(d) The plan will include a continuous evaluation plan. The primary evaluation for course materials will lie in their ability to have the student reach desired levels of competence, and acceptance by faculties on the basis of the academic soundness of what is being taught. These will be assessed by test scores, enrollment and retention rates, and faculty judgments of the materials.

For other aspects of the plan, evaluation criteria and methods will be prepared. In general, the best evaluation of the project will be the extent to which further cooperation is generated and realized. To this end, the evaluation component of the final report will document the extent and prospects of long-term cooperation among the institutions.

2. *Development of a Single Course.* Planning can become disconnected from reality. For this reason, we propose that a single course be developed in order to provide an important task in which various problems of co-operation will have to be worked out. By the end of the project year, the first draft of the course will be completed. We would like permission for the revision and final version preparation to extend beyond January 1, 1975. No additional funds will be required, but the expenditure of the funds should be stretched for this component of the work.

The course materials will be designed to be adaptable to as many different media formats as possible. Motivational aspects will be part of the course design. Selection of the course to be developed will be the first order of business for the policy council if the proposal is approved and funded. The course production will be administered by the project coordinator. Key academic decisions will be made by the course team which will have a course team leader named by the policy council.

3. *Development of a Collaborative Model.* There are many details to be worked out if large-scale cooperation is to become a reality. Academic faculties and administrations of each institution have certain procedures which require prior approval for new courses and new ways of dealing with students. In addition, certain legal and monetary questions will arise and need to be worked out. For example, if government contracts are obtained, over-head will need to be shared according to some acceptable formula. If the program is used commercially, authors, and the participating schools will have to figure out a formula for royalties. Still another important function of the

model building will be the design of ways to stimulate and reward collaborative activity by the faculties of the participating institutions.

4. *Preparation of Proposals to Other Agencies.* Individuals in several government agencies and foundations have expressed interest in proposals for research and development in the area of educational technology which involve cooperative efforts among several schools. Chances for funding are usually improved if prior work can be documented in a proposal. Therefore, the evidence of cooperation among the institutions and the support by the State Board will significantly improve the chances of being funded. Several national panels have called for regional course production and educational technology centers. This effort could grow into such a center for the upper midwest area.

5. *Impact upon Campus Instruction.* There are many ways that on campus instruction could benefit from the products of this effort. The course team will be learning new aspects of instructional design, learning psychology, and ways to use the media. Thus it will have a faculty development aspect. Because being named to the course team will have a high status, course development and teaching will be looked upon with greater favor by other faculty members.

The techniques of course development and the use of media have important applications to courses on the campus. The visibility of the cooperative effort should increase the chance that these techniques will be used. The course which is developed will probably be used on the campuses in order to provide greater flexibility and to deal with campus instructional problems.

Under current or slightly modified administrative procedures, students will be able to select for themselves a program of study involving both external courses and campus courses. This aspect of the cooperative program would increase the options and the opportunities for many students who work or have other responsibilities which keep them from becoming full-time campus students.

6. *Contributions by the Institutions.* Since the interinstitutional proposal does not provide any overhead, the cooperating institutions will be making this obvious contribution.

Facilities. Media production facilities will be provided by the institutions involved. These include extensive studio facilities at UICC and the City Colleges of Chicago, as well as those of other institutions. We have not asked for secretarial help and will provide this from internal resources. Travel costs will be assumed by the institutions. Supplies and technical costs will be considerably greater than the amount requested. While released time to the extent of $50,000 is requested under the grant for the course team, additional support will be forthcoming from a variety of experts on all the cooperating institutions. Individuals such as Dr. Zigerell, Dr. Andrews, Dr. Markle, and others will contribute their knowledge and experience to the project. The project will, in fact, act as the catalyst for focusing talent and resources from all the institutions. Only by such cooperation can we begin to realize the promise of educational technology.

7. *Evaluation Procedures.* Evaluation records will be developed by the project coordinator in the following categories:

(a) Milestones of agreements for collaborative development of alternative education systems. (Cross registration agreements, agreements for course development, cooperative proposals, agreements to share facilities, etc.);

(b) Proposals submitted to other agencies. Proposals approved;

(c) Milestones of course development;

(d) Review of the quality of course elements by experts. Results of formative evaluation of course elements tried out with students;

(e) Evidence of impact upon campus communities: use of new techniques, increased interest and activity in course development and new approaches to teaching, reallocation of resources into course development and teaching, change in attitude. Evidence will include articles, student newspaper notice, letters of inquiry, attendance at meetings, applications for participation, etc.;

(f) Documents developed and approved by the policy council. These will include, in particular, the planning documents and the model for cooperative action.

Budget

Personnel

Project Coordinator	$20,000
(Salary for one year)	
Faculty and staff, released time to prepare course materials	50,000
(5 x $10,000 for ½ year released time for five individuals)	
Supplies and technical services for the production of one course	10,000
(production)	
Total	$80,000

Explanation of Budget

Project Coordinator. By having funds for the project coordinator, the policy council of the participating institutions will be able to select an individual whose primary allegiance is to the project and not to any single institution. Thus, in turn, will dominate or preferentially benefit from the collaboration. *The individual will know that his career will depend upon the growth of cooperation among the institutions.*

Course Team Support. These funds will allow us to attract one outstanding individual from each of the participating institutions. The course team approach has worked extremely well in the British Open University development, and these funds will allow us to explore a model for this kind in the cooperative mode.

Supplies and Technical Services. This relatively small amount for supplies and technical services will give the project some flexibility in the purchase of items which are not available from one of the participating institutions. If we need some animation, special art work, the time of outside reviewers, or more film or videotapes than we can obtain from the stores of the institutions, these funds will allow us to act quickly in the interests of the project.

Part Two

GROUPED AND BOUNDED

LEARNING ENVIRONMENTS

READING, WRITING, ARITHMETIC AND COMPUTING

Arthur Luehrmann
Professor of Physics
Dartmouth College

The Proper Role of the Computer in Education

In the vast majority of universities the computer is virtually isolated from the principal clientele, the students. The computer may serve the needs of administrative data processing, such as handling student records or the biweekly payroll. It may be a laboratory instrument for the computer science department. In the most prestigious universities the computer serves exclusively the research needs of a small group of "big users" with grant money.

Educational computing is given short shrift, and when it *is* served it is often done so in a misdirected fashion, based on the following false premise:

Educational computing requires only a fairly simple computer capable of running computer assisted instruction (CAI) drills and other teaching programs.

To many people in decision-making positions, educational use of the computer is equivalent to CAI—nothing more and nothing less. University administrators look to CAI as a way of reducing the cost or increasing the efficiency of the teaching staff. Teachers look to CAI to relieve them of tedious jobs, such as teaching remedial English or French verbs. Even students often show a preference for CAI over conventional instruction, and some studies show that they learn better from CAI.

Nevertheless, the premise is faulty for two reasons. First, documented examples of effective CAI are few. Institutions have based a decision to install a computer to deliver CAI on the belief that there now exist thousands of hours' worth of good CAI programs waiting to be run on their system. Actually very little exists and much of it is so system dependent that it is not easily exportable.

Even if it were true, however, that dozens of high-quality, well tested CAI courses now exist, there remains a second reason why the CAI premise is a faulty one. It presumes that the only educational role appropriate to the computer is that of the *teacher,* the deliverer of instruction. It is because of this presumption that one so often hears the educational use of computers described as being competitive with conventional teaching. Such discussions usually fall into an uncertain quagmire where questions of cost-effectiveness and labor-intensiveness are debated endlessly.

To become bogged down in such an argument is to miss the whole point of educational computing. Instead of focussing on possible ways in which the computer might affect *the content and subject matter of education,* one is limited to considering only the economics and technology of *delivering instruction* of an otherwise perfectly conventional content. I do not say that the economics and technology of delivery systems is unimportant to education; rather that there is more to computing than delivering instruction.

It is the principal thesis of this paper that computing has new and unique implications for teaching and learning. CAI only begins to reveal the smallest part of those implications and should not deviate our attention from grander potentialities. Worse yet, a computer system optimized to deliver CAI drills may be very poor at handling the more important educational functions to be described later. The ironic result may be that the computer system acquired for educational use is inadequate for educational use.

Upon what premise, then, should university computing be founded? If the campus computer is not to be merely an administrative data processor, if it is not to be just an adjunct to research, if it is not to be mainly a laboratory for computer science, and if it is not to be simply an automated drill instructor, then just what is it to be? The answer to these questions derives, in my opinion, from the following premise:

> Computing is a new and fundamental intellectual resource in the same sense that reading and writing are fundamental intellectual resources. Universities need computers for the same reasons that they need libraries.

This may seem a mildly bizarre claim. After all, a computer is an artifice, a mere machine, a piece of technical apparatus. Isn't it pretentious to identify a box full of wires and transistors with the world of intellect? I think not. All of the objects of intellect are artificial. What could be more arbitrary or artificial than an alphabet or a system of numbering? What word has intrinsic meaning? Yet out of these artificial elements people have built all of the linguistic and mathematical edifices that we know.

Computing likewise begins with artificial, intrinsically meaningless elements, of which the machine itself is the least important: variable, constant, instruction, branch, conditional branch, input, output. At a slightly higher level, there are more artifices: algorithm or procedure, iteration, subroutine, recursion. Just as alphabets, words, sentences and paragraphs are the means by which we give linguistic expression to certain of our ideas, in the same way the elements of computing give us a new form for the expression of old and new ideas. Like language and mathematics, computing is a way of thinking[1].

Examples of non-CAI Computer Use

A few examples may clarify the philosophy of computing prevalent at Dartmouth and a growing number of other schools.

Historically computers found their first applications in the physical sciences, so it is not surprising to find the first interesting educational applications there as well. Eight years ago this fall a group of physicists convened at Irvine, California, to discuss ways in which computers might affect physics teaching[2]. Several of us came away convinced that in a few years the entire pedagogy of freshman mechanics would be transformed.

In the past a clear understanding of Newton's Laws of motion had required a firm grasp on the fundamental ideas of the calculus. This is true because Newton's Second Law is usually represented as a differential equation. Now, the plain fact is that few freshmen have enough experience with calculus to be able to tolerate a presentation of motion in terms of differential equations. As a result all textbooks and most teachers have settled for using the symbols and nomenclature of the calculus; but very rarely have they actually asked students to solve for motion by *using* the calculus. (Check the problems in any textbook, for example.)

But the fact of the matter is that Newton's Second Law has an alternate representation that avoids the whole calculus problem. It can be thought of as an *algorithm* or *procedure* for determining the position and velocity of a body a "small" time later, given the current position, velocity and the force acting on it[3]. The steps of the algorithm are simple algebraic statements that a tenth-grader can understand. Of course, an algorithmic approach only makes practical sense if one has a computer handy to carry out all the tedious calculations.

The payoff of this fundamental change in pedagogy is enormous. For the first time it is practical to teach the essential idea of mechanics instead of cheap imitations—all those awful inclined planes and pulleys. The subject matter, motion, can be taught *generally,* without having to worry whether a particular force law will lead to a

---

[1] A.W. Luehrmann, "Should the Computer Teach the Student, or Vice Versa?" Proc. AFIPS SJCC 1972 Vol. 40 pp. 407-410.

[2] The Computer in Physics, Report of the Conference on the Uses of the Computer in Undergraduate Physics Instruction, University of California, Irvine, 1965. (Commission on College Physics, 1966).

[3] A.M. Bork, A.W. Luehrmann, J.R. Robson, "Introductory Computer-Based Mechanics." (Am. Inst. of Physics, Information Pool, SUNY Stony Brook, 1968).

mathematically soluble problem. The algorithm applies to *any* force law, and it even generalizes easily to handle two and three dimensional situations. Our freshmen especially like to program the computer to display artificial satellite orbits and to find the right launching conditions to send a vehicle to the moon and back—something unheard of under the old pedagogy.

Students in the social sciences at Dartmouth vie with those in the sciences for largest computer use. In sociology a student, using the IMPRESS system[4], learns to do quantitative research on actual data, not different in kind from that carried out by professionals. Sitting at a terminal the student can reach any of sixty different data bases and can direct a sequence of inquiries aimed at finding out, for example, who in the spring of 1973 believed in capital punishment. He can look at overall results and he can begin to cross tabulate belief in capital punishment with age, sex, income, race, religion, etc. Inside a few minutes such a student-researcher will have formulated several hypotheses and checked them out against the data.

As in the physics example, we see here a student *doing* sociology and not merely hearing about it or being drilled on it via a CAI lesson. The situation in music is similar.

A joint project between the music department and the engineering school has been the development of a musical terminal—a computer-driven electronic music synthesizer, now in use with over a hundred students[5]. Sitting at the terminal a student can specify a composition by typing a sequence of commands and parameters that tell pitch, loudness, duration, attack, timbre, etc. He can edit the composition using the standard DTSS editors. When ready he runs a program that converts his composition to information transmitted to the minicomputer-driven synthesizer. The sound is heard in a few seconds via a standard stereo system.

Several surprising things have happened. First the course in composition is now attracting students with little or no ability as performers, since the computer is now the performer. Second, a few students are exploring the idea of music as a list of data that can be transformed by means of algorithms that transpose pitch, invert pitches, change the sequence, etc. In short, they are *doing* music with the same excitement as, and better tools than many professionals have.

The list of examples could be extended easily—river basin ecosystem simulations, economic simulation games[6], computer experiments in genetics[7], computer graphics as a medium for artists—but space and time do not permit. What all these examples have in common is a use of the computer in which the student *masters* a computer-based system in order to *do* problems and projects in various fields. He is not merely the slave of an automated lesson, however personalized and with however much feedback. If my convictions on this point are not clear, I will conclude this section with a Chinese proverb:

> I hear, and I forget;
> I see, and I remember;
> I do, and I understand.

The "Library Model" Taken Seriously

The claim that a basic facility in computer use is every bit as necessary as reading and writing or arithmetic, has far-reaching consequences. For if basic literacy is not the exclusive property of university administrators, nor of researchers in the humanities division, nor of the department of linguistics, nor of the teaching faculty, then for

---

[4] The IMPRESS Primer, 3rd ed. (Project IMPRESS, Dartmouth College, Hanover, NH, 1973).

[5] User manuals are available from J.H. Appleton, Music Dept., Dartmouth College, Hanover, NH.

[6] G.B. Pidot, J.W. Sommer, "ACRES: A Land Development and Environmental Game" (in P. Patterson, Ed., *Recent Developments in Urban Gaming*, Simulations Council Proceedings, Vol. 2, 1973).

[7] T.B. Roos, "Computer Models in an Introductory Course in Biology." *Proc. Conf. on Computers in the Undergraduate Curricula*, 1973 (Computer Center, University of Iowa, Iowa City, Iowa, 1973).

the same reasons university computing must also not become the exclusive captive of any of the analogous groups. Literate, competent and even creative use of computing ought to spread through most parts of the university.

The best institutional model for a computer center dedicated to this goal is the university library, which has always served the literary needs of the entire academic community.

The university library is an interesting object. Its director, the librarian, usually reports to the provost (or academic Vice President, or equivalent), who represents the broad academic interests of the institution. The librarian seeks advice and counsel not only of the linguistically based departments, or of the directors of research programs, but of members of the entire academic community. Typically there is a committee on libraries with faculty and sometimes student membership. The committee makes recommendations to the librarian and to his boss, the provost; and it reports back to the faculty. In effect it acts as an academic watchdog on the accountability of the library.

Access to the library is granted to all members of the university, as a rule. Some basic level of service is offered equally to everyone, independent of rank or prestige or source of funds. More precious services, such as the rare-book collection, are limited by an assessment of the need of an individual to use them, not by his ability to pay. Library hours are determined by the demand of the clientele and not the convenience of the staff. Library use is not batch-processed.

Funding is the critical factor. A university library is a cost center, not a profit-and-loss center. It is not expected to generate significant revenue. The fact that it is one of the largest cost centers is justified on the value of the service it supplies to its varied users. Imagine what your university library would be like if its fiscal operation were modeled after the average computer center. Use of the library would be on a pay-as-you-go basis. At my university the cost of the library, if distributed over the average number of books circulated, amounts to about ten dollars per book borrowed. How much use of your library would you make if you had to pay ten dollars for every book you withdrew? Clearly, only those with substantial research grants could afford such use. And with a greatly shrunken user community, the cost per circulation might go up five or tenfold. Massive educational use of such an expensive service would be utterly unthinkable. In the end the type of library service available would be dictated by the interests of a handful of big research users and the department of library science. It would not be the library that you know.

Though one has only to go back a few centuries to find it in practice, such a model for administration of a university library is heretical today. Paradoxically, the application of today's library model to the administration of the computer center is viewed by most people as equally heretical. Yet in my opinion the logic that leads universities to support costly libraries available to all must also lead them to support costly computer centers available to all.

Dartmouth College is an exceptional university in this respect. Ten years ago Dartmouth decided that computing should be as accessible to students and faculty as a book on its open-shelf library. Ease of access meant the adoption of two radical ideas. First, a user's decision to use the computer had to be divorced from questions of payment or formal justification. Second, the operating software had to be designed to serve a community of four thousand potential users.

The result today is the Dartmouth Time-Sharing System (DTSS)[8-10]. In 1964 the first practical time-sharing system freely accessible to an academic community was created at Dartmouth. Two mathematics professors led a small squadron of undergraduates in designing the time-sharing operating system and defining a new easy-to-learn

[8] R.F. Hargraves, A. Stephenson, "Decision Considerations for an Educational Time-Sharing System." *Proc. AFIPS, SJCC,* 1969, Vol. 34, pp. 657-664.

[9] J.G. Kemeny, T.E. Kurtz, "Dartmouth Time-Sharing." *Science*, 162, 11 (1968).

[10] Biennial Report. (Kiewit Computation Center, Dartmouth College, Hanover, NH, 1973).

programming language — BASIC. The system could support the then unheard of maximum of 24 simultaneous users. That system, which was designed around the General Electric 200 computer series, became the prototype for GE's Mark I time-sharing service, the first commercially successful time-sharing service.

Today DTSS operates on a much larger and faster Honeywell 635 computer. On this machine DTSS now supports, measurably on any afternoon, over 140 simultaneous users. Between one and two thousand different people use the Dartmouth computer in a day — about four thousand in a month. Between fifteen and twenty-five thousand jobs are executed each day. About thirty institutions other than Dartmouth use our computer via a multiplex network that extends to New York, Boston, Chicago, Montreal and Toronto. There are about three hundred computer terminals on our campus and perhaps another hundred at remote locations. DTSS comes on at 7:00 a.m. each weekday and remains on for twenty hours, until 3:00 a.m. the next day — a total of a hundred twenty hours each week. Service interruptions are rare — perhaps one a week — and recovery is rapid — usually under ten minutes.

So much for system statistics. The upshot is that DTSS is a large, heavily used computer system. Administratively, the computer center follows the library model quite closely. Both the librarian and the computer center director report to the Vice President for Student Affairs, a fact which emphasizes our concern for the educational program. (The computer center director, Thomas E. Kurtz, was one of those two mathematics professors who originated the system. The other, John G. Kemeny, has left computing, though he still has a computer terminal in his office as President of Dartmouth College.) Like the Council on Libraries, there is also a Council on Computing largely composed of faculty members. Like the library's public reading room, the computer center operates a public terminal room open to anyone, with or without a Dartmouth connection. In addition it "circulates" computer use around the campus via the regular telephone network.

Money, Budgets and All That

"What about funding?" you are sure to ask. "How is it possible to just give away such a costly service?" In fact we do not just give away free computing. A substantial minority of the use of our system comes from federally supported projects, and there is a law against charging the U.S. government for something that is free to another customer. Therefore, we carry out a detailed billing on every user of the system, and we have an auditable rate structure based on costs and aggregate usage. The individual student never sees a bill, however, and so to him the service appears free. The faculty member without support funds for computing likewise charges his use to a general unsupported teaching or unsupported research account. The bills for these unsupported accounts are paid in the end by transferring general funds of the College into them.

The principal point to emphasize here is that computer use is not allocated by agreeing in advance on a computing budget item for each academic department or other unit. We believe that such a strategy, while it may appeal to a cost accountant, is simply wrong for educational computing. It assumes that the user of the resource and the allocator of the resource have a good idea of the probable value of each quantum of use. This is true when allocating food in the cafeteria and so food should be charged and paid for by the meal. But this is not true of book-borrowing or computing. Worthless humdrum hours often precede priceless seconds of insight. Value is hard to put in economic terms.

On the other hand, any computer center has a finite resource, and an allocation problem must exist. In fact, while Dartmouth gives free *access* to the computer to anyone, we nevertheless ration *use* by other means, some of which are only possible with a large time-sharing system[11]. For example, we set a maximum run-time limit per job for each user. For students it is 32 CPU seconds per job. For faculty it is 64 seconds. We set a limit on number of characters of saved files on the disks. For students it is 8000 characters. For faculty it is 80,000. (Total disk storage is 400,000,000 characters.) Access to system peripherals, such as the line printer and card reader and punch is also rationed. We do not place limits on total CPU use per session or per month, nor do we limit the number of sessions at a terminal.

[11] J.S. McGeachie, "A Flexible User Validation Language for Time-Sharing Systems." *Proc. AFIPS*, SJCC, 1969, Vol. 34, pp. 665-671.

The vast majority of our users rarely encounter their limits. Those that do frequently find ways to make their programs more efficient. In the end if all else fails a user can appeal to have any of his initial limits increased. As a general rule his request is granted, but if he needs still more, some supporting evidence is required. New limits are usually viewed as temporary adjustments.

With our resources and in our user community this system works. To the beginning user the computer seems to be a free resource. The sense of freedom enables the user to approach computing on his own terms and with his own sense of values. It permits game-playing and trivia. At the same time it protects the serious user against unrestrained use and abuse by the more frivolous user. In a large-scale time-sharing system, after all, one user's frivolity can consume at most a few percent of the resource. By contrast, one "big user" with a fat government grant can not only consume a larger fraction of a batch system; he can also dominate the computer center and distort its priorities.

Still, I have said nothing of the net cost of computing at Dartmouth. Isn't it very expensive to provide this type of service? Our view is that it costs about as much as it should. We generally agree that it is as important to us to have a good computer center as it is to have a good library; Dartmouth budgets roughly the same amount for each. The total computer center budget is about $1.5 million. This includes rental or depreciation of hardware, all staff salaries, heating and maintaining the building, and all other items attributable to computing. Certain income should be removed from that figure immediately, since a great deal of our use is sold to non-Dartmouth users. Currently about $300,000 comes from this source. The cost for Dartmouth use is therefore about $1.2 million. With 4000 students, that comes to an average of about $300 per student or about 9% of our annual tuition fee.

This figure is computed in the most conservative way possible and is the upper limit on our cost of computing. Note that it takes the cost of *all* computing at Dartmouth and loads it on the *student.* The fact is that student use amounts to only 30% of total Dartmouth use. Therefore *student use* costs only about $100 per enrolled student per year, which in 1964 dollars is exactly what the Pierce Report[12] recommended ten years ago for educational computing in the United States.

To conclude this section, we believe that Dartmouth's experience proves that computing can safely be made freely available to all members of a university at a current cost that compares favorably with that of the library. Since computing is one of the few areas in education where costs are going down, the situation in the future should actually improve.

Project COMPUTe: a Tactic for Educational Change

Even though the mere act of installing a large free-access time-sharing system has by itself caused profound changes in education at Dartmouth, the rate of change has been slow and the impact on other universities, slight.

Now I want to describe a modest project that might serve as an element in a national strategy for bringing about the sort of change I have been talking about. Project COMPUTe[13] is an effort to develop and distribute course materials dealing with computer use. The project is located at Dartmouth College and has three-year funding from the National Science Foundation.

Publication and wide dissemination of approximately twenty textbooks or monographs is the immediate goal of COMPUTe. The writing, testing, technical documentation of, or dissemination of computer *programs* is of comparatively little interest to COMPUTe. Equally uninteresting to COMPUTe is the problem of developing new strategies for *using* the computer in education.

---

[12] Computers in Higher Education, President's Science Advisory Committee, The White House, Washington, DC, 1967.

[13] NSF Project GJ-28456. Information about the project or for prospective authors is available from Project COMPUTe, Dartmouth College, Hanover, NH.

Instead, the project assumes that good computer uses already exist and that technical transportability—i.e. moving programs to a new computer and supplying operational documentation—is not a serious problem. At least, we think it is not the principal obstacle to the spread of computer use.

What *is* the principal obstacle is the shortage of good materials for use in courses where computer use makes sense. At the university level educational change is almost always accomplished by the appearance of a new, commercially available textbook. Change happens when faculty members decide to adopt the new book instead of the old one. There is no reason to believe that widespread computer use will happen in any other way. During the last five years hundreds of teachers have developed thousands of interesting applications of computing to their courses. Over two hundred papers on the topic have been presented at four annual national meetings sponsored by NSF[14]. Yet, for the most part, enthusiasm has been confined to the originators and has not been transmitted to colleagues. Interest has been generated, but not sufficient enthusiasm to yield widespread imitation.

The reasons are simple. The amount of faculty time and effort that goes into development of computer uses is enormous. It is unreasonable to expect that kind of investment every time a course is given. On the other hand, if teachers were able to get from their local textbook purveyor a few readable, pedagogically practical examples of course materials in their own disciplines, I believe that we would see an enormous growth in educational computer use. That is the working premise of Project COMPUTe.

Now a word about our operational strategy. On the basis of formal proposals submitted to us and referred by others, we select six or eight people for summer writing projects. These authors leave their home institutions, friends; secretaries, telephones, and in-baskets and come to the woods of New Hampshire for one or two months. The mission of each is to write as much of a monograph or text book as possible there and to agree to see it through to completion when they go home.

For its part the project gives up to two months summer salary to each author, and the staff attempts to create a stimulating climate for thinking and writing. Weekly seminars allow each author to learn what the others are doing and to discuss problems together. Access to the Dartmouth computer is freely available to all, and we supply a student programming assistant for any author who needs one.

Much of the contact is informal and centers around the computer center coffee pot, corridor conversations, and weekend outings.

Beyond direct salary support, our principal service is editorial. As each author finishes a draft of a chapter, the project editor types it into a computer file. From thence forward all changes are made by modifying that original file, using built-in editorial features available on the computer system. Another computer-based system types out a neatly formatted, paginated copy of the current state of the manuscript whenever requested to do so. The result is that even in our nine-week period of intense work, an author can see drafts of his work in progress, and can improve the quality of his product.

At the end of summer, or more typically, six months later, the project has a completed manuscript from each person. Several options now exist. From the computer file it is easy to produce multilith masters for immediate use on a small scale by the author or others. One level higher, it is easy in the same way to generate automatically camera-ready copy with the quality equivalent to carbon-ribbon typing. This makes possible an inexpensive format for large-scale printing. Finally, it is possible to go to automatic or manual typesetting and produce the standard sort of published book.

The role of the project at this stage is to act as author's agent in dealing with commercial publishers and university presses. A unique and experimental feature of Project COMPUTe has to do with royalty payments. We are empowered to negotiate the best terms with each publisher and then to negotiate separately with each

---

[14]Proceedings of the conferences, held at Univ. of Iowa, Dartmouth, Atlanta, and the Claremont Colleges, 1970-1973 are available from the Computer Center, University of Iowa, Iowa City, Iowa.

author an appropriate division of the royalty between the author and the project. We believe strongly, and our authors agree, that royalty incentives are very important in any curriculum development project, since the regular academic rewards are so meager.

Now I want to say a few words about why I believe that Project COMPUTe is a model for one element of a larger strategy for bringing about educational change.

1. *Change is produced by active teachers with ideas that come directly out of their experience.* The necessity to teach some subject is the mother of their curricular invention, not the necessity to write scholarly papers on educational change.

2. *Each author is tightly allied to his particular academic discipline.* Each is a member of an ordinary academic department. As a result each is an *insider* and can carry out a program of change in a way that *outsiders* cannot. Each will go back to his department and teach courses there. He may influence others at his own university; but, more likely, he will influence others in his own discipline at dozens or even hundreds of other universities. Communication within disciplines is far more profound than communication within universities.

3. *The creative staff is a temporary staff.* There are no permanent *innovation* experts, only *discipline* experts who temporarily leave their conventional roles to address a problem of pedagogy. Before they fall prey to thinking of themselves as innovation experts we send them home for more contact with the sources of their inspiration.

4. *Rewards for work in curriculum are not confused with rewards for traditional academic good behavior.* Authors are paid to write, and if they write well further royalty benefits accrue. There is no pretense of enhancing professional prestige or tenurability. Simple rules are the basis of good behavior. We want our authors to behave like authors, not prima donnas.

National Model for Educational Change

A natural question is this: is it possible to extend the key features of Project COMPUTe into a full-scale national model for educational change and development? I believe that the answer is yes.

The Carnegie Commission on Higher Education in a recent report[15] calls for the establishment of several regional centers focussing on uses of technology in higher education. The structure proposed there is the starting point for the full-scale model that I would like to promote. Briefly, each center is to be funded at a level of a small university, such as Dartmouth, for example. It is to have a permanent staff of educators, writers and specialists in video, film, audio, graphical design, and computing. The long-range goal of each center is to develop and distribute applications of technology that increase the quality or reduce the cost of education. Each center would provide educational computer service to its entire region. The centers would be situated in major metropolitan areas so that they would have access to real, live students in the way that the Open University does in Great Britain.

As far as it goes this is a good plan, but it does not go far enough. In particular, the relationship between these essentially research and development centers and the production oriented conventional universities is not clear. At some points in the Carnegie report the centers appear as service organizations for the universities. At others, they seem to be competitors, having their own staff and their own student clientele.

It is here where I believe that our Project COMPUTe experience can be of help. Suppose that each center had, in addition to the *regional* tie suggested by the Carnegie Commission, a very strong *discipline* tie as well. That is, each center would be targeted to produce applications in a specialized group of closely related academic fields.

[15] *The Fourth Revolution: Instructional Technology in Higher Education.* (McGraw-Hill, New York, 1972.)

Persons representing those disciplines, possibly via the professional societies, or perhaps through editorial boards of the respective journals, would serve as an advisory panel or even a policy review board for the corresponding center. Such a group might advise the center on needs, priorities, and marketability for new educational developments in their disciplines. It might also serve as an *insider* group for the promotion within the disciplines of new developments coming out of the centers.

The actual development process in the centers would be a partnership involving people with technology and media specialization, education theorists, evaluators, economists, and, finally, discipline experts with teaching experience. The latter should usually be the senior partner, in my opinion; the others should serve as resource people. For the reasons stated in describing Project COMPUTe, it is better that the discipline specialists be cast as "Visiting Fellows" rather than "Tenured Faculty." In the first place, a permanent staff of innovators is hard to imagine. Second, the discipline tie of the permanent innovator would become thin if not replenished by renewed contact with peers in the discipline. Third, the number of people in direct contact with the center and its work would be vastly larger if the number of Visiting Fellows was large. Fourth, the return of visitors to their home universities would serve to spread the word and market the products of the center. Fifth, the mere possibility of becoming a Fellow at the center would cause many more people to become conscious of and interested in the activities of the center.

Since, in the conventional university at least, the *effective* consumer of educational change is not the student but the teacher who selects course format and materials, it is crucial that any large educational development centers have powerful ties with the teaching faculties. That means, in our vertically partitioned universities, powerful ties with academic disciplines.

It might be argued that educational change cannot happen within universities any way, so why worry about good relations with them? Why not set up centers that will compete with them in doing the job that they now do?

I would hope to see a healthy element of competition between the centers and the regular universities. The presence of "Open University" students is a good idea and would foster that competition. But there are two reasons not to cut off the ordinary universities from the start. First there is no need to. The model I have proposed poses little threat and even offers opportunity to the academic disciplines. Second, I seriously doubt whether a frankly competitive organization could attract a staff of sufficient competence to win in a struggle with the conventional universities. It would be attacked by academic specialists as an illegitimate upstart, and that would deter most of the best people from taking a job at the center.

In summary, then, I propose several large regional curriculum development centers, each with very strong discipline ties. These ties would be achieved by being held *accountable* to representatives of the disciplines in exchange for *legitimacy* in their eyes. Apart from the question of ties to academic disciplines, the remainder of the model is essentially that proposed by the Carnegie Commission for developing uses of instructional technology. Since that proposal is probably well known, I shan't elaborate it here.

Meanwhile, Back at the Closed University

Unless someone in the audience knows something I don't know, it would be poor judgment to do nothing until massive support becomes available for such national centers. One works with what is at hand, and it appears that traditional, closed-wall universities are apt to be at hand for a while. Yet all is not gloomy there.

Dartmouth College has made a recent commitment of resources and personnel toward educational change within a conventional university environment. Operating on the premise that the best source of ideas about education is the regular teaching faculty and the best testbed is found in courses offered in the regular departments, Dartmouth has defined a new office charged with promoting faculty experiments in teaching. Particular emphasis is to be placed on experiments that will lead to qualitative or quantitative increases in productivity through use of technology.

In view of the well-known professional and political problems faced by education-minded faculty members in regular departments, one of the principal functions of the new office is to serve the interests of such people. This will be accomplished in several ways. The first and most important way is organizational. The director of the new office—names and titles are not yet settled, but for present purposes let me call him Dean of Instruction—reports directly to the Dean of Faculty. He thus has the ear of the university officer most directly concerned with the quality of the faculty and with departmental practices and standards for hiring, promotion, and tenure recommendations. Hence an organizational mechanism exists for influencing those practices when they are in conflict with the purposes of the office of Instruction. Obviously, this mechanism must be exercised with considerable skill and political wisdom if it is to be effective. But the point is that it now *exists.* There is a way for a faculty member to hold the university to account for its claim that innovative teaching is rewarded.

But accountability applies in both directions. Teachers who expect the support of the Dean of Instruction must be held to account for the quality and effectiveness of their work. For this reason the Office of Instruction is charged with responsibility for evaluating new educational projects. A mere willingness to experiment is no guarantee of quality or effectiveness; and, if only to protect his credibility, it is essential that the Dean of Instruction distinguish between good work and bad work before making a recommendation to the Dean of Faculty regarding particular faculty members. In this way faculty who work with the Office of Instruction will be under the same kind of tension experienced in a regular department, where they expect support if they do well and not otherwise.

Evaluation, then, is the second way in which the new office will promote effective experiments in education. The third contribution is technical and informational. Physical resources, including standard audio-visual equipment, are being expanded and the staff increased. The campus will be linked with TV cable and more origination and playback equipment will be added. Inexperienced faculty members will find technical assistance.

The fourth activity of the Office of Instruction is to coordinate its educational goals with the purposes of the computer center. Not surprisingly the majority of educational technology projects at Dartmouth have been and are likely to continue to be based on some aspect of computer use. Hence it is essential that, for example, a proposed project be examined for additional demand it will place on computer resources. Fortunately, the primary mission of the Dartmouth computer center is to serve educational needs; and there is no conflict of purpose with the Office of Instruction. (One wonders how many other universities can make that claim.)

The final role to be played by the new office is that of fund raiser. It is currently assisting faculty members in four different departments in gaining foundation support for specific projects dealing with educational technology. Its success in this regard can be expected to give the Office of Instruction considerable political leverage when the time comes to speak out for faculty members who have carried out projects under its auspices.

While it is premature to report results for the Office of Instruction, I believe that the basic organizational structure is sound. It is the best way that we can think of to promote experimentation in education within a traditional university, using regular students and faculty with expertise in regular academic disciplines. If successful it will not be as an isolated institute for educational research, but as a practical model for fostering and managing educational change across an entire university.

THE AUDIO-TUTORIAL SYSTEM OF INSTRUCTION

Robert N. Hurst
Professor of Biology
Purdue University

Let me begin with a rather pointed statement which appeared in another paper I prepared on the Audio-Tutorial System of instruction: "Neither its strongest supporter nor its severest critic could deny the impact of the Audio-Tutorial System of instruction on education." Since its birth in 1961, A-T has indeed exerted an influence on educational thought and practices; it has indeed garnered its share of devotees and critics. Most assuredly, it has contributed enormously to the interest in and unrest resulting from the "fourth revolution" described by Eric Ashby and canonized by the Carnegie Commission on Higher Education.

We *are* in the midst of revolution in education and it is an exhilarating and exciting time to be involved with technology, teaching, learning, people and students — who are after all, "a lot like people" (Postlethwait, 1972). Those beautiful, bright, demanding souls, eager, yet hesitant to learn, tired of tradition, daring instructors to teach them. It *is* a time for innovation, for change. In fact, in many educational settings, innovation and change are being legislated by well-meaning but ignorant trustees, boards and administrators who do not understand that change cannot be legislated but must grow as did Audio-Tutorial from an instructor's concern for his students and how they learn. To place the unconcerned or the doubter into an "innovative" setting and tell him "now be innovative" is to assure failure. So many must be permitted, in spite of the knowledge explosion, to disregard the biblical admonition and continue to put new wine into old skins. The old skins being, of course, the lecture-lab or lecture-lab- recitation format, the *"spray* and pray" system where the professor as the font of knowledge spews forth while each and every eager learner dutifully copies, swallows, digests and then upon command, regurgitates.

But for the rest of us, there are other possibilities that make new promises. This is where the Audio-Tutorial System of instruction makes its debut as only one of a whole host of possibilities. As does every other innovative educational practice, Audio-Tutorial has only one goal or purpose *"To Help Students Learn."* We all realize of course, that as facilitators of learning, or teachers, or educators or whatever title we take upon ourselves, helping students learn is the whole purpose for our existence. If we do not help students learn, we ought not to be in the business of education. Therefore, allow me to preface my remarks about the Audio-Tutorial System with some concerns we should all have about technology-oriented instructional systems be they A-T, CAI, video or some combination of these.

Technology must not be used for the sake of novelty of the technology itself. It must extend, not further restrict, our educational flexibility. It must enhance, not cramp, our educational style. It must help students learn, not entertain, humor or occupy them. It must, in other words, have a positive effect on learning. If it meets this final criterion, perhaps the use of that technology is justified, because as Eric Ashby has said: "Any Technology which increases the rate of learning would enable (as Comenius put it centuries ago) the teacher to teach less, and the learner to learn more." Yet it is essential that we examine a technology, weigh its costs and its benefits to ascertain its value as an educational tool now and its potential value ten or twenty years from now. Technology must be kept in its proper perspective and as indicated by the Carnegie Commission, "it should not be adopted merely because it exists, or because an institution fears that it will be left behind the parade of progress without it."

The Carnegie Commission in its Fourth Revolution report (1972, p. 11) lists two tests which ought to be applied to determine whether technology should be used in an instructional program. Let me commend them to you. First, the learning task to be performed should be essential to the course of instruction and, second, the task should be performed better with the use of technology. Perhaps the task could not be performed at all without technology. If so, then only test one need be applied and the instructor has his answer.

Technology *is* having its effect on the educational process and the field of technology promises bigger and better things yet to come. Communication satellites, video cassettes, miniature computers and cable television are just a few of the new tools promised and in some instances already delivered.

Slide 1

This special issue of *Electronics* magazine is illustrative of the directions some tools are taking. A special report of tomorrow's communications.

No one would deny we are indeed a tuned-in, wired-up, plugged-in, hyperarticulate speed-of-light society. And tomorrow's education may well start with today's design.

We could have no more pencils, no more books, and we could write and read electronically.

The goals: A communications system that replaces person-to-person contact. The tools: Satellites, facsimiles, computers, telephones, and microwave. This sounds exciting on the surface, doesn't it? Yet one has to ponder whether or not this is the direction we want to move. What are the roles of or the limitations of instructional media? Do we really want to replace person-to-person contact with all of those very elaborate tools? I don't know; maybe we do.

Slide 2

Slide 3

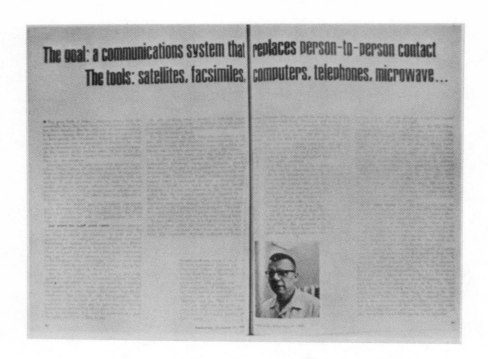

Slide 4

Perhaps however, the most important point of this particular report was a comment that appeared near the end, where Albert Einstein was quoted as having said that the container would never be more valuable than its contents. I submit that media, that technology must be scrutinized carefully and their value documented, else the container may well become more valuable than its contents. If a computer program is designed to operate as an electronic page turner, I'm not sure it is really worth the money. The container becomes more valuable than its contents. At Purdue we program students to turn their own pages. Do we really want to replace this person-to-person contact?

Slide 5

46

In the final analysis we are still dealing with people, students like this typical, average run-of-the mill pre-vet student. I for one, am not ready to give up meeting this student on a one-to-one basis in a person-to-person contact.

But where is this talk about the use and possible misuse of technology leading to? After all, my mission is to inform you of a technology-based system of instruction called Audio-Tutorial. My assignment is not to bias or prejudice your thinking in terms of what you hear from others during this symposium and I'm sure I have not. I do have real concerns about how and why technology is used as I know the other presenters do. These concerns lead me to believe that the best way to help my students learn is through the use of the Audio-Tutorial System, just as the concerns of other innovators dictate the use of their systems to help their students learn.

Perhaps a discussion of the modes and media of the Audio-Tutorial System should begin with a history of its evolution, because like a viable living organism, it evolved.

The entire program grew and developed because a single individual, Dr. S.N. Postlethwait of the Department of Biological Sciences at Purdue University, was concerned for his students and their varying abilities. Dr. Postlethwait had for many years been involved with introductory courses for beginning freshman students and for many years had not been completely satisfied with the lecture-laboratory technique of presentation. It was obvious to him that though he was an excellent lecturer (we are all excellent lecturers of course) he was not reaching all of his students. The course he was teaching encompassed a broad spectrum of ability levels from the very low level achievers through the very bright pre-veterinary students. Dr. Postlethwait knew he was talking over the heads of many of those at the low end of the spectrum and at the same time he was not stimulating those at the high end.

In order to better meet the needs of the individual student, he began to experiment by preparing a tutorial on tape. (Not a lecture on tape, contrary to many people's beliefs.) He prepared a tutorial—a one-to-one discussion— as if the student were seated on the other end of a log from him or at his side or on the other side of the table.

He made the taped tutorial sessions available to students in the Audio-Visual Center which was open from 7:30 in the morning until 10:30 at night. He then announced to the students in his lecture sessions that if they had difficulty in keeping up with him or if they found themselves not being stimulated by his lectures, they could go to the Audio-Visual Center, check out a tape and listen to the week's material as it came to them in a different format. They could individually pace themselves, by deciding just how much of S.N. Postlethwait they wanted to listen to in any given period of time, by repeating those portions that they didn't understand the first time, by taking notes if they cared to, by isolating themselves in a booth with head sets from all extraneous noise and primarily by deciding when they wanted to learn botany.

Being the sage that he is, Dr. Postlethwait soon realized that he had a very important tool at his hand. It gave him the opportunity to involve the student with the things of his discipline, with plants. He couldn't do this in a lecture of five hundred students, but it was quite possible to carry some plants over to the Audio-Visual Center and put them in the booth with the students. He could actually tutor him now through botany by manipulation of text materials, laboratory manual and short exercises that could be done in the booth by involving the student with the tangible items of the discipline. It was a true multi-media approach.

A very peculiar thing happened; students stopped coming to his lectures. More and more students decided that this kind of format had something to offer. It was nice to be able to go to the Audio-Visual Center at 7:30 in the morning or 8:30 in the evening, anytime they wished, check out a tape and be programmed through a series of learning activities.

We can conceptualize the Audio-Tutorial System perhaps with the diagram now on the screen. If we know what it is we want the student to be able to do at the end of his period of instruction, we should tell him what is expected of him. The numbers 1 through 4 on the right side of the diagram, signify the performance objectives which are spelled out precisely for the student. The letters A,B,C,D,E,F signify learning activities which will help the student

47

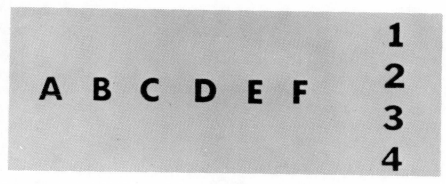

Slide 6

arrive at the performance level designated by the objectives. These activities may include some reading from the study guide, some demonstrate materials, examining a slide or live specimen, viewing a sequence of film or doing an experiment.

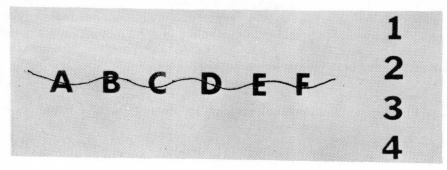

Slide 7

The wavy line weaving A, B, C, D, E and F together signifies the audiotape which is simply the vehicle whereby one programs the student through activities A, B, C, D, E and F. It is not a lecture on tape; it is never a lecture on tape, but it is a device, a programming device, to lead students, quite logically from one activity to another, one experience to another, to get him to the performance level specified by objectives 1 through 4. The tape is not the most important aspect of the program, the objectives and the activities are. Individuals who do not have a sound grasp of the Audio-Tutorial philosophy, fail to comprehend the meaning of those words. Any technology which could deliver this unifying thread that ties activities together could be plugged into the system, video, film or a combination of these.

Why audiotape, why not video or film or print? Audiotape is a *now* technology, a low technology. It is extremely reliable, inexpensive, durable and available *now*. It lends itself to the tutorial aspect of teaching, which means a conversational presentation not a formal lecture, which also means individual pacing not group participation. This also means that the student may stop, back up, and replay any portion as often as needed for understanding. These attributes are difficult to achieve with video or film and too expensive for most schools to achieve with the computer. When the technology of any or all of these formats permits the same flexibility as the audiotape at a comparable cost, then individuals like myself would be willing to become advocates of video-tutorial or computer-tutorial. What I am trying to impress upon you is the tutorial aspect of the program and to indicate to you the audio tape is simply the most convenient, inexpensive, reliable technology available *now* with which to function.

Hopefully you are asking yourself, "Why technology, why not print?" Print works; we know it does. It has served as the bridge among scholars and between scholars and students for centuries—and it does work. Just about everytime I convince myself that it ought to work as well as the audiotape, I find something like this in the newspaper.

48

Recording An Increase

LONDON (UPI)—Gordon Jones, concerned because many of the potential customers who drive into his self-service gas station drive off again on reading the instructions, installed a tape recorder to explain how to operate the pumps. Business shot up 300 per cent, he said.

Slide 8

So we are an aural beast as well as visual.

Slide 9

But it really isn't just to titillate the aural sense that the audiotape is used, another real function comes in freeing the hands and eyes to integrate experiences as this student is doing—manipulating a tangible item and study guide while listening to her instructor talk to her in a one-to-one discussion. What would you do if you had one student to teach? Would you sit her in a lecture room and lecture for fifty minutes three times a week, then have her come into your lab on Tuesday at 1:30 for a three hour lab where you would attempt to integrate what you had told her in the lecture with some lab experiences? I think not. You would probably try to arrange some equally convenient times with no set definite boundaries and tutor her through a series of learning activities which would include laboratory experiences at the time they would be most meaningful in the learning sequence. You probably would not tell her about cell structure on Monday and Wednesday and have her come in the following Tuesday at 1:30 to examine some cells under the microscope. Well, if we would not lecture to one student, why do it for 1000? If we can tutor one student, can we not tutor 1000?

Slide 10

Obviously, we cannot as a single individual sit on the other end of a log and tutor 1000 students through a concept in biology. But we can place a tape recorder on the other end of that log with a recorded tutorial which will tutor him through a series of learning activities — a one-to-one conversation with the student using all the available media at our disposal. What media are available to us as educational inputs?

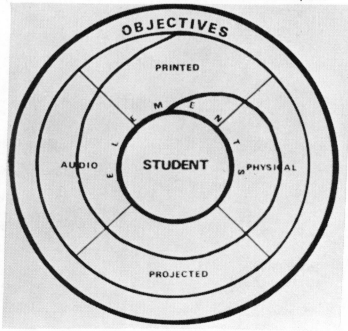

Slide 11

50

Really there are only four major kinds of inputs—the printed, the physical or tangible item or model, projected materials and audio. The developer in the Audio-Tutorial system determines some real objective then surrounds the student with any or all of these inputs and tutors him using these media to reach the objectives set. Any given instructional package may utilize one or all four of these inputs depending on the objectives, the availability of the medium, the educational value of a given medium in a given instructional package and cost. We would not project a four minute 8mm film when three color slides might be as effective. We should not use a set of slides when a page or two of line diagrams in the printed study guide would probably do the job as well. On the other hand, if motion is an integral factor for illustrating a given procedure, the student should have motion available to him. In our situation, this would be 8mm film.

A-T involves the student with an audio input,

Slide 12

and with printed materials

Slide 13

51

when printed materials are appropriate. It involves the student with projected materials

Slide 14

when projected materials are appropriate.

Slide 15

And it involves the student with tangible items,

Slide 16

when tangible items are appropriate.

Slide 17

My choice of the word involve in the past few sentences was not accidental, for this is a major responsibility of the developer of an Audio-Tutorial instructional package — to involve the student with the things of the discipline. Immerse him in botany and things botanical if your intentions are to teach him botany. Have him wrapped up in all the media appropriate to the learning task. In fact, it is my contention that any "new and exciting" program we think to involve ourselves with when we attempt to innovate, ought to have built into it the potential for using as many of these available inputs as possible. No system should work to the exclusion of any one of these instructional inputs if they indeed have any potential value.

So we surround the student with all these media in a Learning Center where he can be himself, take off his shoes

Slide 18

relax

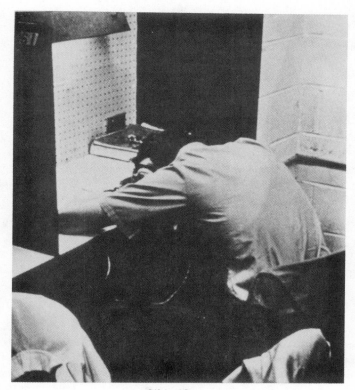

Slide 19

and become involved with the learning activities.

Slide 20

The student becomes isolated from extraneous noise, proceeds at his or her own rate and yet is able to get help from an instructor who is always available

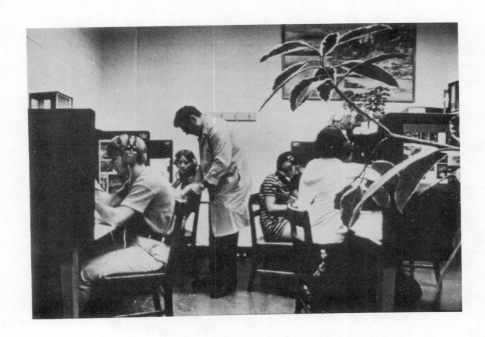

Slide 21

for immediate and personal help when needed,

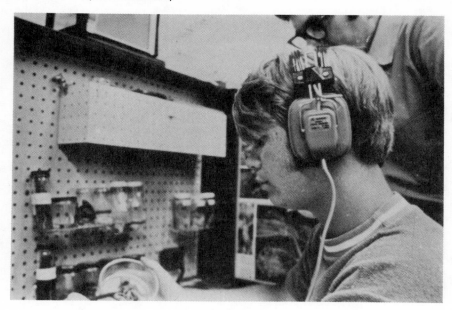

Slide 22

at a time in the learning sequence most meaningful to the student. Exchanges with other students are both encouraged and programmed

Slide 23

as in the case of this student who has satisfactorily completed an instructional package we call a minicourse and is now helping a student having difficulty with the same minicourse. The student will receive points which can contribute to a higher grade in the course through this teaching activity.

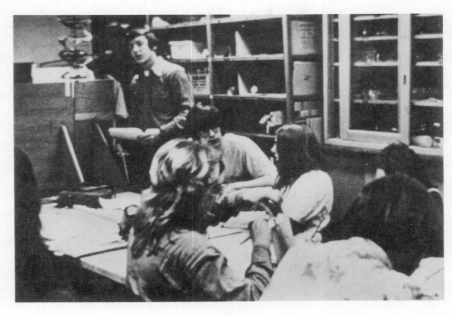

Slide 24

Or exchanges like these taking place informally in the coffee and waiting room adjacent to the Learning Center. Many exchanges here are related to biology, but we are not certain how many are related directly to the course.

Well, those are the modes and media of A-T; now what are we doing with this system that capitalizes on the flexibility and the chance to experiment with learning that it affords us? Can we zero in on some of the things we are doing with the system that we cannot do with a traditional format?

In 1969 we decided it was time to try some other new exciting ideas and we introduced the concept of learning for mastery into our Audio-Tutorial program. This particular concept opens a whole new field of possibilities. The opportunity, for one thing, of making time, not performance, the variable. One can set a performance standard at the level desired, then make time the variable in allowing the student to reach that minimal level. What happens in the process is that students are not branded failures, they are not told "you did not or cannot succeed." Back in 1963 a gentleman named Carroll pointed out that this attribute we call aptitude which is apparently so important to so many people is really nothing more than a measure of time, "the time it takes a student to learn a particular task."

Benjamin Bloom points out in his article "Learning for Mastery" that one thing we can do when we employ this particular concept is document at some measurable minimal level of performance, that our students can at least accomplish certain physical or mental tasks. In so many teaching situations this is not possible and grades are meaningless. I wouldn't want to go to a surgeon for an appendectomy who had A's in vasectomy and tonsilectomy but who failed appendectomy. His overall grade might be a C in surgery, but I would prefer a learning for mastery format so I could know that at least at one time, he could do an appendectomy satisfactorily. Obviously, this is a grossly contrived example, but when one employs the concept for learning for mastery with precisely stated objectives, it is easy to document for anybody who cares to examine the program precisely what it is students can do. Students do not complete an instructional unit until they reach a minimal acceptable performance level.

A learning for mastery format requires a smaller instructional package so a student does not repeat complete units of material when perhaps only one or two points are not well understood his first time through the instruction. At Purdue University we use an instructional package we call a minicourse, which is a unit of instruction that takes the average student anywhere from ½ hour for some minicourses and up to 3 hours for other minicourses to complete, depending on the principle or concept being discussed.

Minicourses are, just as their name implies, little courses. Each has a beginning and an end and each relates to another in virtually the same pattern as one course in any college curriculum relates to another. Thus some have prerequisites, others do not. Some carry more credit and so are more intense or longer than others. Just as some courses involve labs, field trips or demonstrations or as some are more visual than others, minicourses may vary one from another.

Minicourse content is perhaps more logical than the content of some courses (which may be artificially inclusive of specific topics within a given discipline). Minicourses are designed around a single topic or idea or principle. These divisions are much more natural.

Upon the completion of a minicourse, the student receives immediate feedback in an oral and written quiz on his performance in that particular instructional package and is allowed to move on to the next if he is successful. Some students do better if given frequent feedback of success and this system has great potential as a motivating factor for that kind of student. If a student does not do well the first time, this tells him something about his study habits—something he does not have to wait until the end of the semester to find out. It also tells him something about his own abilities. For example, it may not be enough for him to go through the material only one time. It gives him a chance to get started in the right direction in a course and to work at some of these early instructional packages until he achieves the study procedure needed for him to succeed.

At the same time, this kind of course will serve as a winnowing agent for those students not capable of completing the program. Bloom (1968) points out that whenever the pain of remaining in a program becomes unbearable to the student, he simply will quit the program. So the winnowing factor would probably still be present, but it would be the student's decision not to remain in a given curriculum — the student decides "it's not for me," he's never told "you're not quite up to our standards" which does nothing for the student or the school.

I'm sure the idea of making time a variable rankles many individuals involved in professional curricula who feel there's something sacred about a time sequence, about a semester or about a year. But let me pose this question: If we can designate what terminal behaviors or what terminal kinds of performance we expect from the graduates of any kind of instructional program (whether it be a course, or a baccalaureate degree or a professional degree) are we not better off if we can assure those who use the services of the graduates that those individuals can perform at some specified level rather than stating that they completed this program in a semester, year or a period of any designated length?

The courses in which I function are a botany course, Biology 108, and zoology course, Biology 109. When we converted to the concept of learning for mastery in 1969 and looked at the content of these two courses which were always considered sequential courses but taught by two different individuals, we discovered a very interesting phenomenon. Apparently neither instructor trusted the other completely and both instructors were teaching their students several principles common to both plants and animals. Students found themselves repeating much of the same material and thus, there was the problem of redundancy.

With the concept of learning for mastery, when you can assure yourself that those students cannot move on until they reach some level of proficiency with a given topic, it is possible to eliminate all redundancy. In 1969, we actually eliminated about one-fourth of the redundant content of these two courses and this gave us just what the Carnegie Commission promised in their report *Less Time-More Options.* In reality, our program predated the Commission's report but our findings supported their contentions. We had some time left over. We had some optional time to let the student pursue some topics in biology which were of interest or concern to him while working in the same semester credit hour framework.

In their second course of the sequence, students choose about 40% of their curriculum from a whole host of optional minicourses, many of which were evolved upon direct request from the students. They tell us what kind of biological topics they want to study; we develop a minicourse and make it available to them. For special interest groups, like the pre-vet students who wanted more anatomy because they wanted to better prepare themselves for their admission examinations, we had the vehicle to make this possible. We have also developed minicourses upon request from professors of courses taught subsequent to ours in major areas. Often these professors have served as consultants in the preparation or have taken an active developmental role with us.

With a smaller package of instructional materials, one also introduces a flexibility that is not possible in a traditional lecture-lab situation. Just as college students in the still remembered past were offered more individualized curricula when a variety of courses replace the single curriculum all students were expected to follow, so too, do minicourses further individualize the curriculum. The development of the minicourse or conceptual package made it possible for us to individually prescribe instruction for any student for any option within the School of Agriculture and the School of Pharmacy which are the Schools serviced by our two courses.

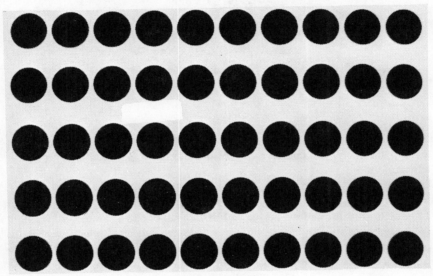

Slide 25

We now have a bank of these minicourses from which we are able to individually prescribe a course in biology suited to the need of any specific individual or option.

Students with guidance can build their own course. We can offer variable semester credit hours from 0.1 of a credit up to 10 or 12 semester credit hours. This year we are offering either 1, 2, 3 or 4 semester credit hours in either course and we individually counsel a student into a package of minicourses commensurate with needs, interests and credit hour enrollment. One of the most surprising aspects of our new variable credit hour offering is just how many students in home economics or sociology or whatever, would like to have 1 or 2 credit hours of biology.

Consider also the disadvantaged student. Specific minicourses designed to eliminate specific deficiencies make more sense than enrollment in an entire course when the deficiency may not be nearly as broad as the course content. Instead of giving the patient one of each pill on the shelf to cure the condition, diagnosis followed by prescription of fewer specific pills, possibly even one, is the treatment required. Instructional packages like the minicourse can function in this capacity.

What about the housewife or the business man or the farmer who would like one semester credit hour in biology, or who would like to know "something" about genetics, or mineral nutrition or photosynthesis or birth

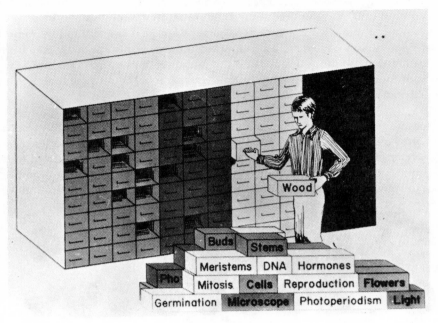

Slide 26

control? The minicourse format permits that kind of student access to specific areas of interest or need without the necessity of an enrollment in and completion of an entire course. The potential then in continuing or extension or adult education is unlimited.

What about the management of such a wide open system of instructions; is it impossible? No, but it is beginning to tax my graduate students and secretarial staff. Open lab hours, a cafeteria of learning which any week could potentially offer students about 80 different minicourses, but more practically offers about a dozen, a student body enrolled for differing credit hour values, each pursuing a package of minicourses perhaps unique to himself, all contribute to the management problem. We have long been ready for computer assistance and in fact have programs written or available to manage the system for us, but alas, we find no federal, state or private agency with $200,000 to $300,000 to put into computer managed instruction.

The computer is destined to become the most important factor in any major innovative instructional under-taking, if not as an integral part of the instructional process, then as the manager of student records and testing, willing to deliver progress reports, prognoses and diagnoses. The present problem with obtaining computer assistance is the vast federal funding for some major CAI programs and the lack of any kind of funding for the mundane com-puter management tasks our own program now stands in need of. The real problem will arise when further educa-tional experimentation, which is sorely needed, will be curtailed by the lack of computer assistance in many innovative programs such as our own.

Management problems increase with each new venture as they have this year by our movement into an experiment with residence hall learning. For two years we have had a take-home kit for all those minicourses whose tangible items lend themselves to packaging. Beginning this year we are making minicourses, complete with all demonstration table and booth tangibles, available in some of the major residence halls. The Audio-Tutorial sys-tem need not be bounded by the institutional environment and indeed is not in our program. Our materials are already affecting those outside the institutional and course setting without our intentional design. Students involved with take home packages now come to us and say "my husband, brother, wife, mother or whoever listened to mini-course Op 11 and wanted me to ask," and so on. Beautiful! Think of the effect we could have if we designed this kind of non-institutional encounter.

Let us ask another question to which the organizers of this symposium have requested we address ourselves.

What about costs of a technologically oriented program like Audio-Tutorial, are they high? The answer is, they need not be — I've already alluded to the low-technology aspect of A-T. In fact, one can move into A-T and stay almost entirely out of the hardware business. That sounds contradictory perhaps, but students can provide their own tape players or buy or rent them from book stores. A reliable inexpensive playback-only device with no record function can be made available to students for about $20. With a two to four student cooperative venture this cost figure is not overly burdensome. A master recorder and duplicating system, and the needed projection equipment are the only pieces of hardware absolutely necessary for an Audio-Tutorial program and many of these are already available on most campuses.

On the other hand, one can go "first cabin" and for $20,000 to $25,000 completely equip a facility with 32 booths—enough equipment and space to tutor about 500 to 600 students through a 4 semester credit hour course by remaining open 70 hours per week. In the cost category, Audio-Tutorial is just not in the game with video formats for CAI. Perhaps to some potential innovators, the lack-lustre hardware needs are a negative factor of A-T. Hopefully this is not the situation.

I have had your attention for a considerable span of time and you have been patient. Let us end the A-T story here, overamplified in some areas perhaps and underamplified in others where you may have some questions. I thank you for your time, but before I answer any questions, let me make my position clear.

Slide 27

Like my amphibian friend here, I feel fairly comfortable with my stance on innovation; I think I'm on top of things, resting on a fairly firm foundation and perhaps sitting a cut above those who, in spite of the virtue of their advanced design like the turtle here, still have to go some to beat my position. Now you ask, "what happens when this advanced design really moves?" I jump and if I jump high enough and this turtle doesn't move too fast, I may maintain my position. Thank you.

REFERENCES

Ashby, Eric. Machines, understanding, and learning: reflections on technology in education. *The Graduate Journal*, 1967, *7* (2).

Bloom, B.S. Learning for mastery. *Evaluation Comment, Center for the Study of Evaluation of Instructional Programs*, UCLA, 1968, *1* (2), 1-11.

Carnegie Commission Report on Higher Education. *Less Time-More Options*, 1971.

Carnegie Commission Report on Higher Education. *The Fourth Revolution: Instructional Technology in Higher Education*. McGraw-Hill, New York, 1972.

Carroll, J. A model of school learning. *Teachers College Record*, 1963, *64*, 723-33.

Hurst, R.N. The potential of audio-tutorial systems of instruction. *Plant Science Bulletin*, 1973, *19* (1), 2-3.

Postlethwait, S.N. Students are a lot like people. *University Vision*, 1972, *8*, 1-6.

LOW-COST EDUCATIONAL TECHNOLOGY

David C. Miller
Director, Instructional Resource Center
University of Illinois, Chicago Circle

INTRODUCTION

A major concern regarding the future of educational technology in higher education is the apparent low level of use, particularly in the traditional university programs. Because substantial funds have been devoted to encourage the adoption of various technological tools, over the past 20 years, most support agencies have been reviewing their programs to see if better ideas and approaches might be available. The recent report[1] prepared by the NAE for the Office of Education is an example of the studies that are under way.

I used the term "apparent low level of use" to highlight the difficulty that anyone experiences in trying to determine what actually is the level of use and perhaps, as equally important, what is the rate of increased use. Social changes have time constants of decades and some sponsors of programs have failed to realize that short programs, even those supported at a high level of funding, may be counterproductive in the short term. Norman MacKinzie[2] has defined educational technology as "the systematic study of the means whereby educational ends are achieved." If we were able to measure the rate of increased use of educational technology so defined, I believe this measure would provide an optimistic index of the future for technology in higher education. However, the fact remains that, to date, the vast majority of students in higher education are being taught by a lecturer unaware of or uninterested in instructional technology who uses books and a blackboard as his only teaching aids. There are important pressures being applied to change the situation because of perceived potential economies by administrators and legislators, demands for better instruction by students and the desire of individual instructors to cope more effectively with an increasingly complex task.

What then are the constraints that slow up the more rapid adoption of technology in education? Perhaps a review of one or two highly successful technological invasions of education will provide some guidance. The paperback book has become so common it may not be recognized as the great revolution in book publishing that it has been. While books have been a vital part of the instructional process for several centuries, the availability of low cost editions in a very convenient format for carrying to and from classes has made it possible for instructors to require students to buy more than just one textbook in a course and thereby provide the student with broad, readily available study resources. The educational need and familiarity with the product combined with low cost borne by the student, the easy availability and convenience of use all contributed to rapid adoption and very widespread use.

A more recent technological invasion of the academic world is the dry copy duplicating machine. The use of these machines has been so great as to give the publication industry great concern and has further complicated the already almost impossibly complex problem of devising a new federal copyright law. Evidently an educational need

---

[1] To Realize the Promise, Advisory Committee on Issues in Educational Technology, Commission on Education, National Academy of Engineering, June, 1973.

[2] Educational Technology and the University, 1966-1970—Centre for Educational Technology, Univ. of Sussex, Brighton, October, 1970.

exists for the rapid copying of many documents. The dry copy process is clean and quick and except for photographs gives excellent copies. It is simple to use and available for use by any instructor at his convenience. Finally, it usually is used with an illusion of no cost because the operating cost is covered by an overhead account and no money passes at the time the copies are made. Furthermore, the per copy cost actually is relatively low when only small numbers of copies of any given document are needed.

The conclusion we can draw from these two examples is that technological developments can penetrate educational institutions and do so fairly rapidly if they satisfy three criteria. First, they must satisfy an educational need as perceived by instructors. Secondly, they must be readily available and convenient to use. Thirdly, they must be relatively low in cost to the student, to the instructor and to the institution.

Low Cost Technology

With these three criteria in mind, what can be said of the technological systems that educators have been exposed to for the past twenty or thirty years? Few, if any, have met all three of these goals. The cost criteria may be satisfied if the cost per student hour of system use is low, say 50 cents or less. In that case, several of the computer based systems may operate at this cost level. However, capital intensive systems in the academic environment have difficulty in raising first costs, creating and maintaining the operating and repair staffs required and perhaps most serious, do not have appropriate amortization programs to cope with rapid obsolescence of complex equipment. Even if all of these capital and operating budget needs are included in the student hour cost calculations, unless university accounting practices recognize the special nature of these systems, the necessary funds for replacement and maintenance are not made available and long-term operation becomes increasingly difficult.

Obviously, all systems involving software and hardware require capital investments and operating support. However, there is a spectrum of costs of this nature and in those programs that have been showing steady growth over the past ten years without major forced feeding from the foundations, the capital investments are relatively modest. One of the best examples is the auto-tutorial system which is being discussed in another paper at this symposium. For some time now, I have been studying educational systems that incorporate low cost technology to see how they could also meet the criteria of perceived need, availability and convenience. Two models, each of which is adaptable to conventional institutions will be described. All of the low cost technological innovations of which I am aware can be used in one or both of these models.

LARGE CLASS MODEL

Each model offers a way to increase the student faculty ratio. The first model uses the obvious approach and merely increases class sizes. This is not a new approach but concern for the quality of education in large group lectures is common among educators and students. There are lecturers who cope successfully with classes of several hundred students, but many instructors are not comfortable with such large groups or are not particularly concerned with the effectiveness of instruction in such circumstances. Since such classes are the delight of administrators and deans because of the massive FTE contributions they produce, the use of large classes will probably continue to increase. However, as higher education continues to be faced with static or even shrinking enrollments, student concerns about instructional quality may become increasingly important and if so, these concerns will clash with administrative desires to use more large classes.

A possible resolution of this conflict of interests could be achieved by the more extensive use of technology in these large class situations. Again, this is not a new idea, it is being done and has been done for many years. However, the extent and nature of use varies greatly. I am sure my premise that technology can improve effectiveness will be challenged and I realize that the research literature on this point is inconclusive. However, the rapid move toward highly flexible curricula provide students with the opportunity to express their preferences in the one way that is incontestable; they can and are refusing to sign up for poorly taught classes. This is still a new phenomenon and the effects are muted by the still large residual of "required courses" but the trend toward a more open curriculum is accelerating and protected havens are likely to decrease in number quite rapidly. Therefore, I am confident that courses using technology properly will continue to attract students and this fact alone will verify its contribution to the "effectiveness" of the instruction.

Use of Motion Pictures

The term "using technology properly," is a key concept. In terms of the previously noted three criteria—cost, convenience and perceived need—what technology is best adapted to large group instruction? Starting from the consideration of perceived need, the instructor should desire to gain and hold attention. The most widely used technology with the proven capability of holding the attention of very large audiences for several hours at a time is the motion picture shown on a big screen. Holding attention, however, is only a start on the learning process. The availability of a large color moving image that all students can easily see can also satisfy a number of other instructor needs by providing unique learning experiences. Some of the more obvious examples capitalize on bringing remote or unusual or dangerous environments into the classroom. One of the most successful films[3] used on the UICC campus was made by Prof. R. Simpson of the Political Science Dept. and chronicles in some detail the organization and conduct of a political campaign for a state level office.

Another important capability of film is to allow a class to relive a one-time event in history, either from an actual filming of the episode or through a dramatic recreation. Technical uses include a wide variety of demonstration experiments that require no set-up time and always work. In this regard, the ability of the camera to magnify or see into normally inaccessible environments can also add substantially to a lecture presentation.

Most people are aware of the educational possibilities of film. Why then is it not used more often? Perhaps a review of how the use of film fails with regard to convenience of use, availability and cost will help to clarify the situation. If we limit the use of film to large lecture classes, showing of the film may be reasonably convenient. Many large classrooms have a large screen, projector, and even, in some cases, a projection booth. A projectionist is very helpful if the film is used for only parts of the class period and may or may not be available. Finding and obtaining appropriate films can be a serious problem, but if the campus has a good reference service, data on a wide variety of available films can be provided. However, if the film must be rented from off-campus, scheduling becomes a factor and decision lead times may be viewed by the instructor as a serious inconvenience. If previewing of films is necessary, additional time is required and the convenience factor suffers still more. The cost of a rental film averages about $15 a showing and the cost of providing an operator may add another $5 to $10 to this amount. If ten films are used in a given course during a semester, the total cost would be between $200 and $250 or, for a large class, about $1 per student per course.

If custom film making is required, the cost increases substantially. Commercial film production costs about $2,000 per minute of finished film and even low cost campus production if fully costed can run $400 per minute. However, an instructor may feel the need for a specific film that can serve to tie together the other films used in the course and a major part of the lecture materials. Assuming a film would be current in content for 5 years, a 30 minute film locally produced would add about $2,400 to the course cost or about $10 per student per course.

To summarize, if the need exists to use film, the convenience of use and availability is only fair, while the cost ranges from low to fairly high. Given optimum conditions film can and is providing strong support for large classes. Unfortunately optimum conditions are not widespread in higher educational institutions and the cost, inconvenience and unavailability factors militate against such use.

Slides

An alternative to the use of film is the 35mm slide or one of its variants. The list of possible perceived needs for the use of slides is similar to the one detailed for film. The lack of motion does introduce an important

---

[3] By the People, produced by R. Simpson, directed by W. Mahin. Distributed by Film Images/Radim Films. Released 1972.

limitation, but can be partially compensated for by the use of a special technique[4] that uses two projectors and a lap dissolve switching unit. By using alternate superimposed images from two slide projectors and sequencing them rapidly, an illusion of motion can be generated that will suffice for many applications. Even for just showing a sequence of slides at a slow pace, the technique allows the same sort of transition from one image to the next that people are accustomed to in films and television.

Once more, however, I must admit that slides are not used extensively in higher education and while there does seem to be a trend toward increased use, a major problem is still inconvenience. Actual viewing of slides in a big classroom may not be much of a problem and a dissolve unit may even be available. The projectors can be remotely controlled by the lecturer and trays of slides easily loaded and unloaded. However, it is in the preparation or procurement of slides that the major inconvenience ensues. Slide collections can be purchased but content and availability is usually more difficult to determine than in the case of film. If purchased, slides will cost about 50 cents to $1 each and if they are used extensively in a course, this can exceed the cost of a film rental. On the other hand, slides can be used many times and collections of slides can be easily edited, so the long-term cost is probably lower than for film.

If the instructor wants to use custom-made slides, he must provide the raw data. Then the slides will cost about $2 to $3 each. This cost can be reduced by the do-it-yourself instructor, but ready access to art materials, drafting tables, varitypers and copy cameras may be a problem and in any case will constitute an inconvenience. Considering only film and processing costs, a slide might be prepared for as little as 10 cents. If, however, the lap dissolve technique is used, two 80 slide trays can be used during a single lecture and would represent a first cost of about $16. Assuming a once a year use and a five year life, the maximum cost for forty-two one hour class sessions would be $135 or, again, for a large class about $1 per student per course. In most cases, slides would cost more than this minimum amount but intensity of use would probably also be much lower, so these two factors would tend to cancel and the $1 cost figure is probably a good average.

To summarize for slides, they can meet many of the same needs as film does. They are more convenient to show, more difficult to buy or rent and easier to custom design and make. However, slide making is a time consuming inconvenience great enough to discourage most instructors. Costs are about the same as film rentals and could be considered low if used with large classes.

Overhead Projectors

Probably the most widely used classroom presentation device is the overhead projector. Interestingly, it also combines the greatest convenience of use with the lowest operating cost of any large class presentation device. The projector is totally under control of the lecturer and can be used as he would use a blackboard. Transparencies can be readily prepared prior to class use on plastic sheets that cost about ten cents each. If erasable markers are used, the sheets can be reused many times. Colored line drawings are easy to prepare with appropriate pens. Colored pictures are possible but represent a much more difficult problem. Moving images are possible in the film mode but motion of the pen in drawing curves or writing usually imparts a higher interest level than a still image. Students often object to the use of prepared transparencies on the overhead projector because it allows the lecturer to present materials much faster than they can put it in their notes. This problem can be overcome if the lecturer also provides copies of notes covering everything presented on the screen, but this involves extra time and eliminates what may be an important learning process. An alternative solution is to pace the presentation of material to allow time for note taking.

Rated in order of low cost, convenience and availability, the overhead projector is clearly the first choice, the slide presentation is second, and movies come off third. However, a well-balanced presentation strategy could find unique need for each of these modes in any given course. The ability of the film to engender affective

---

[4] "Lap Dissolve Projection: A Technique for Teaching Spatial, Temporal and Organizational Relationships," J.S. Daniel, J.P. Bailon, U. of Montreal, Proc. of Third Annual Frontiers in Education Conference (IEEE), p.297.

as well as cognitive responses is particularly important and often is not fully appreciated. Properly orchestrated these three presentation techniques can be used at a cost level that is acceptable and, by so doing, can generate a high interest level and broaden access to content thereby making the large class format quite acceptable and educationally profitable to students.

The use of television in the large class situation has been purposely neglected. Projection television is expensive, technically complex and until very recently, has lacked color capability. Use of individual monitors scattered throughout a large classroom can provide an alternative presentation mode, but I object to the small screen and often poor color that such television offers. Future developments may change the situation, but in that case cost, convenience and availability will be very similar to the film situation. The only possible exception might be when a closed circuit television system is used as an overhead projector with a camera focussed on the desk pad of the instructor. While cheaper than filming such an event, the cost is still not competitive with a simple optical overhead projector.

INDIVIDUAL OR SMALL GROUP STUDY MODEL

A second model of an instructional system that can use low cost technology is based on the assumption that the major fraction of student learning occurs in the self-study or peer group mode and that if efforts are expended to structure and aid this learning activity more effectively than has been the case in the past, an important amount of time that has been devoted to information processing in lectures can be eliminated. The audio-tutorial system, which is a specific execution of this model, has given the impetus to a wide variety of related approaches. A common pattern in all of these systems is a reduction in formal lecture time and varying degrees of individual student assistance.

As noted in the large class model discussion, the only way reasonable costs of technical sub-systems could be achieved was by spreading the costs over a large student population for each application. Even under these circumstances, some costs such as those associated with the production of custom made films are difficult to cover. Therefore, if a system of instruction proposes to provide technology mediated learning for individuals, the necessary duplication of both software and hardware becomes a very serious problem. One of the first systems devised to provide individual instruction was the language laboratory. Unfortunately, the inflexibilities in use that were introduced by cost considerations have contributed to its reputation as one of the less successful educational innovations.

So the challenge of designing successful systems that provide individualized opportunities for guided self-study depends heavily on low cost people and when appropriate and available, low cost technology. The use of differentiated staffing, even to the extent of unpaid undergraduate tutors has provided a component of lower paid instructional staff. The problem of providing lower cost technology has been more difficult because most of the hardware was designed for large group use and even software costs were justified on the basis of only one copy being needed for a class of thirty or more students.

In regard to projected images, the ultimate low cost device is not yet available, although there are some systems such as the Philips PIPS units that recognize the need and have made a start in the right direction.

Audio Tape Cassettes

In the audio field, the cassette format has made possible a variety of applications that support individual study efforts at a low cost. Several applications have been mentioned in previous papers[5,6,7] but for the sake of completeness, will be reviewed.

[5]"A Systems Approach to Individualized Instruction," D.C. Miller, Proceedings Second Annual Frontiers in Education Conference, 1972(IEEE).

[6]"Technology and Self Study," D.C. Miller, *J. Educational Technology Systems*, Vol. 1 (1)pp. 73-80. June, 1972.

[7]"The Audio Tape Cassette in Education," D.C. Miller, *Engineering Education*, Vol. 63, No. 6, March, 1973.

Perhaps the technical sub-systems having the lowest costs to the institution, are those that can use student supplied equipment. Audio tape cassette record/playback units are widely available and less costly than a typewriter. If the assumption is made that each student can find access to a playback unit, cassettes can be used in several ways to promote the effectiveness of the self-study mode. For example, immediate answers to problem sets that are assigned in courses in math, science and engineering can be provided if a commentary tape and an answer sheet is given to the student when he hands in his work. This enables the students to immediately check their results, alternate methods of solution and relationships to lecture materials. The instructor then need only check who handed in a paper and spot check some of them for feedback. If graded papers for all students are considered essential, the students can be asked to keep a copy of their solutions, grade it and report the result. Again, a spot check of the papers turned in could keep the responses honest.

The trade-off, of course, is the effort required to prepare the tape. However, once a master tape is prepared, it can be reused each time the course is taught. An average cassette commentary is about 30 minutes, so the production time should not be more than an hour. There is no need for scripting although a few notes on each problem are helpful, particularly if previous feedback from students had indicated difficult concepts or computational "booby traps." Often a tape dialogue is a good format, where a student or another instructor serve as a surrogate for the listener by introducing questions or comments.

If the campus has its own audio studios, the recording can be done there. If not, tapes can be made in a classroom or in an office if the instructor has a recorder. The principal cost to the school for such a practice is the duplication of the cassettes. Cassette duplicators may cost as much as three or four thousand dollars, but can be used with student labor. Thirty minute cassettes for a class of 40 students could be duplicated in about one hour depending on the particular type of duplicator used. Cassettes can be provided by the school with an understanding that the student return a cassette for each different one he receives. Thus, the school need only buy as many cassettes as students in the class. If a student wants to keep one or more tapes, he is asked to substitute a blank cassette for each one he wants to save. Tapes for a 40 person class can be purchased for about $35 and can be used for four or five courses in sequence. The cost per student hour for such a system would be 5¢, so it is truly low cost.

Learning Laboratories

If the school is able to set up learning laboratories where students can come to listen to prepared tapes, using them in concert with visual materials, the capital costs are somewhat greater but still low. A thirty carrel unit could be assembled for $20,000 to $25,000. Assuming 12 hour a day availability, the cost per student hour could be as low as seven cents although 100% utilization would be required to reach this figure. But even at 50% utilization, the cost is low. However, the cost of software must be added to this capital cost. If the school provides the learning software in the tape/slide format and each set requires about one student hour to complete, ten copies of each set could serve the needs of a class of two hundred. A tape/slide combination could cost about $30 a copy and could be used for at least five course repetitions. So the cost per student hour use is about $.03. Costs for preparing the software should be added to this figure, if the materials are not commercially available. Using a preparation cost of $500 per tape/slide set, and again spreading this cost over a five year period, the cost per student hour of use would be about $.50. Added to the capital costs and duplicating charges, this cost level would be marginal in meeting the low cost criterion. The software preparation time is the major cost factor and is seldom fully costed, since the instructor will contribute time and often campus media services are available from overhead accounts. Thus the perceived cost usually does fall within the low cost category.

It is also interesting to note that for a given tape/slide combination, the cost of the slides comprises about 80% of the total. The 35mm slide is expensive to use for individual viewing and alternate formats are needed. The film strip is one such alternative but lack of highly reliable display equipment, difficulties in editing and the high cost of small numbers of copies are serious limitations.

Some applications in the learning laboratories do not need or use projected visual software and depend on audio cassettes and accompanying printed materials. Such a combination not only greatly reduces cost but for some applications can be the best mode of instruction. "Hands on" experience is often the best way to learn how to operate a wide range of devices and the tape/workbook is particularly well adapted to assist such learning activities. For example, familiarization with electronic laboratory equipment such as an oscilloscope or a signal generator is very effectively conducted by use of a cassette/workbook combination and several versions have been prepared and used. Some video enthusiasts feel that if audio cassettes are good, video cassettes must be better. I think that when a learning situation already requires full visual attention by the student, to offer competing visual information may slow down rather than aid the learning process. It certainly adds to the cost.

Interactive Lectures

One of the earliest uses of the audio cassette recorders was the recording of classroom lectures. Most students and many instructors learned that this procedure was not the learning boon it was expected to be. Listening to audio can be very dull and without a visually related image can be subject to many distractions as the visual sense demonstrates its dominance. Also a one hour lecture requires one hour to review. Thus, the ability to provide individual oral versions of a lecture at a low cost was an attractive solution in search of a problem. One of the most interesting approaches to resolving this situation has been the "interactive lecture"[8] developed by Dr. Stewart Wilson of the Polaroid Corporation.

Most mediated instruction guides a student through a long series of learning steps and depends upon the frequent use of program specified questions to provide learning reenforcement. However, in many successful learning environments, the inverse occurs—the questions are student formulated based on his rate of comprehension and previous background. The system devised by Dr. Wilson creates as nearly as possible with media, a situation whereby a student can learn content by listening to a lecture, can initiate appropriate questions of his choosing and readily obtain answers to these questions. The system is based on the concept that for a given lecture, there is a finite number of questions that any student hearing the lecture is likely to ask. By having a reasonable sized sample of students listen to a given lecture and list their questions, a bank of questions can be generated. Furthermore, it seems reasonable to expect that if a large number of students participate in the preparation of the question bank, any question a student might have subsequently while listening to the lecture would have a high probability of being in the question bank. Then, by recording on cassettes answers to all the questions in the bank and arranging a method of fairly rapid access for any specific answer, the system can provide the student with a low cost interactive learning resource.

Dr. Wilson also uses a modified Flexiwriter which operates from one track of the tape cassette and draws on a sketch pad any visual materials the lecturer wishes to use with his presentation.

I have adapted this idea to a somewhat less sophisticated system with the hope of making it more attractive cost-wise and somewhat easier for a student to use. By recording instructional lectures, editing out all questions asked by students and repetitive or irrelevant materials, a fifty minute lecture can usually be reduced to about thirty minutes. Using speech compression equipment, the lecture can be further reduced to about 25 minutes. A workbook is prepared for the visual materials that accompany the lecture. Using the question set generated by students during the lecture as a nucleus, additional students are asked to listen to the condensed lecture and add questions. The final set of questions and answers to these questions are put together as a part of the final workbook. If desired the question set can be added to and answers can be modified as the lecture is made available to additional students. Thus the unit can be kept up-to-date with relatively little additional effort.

The interactive lecture in this modified format is particularly suited for individualizing instruction. The only contribution required of the instructor is to give permission to record his lectures and to write answers to the questions in the question bank. However, the tape editing must be done by someone quite familiar with the

---

[8] "Interactive Lectures" S.W. Wilson, *Technology Review* (MIT), January, 1972.

lecture content and consultation with the instructor is essential. The system is particularly suited to optimize student time since a bright student can spend about half as much time listening to lectures as he normally would whereas the slower student could review all of the available questions if desired and never risk exposing to the instructor his inability to quickly grasp the material. The portability of the tape/workbook combination allows the material to be studied almost anywhere it is convenient for the student to do so.

Unfortunately, while the system is low cost and can be used conveniently, the perceived need by instructors has not yet materialized in any significant number of cases. One problem is the acceptance of the desirability to move the data transmitting function from the group lecture mode to the individual self study format. Another problem is the availability of skilled tape editors who are also reasonably knowledgeable in the content to be edited. However, students can learn editing quickly and can do a fine job on content with a little experience, but convincing instructors to use the technique is much more difficult.

Calculators

No discussion of low cost technology can ignore the potential and real impact of the new solid state calculators, particularly the hand held units. Costs range from $50 to $400 depending upon the sophistication of the calculations desired. It seems likely that almost every student that takes courses involving calculations sooner or later will obtain such a unit for his personal use just as students now buy typewriters, slide rules and cassette recorders.

The impact of the greatly increased computational capability these devices can provide to students will certainly allow a substantial change in the level and number of problems assigned in technical courses. In those schools, such as Dartmouth, where students have had ready access to the computational power of the digital computer, substantial course modification has already occurred and might serve to guide future steps in this direction.

Cost and convenience would lead one to expect a rapid incorporation of these inexpensive calculators into the curriculum but, again, perceived need by instructors may not be sufficient to push the acceptance of this innovation as quickly as some of us would like.

Television Monitors

The use of TV cassette players and color monitors is a very attractive presentation mode and is receiving a great deal of attention at the present time. I think it is particularly well adapted to use by individuals or perhaps small groups. However, the cost of a playback unit with color monitor is at least $1,500 and each unrecorded cassette costs about $25. Therefore, while I hope money can be found to outfit at least portions of learning labs with TV cassette players, I cannot classify it as a low cost technology — at least not in the near future.

CONCLUSION

Two models of an educational system have been reviewed for needs that could be satisfied by some form of technology. Some needs were identified and possible technological solutions were discussed. The criteria of low cost, convenience of use, ease of availability and perceived need by instructors were applied to each technological approach and the degree to which the technology under consideration met these criteria was assessed. None of the technological systems presently available met all of these criteria to a high degree, although the overhead projector use in the large group model and the audio cassette use in the individual study model came close to satisfying the criteria posed as necessary for successful widespread adoption.

REFERENCES

1. "A Systems Approach to Individualized Instruction," D. C. Miller, *Proceedings Second Annual Frontiers in Education Conference,* 1972 (IEEE).

2. *By the People,* produced by R. Simpson, directed by W. Mahin. Distributed by Film Images/Radim Films. Released 1972.

3. *Educational Technology and the University, 1966-1970* — Centre for Educational Technology, University of Sussex, Brighton, October, 1970.

4. "Interactive Lectures," S.W. Wilson, *Technology Review* (MIT). January, 1972.

5. "Lap Dissolve Projection: A Technique for Teaching Spatial, Temporal and Organizational Relationships," J. S. Daniel, J. P. Bailon, University of Montreal, *Proc. of Third Annual Frontiers in Education Conference,* (IEEE), p. 297.

6. "Technology and Self Study," D. C. Miller, *J. Educational Technology Systems,* Vol. 1 (1) pp. 73-80, June, 1972.

7. "The Audio Tape Cassette in Education," D. C. Miller, *Engineering Education,* Vol. 63, No. 6, March, 1973.

8. *To Realize the Promise,* Advisory Committee on Issues in Educational Technology, Commission on Education, National Academy of Engineering, June, 1973.

LATENT ENVIRONMENTAL EFFECTS OF EDUCATIONAL TECHNOLOGY

James Bess
Director of Planning Studies
SUNY at Stony Brook

In most cases, measurement of the effects of new or experimental instructional technology involves the assessment of changes in the subjects undergoing the special treatment. Seldom is there an examination of others in the educational environment with whom either the subjects or the technology itself interface. This paper looks at some of the potential relationships between the subjects in an experimental instructional setting and students, faculty and administrators whose relationships to the new technology are initially indirect and tangential. The paper is concerned particularly with these relationships in a conventionally bounded higher education system where new teaching-learning technologies represent only a relatively small input to the total environment. It concentrates mostly on the impact on students.

The paper begins with a discussion of some of the variables which might be explored. In particular, needs of students and aims of the curriculum in a conventional system are contrasted. Next, the typical objectives of new instructional technologies on these campuses are discussed. An attempt is made to show how these technologies usually assume a limited set of aims at traditional colleges. The nature of the environment which is needed to support the broader aims of liberal education are then suggested, followed by some hypotheses about the impact of new instructional technologies on that environment. A short section on environmental measurement is then offered. The paper concludes with several recommendations about how technologies must be adapted to recognize not only curricular aims and student needs but also the environmental conditions which are conducive to their satisfaction.

Changing Needs of Students

One way of evaluating the effect of new instructional technologies on a student body is to determine if and how they meet both the aims of the institution of higher education and of the needs of its students. Curricula in post-secondary education are typically designed with each of two broad sets of objectives, though it is sometimes claimed they are in conflict with one another. Depending in part on the kind of institution, conventional courses addressed at meeting institutional needs are intended to have an immediate effect on the student's store of knowledge in a particular field, which in turn, it is presumed, allows him to be more adequately prepared for his post-graduate life. In addition, conventional courses have the objective of increasing the student's critical capacities — his abilities to think objectively and creatively. Frequently the curriculum as a whole attempts to instill some awareness of alternative value systems, particularly as these relate to the duties of good citizenship. It is hoped that the student will, in addition, benefit from his courses by having his overall awareness and appreciation of the fine arts enhanced. Finally, conventional curricula often are designed to allow students opportunities to learn to act with independence and autonomy. It should be noted that these institutional objectives look mostly to the preparation of the student for the future, rather than to his development in the present. Moreover, the pedagogical style which has appeared most conducive to learning under this assumption is one in which learning takes place through the acquisition of "bits" of information, arranged sequentially according to any of a number of theories of cognitive development.

But students often have their own sets of needs in addition to those commonly assumed by institutional educational planners in their design of formal curricula (Katz, 1968; Chickering, 1969). Young people coming to college are seeking to find out who they are and what they are "good" at. More than simply vocational identification, college students look for a deeper sense of the continuing stable set of personality traits they can call their own. They want also to explore alternative living styles, often a frightening prospect for them in which internal conflicts lead to confusing tergiversation. Students are interested in developing their interpersonal competencies — i.e., their capacities to communicate intimately with other human beings. Similarly, they are concerned with the ways they handle their emotions, desiring to feel more comfortable when they express themselves openly or when they find it necessary to be restrained. Finally, they search for meaning in their lives. A never-ending life-long quest, in the college years, this drive is particularly salient.

These two sets of objectives (of the institution and of the student) are clearly related, but often in contemporary higher education they are unfortunately opposed to one another. The more subtle and often undefined and usually unstated educational objectives of the institution are translated into a formal curriculum which is so geared to the meeting of students' future needs that it may ignore those most urgently felt by the students as they pursue their daily lives. That this apparent dualism is more myth than reality was, of course, Dewey's theme in much of his writing (e.g., Dewey, 1916). The artificial separation of future and present, of institution and student, of object and subject is accentuated by the differences among the disciplines where faculty have quite different pedagogical assumptions and objectives (Gamson, 1967). The dichotomization of institutional and student needs leaves unexamined the relationship between motivation and learning, between emotion and reason and between the urgency of the student's present and the practicalities of his future and that of his society. One important test of new educational technologies, then, is to see how well they address themselves to these interlocking sets of needs. To the extent that they can meet this challenge, they will have facilitated the needs of the society for an educated and informed citizenry, the needs of the students for personal growth and development and the needs of a pedagogical system which accounts for the relationship between the two.

It seems reasonably clear that particularly in bounded, conventional systems of higher education, designers of new technologies have not adequately comprehended the synergetic nature of institutional and student needs and have chosen to concentrate on the former. The impetus for experimentation in pedagogical forms on these campuses has been spurred by financial pressures on colleges and universities to find ways to teach more "efficiently" — i.e., to reach out to greater numbers of students at less cost. It can be demonstrated (though it will not be here) that in back of these demands for economy are the restricted set of assumptions about the purposes of the curriculum noted in the first of the set of objectives described above (i.e., those that are oriented toward the preparation of the student as a future citizen). To the degree that teachers and researchers are naively responsive to federal agencies and others who would sponsor such efforts, the experimental technologies will be geared predominantly toward improving the more pastoral functions of higher education—the passing on of information to students for their future use as adults and citizens. This cognitive and future-looking orientation neglects not only the linkages between cognitive growth and total individual development but the manner in which both take place in a complicated social context outside the classroom.

Supportive Educational Environments

A much more comprehensive conceptualization of the environmental conditions requisite to the satisfaction of both affective and cognitive learnings seems to be needed. When new instructional technologies tend to reinforce the more traditional objectives of curriculum makers, they assume a more limited role for the teacher and demand far less of the institutional culture in support of student growth and development. Computer-assisted instruction or self-paced learning devices tend to (though they do not always) ignore the deeper needs of the student for personal growth. While they may recognize in passing that students may develop greater independence or that feelings of personal competence may be enhanced when students proceed at rates compatible with their learning abilities, such benefits are usually treated as fortuitous events rather than as achievements of planned objectives.

Both apocrypha and research (Newcomb, 1962; Newcomb and Wilson, 1966) support the view that peer influences as well as other non-curricular experiences contribute as much to student growth and development as does exposure to formal course work. For example, Bolton and Kammeyer (1967, p. 80) report that in "bull sessions" outside of class, students talk about intellectual matters only about 9% of the time, about popular culture and campus topics (including academic matters) about 24% of the time and about personal concerns for the remaining two-thirds of the time. Despite Newcomb's strong urgings in 1962, little research has been done (or at least reported) which documents the kinds of effects such interactions have on long-term student growth and development. There is strong reason to believe that in "bull sessions" per se (i.e., not "study groups") the intellectual activity which takes place does less to aid students in acquiring the knowledge prescribed by the curricular objectives than it stimulates, provokes, challenges and teaches values and beliefs operating at a more profound level in the individual's motivational and personality nexus. That is, students are more likely to engage in conversations in bull sessions which touch on their deeply felt feelings about issues of importance to them — feelings which frequently stem from prior socialization in earlier parental and educational settings. Yet these intellectual exchanges are of immense value when they can be related to the curriculum, especially when curricular (or institutional) objectives are addressed to individual needs. As Newcomb (1962) notes, "Teachers' influence, if it is to be effective, must be caught up in the norms of student groups. . ." The relationship between academic and non-academic life must, in other words, be consciously considered in the planning of educational objectives. Needless to say, in bounded, conventional systems of higher education, such connections are rarely made. The climate for establishing new instructional technologies on such campuses with this relationship in mind is not, therefore, a favorable one.

Another example of student activity outside the classroom is in "dating." Though on different campuses, interaction with the opposite sex may be called by other names. Bolton and Kammeyer at the University of California-Davis found that their sample of students averaged about 17 hours a week in this activity (either in dyads or in larger mixed-sex groups). Their finding that students on dates tend more than in bull sessions to talk about serious and self-revealing topics is not surprising. They report:

> On dates, students are more likely to discuss personality or identity problems, long-run orientations, and intellectual topics, especially those dealing with religious and philosophical questions. The latter discussions are often attempts by the students to work out their own values and ideologies. (p. 231)

Clearly, dating is potentially one of the most important learning modes for students. There are some who would argue that together with all "non-academic" activities they are not and should not be the responsibility of educational planners. While few would suggest that the dating encounter should be heavily structured as a self-paced learning device (properly videotaped for later feedback to student and instructor!), it does seem reasonable to acknowledge that the quality of the learning that can take place is affected by the prevailing informal student (and faculty) values and norms about the activity. For example, a campus atmosphere dominated by traditional machismo and mannered male-female relations will result in far different kinds of student development than will one which is characterized by equality, honesty, directness and caring.

The main point of these two examples, bull sessions and dating, is to illustrate that the out-of-class activity of students has a direct relationship to the in-class learning. If in the preparation of instructional objectives for courses, faculty are not cognizant of the kinds of growth and development which can take place in other settings and of the relationship of that learning not only to curricular objectives but to student need satisfaction, their design of new instructional technologies will be deficient. More, it may even have a negative effect on the quality of campus life in which it is introduced. As Janowitz and Street (1966) remark about educational television,

> Rarely (if ever) is the crucial question asked: What is the impact of television instruction upon the teaching staff, the student body, and the whole organizational capacity of the educational institution? What are the effects on socialization of television instruction? In short, what are the side effects — when the side effects may be more powerful than the direct effects.

Measurement of the Environment

Those interested in experimenting with new instructional technologies are quite naturally concerned with measuring the effects of their experimental treatments. The hypothesis of this paper is that such measurement must include not only cognitive changes in students, but their affective development and the nature of the environment which supports it.

This raises a number of serious problems. New instructional technologies in bounded, conventional systems of higher education commonly take as their time frame for measurement the semester or quarter — i.e., the unit of time in which a "course" is offered. In the evaluations, pre- and post-course testing of treatment and control groups is performed in order to determine whether the course material has been acquired with greater efficiency. Rarely are efforts made to retest at later times, except perhaps by test-makers concerned with increasing the reliabilities of their scales. Seldom, too, are measures taken of the long-term effects on the thought processes or behavior of the student or of the ways in which his new knowledge has or has not been integrated into his personal value system. There is little research which shows, for example, correlations between achievement scores in courses using new instructional technologies and changes in personality growth and development taken at significant points in the student's college career. In short, evaluations of new instructional technologies do not usually look beyond the course as the time unit of measurement, and they rarely make connections between the objectives of the course and the broader aims and objectives of curriculum and student (c.f. Born et al., 1972).

Nor does the research to date seem concerned with the relationships between new technologies and the "press" of the campus environment. Fortunately, some considerable research has been reported on the nature of the relationships between incoming student characteristics and the effect of the college environment on them (Astin, 1968; Feldman and Newcomb, 1969), though critics of this kind of research are also becoming more vociferous (Feldman, 1972). In grossly oversimplified diagrammatic form, the figure below shows some of the difficulty in measuring the impact of new instructional technologies:

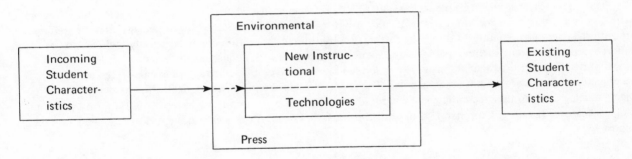

Figure 1. Instructional Technologies of Total Environmental Press

The figure reveals how the new instructional technologies are set in a context of a total environmental press, both affecting and being affected by it. Students entering the institution help determine the press and are affected differentially both by the press and by the new instructional technologies which they may undergo.

It will be helpful at this point to illustrate how measures of the campus environment can be related to evaluations of new instructional technologies. Since the early anecdotal-type research of Boroff (1958) and Jacob (1957), many instruments have been developed to provide valid and reliable information about college campuses. Approaches to the study of college environments vary. One is the method of perceptual analysis, in which various constituencies on a campus indicate the degree to which they feel activities of one kind or another are present in varying degrees (Stern, 1970; Pace, 1972; Pervin, 1967; Chickering, 1970). The several instruments used by the American College Testing Service and the Educational Testing Service (e.g., Peterson et al., 1970) are perhaps the most widely known and readily available of this type, partly because the scales have been well-tested and nationally normed. Through these questionnaires, it is possible to obtain a picture of a campus in terms of its relative emphasis on certain goals, its efficacy in functioning and the quality of its environment measured by perceived characteristics such as scholarship, awareness, community, propriety, practicality, quality of teaching and campus morale.

Another approach to the study of environments is the stimulus approach (Astin & Holland, 1961; Astin, 1968; Pace, 1972). Here, members of the campus are asked to describe their own activities, and/or researchers ascertain the degree of presence or absence of key environmental features (e.g., number of faculty, number of books in the library). Still a third, but related, avenue of investigation is the depiction of the character of an environment by describing the personality characteristics of the individuals who comprise it. Thus far, this approach has been developed primarily for students. Using one such instrument, The Omnibus Personality Inventory (Heist & Yonge, 1968) it is possible to describe a campus in terms of its students' dispositions toward intellectuality, autonomous action, introversion-extroversion, estheticism, impulse expression and altruism, and the degree to which they are personally integrated, religiously liberal and oriented toward practical matters. The instrument is also of value in allowing longitudinal assessments of the student body, thus permitting evaluations of growth and development resulting (presumably) from exposure to the campus or selected portions of it (e.g., different majors or alternative residential arrangements).

Each of these approaches can be of use in the evaluation of new instructional technologies. Again, if the assumption is made that there is an interactive effect among the technology, the environment and student growth and development, then inquiries can be made of the nature of the relationships. If the designers of experiments using the new technologies include in their planning the notion that important, long-lasting liberal education requires supportive environments, then it should be possible to control for the environment in the evaluation. For example, selection of certain dormitories for activities supportive of in-class technologies can be made. Assessment of the quality of the dormitory environment compared with control groups can be made before and after the introduction of the new technology. Similarly, student personality dispositions can be ascertained in these controlled environments, permitting later testing for changes.

Beyond the measurement problems in evaluating the effects of new instructional technologies on students are a whole host of other environmental factors particularly those involving faculty. This is especially true on bounded, conventional campuses. Faculty in the social setting of a traditional institution are not generally inclined nor encouraged to share their teaching methods, problems and successes with colleagues. It is somewhat surprising, then, that new instructional technologies are not looked on more favorably, since as noted earlier, the assumptions and objectives of each are actually quite similar. The problem is compounded when, or if, the broader set of objectives suggested for new technologies is proposed. Faculty on these campuses will resist not only new technological features (Evans & Leppmann, 1967) but the expanded set of objectives and the necessity of environmental support for them.

SUMMARY

To summarize, learning which affects the whole person requires careful design of the total environment in which the process takes place. In bounded conventional systems, it is unlikely that new instructional technologies will result in profound benefits without positive social system reinforcement. The absence of reinforcing contingencies in dormitories and other student-dominated settings results in a narrowed intellectual focus and a shortened time dimension into which new material is integrated. Students, are led, in other words, to view their current academic experience as a shortrun hurdle to be conquered and quickly forgotten, or perhaps stored in memory for some as yet unrecognized future need.

Measurement of the attitudes of those in the environment in which new instructional technologies are introduced will reveal the presence or absence of values which support long-lasting learning and which encourage attention to student growth and development. The bifurcation of institutional objectives (which on traditional campuses are geared primarily toward preparation of the student as a future citizen) and individual student needs (which are temporally situated in the present) is accentuated by new instructional technologies which tend to neglect the latter. Only when those concerned with innovative teaching and learning methods incorporate a broader set of educational objectives will the need for supportive campus environments become of sufficient importance to produce them. In sum, attention to the sociology of learning as well as the technology of teaching in the light of a comprehensive set of institutional objectives is needed for a truly successful educational enterprise.

REFERENCES

1. Astin, Alexander & John L. Holland, "The Environmental Assessment Technique: A Way to Measure College Environments," *Journal of Educational Psychology,* 1961, Vol. 52.

2. Astin, Alexander W., *The College Environment,* Washington, D.C., American Council on Education, 1968.

3. Bolton, Charles D. and Kenneth C. W. Kammeyer, *The University Student,* New Haven, College & University Press, 1967.

4. Born, D. G., S. M. Gledhill, M. L. Davis, "Examination Performance in Lecture — Discussion and Personalized Instructional Courses," *Journal of Applied Behavior Analysis,* 1972, Vol. 5.

5. Boroff, David, *Campus USA,* New York, Harper & Brothers, 1958.

6. Chickering, Arthur, *Education and Identity,* San Francisco, 1969, Jossey-Bass, Publishers, 1969.

7. Chickering, Arthur W., *The Experience of College Questionnaire,* Saratoga Springs, Center for the Study of Educational Change, 1970.

8. Evans, Richard I. and Peter K. Leppmann, *Resistance to Innovation in Higher Education,* San Francisco, Jossey-Bass Publishers, Inc., 1967.

9. Dewey, John, *Democracy and Education,* New York, The Macmillan Company, 1916.

10. Feldman, Kenneth A., "The Assessment of College Impacts" in Kenneth A. Feldman (ed.), *College and Student,* New York, Pergamon Press, Inc., 1972.

11. Feldman, Kenneth A. and Theodore Newcomb, *The Impact of College on Students,* San Francisco, Jossey-Bass, Publishers, 1969.

12. Gamson, Z. F. "Performance and Personalism in Student-Faculty Relations," *Sociology of Education,* 1967, Vol. 40.

13. Heist, Paul A. and George Yonge, *Manual for the Omnibus Personality Inventory,* New York, The Psychological Corporation, 1968.

14. Jacob, Philip E., *Changing Values in College: An Exploratory Study of the Impact of College Teaching,* New York, Harper & Brothers, 1957.

15. Janowitz, Morris and David Street, "The Social Organization of Education" in Peter N. Rossi and Bruce J. Biddle (eds.), *The New Media and Education,* Chicago, Aldine Publishing Co., 1966.

16. Katz, Joseph, and Associates, *No Time for Youth,* San Francisco, Jossey-Bass, Publishers, 1968.

17. Newcomb, Theodore M., "Student Peer-Group Influence in Nevitt Sanford (ed.), *The American College,* New York, John Wiley & Sons, 1962.

18. Newcomb, Theodore M. and Everett K. Wilson, *College Peer Groups,* Chicago, Aldine Publishing Co., 1966.

19. Pace, C. Robert, *Higher Education Measurement and Evaluation Kit,* Los Angeles, Center for the Study of Evaluation, University of California, 1972.

20. Pervin, Lawrence A., "A Twenty-College Study of Student X College Interaction Using TAPE (Transactional Analysis of Personality and Environment): Rationale, Reliability, and Validity," *Journal of Education Psychology,* 1967, Vol. 58.

21. Peterson, Richard E., John A. Centra, Rodney T. Hartnett and R. L. Linn, *Institutional Functioning Inventory Technical Manual,* Princeton, Educational Testing Service, 1970.

22. Stern, George G., *People in Context,* New York, John Wiley & Sons, 1970.

THE COMPUTER AND THE FOURTH REVOLUTION

Dr. Andrew R. Molnar*
Program Director for
Applications and Courseware, T.I.E.
National Science Foundation

I. THE FOURTH REVOLUTION

The Carnegie Commission on Higher Education has recently published a report entitled the "Fourth Revolution" which takes its title from Eric Ashby's observation that four great revolutions have been taking place in education.[1]

The first revolution was the differentiation of adult roles so that the task of education for the young was shifted in part from parents to teachers and from the home to the school.

The second revolution was the adoption of the written word as a tool of education and with some reluctance writing was permitted to co-exist with the spoken word.

The third significant change was the invention of printing and the widespread availability of books.

And the fourth revolution is the development of electronics, notably radio, television and the computer. The computer, however, is the imperative in the fourth revolution.

II. THE GROWTH OF COMPUTING IN EDUCATION

In a little over 15 years, academic computing has grown at a phenomenal rate such that in higher education:[2]

Access to Computers

All major universities and most colleges provide computing services to their students either through local facilities or access to off-campus facilities.

Expenditures

Expenditures in the last decade have increased over ten fold with 50 million dollars spent on computing in 1963 and an estimated 540 million dollars being spent in 1972.

Type of Computing

Of that amount spent, 30% was spent for instructional use; 32% for research use; 34% for administration and 4% for services to other institutions.

*The views are those of the author and do not necessarily represent those of the National Science Foundation. This paper is based on comments made at the April 17, 1973 Annual Convention of The Association for Educational Data Systems in New Orleans, Louisiana, and further illustrated at the Educational Technology Symposium at Stony Brook, New York.

[1] *The Fourth Revolution: Instructional Technology in Higher Education*. A report and recommendations by The Carnegie Commission on Higher Education. (New York: McGraw-Hill Book Company, 1972).

[2] John Hamblen, Inventory of Computers in U.S. Higher Education, 1969-1970. (Atlanta, Georgia: Southern Regional Education Board, 1972).

Sources of Support

This growth has occurred in spite of a diminishing percentage of contributions from Federal sources. Currently, 70% of expenditures for computing comes from institutional funds. In 1965, 36% of the funds came from Federal sources; in 1967, 23%; and only 17% in 1970.

Computer Science Majors

In the last five years the number of computer science degree majors has increased by a factor of 15 from approximately 5,000 to 75,000 students.

Language Substitute

Four hundred and seventy departments now permit the substitution of computer languages for foreign languages. This is a three fold increase in the last two years.

Curricula

Computer-based curricula have grown from less than 100 computer-based packages in 1965 to over 6,000 in 1972—an increase of a factor of 60 over a seven year period.

In secondary education while the figures are less complete, we do know that in 1970 34% of the Nation's secondary schools had access to a computer for administration and/or instructional purposes.[3] In 1963, a survey estimated only one percent of our Nation's secondary schools used the computer for instructional purposes; in 1966, that increased to 1.7 percent and finally to 12.9 percent in 1970. This represents a growth in instructional uses of over 12 fold in little over seven years. This amazing exponential growth of academic computing has come about in spite of a growing financial problem faced by education.

III. NATIONAL SCIENCE FOUNDATION PROGRAMS

Dr. H. Guyford Stever, Director of the National Science Foundation (NSF), says that the Foundation's programs provide for continued strong support for science with an effective balance between research and education programs.[4] The higher priority, however, will be research programs. The NSF budget for Fiscal Year (FY) 1972 was 600.7 million dollars and the FY 1973 expenditures are estimated at 615 million dollars. The requested FY 1974 budget of 641.5 million dollars includes 58.9 million dollars of FY 1973 carryover funds.

The new restructured Science Education Improvement Programs provide support for programs that are designed to (1) increase science education effectiveness; (2) help provide the essential number and variety of trained scientists and engineers; and (3) make the general public more knowledgeable as to the potential uses of science and its limitations so that they can deal more effectively with problems requiring an understanding of science and technology. NSF Science Education Improvement activities in FY 1973 are estimated at a level of 47.0 million dollars versus the planned 80.8 million dollars and compared to a FY 1968 high of 125 million dollars. In FY 1972, the budget was 73.4 million dollars. The requested FY 1974 budget is for 60 million dollars.

The Office of Computing Activities

The Office of Computing Activities was established in July, 1967 to provide Federal leadership in exploring and developing computer technology and the uses of the computer. The Office administers a program in Computer Science and Engineering which supports basic research in Theoretical Computer Science, Software and Programming

---

[3] Charles A. Darby, Arthur L. Korotkin, Tania Romashko. "A Survey of Computing Activities in Secondary Schools." (Washington, D.C.: American Institutes for Research, 1970).
[4] National Science Foundation, Budget Highlights for Fiscal Year 1974.

Systems and Computer System Design. Another program, Computer Applications in Research, seeks to support research studies which focus on the exploitation of advances in computer technology to further research in science. Support is being provided for exploratory studies to develop a National Network of computer-based resources in support of research and education. A new program, Computer Impact on Society, is concerned with studies of the impact of computers on organizations and individuals. The FY 1972 budget for OCA was 12.5 million dollars. In FY 1973, the Office will spend 10.0 million dollars and 10.0 million dollars is requested for FY 1974.

Technological Innovation in Education

The Computer Innovation in Education program has been transferred out of the Office of Computing Activities to the Education Directorate of the Foundation and renamed the Technological Innovation in Education Group. The objectives of this group are to explore and develop new innovative uses of the computer and related technologies in education. In FY 1972, 8.4 million dollars was spent for this activity and 6.0 million dollars is estimated for FY 1973. In FY 1974, 7.0 million dollars is requested for the expanded functions. I would like to briefly describe some of the activities currently being supported.

IV. COMPUTER-BASED SYSTEMS

We have supported the development of a wide variety of instructional systems. Oregon State University has developed an on-line, interactive, graphic system for classroom use in science. The system permits the instructor to dynamically control the graphics terminal with a joystick input device. A large screen television projector enables the instructor to display the computer output on a 6 foot by 8 foot screen which is clearly visible to a class of 200 students. This classroom use of a sophisticated terminal significantly reduces the cost-per-student hour of instruction.[5]

Project IMPRESS at Dartmouth College is a conversational, interactive package for the social sciences.[6] It permits the student to have access to over 100 files of social science data on a variety of topics. Rather than hear a lecture, the student formulates hypotheses about current social problems and tests them using a variety of statistical packages using current social data. The system includes pedagogical routines that guide a novice through complex statistical programs in a conversational manner with minimal previous experience and permits undergraduates to perform learning activities which would not otherwise be introduced until later years. This approach is unlike CAI and yet different from traditional problem-solving. The potential for IMPRESS and more advanced systems to reduce costs and offer a new instructional format is very attractive.

Currently, Dr. Seymour Papert of MIT and Dr. Robert Davis at Syracuse University, now with PLATO, have demonstrated the use of LOGO, a computer language, to teach and assist fifth grade children to compute functions and solve calculus-like problems. This activity seeks to avoid the rigid sequential presentation of mathematical concepts and through the use of the computer and computer artifacts introduce higher order concepts at a much earlier age. With this system children have demonstrated their ability to write programs to draw simple figures, construct complex geometric designs, write a frame-by-frame movie, generate music, write computer generated poetry, solve motion problems in physics and program the movements of a marionette.[7]

NSF has developed a number of experimental models of computer networks for developing and sharing computer networks for developing and sharing computer resources for instructional purposes. Some use batch processing, others are interactive. One network combines closed-circuit television with remote computing. One experiment involved a nationwide disciplinary network for Chemistry departments while still another uses a network of minicomputers for small colleges. In the past four years, some 30 regional computing networks were

---

[5] Tim G. Kelley *et al.*, "Interactive Classroom Graphic." Oregon State University, 1972.

[6] James A. Davis, Using the IMPRESS System to Teach Sociology. In "Proceedings of the Second Annual Conference on Computers in the Undergraduate Curricula," (Hanover, N.H., Dartmouth College, 1971).

[7] Seymour Papert, "Teaching Children Thinking," IFIP World Conference on Computer Education, August, 1970 and "Twenty Things To Do with a Computer," Artificial Intelligence Laboratory, Massachusetts Institute of Technology, Cambridge, Massachusetts, 1971.

established involving 300 institutions of higher education and some secondary schools. The program has provided members with access to a large computer with a library of instructional and problem-solving programs as well as technical assistance and training. Today, approximately three quarters of the networks are self-sustaining and continue to operate after the termination of Federal funds. This highly successful experimental program is now being phased out.

The research and development of the 1960's, although severely limited by technology and pedagogy, demonstrated that students could learn using CAI at least as well as and in some cases better than by more traditional methods. However, the equipment lacked graphics and audio capability. Software systems were not flexible or easy to program and were much too costly — probably by a factor of ten. In order to remedy this situation NSF sponsored the development and demonstration of two advanced systems; one following a centralized, utility approach and another following a modular or decentralized approach. The projects will take five years and ten million dollars of NSF support.

The University of Illinois PLATO IV (Programmed Logic for Automatic Teaching Operations) system is controlled by a Control Data Corporation 6000 series computer with up to 1,000 terminals connected to the computer through a single television channel.[8] The terminal consists of a keyset and a plasma display for computer generated information. The plasma display panel consists of two sheets of glass separated by a thin layer of gas. Points on the display are fired by the computer to generate words, figures and drawings. Up to 256 colored pre-recorded microfiche slides can also be displayed on the screen as well as dynamic information superimposed over the static display. More than 4,000 random access audio messages of up to 21 minutes in length can be recorded and selectively presented under computer control.

A touch sensitive panel permits a child who is reading and doesn't recognize, for example, the word "elephant" to touch the word on the display panel and have a picture of an elephant appear and hear the word in his earphones. The system will provide courses in elementary and secondary school curricula as well as community college and university level courses.

One hundred and fifty terminals are up and operating at Urbana and 400-500 terminals will be installed from Urbana to Chicago by September of this year. The system was also demonstrated via satellite in Italy and Switzerland last summer and the Organization for Economic Co-operation and Development (OECD) now has a terminal in Paris.

The TICCIT (Time Shared Interactive Computer Controlled Information Television) system is operated by a Data General, solid state, minicomputer with 128 student terminals.[9] The terminal consists of a keyboard, a small color television to display computer generated displays, video tape or slides and audio. The courseware will consist of two years of Mathematics and English and will be written to follow a prescribed set of design procedures. The intent is to design and validate procedures that will yield high quality courseware which will be useful to large numbers of students in standard courses throughout the country. The system will be installed and tested in 1974 at two community colleges — Northern Virginia Community College and Maricopa Community College in Phoenix, Arizona.

The Education Testing Services of Princeton, New Jersey will evaluate and report their findings for both the PLATO and TICCIT project.

---

[8] Donald L. Bitzer and D. Skaperdas, "The Design of an Economically Viable Large-Scale Computer-Based Educational System," pp. 14-34 in *Computers in Instruction*, (Ed.) R.E. Levien, Rand Corporation, Santa Monica, California, 1971.

[9] Kenneth J. Stetten, "The Technology of Small Local Facilities for Instructional Use," pp. 35-41, in Computers in Instruction, (Ed.) R.E. Levien, Rand Corporation, Santa Monica, California, 1971.

The MITRE Corporation is currently demonstrating the feasibility of interactive, computer-controlled television systems for home use.[10] They have coupled a cable television system with a computer to demonstrate the feasibility of using a standard television receiver for home computer driven displays for homes in the new town of Reston, Virginia. Cable television permits two-way conferencing. The home user communicates with the computer through a touch-tone telephone. Lessons are addressed directly to his television receiver and he may use his touch-tone phone for calculations or answering questions. The demonstration includes the home use of 27 lessons for fourth grade arithmetic drill practice. A simple computing language, Mr. Computer, is also available for writing student originated programs. Since cable television permits two-way conferencing, the teacher may work directly with students at home during the day or conduct adult education in the evening.

It is foreseen that 2,000 individual homes may be served for a nominal monthly fee. The home user will be able to shop remotely by television. He will be able to receive his mail automatically by dialing his post office box number. His salary will automatically be deposited in his bank account by his employer and he will be notified through his television set. Upon his authorization, bills such as mortgage payments will automatically be transferred to his creditors. The computer controlled television will display this information and he may take a polaroid snapshot for a hard copy receipt. The system can provide fire and security monitoring. The user will be able to interact directly with his doctor and thereby reduce the number of office calls or home visits. He will also be able to make home movies using a small low-cost video camera and later play it back through his home receiver. Demonstrations of these services are currently being conducted at Reston, Virginia.

V. COURSEWARE AND TRANSPORTABILITY

Based upon a number of NSF initiated studies, it became clear that courseware was a critical problem. EDUCOM, using 35 experts in a Delphic seminar, concluded that the most critical factor inhibiting the use of instructional computing was not cost but the lack of good, readily available computer-based educational materials.[11] This led us to initiate a more purposeful attack upon both the short-range and long-range solutions to courseware development and transportability problems.

First, we initiated a state-of-the art study to determine what existed and how useful it is. Second, for the short run, we emphasized the development, documentation and testing of existing, but yet unpublished packages. Third, for the long run, we supported the development and analysis of experimental models for creating incentives and transportability in order to better understand the characteristics of this rapidly changing field. We have encouraged interdisciplinary conferences for diffusion of computer-based instruction through hands-on experience and face-to-face discussion, with curriculum developers. Finally, we continue to develop computer courseware for classroom use.

Strategies for Curricular Development

The Human Resources Research Organization (HumRRO) of Alexandria, Virginia is conducting a state-of-the-art survey identifying all computer-based curricula by discipline, level, language, machine, and instructional use.[12] Compelling examples of computer-based instruction and associated costs of development have been identified. Surveys of publishers and vendors were made. Currently, alternative strategies, their associated costs and consequences are being evaluated. One recommendation HumRRO has made is the creation of a National clearinghouse for computer-based materials for higher education.

---

[10]Kenneth J. Stetten and Rodney K. Lay, "A Study of the Technical and Economic Considerations Attendant on the Home Delivery of Instructional and Other Socially Related Services Via Interactive Cable TV," MITRE Corporation, McLean, Virginia, December, 1972.

[11]Ernest J. Anastasio and Judith S. Morgan, "Factors Inhibiting the Use of Computers in Instruction," (EDUCOM: Princeton, New Jersey, 1972).

[12]Robert Seidel et al., "A Study of Computer-Based Curricula," Human Resources Research Organization, Alexandria, Virginia, 1971.

Curriculum Development — Project COMPUTe

Based upon our survey of publishers, it became apparent that they were uninterested in developing and publishing computer-based modules. Also, the most compelling materials used in classrooms were found to be undocumented and only locally available. Further, neither institutional incentives, such as release time, nor royalties were available to stimulate individuals to document, debug and test their programs. Through a grant with Dartmouth College a national search was made for exemplary materials in the environmental and related sciences. The authors were invited to Hanover for the summer and the College provided computer time, programming and editorial services. Standard formats were devised for student, teacher and computer program materials. Publishers are being contacted about publishing an edited series as a package. Through special arrangements, both the authors and Dartmouth may receive royalties. The project we hope will accelerate the number of quality packages available and could create a commercial model for curriculum development efforts which the College could pursue after the termination of the grant.

Transportability Problem — CONDUIT

One of the most serious obstacles that we face is the problem of transportability of programs. Programs that run at one location are rarely available on request and if available, seldom work elsewhere. One solution is a National Academic Network which permits the field to develop but also permits others to have access to the materials. Short of interconnection, however, standards must be adopted to make materials compatible for a variety of existing systems and machines.

CONDUIT is a consortium of five regional networks involving 100 colleges and universities with an enrollment of 300,000 students.[13] It seeks low-cost solutions to the problem of transportability. Disciplinary committees have identified 100 packages in eight disciplinary areas. CONDUIT-Central in cooperation with the computer center director, and curriculum coordinator in each of the five networks have documented and certified the instructional packages, established procedures and costs for transporting the materials and created self-instructional videotaped materials based upon workshop experiences and are moving the materials from center to center and ultimately into the classroom for use and evaluation. An independent organization, HumRRO, has devised numerous hypotheses concerning organizational structure, transportability, information needs, training and accounting procedures and will evaluate the entire system.

Conferences

The dissemination of information concerning computer-based curricula, is, at best, very difficult. From experience, one of the most successful mechanisms for rapid dissemination has been through annual multi-disciplinary and disciplinary conferences at which users present and tryout on computer terminals a wide variety of materials. The annual Conference on Computers in the Undergraduate Curricula produces 60 to 80 published papers on computer applications in approximately 20 disciplines and attracts approximately 1,000 attendees. This year's conference will be held June 18-21 at Claremont Colleges, Pomona, California. Disciplinary conferences have been held in Physics, Chemistry, and the Humanities.

Courseware

The NSF Science Course Improvement Program is currently supporting a four year project on Computer-Based Education (C-BE) at the University of Texas which is aimed at evaluating the impact of a critical mass of computer-based education on a broad range of academic subjects. Courseware will be developed in approximately 16 interrelated academic disciplines. The Foundation is providing 1.3 million dollars and the University is providing a like amount to develop and use the courseware in the classroom.

---

[13] Joseph R. Denk, "CONDUIT—A Concrete Pipeline for Software-Starved Little People," in the "Proceedings of the 1972 Conference on Computers in the Undergraduate Curricula," Atlanta, Georgia: Southern Regional Educational Board, 1972.

VI. COMPUTER LITERACY

Approximately 60% of the world's computers are used in the United States. The United States is the prime user and principal producer of computers and computer-related equipment. Exports of computers are approaching one billion dollars and with respect to balance of payments, the United States is the only net exporter of computers in the world. A recent National Bureau of Standards study found approximately 2,300 different applications of computing in business and industry. The computer is fast becoming a national basic industry.

While the printed text was important to civilization because it permitted man to extend his immediate memory and to accumulate his past experiences, its true impact on society was not realized until there was a literate populace.

So it is with computers. The computer in its short span of history has been one of the most significant amplifiers of man's productivity. However, the widespread use of this powerful tool may be limited by the lack of public understanding and the public's inability to see how the computer may benefit them and society.

A recent AFIPS-Time Magazine study, "National Survey of Public Attitudes Toward Computing," showed strong public anxiety toward the computer.[14] Approximately one-third of the Nation's adults still believe that the computer is some kind of "thinking machine" and has the power to think for itself. More than half believe that they are too dependent on the computer and that computers are changing their lives too rapidly. Fifteen percent believed that their lives are worse because of computers; this is twice the number who feel technology in general has made life worse.

Federal programs in science and technology aimed at making significant gains in productivity and the general well-being of the public must also be concerned with public understanding of these developments. An informed populace can better understand the strengths and limitations of new technological innovations such as computing. The degree of "computer literacy" among the general populace may be the limiting factor in rapid technological advances and with it, national productivity.

A recent report to the National Science Foundation by the Conference Board of Mathematical Sciences (CBMS), entitled "Computers in High School Education," has also strongly recommended the development of a "computer literacy" curriculum for secondary schools.[15] They recommended specifically the preparation of a junior high school course in computer literacy; materials for an introduction to computing; materials for a number of science courses; special programs for students with unusual aptitudes in computing; vocational education; teacher training and the creation of an information clearinghouse.

VII. WHAT IS TO BE DONE

While the fourth revolution is gaining ground, the current financial crisis in education offers a challenge and a major opportunity to advance the educational use of computers to a new plateau and in the process increase the quality of instruction while significantly reducing the costs. However, much remains to be done.

What we need is a complete system and a total curricula. Anything less will be costly and ineffective. At many locations, educators are still working with cast-off business machines and providing rigid one-dimensional instruction. Through the persistence of a number of educational innovators, we are on the verge of a "first generation" computer-based system. When this is accomplished we will have a medium without a message. What is needed is a critical mass of quality materials — a total curricula. Then and only then will we be able to demonstrate significant cost-benefits.

---

[14] "A National Survey of the Public's Attitudes Toward Computers" (New York: Time Magazine, Time Life Building, Rockefeller Center, 1971).

[15] "Recommendations Regarding Computers in High School Education" (Washington, D.C.: Conference Board on the Mathematical Sciences, 1972).

Marshall McLuhan argues that the electronic revolution is totally new and is changing the very nature of human perception and experience. In the age of television and computer, McLuhan says that we move into the world of pattern recognition and out of the world of mere data classification. We cannot merely convert old programmed texts into computer formats. We must retool our curricula to take advantage of the new degrees of freedom the computer offers. This trend is already becoming evident in much of the new curricula.

We need a market mechanism to develop and distribute instructional material. Currently, publishers find the distribution of computer-based materials uninteresting. Equipment manufacturers, especially in the mini-computer field, find that the availability of computer-based materials is important in the sale of equipment systems and they have done a good job in providing simple programs and materials. However, equipment is the manufacturer's business — not curricular development. Therefore, unless there are some major mergers between publishing houses and vendors, we are unlikely to see the commercial sector play a vital role in education. Education will have to create its own organizational mechanisms specifically designed to create, develop and disseminate curricular materials or face the prospect of becoming the world's largest and most expensive cottage industry.

We need a new organizational mechanism to handle the new technology. John Gardner once observed that most organizations have a structure that was designed to solve problems that no longer exist. We must go beyond current arrangements if we are to develop. There are still no incentives to write programs on courseware which upgrade the quality of education or reduce the cost-per-student hour of instruction. Writers seldom get royalties or promotions and seldom share in any cost savings which may accrue to the University. Instructors are better advised to write research papers in their discipline than to develop computer courseware. Educational institutions that are serious about cost-effectiveness will eventually have to devise institutional rewards and/or monetary incentives if they wish to reap the benefits of instructional technology.

While there is a revolution in technology, there is an even greater revolution taking place in education. Just because we are on the right track doesn't mean that we will not be run over by changing events. Obsolescence is becoming a major problem in our knowledge society. The average man in the work force can be expected to change jobs six or seven times in his lifetime. The half-life of professional man is only about ten years.

Paul Armer proposes the "Paul Principle" which he contrasts with the "Peter Principle"—individuals tend to rise in organizations to their level of incompetence.[16] The "Paul Principle" states that individuals often become incompetent over time because they become uneducated or obsolete. He says that higher education is not even remotely prepared to take on the continuing education as a major task. He suggests that universities of the future will operate somewhat like hospitals. They would admit students not just one or two times a year but continually. On arrival a diagnosis would be made of the deficiencies in the student's knowledge and the educational process of individualized instruction would be designed to fill the gaps. Modern technology is now capable of delivering instruction to an individual's home, place of employment or any other location. Education is no longer restricted to the classroom and must seek a new role in the knowledge society.

What is the Federal role in these developments? While there is no explicit Federal policy toward computing and while it is difficult to identify programs with computing in their title, there are many activities being initiated at the Federal level. The Federal programs tend to favor innovation and research and tend to look at technology as a whole rather than at computers in particular. Currently, programs tend to focus on increasing productivity, that is, improving quality while reducing costs. They seek to support projects which benefit many institutions and many disciplines. Programs of institutional support, equipment grants and support for the acquisition and upgrading of computers have been greatly reduced or completely eliminated. The acquisition and development of technology and systems will fall to the States and to the education institutions involved.

How will this affect the future of computing? My prediction is that the development of instructional computing will follow the Xerox model. That is, in spite of the fact that the initial dry process copying machine was more expensive than the wet processing machines, it was adopted because of its convenience and its ability to meet a

[16]Paul Armer, "The Paul Principle: When Technology Outgrows Man," *Geriatrics*, 24, No. 6, Dec., 1970, pp. 29-30, 34.

compelling need. Similarly, computing is so compelling a tool that it cannot be stopped. How fast it will take to develop and how expensive the development will be are the only questions to be answered in the fourth revolution.

Part Three

INDIVIDUALIZED, BOUNDED

LEARNING ENVIRONMENTS

THE TICCIT PROJECT:

DESIGN STRATEGY FOR EDUCATIONAL INNOVATION

C. Victor Bunderson
Director of Computer Uses in Education
Brigham Young University

The term TICCIT refers to the MITRE Corporation's "Time-shared Interactive Computer-Controlled Information Television," a hardware concept employing conventional television and cable technologies and minicomputers. Being derived from a hardware description, the term does not signal what we at Brigham Young University regard as the educational contributions of the project. The purpose of this paper is to place the hardware contributions of the MITRE Corporation in context with the educational contributions and courseware design strategies which have been evolving at Brigham Young University and to show how these strategies apply to the needs and goals of the project, including those of teaching community college English and mathematics more productively.

Experience in conference presentations, workshops and visitor orientation to the TICCIT project has proved to be difficult in conveying all of the essential features of this project to a new audience. The TICCIT project is not just another computer-assisted instruction (CAI) project; it is a hopeful but radical departure. Those familiar with existing CAI projects may be deceived when they attempt to apply familiar generalizations about hardware, CAI languages, tutorial, drill, simulation and other instructional strategies and utilization models to TICCIT—for most of them do not apply. Those who have seen samples of "learner control" must be prepared to redefine their understanding of this concept when discussing TICCIT. Taken alone, each innovation in hardware, software, courseware and implementation seems simple and natural enough. However, one must perceive all of these facets, working in harmony toward educational goals, to understand all of this "elephant," rather than like the blind men, some discrete part of it.

Some History of the TICCIT Project

If TICCIT is indeed different, it is different because of the disciplined design approach to the solution of educational problems and the interdisciplinary cross-fertilization between the designers and developers at three institutions, the MITRE Corporation, the University of Texas CAI Laboratory and Brigham Young University (BYU). The systems engineers and computer scientists at the not-for-profit MITRE Corporation provided the know-how in hardware and software development and integration. Unlike a manufacturer of existing hardware, MITRE was not bound by the constraints of an existing product line. Education for too long has had to make do with computer products designed for business and science and willingly marketed to educators as an instructional tool despite the inappropriateness of the hardware and software capabilities. Unlike a laboratory at a single university, the system engineers at MITRE are experienced at the process of working backward from a problem to be solved in society at large, to a concrete solution and seeing this solution all the way through to system integration, installation and testing in a real-world environment.

Aware of its own educational and social-science limitations, MITRE looked elsewhere for partners to specify educational goals and strategies. The University of Texas CAI Laboratory, one of the older and more successful of its kind, contributed a learner control philosophy and an educational design science approach. This included the identification of needs, the specification of goals and the development of cost-effective CAI programs (courseware).

A hybrid approach was employed which fell somewhere between the disciplines of computer science and educational psychology. The Instructional Research and Development Department at BYU also contributed greatly to this design science approach and contributed a perspective that media hardware must be clearly a function of instructional strategy, and that old models of CAI, developed on yesterday's slightly adopted business or scientific computer systems, may not teach effectively. The graduate program in Instructional Psychology at BYU provided a cadre of trained developers, researchers and theorists who ultimately contributed major theorems of instruction on which the novel design of learner-controlled courseware was based. Most of the key personnel from Texas moved to BYU in 1972 to consolidate the courseware project, effecting a mitosis of the Texas CAI Lab and transplanting it at BYU as the Institute for Computer Uses in Education.

This paper takes the perspective held by members of this interdisciplinary group of instructional psychologists, computer scientists, and others who have gathered to the mountains at Brigham Young University. Since its establishment in 1972, the Institute for Computer Uses in Education (ICUE) has become a department in the new Instructional Research, Development, and Evaluation Division (IRDE). This division is one part of perhaps the largest educational technology group assembled at any major university. A sister Production Services Division provides production facilities in motion picture, television and any of the conventional sorts of media. A third sister division includes the library and learning resource centers. Computer-assisted instruction (CAI) is the newest addition to BYU's learning resources capability. In addition to ICUE, the IRDE division houses instructional evaluation, research and development activities not tied to any kind of media. The Department of Instructional Development is headed by Dr. Edward Green. The Department of Instructional Evaluation and Testing is headed by Dr. Adrian Van Mondfrans. Collectively, these departments are organized under an administration at the equivalent level of Dean by Dr. R. Irwin Goodman. These three departments add a research and development focus to the more conventional production activities of the educational technology operations of BYU. Research is enhanced by a graduate program in instructional psychology, in cooperation with the College of Education. Dr. M. David Merrill heads this department.

One result of the rich selection of possible media and methods and the instructional research and theory behind their use is that we place our group clearly in that camp which believes that instruction can be approached as a design science and that the form of the hardware and software, not just the courseware, is a result of that design science approach.

The design science approach to education now evolving at BYU and elsewhere attempts to apply a discipline within each of the following stages of design:

1. Analysis of Educational Needs

2. Specification of Project Goals (based on needs and values)

3. Design Strategies

   Instructional Systems Design
   Courseware, Hardware, Software
   Organizational Design (Roles for Teachers and Others)
   Evaluation Design

4. Realization of Designs in Hardware, Software, Courseware and an Organization of People and Machines

5. Subsystem Integration and Testing (for TICCIT, evaluation and revision of hardware, software and courseware occurs at BYU during 1974)

6. System Integration and Testing (for TICCIT demonstration and evaluation occurs at Phoenix College and Alexandria, Virginia, campus of Northern Virginia Community College, 1974-1976)

This paper is organized into three sections according to the first of the six stages of the design process listed above.

Analysis of Educational Needs

Few educators now believe the idealized model of the "systems approach" which asserts that the process of innovation design begins with an analysis of needs in society, narrowing to needs or problems in some class of educational institution, then deriving goals from needs. This rational, ideal model can only be approximated in real life. Actually, a project like TICCIT begins when certain individuals become convinced that computer-assisted instruction (CAI) has tremendous potential to restructure and improve education. These individuals are able to formulate a plan which is logically related to some real needs and are able to obtain resources to evolve and test that plan. Extensive research on CAI was conducted at many CAI laboratories and centers, in universities, government, industry and schools. By 1970 this work had established by data and argument that CAI could be extremely effective, efficient and motivating, and that its cost could become quite competitive. The National Science Foundation's Office of Computer Innovations in Education, guided by the advice of experts, invested $10 million, starting in 1971-72, in two major demonstrations of CAI. One of these, the PLATO project at the University of Illinois uses a giant computer with upwards of 1,000 student terminals of completely new design. Their approach is to provide teachers with this resource, leaving it up to the users to develop the instructional designs and organizational designs. No attempt is made to restructure the roles of teachers in any major way. By contrast, the TICCIT project uses state-of-the-art computer and television technology. The hardware consists of two minicomputers and 128 color TV student terminals. The hardware, software and courseware are reflections of a strategy for restructuring education toward a learner-centered, individualized model. Men and machines are organized to serve as a source of help for students who are learning and growing in a number of dimensions. The concept is that computers cannot merely be added as an adjunct to teachers in present educational structures, but that a larger redesign must be undertaken. In the words of Peter Drucker:

> The educators still talk of minor changes, of adjustments and improvements. Few of them see much reason for radical changes. Yet education will in all likelihood be transformed within the next decades by giant forces from without.
>
> It will be changed, first, because it is headed straight into a major economic crisis. It is not that we cannot afford the high costs of education; we cannot afford its low productivity. We must get results from the tremendous investment we are making. . .
>
> Teaching is where agriculture was around 1750, when it took some 200 men on the farm to feed one nonfarmer in the town. We have to make the teacher more productive, have to multiply his impact, have to increase greatly the harvest from his or her skill, knowledge, dedication, and effort. . .(P. F. Drucker, *The Age of Discontinuity,* New York: Harper & Row, 1969).

Given a vision of what can be accomplished and the resources and opportunity to do it, a needs analysis is the application of discipline in data collection and rational analysis to guide broad design decisions, rather than the process of inscribing focus and direction on a blank tablet.

The data collected had to focus on the following questions: Is higher education the most strategic sector of education for the initial introduction of a CAI system designed for major positive educational impact and mass dissemination? Within higher education are the community colleges the sector which initially can best be served by systems like TICCIT? Will they prove more receptive to this type of innovation? Are the costs associated with various kinds of instruction in community colleges high enough that certain of them could be replaced by CAI? What courses have the heaviest load of students, and the greatest need for individualization and deeper levels of remediation? What are the socially and educationally valid motives and aspirations of teachers and other educators which must be served in a system wherein old roles are changed? What are the needs of students which must be served by a man-machine system involving CAI?

Some data and analysis bearing on these questions is documented elsewhere. For this overview, it is sufficient to observe that higher education does have high costs, high volume and students who are free to take or leave CAI. It is suffering from serious financial problems and social pressures which call for rapid and dramatic change. Within higher education, community colleges are the most rapidly growing sector. They are dedicated to teaching students and to new forms of community service, not graduate research, and are fairly receptive to innovative approaches to accomplish these goals.

Within community colleges, instruction in Freshman and developmental mathematics and English usually accounts for at least 25 percent of the total contact hours of instruction. A large portion of this (about 80 percent) could be served by two modular systems of CAI lessons in math and English covering from 12 to 25 credit hours of instruction, depending on how these lessons are allocated to course titles. Educational costs in community colleges average $3.26 per student hour, $1.50 in direct instructional costs. Much of this cost could potentially be replaced by a man-machine CAI system with greater effectiveness and a potentially lower cost.

Community college students share with other students the desire for instruction which is relevant to their needs and interests and respectful of their time. They resent phoniness, lack of preparation and arbitrary treatment on the part of teachers. On the other hand, they value productive human interactions with teachers and other students and few would like all college instruction mediated solely by a machine. Open enrollment policies of community colleges introduce large numbers of students who are inadequately prepared in basic math and English skills and thus are unready to take Freshman-level courses in these subjects, or other college courses which depend on these skills. Besides their achievement deficiencies, many suffer from attitudes of avoidance toward study and learning, poor study habits and attitudes that place the blame on others for not teaching them, rather than on themselves as the responsible agents for personal growth.

The motives of teachers are varied. The better ones are rewarded by seeing intellectual and personal growth in individual students, by learning and producing scholarship themselves and by perfecting their teaching skills. Those who love their subject matter believe they can convey some of the imponderable values of a liberal education—a reverence for knowledge and its skillful expression, an excitement in its pursuit, an aesthetic delight in the elegant, attractive nuances of a subject, a discipline in problem solving or scholarship. Teachers seek fair recompense for their labors. They value the respect of their students, peers and administrators and community. Not all teachers are good teachers and not all motives for staying in the teaching profession are as laudatory as those just mentioned. A man-machine system involving CAI should enhance the stature, influence and opportunities of teachers possessed of educationally constructive motives and attitudes. It is probable that CAI can only be a small influence in this regard, but it should certainly be designed to be a positive, rather than a negative, influence.

Specification of Project Goals

Earlier publications on the TICCIT project emphasized the cost aspect of computer-assisted instruction. A panel of NSF advisors, familiar with CAI and other forms of educational technology, had advised that if TICCIT could be no more effective than traditional forms of instruction and could deliver this instruction at less cost, it would be a major contribution. A general goal of the project was then and still is to create a "market success" so that after the application of government funds, private industry will provide efficient dissemination and competition to further drive the cost down.

Despite the more limited aspirations initially held by outside advisors, the design science approach of the TICCIT project started with a set of educational goals that put cost in its proper context. Initially, little could be said about goals which seemed too remote to be accomplished. As the project evolved, however, design strategies became well defined. These strategies now provide basis for optimism that a more ambitious set of goals can be achieved. That complete set of goals is discussed below.

The Derivation of Goals from Needs and Values

In classical statements of the systematic approach to instructional development, goals are derived from the needs of the institutions and the needs of individuals served by these institutions. Preferably these goals are measurable at least through a longitudinal research study. It is clear to any thinking person that this model of the systems approach is an oversimplification. Goals are derived as much from the philosophy and values of the system's designers as from the needs they serve. The needs must be there, it is true, or the product of a design effort will not be used. The goals should indeed be assessable to assure they are achieved.

It is the explicit recognition and use of human goals and values, however, in a rigorous, empirically based process of design and development that provides the critical distinction between a design science and a natural science. Herbert Simon, in his little book of provocative essays on "The Sciences of the Artificial" makes this distinction. While he does not treat the design of instruction directly as one of the artificial sciences, he deals with learning and problem solving in this manner. It is clear from his book that he would consider education as one of those disciplines which could more profitably be viewed from the perspective of artificial science than as a natural science-based field. We prefer the term "Design Science of Instruction" to Simon's term. It would be presumptuous to claim that we have developed a design science for instruction at this time, but it is appropriate to place the designers of the TICCIT courseware within that world-wide group of researchers who believe that such a science can be developed.

There is a diversity in values among the design group which generated learner-controlled courseware. Religious backgrounds include Catholic and Protestant, Mormon and Jewish and a variety of degrees of orthodoxy. Yet there is a core of common values regarding the nature of man in particular, and the roles of students and teachers. Rather than the mechanistic "O" (organism) of behavioral psychology, we see students as agents, using that meaning of the term which identifies the student as one who acts and who has the power to originate action. The student's own goals and values shape his choice of actions and any description of his choice behavior must be incomplete and deceptive without consideration of these constructs. It is felt that students grow when given responsibility for their own choices and that a system which deprives them of choice limits growth.

Limits to intellectual and personal growth, for all practical purposes, are imposed by the teachings of the student's culture. His genetic inheritance provides broad limits within which growth may occur, and with different degrees of rapidity. Educational institutions are now structured both to unfold human potential along certain dimensions and to limit it in others. Treating this assumption as a value which shapes instructional systems design rather than as an hypothesis to be weighted by the descriptive methods adapted from natural science has strong operational consequences. If the limits to growth are indeed far beyond what can be attained by present educational environments, then the designers of new learning environments can expect quite remarkable quantum leaps in student growth as better and better designs are found.

Any design for a new learning environment can include teachers only, or both teachers and machines. Except in rather limited aspects of a total curriculum, instruction completely by machine-student interaction must be incomplete and probably largely unacceptable by students. Since the majority of a student's life is involved in human interactions and education seeks to expand his ability to function with others, the process of education as a total concept must involve human interactions as its dominant feature. The computer is another technological tool to enhance certain aspects of this process, those aspects which deal with information transmission and processing and information management.

A teacher can be both hero and villain, sometimes both, in the process of bringing about growth in students. A teacher can destroy a student's faith in himself and turn him away from learning forever, or break through barriers that limit his horizon and free him to growth. Teachers can learn to use computers and other tools to expand their ability to instruct, to manage, to build students and to produce scholarship. They can also subvert systems which involve technology and quietly but effectively sabotage the potential of such systems. Some proposed roles for teachers who will use systems like TICCIT are described below.

While we are considering the values which influence the design of TICCIT, it is sufficient to say that the same values related to the process and limits of growth apply to teachers as well as students. Teachers are the central agents in this process, and upon the way they define their roles depends the success of the project and the future of technology in existing educational systems.

95

No attempt has been made to annotate the above discussion of values from the more than extensive literature of philosophy, psychology and theology. No excellence in these fields is claimed by the designers of the TICCIT courseware, only recognition of the powerful role of values in the process of design. Given the decisive role of values in the design of systems like TICCIT, having great social potential, it would seem that responsibility exists to make at least the more influential values explicit. Those mentioned above will be seen by the reader to be implicit in the multiple goals for educators discussed below.

Design Goals for TICCIT Courseware, Hardware, Software & Implementation

Table 1 summarizes the design goals. It will be seen that they are grouped into the categories of institution, content, individual student and educator.

TABLE 1

Courseware Design Goals

COST GOAL

> $1.00 per contact hour
> 25% less time
> Increase enrollment significantly

CONTENT GOAL

> Small step forward in content
> Clarify objectives
> Design for flexibility

GOALS FOR STUDENTS

> 85% of students will achieve mastery
> Increased efficiencies
> Improved strategies
> Voluntary approach, reduced avoidance
> Responsibility

GOALS FOR EDUCATION

> Define new roles in management-advisement
> Stimulate teachers to demonstrate humane values in follow-on or coordinate instruction
> Define new professional roles in development
> Instructional research—computer as a tool

Institutional-Level Goals

A. *Cost Goals:* We seek to reduce the cost of a contact hour of community college instruction in mathematics or English to somewhat less than $1 per contact hour, with no loss in effectiveness and with reduced contact time. By reduced contact time, we mean that it is our goal to reduce the time it now takes a student to complete equivalent work in mathematics or English by some 25 percent or more.

This cost goal implies that the teacher-student ratio in the TICCIT courses will be reduced so that computer-assisted instruction need not represent an add-on cost.

B. *Enrollment Goals:* It is our goal to increase enrollment significantly. The quantitative definition of the word "significantly" is to be determined by the Educational Testing Service through its summative evaluation of the TICCIT project. We expect this increase to occur both through reducing attrition in the college as a whole and through increasing enrollment in courses given by computer-assisted instruction over any increase which might occur through traditional modes. If achieved, this factor could give administrators an option other than reducing staff to achieve the cost advantages of TICCIT.

C. *Content Goals:* It was not our goal initially to innovate substantially in curriculum content. We sought an appropriate and accurate representation of the curriculum as now described by professional organizations in the fields of mathematics and English, in textbooks and as taught at community colleges. As the project has evolved, we have found the math content to correspond closely to standard textbook topics. In order to achieve the more important effectiveness goals, the English content has had to depart more substantially from conventional approaches.

We seek a small step forward in mathematics content through encouraging colleges to combine beginning and intermediate Algebra into one modular system of instructional materials, and to replace the College Algebra, Trigonometry, and Analytic Geometry sequence by the "Math O Course" as recommended by the committee on the undergraduate programs in mathematics. In the Math O approach the student learns the concept of function and sees it illustrated by the various elementary functions.

We seek a larger step forward in English grammar and composition, primarily through moving toward a generative approach to composition, and through clarifying the objectives and structure of those subjects around an internally consistent, generative rhetoric. Our analysis of the objectives of English composition and grammar leads to an apparent simplification in what "topics" are considered. Such an analysis does not map as readily into English textbook topics as does the mathematics analysis.

We expect to provide great flexibility through a modular structure in both mathematics and English so that community college administrators and faculties can utilize these materials in a variety of ways.

Effectiveness Goals for Individual Students

A. *Mastery:* At least 85 percent of the students who take the TICCIT courses will achieve mastery, as defined by the mastery tests at the lesson and unit levels.

B. *Efficiency:* Students will improve their efficiency in learning from CAI by a substantial factor as measured between the first two and last two units of any course. We now have no good basis on which to make a quantitative prediction for the magnitude of efficiency increases. It stands as a design goal nonetheless, and is expected to contribute to the decreased time of 25 percent or greater discussed above. Time saving is of value to students, as well as to an educational system.

C. *Improved Learning Strategies:* Learning strategies are defined operationally in terms of patterns of use of the learner control command language described in another section below. Improvement in strategies will be measured by the extent to which the student's efficiency improves simultaneously with the reduction in his requirement for advice.

D. *Approach Rather Than Avoidances:* The students will develop a positive attitude of approach rather than avoidance relative to the subject matter in any TICCIT course. Attitude is measured in part by questionnaires given to the student from time to time, but is measured primarily by the extent to which the student will voluntarily work on optional material. This includes AB level materials which are not required, and games, simulations, "tidbits" and other items which are not required. Approach can be measured in a gross way by the extent to which students who take the Algebra course go on and take the higher level course. This assumes that they would not otherwise have taken it. The same type of measurement can take place in English and can be reflected at a gross level through increased enrollment in the more advanced English courses not taught by TICCIT.

E. *Responsibility:* Students' attitude of responsibility towards learning will increase from the first unit to the last unit. While difficult to measure, it is expected that the extent to which students meet scheduled appointments can be assessed, as can the extent to which they exert continual effort toward achieving goals of mastery and efficiency.

The effectiveness goals for students are very much a function of the learner-controlled courseware concept described below. Rather than being led step-by-step, guided by some all-knowing mathematical algorithm which makes decisions for him, a student is given a command language which allows him to survey freely, establish his own sequence within the constraints set by prerequisites and establish his own learning tactics. Learning tactics are described in terms of the sequence of rules, examples and practice instances a student sees. It is only through this learner-controlled courseware strategy that we hope to be able to help the student achieve improvement in all five of the effectiveness goals discussed above.

Goals for Educators

A long-range goal of this project is to make a modest contribution toward the enhancement of the profession of education toward greater rigor and discipline, in the application of empirically testable principles of instruction and management. Increased productivity and increased professionalism is the key. The basis for new hope lies in further development of a design science foundation for education and a related technology of instruction. Computers are a principal tool to administer, manage, and design instruction and to collect data relative to prescriptive design theorems.

New roles for teachers and modifications of old ones must emerge before these long-range goals can be achieved. Four which are of special interest to the TICCIT project are the following:

1. Manager-advisors for students involved in TICCIT courses and other technologically mediated systems.

2. Master teachers.

3. Designers and developers of courseware.

4. Instructional researchers.

Rather than elaborate on these roles in this section, they will be discussed in the section on design strategy after context is provided by a description of the hardware and courseware design.

Strategies to Meet Design Goals

Since the hardware and software design for TICCIT is so heavily influenced by the courseware, which in turn is designed toward the effectiveness goals described above, the strategy for achieving the effectiveness goals will be discussed first, followed by a discussion of new roles for educators. There will follow a description of the hardware design to meet the cost goals.

Mastery

The strategy to achieve the goal of student mastery is based on the application of instructional theorems to the design of a modular courseware data structure. This data structure, or content structure, is separated both conceptually and physically in the computer from the logic which implements instructional sequencing strategies. Instructional sequencing strategies are largely left in the hands of the student, who is guided by an advisor program to develop his own characteristic strategy and tactics.

The instructional research, and the propositions or theorems derived from it, which shaped the design of the content components is described in Merrill and Boutwell (1973) and Merrill (1973). In the former paper, a review of the literature on learning and instruction led to the development of what is in effect a taxonomy of instructional variables. By means of this taxonomy, any instructional sequence involved in complex cognitive learning tasks may be characterized.

This taxonomy involves three classes of variables: presentation form, inter-display relationships and mathemagenic information.

Presentation form may be of four types, generalities of instances, either of which may be presented either in expository or inquisitory form. The system deals primarily with concept learning and rule using, so a generality is a definition of a concept, of a clear statement of a rule. An instance is an example or non-example of a concept or a rule in use. Expository means to tell, inquisitory to ask. Inquisitory generalities (e.g., "define a concept") are rarely used in TICCIT, since memorization of rules is not sought and since it is difficult to analyze by computer open-ended definitions or rule statements in natural language.

Mathemagenic information is information which gives birth (gen-) to learning (mathema-). This category involves prompting and cuing and other attention-focusing techniques. Specific techniques include attribute isolation (use of color, graphics, etc., to highlight key attributes), search strategies (step-by-step algorithm), mnemonic aids, and production strategies (heuristics to guide the production of student-generated products, for example, written paragraphs).

Certain concepts of man-machine instruction developed at the Texas laboratory were combined with the Merrill taxonomy to devise the modular courseware structure. These included the concept of hierarchically indexed data structures and a command language to move about within these structures. A set of content files indexed within these structures was defined. Since the content files were developed along the lines of the taxonomy of instructional variables, the idea was that students could use the command language to sequence these files themselves, thus manipulating instructional variables.

The TICCIT courseware is hierarchically organized into four levels. These levels are represented to the student by special displays that present the hierarchies, list the topics, provide access to a standardized version of the objectives and display status after the student has worked. These are:

Course Level: Course objectives and status display (course map).

Unit Level: Unit objectives and status display (unit map).

Lesson Level: Lesson objectives and status display (lesson map).

Segment Level: Primary Instruction Components (rule, example, practice).

Objectives and Status Display (Map)

A simplified map is shown in Figure 1. The screen displays a hierarchy on one side and topics on the other. To survey, the student may look at the introduction (either a minilesson, a sequence of digitally generated displays, or a videotape). He may also type integers on P. Typing an integer followed by the OBJ (objective) key gives a cartoon illustrating the segment objective. "P" gives the prerequisites. STATUS is indicated by coloring the boxes red, yellow or green to indicate trouble, uncertainty, or clear progress. Typing "X" gives a similar map for AB test, AB work, and games, simulations and other "fun options."

At the course level, the boxes represent unit objectives, at the unit level, they represent lesson objectives and at the lesson level, they represent segment objectives.

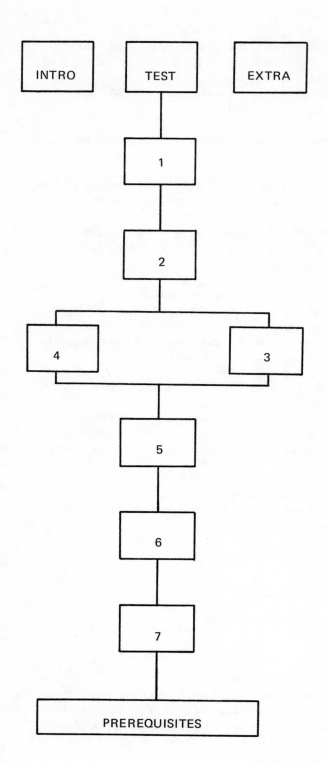

E.8.5

1. The Complete Verb Phrase

2. Uses of the Verb "to be"

3. Memorizing Be Verbs

4. Recognizing Have Verbs

5. Recognizing the Modals

6. Memorizing Modals

7. Identifying Verbs

Figure 1. Lesson MAP

100

To permit the student access to any level of the courseware, a learner control command keyboard was designed. It is illustrated in Figure 2. The ATTN key signals that a typed command is forthcoming (e.g., logon, logoff, calculate). BACK displays the immediately preceding screen image. SKIP permits by-passing a test item and certain other functions. NOTE records a comment for the author and EXIT pops back to a level from which the student exited for some operation. The nine keys at the bottom of Figure 2 are involved in the learner's control of his own learning tactics. The RULE, EXAMP, PRACT, EASIER, HARDER, HELP, and OBJ keys deal with events within a segment while the MAP and ADVICE keys are more general.

On a course or unit map when the student selects a box, he pushes the "GO" button and drops to the next lower map. On a lesson map, when the student selects a segment, he pushes the "RULE," "EXAMP" (example) or "PRACT" (practice) button to interact directly with the content. Following any of these three buttons, he may push EASIER, HARDER, or HELP to vary the instructional variables which he may require for effective learning.

From the lesson map illustrated in Figure 1 and from the primary instruction keys may be inferred the various content files which compose the modular courseware data structure.

The three main primary instruction learner-control buttons are related to the presentation form dimension of the taxonomy of instructional variables as indicated in Figure 3. This figure also shows how the EASIER and HARDER keys are related to inter-display relationship variables, and the HELP to mathemagenic information.

The function of the nine principal learner control command keys is as follows:

RULE   Accesses the main generality for a segment. For a concept, this is a definition, for a rule it is a clear statement, for memorization it describes what is to be memorized.

EXAMP   Accesses the next instance in a file of expository instances. The sequence of instances is constructed so that matching, pairing, and other instructional variables, not appropriate for student control, are built in.

PRACT   Accesses the same instance file as EXAMP, but presents it in inquisitory mode, with necessary answer processing for student-entered constructed responses.

RULE may be followed by:

EASIER   More concrete form of rule (an analogy). Simpler terminology.

HARDER   More abstract. Technical notation and terminology.

HELP   Mnemonic aids to remember the rule. Attribute isolation of key terms or characteristics using color, graphics and audio. These displays may be followed by an information processing sequence for using the rule or testing instances of the concept.

PRACT or EXAMP may be followed by:

EASIER or HARDER   Shifts to easier or harder instances.

HELP   Instance specific attribute isolation using color, arrows, sometimes graphics and sometimes audio. Aids to recall the rule are presented first, followed by a step-by-step walk-through of a good information-processing algorithm for using the rule or testing the concept, specific to this instance.

101

EASIER and HARDER are typically "inter-display relationship" variables while HELP provides "mathemagenic information," although this distinction does not always hold in the case of EASIER.

Matching of examples and non-examples and a default sequence generally going from easy to hard and covering the necessary range of divergency among the instances is built into the instance files and their controlling logic. A principle in the design of learner control was that students should be given control only over those variables for which they had or could learn a basis for intelligent choice.

There are five basic kinds of content files and additional files for display formatting and answer-processing.

Map files include the objectives and prerequisites for survey, and the INTRO content for course, unit and lesson maps.

Generality files provide for each segment a main generality, an easier version, a harder version and a "help" file for the generality.

Instance files include for each segment a sequence of between about twelve and forty instances. The instances are classified as easy, medium and hard and are available in expository or inquisitory modes. For each instance, a help file specific to that instance is available. In inquisitory mode, answer-processing and feedback is available. Instance files may be defined by generative algorithms as well as by a set of discrete items.

Test files for each lesson are made up of instances similar to those found in the inquisitory instance files. AB level tests are also available. Unit and course level tests may be provided, although they are often off-line.

Fun options are games, simulations, tidbits of humorous or interesting information, and options to look at extra videotapes of interest. These are made available on the same map with the AB work, hopefully to induce students voluntarily to choose optional work.

The learner-control command language provides the student with a means to access any file with few restraints. He may be forced to listen to and look at advice if he is going astray, but he is never forced to look at any instructional material that he does not select.

From the above description of courseware content structures, it is possible to summarize the strategy for achieving the goal of mastery. Each student has an idiosyncratic requirement for instruction on the various objectives which constitute a course. Through the map displays and through the status reports using this map display, he can select which objectives he needs and, within broad restraints set by the prerequisite relationships between lessons, the sequence of objectives. Within an objective, which typically teaches a single concept or rule, students vary on the level of abstraction, concreteness, difficulty, and the help they need to understand how to perform on the practice items which test that objective. The tactical sequences possible by various students are unlimited. The slower students will need more EASIER displays and more HELP. They will probably need a *greater* number of instances. Brighter students may use a discovery approach, focusing on the harder practice instances. They will have less requirement for HELP and for the alternate rule displays. Status reports signal the student when he has achieved mastery, so that all students who can read the displays are assured that if they keep working they can eventually reach a mastery state.

Efficiency — The careful analysis of content into learning hierarchies typically increases the efficiency of systematically designed instruction in comparison to classroom instruction, since incidental material is deleted. Furthermore, students can skip those objectives which they already know. At the level of the tactical sequences of primary instruction keys within a segment, we also hope to improve efficiency by helping the student devise his own characteristic plan of attack, modifying it as needed. The advisor program and status displays constitute the design techniques used to achieve this goal. It is expected that learner-control will be less efficient, at first, than would a skillfully designed adaptive sequence based on research and controlled by the computer. The hypothesis is that given adequate status displays, a reasonably good advisor, and practice, students can develop skill in strategy and tactics which will exceed the efficiency possible through program control.

Improved Strategies — Assume that the art and science of mathematical modeling of the learning process should evolve to the point where greater levels of mastery and efficiency could always be obtained by computer control than by learner control (a possible future which we doubt will occur). Even then, learner control would be preferred. The goal of improved strategies and its companion goals, improved attitudes of approach and responsibility, should not be subordinated to the quest for efficiency.

Previous research on learner control at the University of Texas (e.g., Judd, Bunderson and Bessent, 1970) did not seek to establish relationships between the availability of learner control and the growth in strategy competence, approach and responsibility. The conception of learner control was too narrow, both in relation to the outcomes of learner control and the means to implement it. The available CAI programs were too short in duration for much skill in learner control to develop and the courseware data structures lacked the modularity and the relationship to instructional variables inherent in the TICCIT courseware design.

A broader concept of learner control requires better answers to the questions: What is to be controlled? How is it to be controlled? On what basis do we expect the student to learn to control it? The taxonomy of instructional variables described above gives a framework for answering the first question: The student should have control over instructional variables which can make a difference in his learning. The variables reviewed and classified in the paper by Merrill and Boutwell (1973) were divided into those which could readily be manipulated by the student and those which, at least for now, should remain under the control of the authors and the computer.

The results of this decision process are described above in the discussion of the MAP logic, and the primary instruction commands.

How are these variables to be controlled? Earlier learner control researchers had relinquished control to the student in a fairly ad hoc and non-systematic manner. Because of the lack of separation of strategy and content in the various tutorial CAI languages, choice of options was thrust unexpectedly into the hands of students at content specific decision points. A more rational approach developed in later years (Schneider, 1972), but these approaches were still limited in the range of variables placed under student control. The TICCIT design for learner control viewed student-machine interaction as a communication process requiring a formal command language—a language related to the variables which affect learning.

A model for student-machine communication developed by Gordon Pask provided one source of inspiration for the learner control command language implemented in TICCIT. Pask asserted that all communication between student and computer can be described as taking place in one or more special languages. The flow of instructional information sequenced according to fixed algorithms within the computer, and the answers to questions and problems entered by the student comprise what Pask calls the L^0 language. Discussion about the instructional process itself, and attempts by the student to control the process in some way, take place in L^1. It is possible also to define an L^2 language in which control processes can be discussed and modified.

In the TICCIT system, we speak of progressively higher levels of discourse, analogous to Pask's languages.

Level 0 may be implemented primarily within the files of instances where students may look at worked examples or may practice. Level 1 is implemented by means of the MAP logic and the primary instruction keys. Level 2 is implemented by an advisor program, which refers to a set of student historical data (monitor) and communicates by reference to "status displays" at course, unit, lesson and segment levels. The advisor also communicates through audio and through blue-colored visual displays.

The concept of a learner control command language and advisor which permits discourse between student and machine at all three of Pask's levels is the key element in the design approach to improve student strategies. The elements missing from earlier implementations of so-called learner control were the instructional variable-related commands, the status displays and the advisor.

These latter elements provide an answer to the question: "On what basis may the student learn improved strategies?" Given instructionally relevant commands, well-defined goals (objectives and tests on MAP displays), and status reports which reveal the discrepancy between present status and desired status, students have the information necessary to initiate strategic and tactical decisions. The availability of an advisor permits the student to request suggestions on which strategic or tactical decisions might be appropriate at any time during the process of instruction. The advisor also monitors the student's choices and offers unsolicited advice about strategy on tactics when the student departs from a generally useful model.

By means of the advisor, the goal is to help the student learn to use the status displays to guide his own initiation of strategic and tactical maneuvers, until he becomes independent of any requirement for advisor support.

A survey is effected primarily through the use of MAPs at the course, unit and lesson levels. Any MAP permits access to the introduction, videotape or minilesson, to the objectives, the prerequisites, and any rule display. The student may survey any unit and lesson in the course freely, but he may not work on instances or tests on any lesson for which he has not completed the prerequisite lessons.

Learning tactics occur within a segment, and use the primary instruction commands RULE, EXAMP, PRACT, EASIER, HARDER, and HELP in any sequence, except EASIER, HARDER, or HELP must always be preceded by RULE, EXAMP, or PRACT.

Testing tactics take place in the practice files for self-testing, and in the lesson and unit tests. Students get three attempts at the lesson-level working tests. The students with higher aspirations or with greater approach responses may also elect on certain lessons to take the XTRA work. Trying XTRA provides another MAP with fun options and more advanced concepts and rules. An "AB" level test is provided on the XTRA map for which only one attempt is permitted.

Review tactics are permitted at any time. The student uses the survey and learning tactics commands. Within a lesson, review mode is identical to initial learning with the exception that no scoring occurs and the advisor is limited to a few simple, general comments about review strategy.

Approach vs. Avoidance — What variables effect positive affect toward learning a particular content? The taxonomy of variables on which the TICCIT courseware was built is a classification of variables which effect mastery learning, not affect. One point is clear: It is impossible even to measure approach without permitting free choice. Voluntary choice is a requisite for the measurement of an affective objective.

The designers of TICCIT hypothesize that learner control will also contribute to the development of approach responses. The XTRA menu is one means to implement this concept. The AB level test and extra work is designed to be strictly voluntary. The extent to which students spend time on these materials is one possible way to access the growth of approach responses.

Effective instruction may be the most powerful variable in producing approach. A sense of accomplishment, and a recognition of growing skill at strategy and tactics may lead the student to choose optional work during TICCIT instruction and more significantly, elect to take more advanced math or English courses not using TICCIT, which he otherwise would not have taken.

The introductory videotapes and minilessons are designed to produce a positive attitude toward taking each TICCIT lesson. In addition, the use of color, graphics and low-key humor are designed to lighten the task of learning.

Responsibility — Like approach, the growth of a sense of responsibility is an outcome for which the controlling variables are not well understood. The modular design of TICCIT, with its clearly defined outcomes of mastery and efficiency, provides an opportunity to observe variations in indices related to responsible use of time and resources. The extent to which appointments are scheduled and kept provides a gross measure. Day-to-day fluctuations in efficiency provide a more fine-grained measure.

The design strategy is based on the assumption that growth in responsibility occurs when responsibility is clearly fixed and help is provided to assist the individual to carry that responsibility. An over-riding tone pervades the courseware and the advisor program. It says wordlessly that the responsibility of the authors is to provide effective, interesting instructional resources, and helpful advice. The responsibility of the student is to select his own goals (at registration) to plan a sequence of subgoals and to apply himself actively to the task of achieving these goals.

The training of proctors and teachers is a key aspect in the strategy to achieve improved responsibility. An increase in the student's responsibility to control his time and his learning activities is accompanied by a decrease in the teacher's responsibility. The great lesson of parenthood must be learned by teachers: To permit the growth of your children or your students, it is necessary to let go and permit free choice. Freedom of choice means that the child or the student can choose a course that produces failure as well as a course which leads to success. If provided with sufficient information about the process that led to success or failure, the student can learn from his experience. Teachers and proctors must learn not to step in and rescue a student from an impending error, but instead maintain a problem-solving nonjudgmental attitude and provide help when requested.

In summary, the design strategy for effectiveness goals is based on a review of instructional variables effective in complex cognitive learning, particularly in concept and rule learning. Certain of these variables were put under the control of the student by means of a learner control command language. The student uses his language to survey the course, plan an overall sequence strategy, for learning objectives, developing specific learning tactics for each objective and developing his own testing and review tactics. Status displays help him focus his efforts and make strategic and tactical choices. An advisor program helps him learn the command language so that his strategies and his level of mastery and efficiency will improve simultaneously. In addition, improved attitudes of approach and responsibility are sought through global aspects of the courseware design and through the manner in which teachers and proctors are expected to interact.

Roles for Educators

The roles of manager-advisor, master teacher, instructional designer-developer and instructional researcher are not new roles. Good college teachers at many campuses now demonstrate all or most of the skills discussed below in relation to the existing systems of instruction they deal with. TICCIT may cause sharper definitions and distinctions to be made in these roles and will bring to a head issues regarding the distribution of a faculty member's time across various roles. The issue of incentives, both financial and professional, for time spent in new roles will become especially crucial.

The manager-advisor role is a substantial departure from that of being the central figure in the classroom. Management by objectives, as developed by experts in fields other than education, uses similar principles. The teacher helps the student select goals and plan actions, evaluate the success of those actions, and modify plans accordingly. The student grows by assuming responsibility for his own goals and plans. The system of materials in the computer is a resource structured both to facilitate goal setting, strategy planning, learning tactics and evaluation. The teacher is a source of help rather than a dispenser of information and a judge. The teacher and

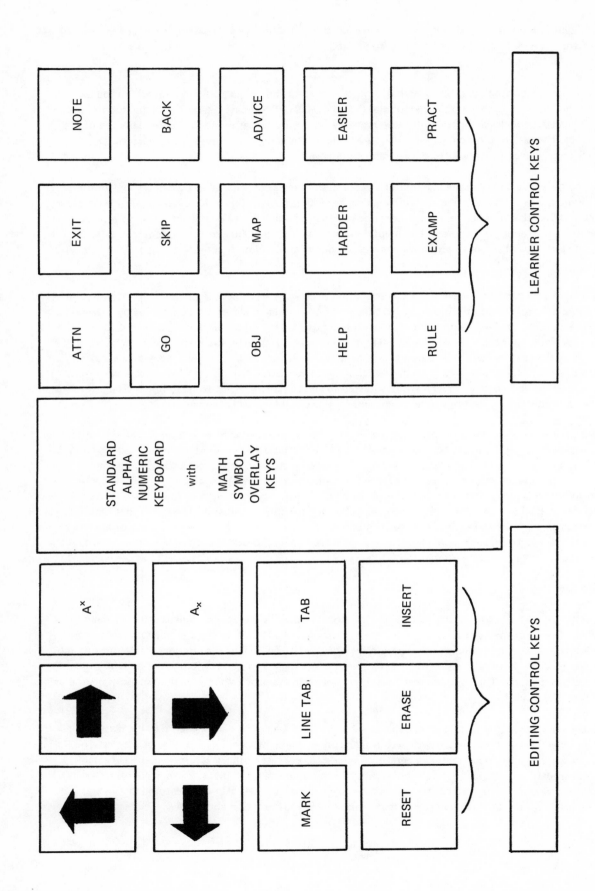

Figure 2. TICCIT Keyboard

106

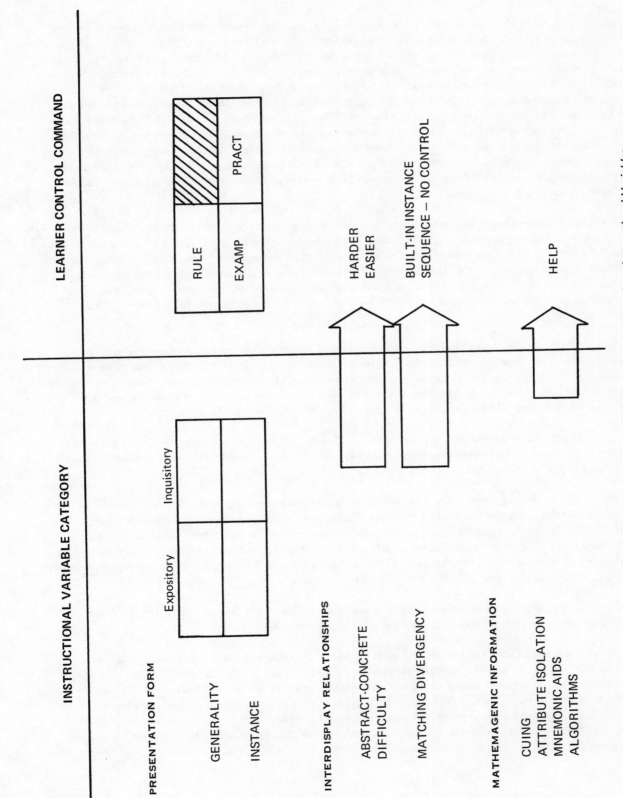

Figure 3. Relation of Learner Control Commands to Instructional Variables

107

proctor training courses to be developed prior to implementation in the colleges are designed to help define the new roles of manager-counselor. As noted above, this role is related to the growth of an attitude of responsibility in students.

Master Teacher — The TICCIT implementation plan does not include explicitly the role of master teacher, for this must occur in more advanced courses which follow the basic TICCIT math and English series. Teachers confronted with the idea of computer-assisted instruction fear that certain of the imponderable values of education can never be conveyed by computers. Most of us have known an outstanding teacher who exerted a strong influence on our lives, either as a model of the kind of person or professional we would like to become, or as someone who conveyed a love for a particular subject, or a creative approach which may have enriched our life or even changed the direction of our career. Confronted with a set of objectives for the TICCIT courseware, or any systematically designed instruction with measurable objectives, experienced teachers immediately fear that something important may have been left out. When the source of this concern can be defined, it often turns out to be a matter of style or of professional judgment in a debatable area. Sometimes it is a complex behavior, like creativity or advanced problem solving, which can best be addressed in more advanced courses. Often it cannot be defined or even clearly articulated.

Computers demand the great discipline of making things explicit and operational. If certain hard-to-define values or goals are not taught by the TICCIT courses, at least now an operational definition of what these things are *not* will exist. Let the master teacher in the more advanced courses demonstrate in the lives of well-prepared students what these values *are.* TICCIT thus offers a friendly challenge to teachers: Take the hopefully well-trained graduates of the freshman math and English courses who have demonstrated explicit operational skills, and convey to them the things which the computer and the teachers in the manager-advisor role could not convey.

The proper questions regarding computers in instruction is not "Can computers replace teachers," but "For what subjects and students should instruction be carried primarily by machine, when primarily by a teacher, and when as a shared responsibility between teachers and machines." By demonstrating courseware and organizational models in two subjects as diverse as high school through freshman college level mathematics and basic college level English composition, the TICCIT project seeks answers to these questions.

Instructional Designer-Developer — It has been noted often that college instructors are not taught how to teach. Yet even the extensive research in teacher education has emphasized interaction skills, and seldom deals with design and development skills.

The invention of learner-controlled courseware was accompanied by the concurrent development of a team approach to the design and development of materials. These roles are described in greater detail elsewhere (Bunderson, 1973). Briefly, teachers may serve as subject matter experts on such teams. Other professionals receive training as instructional psychologists, who formulate strategies and who work interactively with subject matter experts in content analysis and content component design. Technical personnel serve as design technicians, evaluation technicians, graphics specialists and coders or "packagers."

One objective of this project is to provide documentation and later training, so that others can organize teams and develop courseware designed toward their own goals and values.

The availability of TICCIT computer resources for new development also offers teachers a new means to achieve some of the values not accomplished in the basic TICCIT courses. The computer can be used for modeling, simulation and the development of small packages as adjuncts to the teacher in classroom and laboratory, especially in more advanced courses. This mode of computer use has been shown to enrich greatly the educational experiences of both teachers and students. By meeting the cost goals and thus potentially catalyzing a mass market, the TICCIT project can lead to the widespread availability of low-cost computer resources for teachers and students interested in these adjunctive uses.

Instructional Researcher — Research on human learning and instruction as it is practiced in universities can often justly be characterized as being irrelevant to real instruction. Applied research, on the other hand, may be so content specific and situation specific as to possess no generality. The design science approach to instruction, the modular courseware data structure, and the data recording facilities of TICCIT offer a middle ground. Community college teachers, freed of some classroom responsibilities, can investigate the effects of instructional variables, management variables, and social variables on any of a number of effectiveness criteria, with real hope of generality. This type of research has too much of an applied flavor to appeal to most educational researchers in universities, steeped as they are in descriptive natural science-based research paradigms and philosophies. The field is open to undergraduate instructors to make the professional contributions they would like in research. On the one hand, TICCIT provides instrumentation unparalleled at most educational research centers. On the other hand, many college instructors have research training, are getting it in connection with graduate work at nearby universities, or can obtain it.

The TICCIT project as initially conceived made provision budgetarily only for the transfer of the manager-advisor role to the faculty of the test colleges. This was to be done through the development of a teacher-proctor course to be conducted at the colleges immediately following the installation of the equipment and prior to the full-scale demonstration. As the project has evolved, much interaction with the faculties of Phoenix College and Alexandria Campus has revealed the intimate relationships among all four roles. An implementation plan has been formulated and is evolving as of the date of this paper to provide details on how all aspects of physical arrangement, organizational patterns and role definitions at each college will be handled. No faculty will lose their jobs at either college, regardless of hoped-for improvements in productivity which may make a smaller staff feasible in the TICCIT courses. Colleges can greatly benefit by turning the talents of faculty into improvements in more advanced course (master-teacher role), new instructional development and instructional research, but they must establish the professional and economic incentives and organizational structures to make this possible.

Numerous institutional and sociological problems must be solved before state legislators, state boards, trustees, college administrators and faculty committees on tenure and professional development will permit an environment in which the diverse roles and contributions discussed above can flourish. Such social and institutional change is beyond the scope of the present project. As designers and developers, we can only convey some ideas, design the system to provide the opportunities, transfer what information we have and root for the visionary and courageous faculty members and administrators at the two colleges to find ways to accomplish rewarding and productive roles for educators.

For those who fund the colleges, the idea that an institution-specific research and development capability can pay for itself in faculty satisfaction, student growth and increased productivity will require much proof.

Institutional Goals

To achieve the low-cost operation projected as a design goal, the TICCIT hardware had to be unique. As a non-profit systems engineering corporation, the MITRE Corporation was able to select from existing off-the-shelf components. They picked minicomputers and television technology to mediate the TICCIT system. The configuration consists of two NOVA 800 minicomputers, a terminal processor and a main processor. The terminal processor handles communications with 128 color TV terminals. It also provides keyboard echoing from the 128 keyboards and formats and refreshes displays (a television image must be refreshed 60 times per second). These displays may consist of any combination of characters, representing symbols from any language. Special character fonts may be created "on-the-fly" by a sophisticated display generator. This same display generator is able to create digital graphics either of the mathematical function variety or of a free-form cartoon variety. Any of these graphic displays, either character or pictorial, may be colored down to a resolution of ½ character in any of seven brilliant colors. This color display and the graphic capability is extremely powerful for the prompting and cuing aspects of instruction.

The television terminal may also be used as a display medium for videotapes, which may be switched from a bank of videotape players housed at the central computer. The terminal processor handles this operation. The terminal processor also retrieves the digital graphics from a magnetic disk for display on the television sets and retrieves digital audio from disks and switches it to the terminal.

The main processor accesses the large data bases of content files produced by the authors and executes the program logic. The operating system is designed around the educational requirements generated by the design goals and is more efficient for this purpose than a general purpose time-sharing system.

By using these off-the-shelf components and minimizing new development, the MITRE Corporation has been able to keep the cost of the 128 terminal TICCIT system down to a total cost which amortizes to less than 45 cents per student hour for the hardware. The cost goal of the entire TICCIT system is to provide instruction for less than $1 per student hour for hardware, software, courseware and support personnel. By contrast, a contact hour of instruction in a community college averages $3.26. This includes all components including physical plant, library and administration. These components can be reduced by increasing the library and administration. These components can be reduced by increasing the number of students which a given physical plant can support; however, the main target is the $1.50 per student contact hour of this $3.26 total which represents the cost of traditional instruction.

A major factor in achieving the cost goal is how the faculty role, faculty ratio and ratio of support personnel is eventually defined. Depending on the organizational design, TICCIT can end up costing more or less than traditional instruction. Since computer costs will decrease, the major evaluation should focus on the effectiveness goals, which have received the burden of attention in this paper.

Design Strategy for Effectiveness Goals

Previous research in CAI has shown that the average student typically finishes a block of instruction in anywhere from 15 to 60 percent less time. The probable reasons for this finding include the ability of the student to skip rapidly over that which he already knows, and move at his own pace otherwise. In addition, careful instructional analysis simplifies the objectives and structure over what is usually taught in classroom instruction. The modular structure of the system, the large amount of freedom provided by learner control and the built-in attempt to improve learning strategies are those designed features of TICCIT courseware which should lead to more rapid student progress.

The goal of increased enrollment is related to the attitudinal goal of approach vs. avoidance. A positive attitude toward both the TICCIT system and the subject matter conveyed by it can influence enrollment on both the TICCIT courses and those courses for which they are prerequisite.

ACKNOWLEDGMENTS

C. Victor Bunderson is the Director of the Institute for Computer Uses in Education, Brigham Young University, and co-principal investigator with Kenneth Stetten of the MITRE Corporation on the NSF financed TICCIT project. This paper employs the first-person plural in referring to an interdisciplinary design team who developed the concepts in this paper. This team included at BYU Dr. M. David Merrill, Dr. Gerald Faust, Dr. Harvey Black and the various math and English authors. These individuals contributed from the instructional psychology and content perspectives. Stephen Fine provided a computer science perspective. Among the various graduate students who contributed to the design, Fred O'Neal, Andrew Gibbons, Roy Bennion and Rowland Blake deserve special mention. Faculty members, project managers and administrators at Northern Virginia Community College and Phoenix College have contributed both to the courseware design and development and to the implementation plan. The courseware and implementation work at BYU is conducted under a subcontract from the MITRE Corporation and NSF contract #C-729. The contributions of Kenneth Stetten, John Volk, John K. Summers, Ned Burr, Paul Neuwirth and others at MITRE to the educational considerations discussed in this paper are difficult to measure, but very real.

REFERENCES

1. Bunderson, C. Victor, "Team Production of Learner-Controlled Courseware: A Progress Report." Chapter of published proceedings of the International School on Computers in Education (ISCE) based on materials presented at the School, Summer, 1971; published in *International Journal on Man-Machine Systems;* also, Institute for Computer Uses in Education (ICUE) Technical Report No. 1, Brigham Young University, Provo, Utah, 1973.

2. Judd, W., Bunderson, C. V., and Bessent, W. "An Investigation of the Effects of Learner Control in Computer-Assisted Instruction Prerequisite Mathematics (MATHS)." Technical Report No. 5, Computer-Assisted Instruction Laboratory, University of Texas at Austin, Texas, 1970.

3. Lee. B. N. *Writing Complete Affective Objectives.* Wadsworth Publishing Company Incorporated, Belmont, California, 1972.

4. Merrill, M. D. and R. Boutwell. "Instructional Development: Methodology and Research." *Review of Research in Education.* AERA, 1973. Also, Instructional Research, Development and Evaluation Department Working Paper No. 33, Brigham Young University, Provo, Utah.

5. Merrill, M. D., "Premises, Propositions, and Research Underlying the Design of a Learner-Controlled CAI Instructional System: A Summary for the TICCIT System." Department of Instructional Research, Development, and Evaluation Working Paper No. 44, Brigham Young University, Provo, Utah, June, 1973.

6. Schneider, E. W. "Course Modularization Applied: The Interface System and Its implications for Sequence Control and Data Analysis." Presentation given at the Association for the Development of Computer-Based Instructional Systems Conference, 1972.

7. Simon H. A., *The Sciences of the Artificial.* The M.I.T. Press, Cambridge, Massachusetts and London, England, 1969.

PLATO[1]

James Parry
University of Illinois
Urbana-Champaign

The Computer-based Education Research Laboratory of the University of Illinois is developing the PLATO IV system to provide high-quality computer-based education at low cost. When fully implemented, the PLATO IV system will consist of a large control computer facility simultaneously serving several thousand remote users of graphics terminals, with response times of a fraction of a second. The estimated cost per user will be fifty cents per hour, including operating expenses such as communications charges, management, and amortization of capital costs for the computer and the graphics terminals. The research and development effort over the past twelve years has resulted in important innovations in terminal and communications hardware and in system and teaching software.

A sketch of the PLATO IV student terminal showing its major components is shown in Figure 1. The heart of the terminal is the plasma display panel, now being produced by Owens-Illinois of Toledo, Ohio. The panel measures 8.5" X 8.5" X 0.5" and is transparent 512 X 512 dot matrix display with inherent memory. Individual dots can be written or erased without disturbing the rest of the display. Terminals incorporating plasma panels are being built to PLATO specifications by Magnavox, Fort Wayne, Indiana. These terminals contain character and line generators, special keysets, input/output ports for external equipment, and interface electronics to 1200 bit per second telephone line. The terminal writes 180 characters per second or draws 60 connected lines per second, using a data format of sixty 20-bit words per second (a word typically contains three 6-bit character codes or one 18-bit panel address). The character generator has 126 standard characters plus 126 characters whose shapes are transmitted from the computer and stored in the terminal's memory. Each character is an 8 X 16 matrix of dots. There is room on the panel for 32 lines of 64 characters. As of June, 1973, over 200 terminals are connected to a Control Data Corporation Cyber-73 computer. These terminals are located across the country and in Canada, with major concentration in Champaign-Urbana and Chicago.

Computer-controlled accessories, also developed at the University of Illinois for use in computer-based education, are being used with the existing terminals. A random-access image selector projects any one of 256 full-color images onto the back of the transparent plasma panel (access time less than 0.3 seconds). The images are in a 16 X 16 grid on a 4-inch square sheet of film. A random-access audio device records on and plays back from an interchangeable 15" disk made of audio-tape material which holds up to 20 minutes of recorded messages. The access time of any of the 4096 starting points is less than 0.3 seconds. Tone reproduction quality is sufficient for foreign language instruction. An input device defines a 16 X 16 grid of touch sensitive regions at the display surface through the use of light beams. When intersecting light beams are interrupted with a finger (or other opaque object) the position is reported to the computer. Each of the accessories has been developed with reliability and minimum cost in mind.

The novel communications technique presently in use cuts transmission costs by synchronous packing of information for one thousand terminals into a standard television channel (microwave or cable TV). This scheme will permit the central computer to handle one thousand terminals a hundred miles from the computer at a communications cost of less than $10 per terminal per month for 24-hour-a-day dedicated service. Inherent error rates are low, and error-sensing logic in each terminal permits the central computer to correct almost all transmission errors. The communications system is diagrammed in Figure 2.

---

[1] Acronym for Programmed Logic for Automated Teaching Operation.

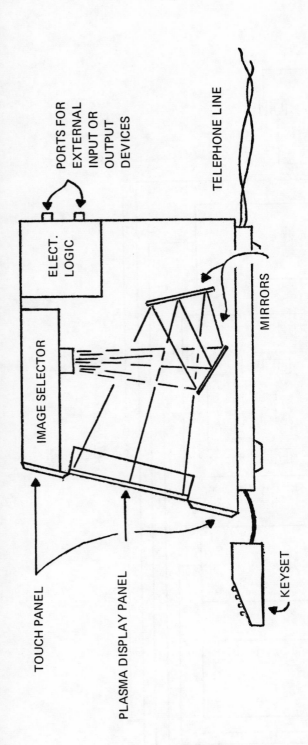

PORTS FOR EXTERNAL INPUT OR OUTPUT DEVICES

ELECT. LOGIC

IMAGE SELECTOR

TELEPHONE LINE

MIRRORS

TOUCH PANEL

PLASMA DISPLAY PANEL

KEYSET

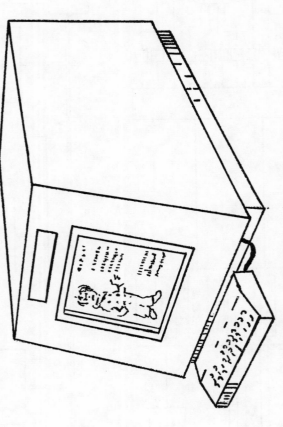

PLATO IV
STUDENT TERMINAL

FIGURE 1. PLATO IV STUDENT TERMINAL

113

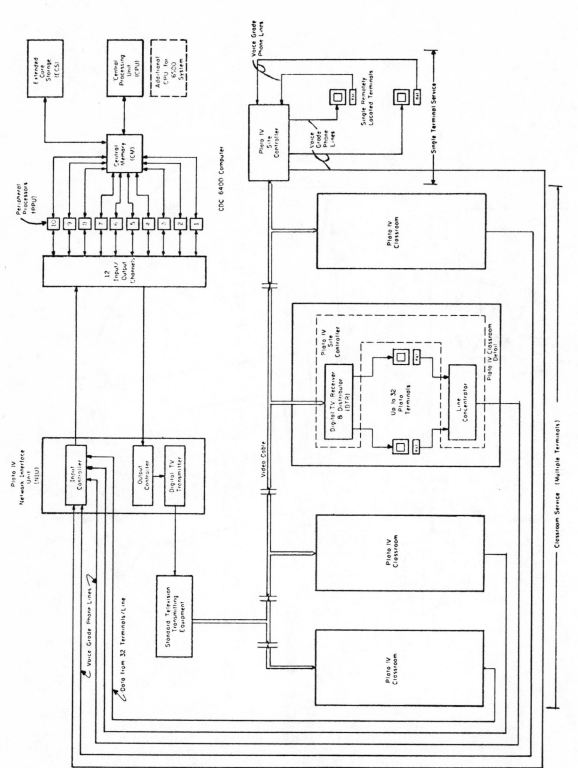

FIGURE 2. PLATO IV

114

The systems software is unusual in that no references to mechanical disk memories are made for student while he studies a lesson. The lesson and the student's individual status reside in Extended Core Storage, a Control Data Corporation device whose access is 5 microseconds and whose block transfers rate to the computer's central memory is 6000 million bits per second. (A fast disk memory has an access time of 15,000 microseconds, and a transfer rate of 5 million bits per second.) These unique transfer characteristics permit greatly enhanced computer utilization (and lower computer costs) and fractional-second response times. Lessons are compiled in such a way that all students studying a given lesson share a single copy. Another unusual feature is that, instead of waiting for "end-of-line," *every* key typed by the student passes through the *complete* software system before causing some response at the terminal, even if that response consists merely of an echo of the typed key on the plasma panel. The result is that the keyboard is completely redefinable by the lesson author. While the system's primary use is to be direct education, the operating system also permits conventional data processing at lower priority, including analysis of accumulated student response data.

Lessons for use on PLATO are written by teachers (as opposed to computer programmers) in the TUTOR author language. Several thousands of hours of lesson material have been written in TUTOR during the past few years. The plasma panel terminal has permitted expanded graphics capabilities, including commands for producing circles, arcs, special erase modes, variable-size characters written at arbitrary angles, etc. Powerful and highly efficient natural-language answer-judging capabilities make it easy for authors to create sophisticated dialogs with students. The computational features exceed those of FORTRAN: calculational statements closely mimic natural algebra (implied multiplication, superscripts for exponents, etc.), and as in older versions of TUTOR all calculations are compiled to machine code for rapid execution. TUTOR is rich in branching and conditional commands. Some major components of the system software are themselves written in TUTOR.

Initial classroom use of the system is occurring at the University of Illinois, and at public elementary schools and community colleges in several cities in Illinois. Subject areas currently being taught include arithmetic, Russian, French, Latin, chemistry, physics, biology, political science, veterinary medicine, economics, accountancy, elementary reading, music, and engineering. PLATO IV is being developed with support for the State of Illinois, the National Science Foundation, the Control Data Corporation, the Advanced Research Projects Agency, and the Ford Foundation.

THE PSI PROJECT AT THE UNIVERSITY OF TEXAS AT AUSTIN

James E. Stice and Susan M. Hereford
University of Texas
Austin, Texas

BACKGROUND

PSI stands for the "Personalized System of Instruction" also known as the "Keller Plan." It was conceived by Dr. Fred S. Keller, a well-known learning psychologist and was first tried at the University of Brasilia in 1964 by Keller, J. Gilmour Sherman, Caroline Martuscelli Bori, and Rodolfo Azzi. Keller and Sherman later continued their development of the method at Arizona State University[1] and their efforts were summarized in Keller's classic paper, "Goodbye, Teacher. . ."[2].

Briefly, the method requires a teacher to make a careful analysis of what his students are to learn in his course. Having established the terminal and intermediate objectives, he then divides the course material into units, each containing a reading assignment, study questions, collateral references, study problems and any necessary introductory or explanatory material. The student studies the units sequentially at the rate, time and place he prefers. When he feels he has completely mastered the material for a given unit, a proctor gives him a "readiness test" to see if he may proceed to the next unit. This proctor is a student who has been chosen for his mastery of the course material. On the readiness test the student must make a grade of 100, but if he misses only a few questions, the proctor can probe to see if the questions are ambiguous and can reword the questions if necessary. If the student does not complete the test successfully, he is told to restudy the unit more thoroughly and return later for another test. He receives a different test form each time he comes to be tested. No matter how many times a student is required to retake a readiness test, he is never penalized; the method requires only that he ultimately demonstrate proficiency. All students who demonstrate mastery of all course units receive a grade of A.

The lecture is greatly de-emphasized as a medium for information transfer. Lectures may be given at stated times during the course, but only to those students who have completed a specified number of units and can therefore understand the material to be discussed. The students who qualify for a lecture are not required to attend them and the material discussed in the lecture is not covered on any examination. Thus the lecture is used as a *reward*. The professor gives his lecture on a topic he is personally interested in and about which he feels he has something worthwhile to say. Those who attend come because they *want* to.

In various articles and presented papers, Keller has listed the following five essential features of the PSI method:

1. The go-at-your-own-pace feature, which permits a student to move through the course at a speed commensurate with his ability and other demands upon his time.

2. The unit-perfection requirement for advance, which lets the student go ahead to new material only after demonstrating mastery of that which preceded.

---

[1] Keller, Fred S., "Engineering Personalized Instruction in the Classroom," *Revista Interamericana de Psicologia*, Vol. 1, No. 3, 189-197 (1967).

[2] Keller, Fred S., "Goodbye Teacher . . .", *The Journal of Applied Behavior Analysis*, Vol. 1, No. 1, 79-89 (Spring 1968).

3. The use of lectures as vehicles of motivation, rather than as sources of critical information.

4. The related stress upon the written word in teacher-student communication; and finally:

5. The use of proctors, which permits repeated testing, immediate scoring, almost unavoidable tutoring and a marked enhancement of the personal-social aspect of the educational process.

PSI at the University of Texas at Austin

At the University of Texas at Austin, PSI was first tried in the Fall of 1966 by Carl F. Hereford, Luiz F. S. Natalicio and Walter Stenning. They used it to teach Psychological Foundations of Secondary Education and although their course was quite successful (and has been taught as a modified PSI course ever since), they made no particular effort to advertise what they were doing. As a result the campus at large was ignorant of their experiment. Thus it was not until 1969 that PSI was applied in another course at Texas. In the Fall of 1969 Dr. Billy V. Koen, Assistant Professor of Mechanical Engineering, used PSI to teach Introduction to Nuclear Reactor Theory, a senior-level elective course. His efforts were met with a certain amount of administrative resistance, but Koen persuaded his department chairman to give him some extra secretarial assistance and some funds to pay for the reproduction of units and readiness tests. His course was decidedly successful and to our knowledge, it was the first PSI course in engineering taught anywhere.

Koen gave a report on his course at a Teaching Effectiveness Luncheon sponsored by the College of Engineering in the Spring of 1970, and in the Summer of 1970 Dr. Lawrence L. Hoberock of the Mechanical Engineering Department used PSI to teach Kinematics and Dynamics of Mechanical Systems. His course was also successful and in the Fall of 1970, two more engineering professors instituted PSI courses. Dr. Charles H. Roth, Jr. of Electrical Engineering taught Digital Systems Engineering I and Dr. Gerald R. Wagner taught a graduate course in Applied Statistics.

There now existed a nucleus of four engineering professors on the Texas campus who had experience with the PSI method. All had obtained results which were superior to those they were accustomed to achieving with conventional instructional techniques and they were enthusiastic about PSI. They began to proselytize and gave unselfishly of their time to acquaint others with the method. In Spring 1971 Dr. Leonard M. Simmon, Jr., of the Physics Department used PSI to teach Electricity and Magnetism. In Summer 1971 Mr. John J. Knightly and Mr. John L. Sayre of the Graduate School of Library Science taught a PSI course in Basic Reference Sources. In Fall 1971 Dr. John M. White taught Principles of Chemistry, Dr. Paul E. Nacozy of Aerospace Engineering taught Engineering Computation and Dr. Robert D. Brooks of Radio-TV-Film taught Audio Environments using PSI. All these course developers sought and obtained the advice and counsel of the original four "experts" from the College of Engineering and all obtained good results and are still using the Keller Plan to teach these courses. In succeeding semesters the number of PSI courses has continued to increase, until at the present time we can identify thirty courses which are taught in 15 departments in six colleges (for a chronological list of PSI courses developed, see Appendix).

The Alfred P. Sloan Foundation Project

Continuing development of Keller Plan courses began to run into snags. Classroom requirements and cost of reproduction of materials, proctor salaries and unusual grade distributions began to focus administrative attention on our activities. This attention was not necessarily hostile, but we were becoming pretty visible and department chairmen and deans had many requests for funds and budgets to balance. They began asking a number of valid questions (which had previously already occurred to us). We also wished to see the development of new courses continue in an orderly fashion and wished to be able to achieve some control over their quality. Thus we began to explore the possibility of attracting grant support to aid our project. Our early efforts were unsuccessful, but the Alfred P. Sloan Foundation of New York City became interested and they ultimately funded a two-year program which had two purposes: the development (or redesign) of twelve PSI courses and the evaluation of course data.

The courses to be developed under the grant are:

1. Introduction to Nuclear Reactor Theory — B. V. Koen (redesign)

2. Dynamic Systems Synthesis — L. L. Hoberock (redesign)

3. Engineering Statics — P. E. Nacozy and W. T. Fowler (redesign)

4. Principles of Audio and Visual Production — R. D. Brooks (redesign)

5. Principles of Chemistry — J. M. White (redesign)

6. Structural Dynamics — R. R. Craig

7. Design of Structural Systems in Timber — D. W. Fowler

8. Process Analysis and Simulation — D. M. Himmelblau

9. Electrical Engineering Laboratory I — C. H. Roth, Jr.

10. Electronic Circuits I — W. M. Clark

11. Basic Library Cataloguing and Classification — Mrs. Billie G. Herring

12. Introduction to Engineering Analysis (Pre-Calculus Math) — G. R. Wagner and Mrs. Nancy Hamilton

The questions for which answers are being sought:

a. Do students learn more (or better) with PSI?

b. Are the higher average grades in PSI courses justified?

c. Does a PSI course result in a significantly different long-term retention of course content by students?

d. Does PSI cause students to learn how to study?

e. Are PSI materials transferable?

f. What are the costs of PSI courses?

g. How can your course be designed to minimize procrastination?

h. How do we reduce the percentage of dropouts?

i. What is the effect of class size?

In addition to course development and study of the questions posed, the project includes a PSI Summer Institute in engineering statics for community college teachers. Engineering statics is a core course for all engineering students and it is normally taken during the second semester or the second year. Few community colleges offer courses in engineering statics, either because the enrollment would be too small, or because no faculty member is qualified to teach it (there are few engineers on community college faculties). As a result, the community college transfer may be at a decided disadvantage when he transfers to a four-year college or university to pursue an engineering degree.

In an effort to alleviate this problem, Wallace Fowler and Paul Nacozy developed a PSI statics course in Spring 1973. In Summer 1973, they revised the course and taught it to 24 community college teachers from 16 states. The materials were further revised and have been distributed to the summer school participants, who are using them to teach the course at their respective campuses. The participants at the Summer Institute were an exceptional group, capable, conscientious, and enthusiastic. This part of the Sloan Foundation project will yield information about Question e. (are PSI materials transferable?). It also disseminates use-tested PSI materials so that the users are not required to develop their own courses. They in turn will be able to suggest further modifications, based upon their experiences in the field.

The evaluation phase of the Sloan Foundation project is under the direction of Dr. Susan M. Hereford, assisted by staff members of the University of Texas Measurement and Evaluation Center.

Trends in PSI-Related Research

The conscientious introduction of any innovative approach to teaching necessitates that the instructor channel increased amounts of his time into preparation for the course. The preceding description of the basic operations of PSI courses should make it apparent that instructors choosing to design and implement Keller Plan courses typically find themselves with little time to devote to thorough and systematic evaluation of the effectiveness of the method or to research directed toward its analysis. Furthermore, it is well known that instructors directly involved in preparing instructional materials or designing new educational environments frequently are unable to analyze them objectively because of their level of belief and personal involvement. These considerations, combined with the relative recency of Keller's published description of the method, have limited research and evaluation activities directed toward systematic analysis of the instructional method itself. Most published papers regarding PSI are descriptive of applications of the method to specific courses. Grade distributions, rates of student progress, unit structure of the course and students' reactions are usually reported.

Other literature describes the effects of various modifications of the method. The impact of such modifications as the removal of self-pacing and the addition of interviews or oral examinations have been reported. Research comparing relative student achievement in PSI and more traditionally taught classes also has been reported. The general conclusions to be drawn from published reports of attempts to apply Keller's system of instruction and modifications of it are similar to those originally presented by Keller. Students appear to learn the content of the course more effectively and leave the course having more positive feelings about it than is typically the case in classes taught by various lecture-discussion methods.

In his 1967 paper (1), Keller suggested that systematic research regarding elements of the personalized system of instruction could begin only after initial problems involved in instituting the approach had been solved:

> The work done thus far to develop this kind of
> individualized teaching within the mass-education
> framework of a large university has been aimed
> mainly at establishing a base-line procedure. Once
> this is done, it will be possible to begin assessing
> the relative importance of some of the variables
> involved. (p. 195)

New Directions in the Evaluation of PSI

Keller's idea of "assessing the relative importance of some of the variables involved" implies an internal approach to research regarding PSI. The evaluative approach in which PSI courses are compared with more traditionally taught courses in terms of student achievement and effective response serves to establish and ensure the credibility of the method and for this reason, should not be abandoned. The internal approach to evaluation requires an analysis of the elements of PSI and the interaction between those elements and factors present in the general academic environment. Critical examination of some of the possible objections to the use of the method is also necessary, as is an objective assessment of some of the claims made in its favor.

Research and evaluation activities are proceeding concurrently with development and implementation of Keller Plan courses at The University of Texas at Austin, with the major source of support at this time being the $340,000 grant from the Alfred P. Sloan Foundation. Research efforts by the evaluation staff focus on individual courses as well as on the project as a whole. At the level of the individual project, evaluation activities are designed primarily to provide the instructor with systematic feedback from his students and his proctors regarding his developing course. More candid student responses are typically obtained when data are collected by persons not directly associated with the course or the instructor. Obviously, data from each course will become part of the final analysis of the total project; however, in order to go beyond typical PSI evaluation efforts of the past, the present study has been designed to cut across course, departmental, and college boundaries, thus focusing on the method itself and the crucial variables interacting with its application. Of necessity, the evaluation effort includes the search for new approaches to educational research since Keller Plan courses by definition rule out many of the assumptions of traditional educational research strategies. One example of this problem is the consideration that an instructional approach which is designed so as to individualize instruction cannot be analyzed completely by means of conventional group methods such as comparisons of class averages. The use of criterion-based testing procedures rather than conventional normative testing further complicates the evaluation.

Research and evaluation work regarding PSI courses at The University of Texas at Austin can be conceptualized in terms of several major areas of concern which should be considered as supplements to rather than substitutes for more traditional forms of evaluative comparisons which are proceeding concurrently.

Student Characteristics

One of the primary concerns of the PSI evaluation project is the relationship between student characteristics and the relative effectiveness of PSI courses. Experience has made it clear that certain students are simply unable to function adequately in a PSI learning environment. A combination of experience and intuition tells us that the critical factors here are probably not intellectual variables. Given an adequate level of intellectual functioning to cope with college level learning experiences, an individual's response to PSI seems to be related to such attitudinal and personality factors as autonomy, need for interpersonal competition, need for affiliation and motivation to earn high grades. Various aspects of a student's background and current life style may also influence his response to Keller Plan courses. We are currently investigating the relationship between student response to Keller Plan courses and background variables, concurrent situational variables such as marital status, employment, living arrangements and preferred place of study, and attitudinal variables such as general acceptance of education. We are also attempting to determine whether students who express initial reservations about taking a course taught by the Keller Plan do in fact perform more poorly than they would be expected to perform as a function of their academic aptitude and grades in other subjects.

The major goal of this study of the relationships between student characteristics and instructional outcomes under the Keller Plan is to obtain data which may assist in future differential placement of students in courses which represent optimal learning situations for them. As the number and variety of available instructional strategies increase, it seems appropriate and necessary to attempt to find relationships which will allow students to be assisted in choosing learning environments which will maximize the probability of their success.

The impact of the proctoring experience on students filling that role is also under investigation along with an analysis of the characteristics of students who become successful proctors. It is predicted that the proctoring experience will be found to have impact beyond the reinforcement of knowledge of the course content. For example, proctoring may in some instances stimulate a developing interest in teaching as a profession.

Cost and Time Factors

One consistently mentioned source of concern with regard to Keller Plan courses has been that they may be prohibitively expensive, particularly in the area of instructor time. In response to this concern, we are attempting to trace cost and time patterns through two or three offerings of a PSI course. It has been predicted that cost and time will be relatively high during the initial offering of a PSI course but will drop in subsequent semesters to a level comparable to that for more traditional forms of instruction. A related consideration is class size. If it is found that large classes can be taught successfully by one instructor and a group of proctors and assistants, it is conceivable that Keller Plan instruction may eventually represent a reduction in the cost of instruction.

PSI Within the Conventional Academic Setting

Many questions about the feasibility of Keller Plan instruction have been concerned with the interrelationships of PSI courses and the remainder of the curriculum. Questions of several types have been raised. Given the high level of required proficiency, how many PSI courses could a student be reasonably expected to take during one semester? Could an entire curriculum be built around Keller Plan instruction? If a student is taking several traditional courses and one PSI course, will he tend to neglect the PSI course in favor of other courses having schedules and precise time requirements? Can complete self-pacing be permitted within the constraints of the semester system? Such questions have implications for student placement as well as curriculum design; therefore, their consideration is crucial to future implementation of Keller Plan courses.

One of the usual results of placing a PSI course within a conventional curriculum is a relatively high drop-out rate in the PSI course. A period of procrastination usually precedes dropping out. A major research and evaluation effort currently is being directed toward analyzing underlying reasons for procrastination and eventual drop-out. Strategies for modifying PSI in such a way as to decrease procrastination and the resulting drop rate are also being explored. Care must be taken in this area, however, since strategies found to be successful in reducing procrastination and lowering the drop-out rate may also introduce elements sufficiently aversive to violate the rationale on which PSI is based.

Transferability

Whether a PSI course developed and refined at one institution can be transported to another institution and used effectively has been another source of concern regarding Keller Plan courses. We are presently investigating the effectiveness of the summer institute which was described previously. Factors under investigation include instructor characteristics, student characteristics and institutional characteristics. The feasibility of transferring PSI materials between institutions has a direct relationship to the issue of cost and time which was mentioned previously. If transfer can be successfully accomplished, much duplication of instructor effort could be eliminated.

General Impact of PSI on Students

Claims, usually based on theory or intuition, have frequently been made that the experience of taking a PSI course has a lasting impact on a student's study habits and orientation as well as on his retention of course material and subsequent academic performance. The present research and evaluation project includes an attempt to assess changes in study habits and orientation and to monitor students' performance in later courses, particularly those for which the PSI course functions as a prerequisite.

Instructional Objectives and PSI Effectiveness

It is well known that instructional strategies must be designed in such a way as to be congruent with the educational objectives of the course. The types of instructional objectives (i.e., cognitive, affective and/or psychomotor) to which PSI is best suited are under analysis. Results to date indicate that objectives in the cognitive and psychomotor domains are most consistent with PSI strategies. It is clear that the 100% mastery criterion would be difficult to apply in areas where correct responses to readiness test questions may vary as a function of theoretical orientation.

Elements of PSI

It was mentioned previously that comparisons of PSI and more conventional forms of instruction typically have indicated higher levels of student achievement in PSI courses, as well as more positive student attitudes. Although somewhat limited at this time, because of the newness of the project, our data indicate similar trends. It cannot be determined from such data, however, just what element or elements of PSI cause such improved performance. If, for example, self-pacing and the use of proctors were removed, would the simple introduction of a criterion testing procedure with a high required level of proficiency yield the same results in the area of student achievement? Would the addition of proctors to a conventional teaching environment yield attitudinal improvements comparable to those found when all PSI elements are applied? Obtaining data necessary for analyzing the relative contribution of PSI elements is difficult since it necessitates experimental control rarely possible in educational evaluation settings. Analysis of the relative contributions of the major elements of PSI to its general success seems to have the greatest potential value in terms of research regarding the instructional method as a whole. Such information, combined with that regarding student characteristics and the interaction between educational objectives and teaching methods, would encourage the establishment of empirical and logical criteria for choosing among teaching methods and placing students in classes designed to facilitate their learning.

Summer PSI Symposia

In order to disseminate the results of the project, two Summer Symposia will be held. These will occur during the Summers of 1974 and 1975 and plans are to invite approximately thirty selected educators to each, paying their expenses. These symposia will last two to three days each.

Advisory Board

An Advisory Board has been appointed for this project, both to provide guidance to project personnel and to serve as another avenue for dissemination of results. The Board consists of six permanent members and varying numbers of temporary members who serve as consultants in particular specialty areas.

The permanent members of the Advisory Board are:

Dr. David G. Born, Professor of Psychology, University of Utah, Salt Lake City, Utah

Dr. Ben A. Green, Jr., Center for Personalized Instruction, Georgetown University, Washington, D.C.

Dr. Fred S. Keller, currently Visiting Professor of Psychology, Texas Christian University, Ft. Worth, Texas (formerly with Western Michigan University)

Dr. David T. Pratt, Associate Professor of Mechanical Engineering, Washington State University, Pullman, Washington

Dr. J. Gilmour Sherman, Professor and Chairman of Psychology, Georgetown University, Washington, D. C.

Dr. John G. Truxal, Dean of Engineering, State University of New York at Stony Brook

Consultants who have served the project so far are:

Mrs. Amogene F. DeVaney, Professor of Engineering and Mathematics, Amarillo College, Amarillo Texas

Dr. Gerhard F. Paskusz, Professor of Electrical Engineering and Associate Dean of Engineering, University of Houston, Houston, Texas

Dr. Bernet S. Swanson, Professor of Chemical Engineering, Illinois Institute of Technology, Chicago, Ill.

APPENDIX

PSI COURSES TAUGHT AT

THE UNIVERSITY OF TEXAS AT AUSTIN

FALL 1966

Educational Psychology 332S — Psychological Foundations of Secondary Education — Carl F. Hereford, Luiz F. S. Natalicio, and W. Stenning. This course has been taught each semester since. It is now taught exclusively by PSI in seven or eight 50-student sections at a time. Contact Dr. Hereford, Professor of Educational Psychology, 305 Sutton Hall.

FALL 1969

Mechanical Engineering 361E — Introduction to Nuclear Reactor Theory — Dr. Billy V. Koen, Associate Professor of Mechanical Engineering, 418C Taylor Hall.

SUMMER 1970

Mechanical Engineering 324 — Kinematics and Dynamics of Mechanical Systems — Dr. Lawrence L. Hoberock, Assistant Professor of Mechanical Engineering, 418C Taylor Hall.

FALL 1970

1. Electrical Engineering 360L — Digital Systems Engineering I — Dr. Charles H. Roth, Jr., Professor of Electrical Engineering, 510 Engineering Science Building.

2. Mechanical Engineering 361E — Introduction to Nuclear Reactor Theory (repeat) — Dr. Billy V. Koen.

3. Mechanical Engineering 390R.1 — Applied Statistics — Dr. Gerald R. Wayner, Assistant Professor of Mechanical Engineering, 201B Engineering Laboratories Building.

SPRING 1971

1. Electrical Engineering 360L — Digital Systems Engineering I — (repeat) — Charles H. Roth, Jr. and H. Kerner

2. Physics 416 — Electricity and Magnetism — Dr. Leonard M. Simmons, Jr., Asst. Professor of Physics (Now at the University of New Hampshire)

SUMMER 1971

1. Electrical Engineering 360L—Digital Systems Engineering I (repeat)—Charles H. Roth, Jr.

2. Library Science 340 — Basic Reference Sources — Mr. John J. Knightly and Mr. John L. Sayre. Mr. Knightly is in the Graduate School of Library Science at UT/Austin and Dr. Sayre is Librarian, Philips University, Enid, Oklahoma 73701.

FALL 1971

1. Aerospace Engineering 211 — Aerospace Engineering Computation — Dr. Paul E. Nacozy (Assistant Professor of Aerospace Engineering, 227 Taylor Hall).

2. Chemistry 302 — Principles of Chemistry — Dr. John M. White, Associate Professor of Chemistry, 119B Chemistry Building.

3. Electrical Engineering 360L — Digital Systems Engineering I (repeat) — Dr. C. V. Ramamorrthy and Terry A. Welch (Using Roth's materials).

4. Library Science 340 — Basic Reference Sources (repeat) — Julie Bichteler and John R. Wheat (using Knightly-Sayre materials)

5. Mechanical Engineering 390R.1 — Applied Statistics (repeat) — Gerald R. Wagner.

6. Radio-TV-Film 341 — Audio Environments — Dr. Robert D. Brooks, Associate Professor of Radio-TV-Film, 210B Social Work Building.

SPRING 1972

1. Aerospace Engineering 211 — Aerospace Engineering Computation (repeat) — Paul E. Nacozy.

2. Aerospace Engineering 367K — Flight Mechanics — Dr. Wallace T. Fowler, Associate Professor of Aerospace Engineering, 227 Taylor Hall.

3. Architectural Engineering 222 — Architectural Engineering Computation (repeat) — Kenneth Armstrong (using Nacozy's materials).

4. Electrical Engineering 360L — Digital Systems Engineering I (repeat) — Charles H. Roth, Jr.

5. Library Science 340 — Basic Reference Sources (repeat) — Julie Bichteler and John R. Wheat (using Knightly-Sayre materials).

6. Mechanical Engineering 390R.1 — Applied Statistics (repeat) — Gerald R. Wagner.

7. Radio-TV-Film 341 — Audio Environments (repeat) — Robert D. Brooks.

SUMMER 1972

1. Chemistry 354 — Physical Chemistry — Dr. John M. White, Associate Professor of Chemistry, 119B Chemistry Building.

2. Communications 380 — Communication Research Design — Dr. Jack L. Whitehead, Associate Professor of Speech Communication, 214A Speech Building.

3. Electrical Engineering 360L — Digital Systems Engineering I (repeat) — William R. Adrion (using Roth's materials).

4. Engineering Mechanics 306 — Mechanics I — Dr. Wallace T. Fowler, Associate Professor of Aerospace Engineering, 227 Taylor Hall.

5. Library Science 340 — Basic Reference Sources (repeat) — Linda C. Schexnaydre (using Knightly-Sayre materials).

FALL 1972

1. Aerospace Engineering 311 — Aerospace Engineering Computation (repeat) — Paul E. Nacozy.

2. Aerospace Engineering 367K—Flight Mechanics (repeat)—Walton E. Williamson (using Fowler's materials).

3. Astronomy 308 — Descriptive Astronomy for Non-Science Majors — Dr. William H. Jefferys, Associate Professor of Astronomy, 15.318 Physics-Math-Astronomy Building.

4. Astronomy 367M — Laboratory Methods in Astronomy — Dr. R. Robert Robbins, Jr., Associate Professor of Astronomy, 17.212 Physics-Math-Astronomy Building.

5. Chemical Engineering 202 — Introduction to Engineering, Dr. Eric Nutall, Assistant Professor of Chemical Engineering, 206 E. P. Schoch Laboratories Building (using Nacozy's materials).

6. Communications 380 — Communication Research Design (repeat) — Dr. Michael R. Chial (using Whitehead materials).

7. Electrical Engineering 360L — Digital Systems Engineering I (repeat) — Charles H. Roth, Jr., A. J. Welch, and Stephen A. Underwood (using Roth's materials).

8. Library Science 340 — Basic Reference Sources (repeat) — Julie Bichteler and John R. Wheat (using Knightly-Sayre materials).

9. Mechanical Engineering 364L — Dynamic Systems Synthesis — Dr. Lawrence L. Hoberock, Assistant Professor of Mechanical Engineering, 418C Taylor Hall.

10. Mechanical Engineering 390R.1 — Applied Statistics (repeat) — Gerald R. Wagner.

11. Physics 416 — Electricity and Magnetism (repeat) — Dr. Austin M. Gleeson (revision of Simmons' materials).

12. Radio-TV-Film 341—Audio Environments (repeat)—Robert D. Brooks.

SPRING 1973

1. Aerospace Engineering 311 — Aerospace Engineering Computation (repeat) — Dr. Paul E. Russell (using Nacozy's materials).

2. Aerospace Engineering 365 — Structural Dynamics — Dr. Roy R. Craig, Associate Professor of Aerospace Engineering, 310 Engineering Science Building.

3. Aerospace Engineering 367K — Flight Mechanics (repeat) — Walton E. Williamson (using Fowler's materials).

4. Astronomy 308 — Descriptive Astronomy for Non-Science Majors (repeat) — Dr. Michael Breger.

5. Chemical Engineering 202 — Introduction to Engineering (repeat) — Dr. Robert S. Schechter and Mr. A. T. Kott (using Nacozy's materials).

6. Electrical Engineering 360L — Digital Systems Engineering I (repeat) — Dr. Stephen A. Underwood and Dr. D. G. Raj-Karne (using Roth's materials).

7. Engineering Mechanics 306 — Engineering Statics — Drs. Wallace T. Fowler and Paul E. Nacozy.

8. Library Science 340 — Basic Information Sources (repeat) — Julie Bichteler and John R. Wheat (using Knightly-Sayre materials).

9. Library Science 351 — Basic Cataloguing and Classification — Mrs. Billy Grace Herring, Assistant Professor of Library Science, 4.224 Humanities Research Center.

10. Mechanical Engineering 364L — Dynamic Systems Synthesis (repeat) — Dr. Lawrence L. Hoberock.

11. Physics 416 — Electricity and Magnetism (repeat) — Dr. Herman Wolter (Gleeson's revised materials).

12. Astronomy 383 — Fundamental Astronomy (Graduate Course) — Dr. William H. Jefferys.

SUMMER 1973

1. Electrical Engineering 321 — Electrical Engineering Laboratory I — Dr. Charles H. Roth, Jr., Professor of Electrical Engineering, 510 Engineering Science Building.

2. Electrical Engineering 360L — Digital Systems Engineering I (repeat) — Dr. Stephen A. Szgenda (using Roth's materials).

3. Engineering Mechanics 306 — Engineering Statics (repeat for PSI Summer Institute for Community College Teachers) — Wallace T. Fowler and Paul E. Nacozy.

4. Library Science 340—Basic Information Sources (repeat)—Linda Schexnaydre and Charlotte Roach (revision of Knightly-Sayre materials).

5. Library Science 351 — Basic Cataloguing and Classification (repeat) — David Shinder and Maurice Leatherberry (using revision of Herring materials).

FALL 1973

1. Aerospace Engineering 311 — Aerospace Engineering Computation (repeat) — Dr. Paul E. Nacozy.

2. Aerospace Engineering 367M — Flight Mechanics (repeat, being given to three students as independent study course) — Dr. Wallace T. Fowler.

3. Architectural Engineering 362L — Design of Structural Systems in Timber — Dr. David W. Fowler, Associate Professor of Architectural Engineering, 310 Taylor Hall.

4. Astronomy 108K — Practical Astronomy (Laboratory Course) — Mr. Tom Connell and Mr. Alan Kiplinger, Teaching Assistants.

5. Astronomy 308 — Descriptive Astronomy for Non-Science Majors (repeat) — Drs. William H. Jefferys and Michael Breger (three sections).

6. Astronomy 367M — Laboratory Methods in Astronomy (repeat) — Dr. Paul Vanden Bout.

7. Chemical Engineering 202 — Introduction to Engineering (repeat) — Dr. Robert Mills (using Nacozy's materials).

8. Chemical Engineering 376 — Process Analysis and Simulation — Dr. David M. Himmelblau, Professor of Chemical Engineering, 211A E. P. Schoch Laboratories.

9. Electrical Engineering 321 — Electrical Engineering Laboratory I (repeat) — Dr. Charles H. Roth, Jr.

10. Electrical Engineering 360L — Digital Systems Engineering I (repeat) — Drs. Stephen A. Szygenda and Stephen A. Underwood (Three sections) (using Roth's materials).

11. Engineering Mechanics 306 — Engineering Statics (repeat) — Drs. Wallace T. Fowler and Paul E. Nacozy.

12. English 301—Freshman English Composition—Dr. Susan W. Wittig, Assistant Professor of English, 4 Calhoun Hall.

13. General Engineering 304 — Introduction to Engineering Analysis (pre-calculus mathematics) — Dr. Gerald R. Wagner and Mrs. Nancy Hamilton, 112 Engineering Laboratories Building.

14. Library Science 340 — Basic Information Sources (repeat) — Linda Schexnaydre and Julie Bichteler (revision of Knightly-Sayre materials).

15. Library Science 351 — Cataloguing and Classification (repeat) — Mrs. Billie Grace Herring.

16. Mechanical Engineering 335 — Probability and Statistics for Engineers — Dr. Gerald R. Wagner, Assistant Professor of Mechanical Engineering, 201B Engineering Laboratories Building.

17. Mechanical Engineering 361E — Nuclear Reactor Engineering — Dr. Billy V. Koen, Associate Professor of Mechanical Engineering, 415 Taylor Hall.

18. Mechanical Engineering 364L — Dynamic Systems Synthesis (repeat) — Dr. Lawrence L. Hoberock.

19. Mechanical Engineering 366L — Introduction to Operations Research — Dr. Charles S. Beightler, Professor of Mechanical Engineering, 201E Engineering Laboratories Building.

20. Mechanical Engineering 390 R.1 — Applied Statistics (Graduate Course, repeat) — Dr. Bernard Most (using Wagner's materials).

21. Radio-TV-Film 321K — Introduction to Image and Sound — Dr. Robert D. Brooks, Associate Professor of RTF, 210B Social Work Building.

COMPUTER-BASED HIGHER EDUCATION: A FIVE-YEAR RESEARCH PROGRAM

Duncan Hansen
Memphis State University[1]

INTRODUCTION

If the CAI researchers who began the initial systems in the early 1960's had envisioned the contents of a current technical report, the image of the table of contents would have centered about "the computer as the teacher." The group mind set was framed about the vision of enriched, detailed, student-computer interaction with learning control via optimization. Now, in the light of a decade time tunnel, CAI investigators can report their principal finding: the context of computer-based training is broader than our original conception and profits best from a management model for instruction. There is no singular way to individualize instruction to its optimal level without employing some of the older techniques, such as group discussion, or the newest ones, such as multimedia split-screen presentations. This requirement for a broader multifaceted approach to learning resulted from our facing research as it evolved through study after study towards "the computer as the manager of instruction." Using a computer-managed instructional (CMI) model to encompass computer-assisted instruction (CAI), simulation, adaptive testing, natural language dialogues, media management, scheduling, record keeping and evaluation, the potential of each of these components as training processes became most enhanced. This paper will report some of the research developments within this CMI framework.

For purposes of review, the studies were organized into four categories: learner strategies, training strategies, validation strategies and computer systems strategies. In learner-oriented research, investigators sought to find the students' cognitive and personality processes reflective within computer-based training. Therefore studies included rule learning behaviors, behavioral objective learning, memory, subjective organization, anxiety and curiosity. Those involved in training strategies studied effectiveness of computer-managed instruction, the possibilities of adaptive testing and modeling and the uses of simulation and information retrieval systems. The focus was on the design, implementation and evaluation of CMI components. The area of validation studies led to the evolution of an interdisciplinary team, an important ideational contribution in its own right, plus the role of CAI/CMI in schools and DOD training. Computer strategies produced, over the years, insight into interactive systems, instructional management systems and data analysis systems.

Brought together, the strategies, the studies and the results lead us to repeat here, and throughout this report, those themes which have led to profitable outcomes.

1. A model of computer-managed instruction yields a sufficient, integrated, and cost-effective approach to learning/teaching.

2. The individual difference variables reflective of the behavioral processes of memory, anxiety, curiosity and rule application are critically important to a CMI adaptive training model. The primary research need is to extend the set of available indices reflecting training in learning behavioral objectives, graphics, etc.

[1] The research described was accomplished at Florida State University; citations such as "(TM59)" refer to Technical Memorandums issued to inform the contractor of the work that was done.

3. The selection and integration of media components and the requirements for optimal resource allocation of training elements (instructors, simulators, peer instructors, etc.) has received limited research attention and represents one of the promising areas of the future.

4. The requirement to build substantive liaison models between the educational system's leaders and university researchers is essential if the design characteristics and requirements of training on the one hand and the theoretical concepts on the other are to merge in productive fashion. An interdisciplinary research team was an exemplary model of this liaison process.

5. In reference to computer strategies, the creation of management or central programs was highly profitable and the need to create training-oriented management systems is of the highest importance.

We turn now to the specific elements and studies within the broad four strategy theme approach. Each topic will be reviewed and summarized by valid CAI/CMI conclusions. Statements as to needed future activity will be made topic by topic.

LEARNER ORIENTED RESEARCH

The primary focus of CAI investigation for the learner strategy research was devoted to studying the internal cognitive and personality processes of the learner while in computer-based learning tasks. Studies of rule learning behavior, anxiety and curiosity and memory lead to positive indications that these searches should be continued. Results of research into the role of behavioral objectives in learning and into subjective organization have led investigators to feel that these are less rewarding areas.

Rule Learning Behaviors

Probably the most common type of learning undertaken by students is the acquisition of principles or rules. By learning rules in a specific situation as one of a class of situations, the rule governed behavior of the learner permits more effective learning strategies that generalize to more than one situation. Because the learning and application of rules has been recognized as a very important component of education in general, a substantial amount of research is currently underway by several instructional psychologists. From this research, several generalizations can be made as to the composition of instruction for complex rule learning.

In this discussion of rule learning behavior, it will be helpful to consider three interrelated concepts. These are the rule statement, the rule and rule governed behavior. A rule statement describes the procedure to be followed in performing a specific operation on inputs from a specified class of inputs to produce a specific output from a class of outputs. The rule is considered to be the procedure or operation described by the rule statement. Rule-governed behavior is that behavior that would result from a student correctly applying the rule. The ambiguous term "rule learning" may now be divided into two appropriately descriptive terms: (a) learning the rule statement which refers to learning to verbalize the rule statement, and (b) acquisition of rule-governed behavior which refers to the correct application of the rule.

A replication study was implemented to investigate prior findings that rule statements presented in the instruction reduced the number of examples needed and total time required to meet a prespecified criterion. Further, presentation of rule statements increased performance on a transfer task and reduced the requirement of reasoning ability in learning the task and presentation of objectives also reduced the number of examples and reduced the requirement for reasoning ability. The replication showed that presentation of rule statements reduced the number of examples required to meet criterion performance, increased posttest performance, reduced total time required to meet criterion performance, increased retention performance, and reduced the level of state anxiety within the learning task (TM59).

A third study in this area found that the presentation of objectives increased the total amount of time spent studying a rule learning task (TM47). The presentation of sample test items within the learning task reduced the requirement for memory, but neither objectives nor sample test items had an effect on post or retention performance.

Implications from these studies for instructional method in acquisition of rule application skills appear to be three fold:

1. Instruction should present general instructional objectives to inform the student as to what is expected of him.

2. Presentation of rule statement can prevent the "discovery" of an incorrect rule.

3. Presentation of sample test items gives the student a chance for practice and immediate feedback.

Further studies revealed that availability of prior examples reduced problem response latency and reduced the requirement for reasoning ability (TM in press). A present investigation, currently being analyzed, appears to show that memorization of work statements reduces both the number of examples and total time to reach criterion performance on complex rule application tasks. However, no memorization effect has been found on the posttest or retention test of rule application skills. Implications for instructional development are (a) the requirement of memorization of rule statements to facilitate the correct choice of a rule when more than one is being learned, and to aid in recognition of operational symbols if they are used; (b) the use of several examples to show the statement instances of the correct application of the rule; and (c) the requirement of reviews if more than three rules are being learned in one session to provide simulated testing and appropriate followup review instruction.

Future

In addition to apparently useful generalizations given for the development of instruction for acquisition of complex rule application skills, implications for fruitful future research in this area have grown out of the FSU investigations. It should be ascertained what type of examples are most profitable presented to the student: non-examples, examples, or both. A second line of research recommended is the investigation of design of rule learning materials dependent upon the abilities of the learner; this would contribute to the adaptive model research. A final area which appears to offer promise is the area of optimal number of examples for presentation before sample test items. All of these studies relating to number of examples would contribute to a drill and practice adaptive model.

Behavioral Objective Learning

Only in the latter part of the decade was research undertaken to examine empirically the claims made for objectives in instruction. Of the approximately 35 studies conducted, about half failed to confirm the hypothesis that providing students with objectives leads to increased learning. Remaining studies showed facilitative effects (TM45). The research on interactions between objectives and type of learning provided few positive findings. No general conclusions can be found in the research which found a few significant interactions between objectives and learner characteristics.

Investigations at FSU found that objectives significantly increased study time with no posttest difference between groups (TM61), and that objectives partially reduced anxiety without affecting performance (TM47). The hypothesis that objectives add structure to learning as is done by advance organizers was not confirmed, although a main sequence effect was found (TM57). A further FSU study found that objectives focused learning on relevant materials and depressed incidental learning (TM66).

To generalize from studies overall, it seems that objectives can have an effect on learning, although this effect does not appear to be as strong or as pervasive as originally assumed.

Future

It is anticipated that research on behavioral objectives will continue the trend away from exploration of their effect on learning. The trend will be toward exploration of interactions with task and learner characteristics. The exploration of hypothesized cognitive functions which may be fulfilled by objectives in the learning situation is anticipated to grow, also. An example of this type of research is the investigation of objectives as an orienting function (TM57). Further research in these areas may prove more productive than that conducted to date.

Memory Research

An important capacity for memory is the ability to discriminate. This is an idea which has been reinforced by the research which we have conducted on directed forgetting. Important to the retrieval of some previously stored event is that we be able to discriminate it from other stored information. We think voluntary forgetting is largely a matter of sharpening one's capacity to discriminate between material which is to be remembered and that which is not (TM19).

This way of looking at things raised the question of the nature of memory storage. If one's ability to discriminate among memories is important, then perhaps encoding is in terms of dimensions which offer a basis for discriminating among memories, and more specifically, in terms of the values of such dimensions. Just what these dimensions are is unknown. The point is simply the proposition that events are encoded according to abstracted features.

Another study (in press) investigated short-term memory (STM) prerequisites to development of more complex mental processes. Of special interest was the possible differences between white, advantaged children (6-7 years old) and black, disadvantaged children. Differences would seem to indicate that memory characteristics are not the same for these two groups.

The findings were also compared with prediction of three of the more characteristic information processing models for STM: Sperling's Visual STM Model, the Feigenbaum-Simon Computer Simulation Model, and the Atkinson-Schiffrin Model. It was found that some of the results could be incorporated into the structure of all the models, but that no one model could account for all the findings. An alternative model was developed which included an IQ parameter, a more complex rehearsal process, and an operational representation of organizing strategies.

Our conclusions for both the directed forgetting and STM childhood research are that they both indicate possible individual differences which could be useful in adaptive instruction. It is necessary to continue research to fully operationalize appropriate memory indices.

Future

In the near future of memory research, the computer will be used to construct theories and to simulate memory performance rather than to assist in the conduct of experiments. This will be particularly true in the areas of semantic and long-term memory. These theories are particularly complex and it will be especially useful to simulate performance. By contrast, experiments to test such theories may be simple and fairly easy to conduct with relatively unsophisticated equipment.

Subjective Organization

The purpose of the research on subjective organization (SO) was to determine if SO is a meaningful individual difference variable in the learning of verbal discourse. Furthermore, we thought to examine the relationship between SO and other aptitude variables thought to be important determiners of learning from prose materials. In order to accomplish this, a new measure of subjective organization had to be developed because previous measures had certain limitations which were thought to mitigate against finding a meaningful relationship between memory organization and recall. Thus, as an outcome of this research, a new measure has been examined and partially validated in relation to other SO measures and other individual difference variables.

The basic research paradigm was one in which SO and other measures were administered to subjects and then those subjects were asked to learn paragraphs which were organized in various ways. The results indicated that high organizers are highly influenced by the external structure of the learning materials and they tended to mirror that organization in their recall. High organizers, however, were able to reorganize the materials, but that was not to their advantage because of the time constraints involved. That is, high organizers actively sought alternative relationships among the sentences, thereby reducing the amount of time spent memorizing them.

Three generalizations can be made on the basis of the studies which were conducted at FSU on subjective organization:

1.   It seems that the ability to reorganize material can be a limiting factor to a learner if sufficient learning time is not provided.

2.   Low organizers need to have learning materials structured to a higher degree in order for them to learn effectively.

3.   High organizers perform equally on materials of high and low structure.

Future

The conclusions of the investigations in this area indicate that future research should consider the following:

1.   A practical, reliable, and valid instrument for measuring SO must be developed. In this regard, the potential use of a computer for real-time presentation and scoring is promising.

2.   Explorations on more complex instructional tasks must be undertaken on the finding that low organizers need highly structured materials whereas high organizers perform the same on both high and low structured materials.

Continuation of research in these areas should provide instructional designers with a set of findings which would guide the structuring of textual materials such that the learning of all students will be maximized.

Anxiety and Curiosity Research

Our investigation of anxiety and curiosity behaviors of a student while being trained was primarily focused on the use of these personality indices as predictors of optimal instructional treatments. While State/Trait Theory initially guided our efforts, the subsequent inconsistencies between replicatable findings and the theory indicated its limited role in a training context. The theoretical study of curiosity did provide us with a new framework which appears to resolve many of these prior unexplicable complexities.

The development of State/Trait Anxiety Theory, based on Drive Theory, allowed a number of derivations for prediction of performance relevant to computer-assisted instruction (TR6, TR7). At the same time CAI seemed an excellent vehicle for testing the theory (TR14). The results were not encouraging for confirming a Drive Theory interpretation of State/Trait Anxiety. However, anxiety was shown to be an indicator of CAI performance and the thrust of research continued in this area (TM20, TM41, TM42, TM49, TM52). Studies included anxiety effects on memory support, test taking, and interactions with response mode, subject matter familiarity, and learning time.

The important results indicated a consistent inverse relationship between state anxiety and learning, differential effects of trait anxiety especially as it revealed learner latencies, the complex role of memory aids and response modes as facilitators under some conditions, and the complex functional relationship of anxiety, curiosity and latencies. This later finding could be a promising future framework for studying latencies within training.

In addition, the anxiety theory and research directly initiated and influenced new work on state/trait epistemic curiosity (TR23, TM34). Curiosity provides an additional indicator of performance within instruction and specifically CMI. The concurrent interests in adaptive instruction models resulted in postulating the value of these personality variables as useful predictors in decision models for selecting alternative individualized treatments. One study, utilizing regression techniques, especially found state anxiety to be a useful predictor for selecting remedial instruction (TR27).

Future

For the future, we anticipate that the effort within adaptive models and the theory of anxiety-curiosity within training will be highly fruitful. The use of anxiety-curiosity concepts to study response latencies may help explain the highly variable results one tends to find.

Graphics Research

In order to employ the research capabilities of computer presentation of graphics in instruction, an initial study at FSU provided the opportunity for devising techniques to code graphics onto the cathode ray tube screen. This general model of graphic encoding was then used to develop studies of selection and sequencing of graphics for realistic training materials(TM14). Further attempts to learn the rules of graphic learning (TM24) demonstrated that the search for such rules is difficult, and can even be considered unprofitable.

Furthering the graphics investigations, FSU pursued research in mapping sentences on to graphics (TM60). Studying this instructional technique provided data which was complex. More appeared to be going on in this instructional situation than could be easily interpreted by learning theory.

Used as a teaching aid, computer graphics proved helpful in instructing engineering dynamics students in the traditional stumbling block of Euler angles (TM18). Graphics proved helpful in assisting in visualization of the angles. Subjects also reported positive attitudes toward the instruction.

Future

Generally, given current constraints, the search for rules in learning from graphics appears to be unsuitable for study. As an aid in problem solving, graphics apparently lend assistance to learning; the experience can be positively viewed by learners.

TRAINING STRATEGIES

A major investigation of computer-managed instruction was conducted as a priority in training strategies, to study training effectiveness, and cost benefit outcomes. Further training strategies in the areas of adaptive testing, adaptive systems, simulations, and information retrieval systems were also researched to various degrees. The research, generalizations, and future trends are described in the following sections.

Computer-Managed Instruction

Throughout the duration of the contract there was a concurrent set of investigations in computer-assisted instruction (CAI) and computer-managed instruction (CMI). The primary purpose of the investigations of CMI was to determine its training effectiveness and associated cost benefit outcome in comparison with CAI and other more conventional means of instruction. As pursued at FSU, computer-managed instruction involves the following:

1. diagnostic assessment and the assignment of individualized learning prescriptions,

2. the use of CAI for practice and remediational purposes,

3. the use of simulation for role and decision-making training purposes,

4. the use of the computer for ease and objectivity of curriculum development, and

5. the development of a record system so that the individualized training process could be effectively monitored and managed.

With this CMI conceptual context, a number of studies were pursued (TR8, TR11,TR12,TR19, TR22, TM23, TM32). All of these studies indicated that CMI at the collegiate level is highly feasible, cost-effective, and provides for learning results similar to CAI. However, due to the mastery level learning approach utilized in the instructional materials, the relationship of individual difference variables to learning rate or performance was more limited. Where extensive media and recitation sections were used, the effects of individual difference variables seemed to be more pronounced. Finally, learning attitude toward the instructional materials was quite positive and could be manipulated by the form of training.

In turn, investigations of CAI indicated that it is useful in a number of technical training areas. It proved especially useful for dynamic graphics such as found in engineering dynamics. However, while CAI was shown to be viable in areas like chemistry, the results did not tend to exceed those found in CMI.

It is important to note the fact that the development process for CMI, while not quite as demanding as that of CAI, still was considerable. The dependency on a sound training model, formative evaluation, and effective monitoring of students in an individualized mode seem to be the critical factors in the design and implementation of CMI.

From this, consequently, the following research generalizations can be derived:

1. Terminal-oriented computer-managed instruction has shown to be more effective than conventional instruction and less costly than computer-assisted instruction.

2. The most significant gains in the quality of instruction have not necessarily been due to the use of computers, but have been through the implementation of systematic approaches to the training process required for application of the computer.

3. Although the computer provides the instructional developer with more information about the instructional process than has been available, the revision process remains the least well understood and utilized component of the systems approach; however, the provision for systematic, reliable data now allows us to turn our attention to this problem.

4. Interdisciplinary collegiate development teams will not necessarily produce better computerized instructional materials than those produced by conceptually integrated teams.

Future

During the time period since the initiation of the Themis Project, educators have come to understand that in order to implement individualized instruction for the learner, there is a need to provide similar training for the trainer. This new form of teacher training has been labelled "competency-based" or "performance-based" training. The implementation of such training programs has more clearly identified the needs which such programs have for a computer. These computer needs, in general order of priority, are listed below:

1. Record keeping of computerized and noncomputerized assessments of student performance for monitoring purposes

2. Scheduling

3. Assessment of "computer-testable" skills

4. Adaptive remediation, including CAI and drill and practice exercises.

If this list is an accurate reflection of the needs of such programs, then it would appear that the role of the computer must be first as a general management system and only secondarily as an assessment and instructional tool.

Adaptive Testing

The initial undertaking with adaptive testing concerned itself with the automation of intellectual and personality measures. This effort successfully resulted in the automation of an individualized intelligence test (Slosson Intelligence Test) (TR21) with satisfactory reliability and validity coefficients. Moreover, a complex personality test, namely, the MMPI, was also satisfactorily implemented (TM28, TM48). These studies indicated that response latency contributed to the score information and concurrent validity when measured against a conventional administration. This line of research eventuated in a systematic review (TM3, TM30) covering the various uses of automated testing.

In turn, the development of sequential testing and tailored testing continues to be investigated. Utilizing simulation techniques, sequential testing can be shown to be a profitable approach. The general goal of sequential testing is to present the smallest number of test items necessary to accurately classify an examinee into two or more exclusive groups, or in conceptual terms, to improve reliability and validity of the decision process within CAI testing. Previous computer-based sequential testing models have been based upon right-wrong measures of performance. The FSU sequential testing effort differs from previous models in that both invariate and multi-variate performance measures are utilized. The multivariate prediction model is expected to increase classification accuracy beyond that possible using binary-coded item response data alone. More importantly, the use of tailored testing is currently being investigated as an approach for the administration of attitude items in a training situation (TM in press). It is conjectured that the number of test items can be minimized and the assessment of learning satisfaction can be improved in terms of its accuracy.

These studies of sequential testing led to the development of adaptive reading comprehension tests. The adaptive reading tests provided for a more dynamic individualized search of the student's current comprehension level especially under paced conditions. The rationale for using paced conditions is based on learning-time savings being pace contingent.

Future

In the future adaptive testing will most likely focus on two aspects. First, an investigation of incorrect as well as correct alternatives via Bock's multiple category model shows great promise. This approach should allow for adaptive selecting of items by items alternative characteristics and the assignment of sequentially derived confidence bands about the student's performance level. Given the improved information from this approach, it is then conjectured that a sampling approach to sequential testing can more effectively provide for the early classification of a subject especially if complex confidence band techniques are utilized. Thus, the future tends to hold a continued seeking for more efficient testing procedures as well as ones which will have psychometric properties appropriate for the individual and not just the group.

Adaptive Modeling

A major theme throughout the ONR-sponsored research has been that instruction should not be fixed for all students either in treatments or time. The alternative to fixed instruction is adaptive instruction which attempts to match an individual's unique characteristics with optimum treatment dimensions. Models for selecting appropriate alternative treatments consist of contingent, mediated, and optimizing algorithms designed to achieve the objectives.

The initial studies of adaptive models at FSU investigated learning and personality variables which might prove useful in predicting and assigning remedial instruction, lesson length, and other instructional variables. Multiple linear regression methods were developed (TR9) and used in an early modeling attempt with predictor variables consisting primarily of performance variables (TR10). Personality variables were added, in a phased approach to determine useful predictors, which resulted in outstanding performance levels for the adaptive group. A major study which manipulated the assignment of remedial instruction was undertaken (TR27). The order of outcomes in terms of superiority were the adaptive model strategy, remediation for all strategy, a learner choice strategy, and a no-remediation strategy.

These results and models were then considered for employment in reading comprehension (TR20). More recently, models based on the experience gained in the ONR-sponsored research, were developed for the Air Force Advanced Instructional System. In addition, ONR adaptive modeling has continued with an investigation of drill-and-practice in terms of lesson structure composition. Further, the study of the utility of measures which relates information processing to reinforcement contingencies for adaptive instruction has resulted in a model which takes into account both memory and motivational processes and procedures.

Future

It is anticipated that investigation of the monitoring and managing aspects of both training resources and of the individual will provide payoff in the future. This will involve managing such things as the problem set size, the sequences among sets, the assignment of media, the assignment of instructor and peer time, and the use of incentives.

Simulations

System Simulation

One of the major methods of using simulation in education, as well as other spheres, is the projection and analysis of systems. By simulating a prototype computerized management system intended as a subcomponent of the FSU elementary teacher training model, the CAI Center examined a number of problems in a data acquisition and instructional system (TR8). The following generalizations resulted from the system analysis: (a) a computer-managed system is technically feasible for use with an individualized teacher training program, and (b) computer processing for trainee scheduling and testing data, as well as program management, is necessary.

Simulating a teacher training system using information from a behavioral simulation (TR16), FSU found advantages in experimentation capabilities and resulting predictions about the teacher training program. Further, advantages were found in the utilization of regression techniques in combination with A Programming Language (APL) for designing, constructing, and utilizing a system simulation.

Behavioral Simulation

A behavioral simulation was used at FSU to train prospective teachers by providing an environment facilitating transfer to the classroom (TR16). Analysis for the behavioral simulation proceeded through assessment of entry behaviors, collection of data on trainee performance during instruction, collection of data on criterion variables and analysis and evaluation of the required training process in terms of the dimensions of simulation theory to estimate the nature and validity of the behavioral simulation. Behavioral simulation appeared to permit change in participant's behavior patterns.

Instructional Simulation

A further major function of simulation is instructional. Much of the debate in this area continues to be over the potential for simulation to affect attitudinal and/or cognitive growth. One game, or simulation, developed at FSU (TR17) was designed to allow the player to relate his knowledge of science to situations in elementary classroom instruction. Use of the game by graduate students indicated that a learning environment of this nature can foster growth in both cognitive and affective areas.

One of the primary advantages seen in instructional simulation is the ability to reduce cost (e.g., by reduction of expensive laboratory equipment) and a second is experimentation without danger (e.g., investigating dangerous chemical combinations without use of the chemical). Investigation into simulating laboratory experiences at FSU showed that simulation, as opposed to traditional laboratory methods, was equally effective as evaluated by posttest performance and total instructional time.

Statistical Simulation

As is suggested in the Computer Systems section of this report, A Programming Language (APL) proves to be an outstanding computer language for the simulating of statistical analyses, due to its mathematical capabilities (SM3). It is possible for a student to explore the meaning of various statistical concepts through sample problems and exercises, which he works as often as he wishes. He can be guided through the hypothesis testing procedure by inspecting data, successively making appropriate inferential decisions as further hypothesis testing information is given him (SM12). This type of APL simulation continues to expand as its utility and appeal are exposed to wider audiences at FSU.

Simulation Development

Investigators of simulation generally predict a more widespread use of the technique, both in education and in other spheres, for research and analysis as well as instruction and training. Advances in the development of such simulations, however, are meager (TM53). The major problems affecting progress are seen in evaluation:

1. Many authors feel that their simulations produce affective rather than cognitive changes and are unsympathetic to stating behavioral objectives. Since an equal number of authors and users request behavioral objectives for simulation, this problem may not be resolved until statements of affective objectives are satisfactorily developed, and can be evaluated.

2. Evaluation of instruction by simulation is correspondingly difficult. A search for satisfactory, new methods of evaluation may be a future activity, or a satisfactory relating of simulation evaluation to existing techniques.

3. The validation of the simulation model itself remains the most difficult part of simulation development. While mathematical simulations appear to have potential to solve this problem through output comparisons, simulations of human behavior, for example, provide a requirement for establishment of other model validation procedures.

137

Information Retrieval

IR for Inquiry

Information retrieval (IR) systems, like simulations, can be developed and used for research and/or instruction. FSU research on a CAI-based information retrieval system containing 5312 social science generalizations was directed toward examination of human inquiry behavior and appraisal of affective factors within the task (TM16). Both the feasibility of the approach to improving inquiry behavior and the positive nature of learner reaction were established in the IR application.

IR Instructional Tasks

In the library science area, recognition of the future growth of automated IR systems led to provision of computer-based IR tasks for advanced students (TM40). Both instructional and research goals were set for the use of the on-line searched coordinate index, which referenced 1856 documents prior to its transfer to the IBM 6400. As a teaching aid in graduate courses, the IR system served several instructional purposes: (a) a demonstration of an on-line search was available to students, (b) the system provided lessons in preparing and searching coordinate indexes, (c) the system permitted students to develop skills in the use of computerized IR, and (d) students were able to perform test searches of the index with reference questions.

For research purposes, all student uses provided data which were collected by the computer system and stored for use in IR evaluation and revision. Data collected on student attitudes were positive, as were professional observations. This system was one of the first implemented in library schools.

Future

Since good inquiry skills are universally useful, the potential of IR systems in enhancing these skills is an area of interest in which future research is recommended (TM16). It is suggested that the new techniques of observation and evaluation gained in participation in these developmental efforts become part of the individual's professional research, development, and teaching approach, thereby enriching members of such groups.

The development and use of information retrieval systems in library science is an example of uses that can be made of specialized IR systems in a number of fields. Since the number of fields which will add computers and IR systems to their requirements continues to grow, the development of this type of instruction should be present in concomitant instructional areas.

VALIDATION STRATEGIES

During the FSU research, every effort was made to interrelate with ongoing institutional activities, its associate problems and its need for research. For example, a team of FSU professors who were also active in the Navy Reserve was formed into a functional CAI research unit. This group represented a bridging process between the various research studies formed at FSU and their application within the Navy.

Navy Research Interdisciplinary Team

The team of FSU professorial investigators who also had active relationships in the local Naval Reserve pursued a number of objectives. First and foremost, the group applied the concepts and procedures of computer-managed instruction (CMI) to local training of the Seaman 1 classification. This CMI implementation study was quite successful in that there was both a significant increase in performance level as well as a significant savings in training time. The results were tempered by the small number of participants, and I am sure, are in the process of being replicated at such bases as the Air-Naval Station at Memphis, Tennessee.

Secondly, the group pursued broad systems concepts for the planning and management of Naval training. This led them to attend many conferences and provide consultation help to the Naval Reserve system itself. In many cases the team members performed active duty, which led to significant plans whereby more effective reserve drills could take place.

Lastly, the team provided leadership for the Navy concerning university and community relationships. As university models, they effectively contribute and are utilized within Naval Reserve operations. Secondly, in regard to community involvement, they advanced the Navy concerning such special training problems as race relations, drugs and other associated behavioral matters. Perhaps more directly to computer activity, they assisted in the design of information management systems and associated adaptive training and testing systems.

In regard to some constraints, the usual problems of communication and lack of goal understanding handicapped the group at many turns. Given a fair degree of isolation in Tallahassee, Florida, the group maintained a vigorous information exchange which undoubtedly led to the successes that it achieved.

DOD Computer-Related Activities

As an indirect consequence of our FSU research effort, the project personnel was also able to serve the Department of Defense on other training projects. The most significant one of these was the AF Advanced Instructional System (AIS). We could not have designed and specified the AIS without the prior work of the Lowry Human Resource Laboratory group or our critical CAI/CMI experience and data. We turn now to a description of the AIS project.

The Advanced Instructional System (AIS) is a development within the Air Force Human Resources Laboratory (AFHRI) to implement the latest demonstrated state-of-the-art in training techniques, media usage, management procedures, and computer technology to Air Force Technical Training. The CAI Center was awarded a contract by AFHRI to develop functional design specifications for the individual multimedia computer-based training system which would provide significant cost-effective improvements in the operation of technical training courses at Lowry Air Force Base, Colorado.

In addition to the goal of providing individualized training, AIS will focus on the managerial processes which can be enhanced by the computer, cost-effective multimedia approaches which may provide time-savings, modular implementation which will provide both flexibility during development and revision of learning materials and additional cost savings during expansion throughout the Air Force. AIS will be implemented within three technical training courses with a total enrollment of over 2000 students. The courses of Inventory Management (inventory and supply), Precision Measuring Equipment (precision electronics measurement and calibration), and Weapons Mechanic (tactical weapons loading) represent a broad range of technical training requirements.

The AIS consists of seven subsystems which reflect the scope and complexity of the effort: (a) instructional materials, (b) instructional strategies, (c) media hardware and software, (d) management components, (e) computer hardware, (f) personnel and training requirements, and (g) related requirements. These subsystems are designed to provide for all aspects of the instructional process from materials development and evaluation through student use and management to review and revision. Operational considerations, including computer systems design and maintenance, CAI languages, and the selection and training of AIS personnel are also considered in the design.

Wakulla School System

The Wakulla County Title III project focuses on two primary goals: (1) implementation of computer-assisted instruction in mathematics and reading for Southern rural students, and (2) development and implementation of CMI for the mentally retarded. Begun in July, 1968, the project is a joint undertaking of the Wakulla County, Florida, Board of Instruction and the FSU-CAI Center. By the Spring of 1970, Ss at Shadeville Elementary School and selected seventh and eighth grade Ss at Medart High School were receiving two to three computer-assisted instruction lessons per week in reading and/or mathematics. Math materials had undergone revision, and reading lesson assignments had been varied to best accommodate needs of the Ss.

As in the Spring of 1969, testing results in the Spring of 1970 indicate the Ss who participated in the CAI instruction showed positive gains in both reading and mathematics. In addition, attitude measures completed on teachers and Ss involved with the computer instruction demonstrated positive reactions to computer-assisted instruction. In the Fall, assessment instruments previously used were eliminated because it was felt that they did not measure the effects of the instruction; and individualized reading tests and a criterion-referenced test, constructed from sample CAI reading items, were administered by project personnel. Spring posttest results on these instruments and the regularly administered standardized achievement test indicated positive results.

The CAI program was the first of a three-phase effort designed to serve between 60 and 70 EMR students in three elementary schools and one high school. The second phase involved the development and evaluation of a computer-managed instruction program in which the computer was used only for evaluations and prescriptions. In Phase III, a curriculum will be developed which does not involve computers.

The Phase I materials were prepared on four reading levels. Each student's progress was monitored daily and each was assigned to the level suggested by that evaluation. The investigators found that the difference between the third and highest levels was too broad, so a new program was developed and evaluated to bridge that gap.

In addition, an experiment was designed to test the effects of picture-stimuli on vocabulary acquisition. The study demonstrated that picture-word matching significantly improved the student's ability to learn new words.

In September, 1972, Phase II began with the writing of programmed booklets to be used in the CMI program. Many materials were written to eliminate gaps found during the Phase I evaluation. A new branching technique was developed which was based on a hierarchical development of reading skills. Also included in the materials were picture-word matches suggested by the study in Phase I, but the concept has been expanded to include picture stimuli to be matched with phonetics, phrases, and sentences.

COMPUTER SYSTEMS STRATEGIES

There are three main areas of design and implementation of computer systems for instruction, namely, (a) interactive programming languages, (b) management schemes, and (c) data analysis systems. The software or language developments employed a common strategy, to maximize the ease of use while devoting a minimum of developmental effort. The topics within this theme will be organized around the above three topics.

Interactive Systems

A Programming Language (APL)

The development of the programming language APL (A Programming Language) on the IBM 1500 CAI system was a project oriented toward determining the capabilities of this type of language for meeting the diverse requirements of computing in education. The elegant and powerful data structures and commands of APL appear suitable to the areas of instruction, data processing, and computer science (Systems Memo 4).

APL Generality

A measure of any programming language is its need for extensions. In the instance of APL, extensions in the form of functions were developed in the areas of programming aids, statistical analyses, character handling, numerical manipulation, and graphic control (SM3). The fact that such APL functions can be created and so extend the language is to its credit; however, the fact that extensions were needed is an indicator of educational requirements for more than one computer language.

APL Instructional Programming

APL's usefulness for statistical analyses and simulation activities (SM12) has been documented by FSU, and demonstrated through certain graduate-level courses in the College of Education in which the majority of students chose to learn APL as a programming language for educational purposes. Beyond the use of APL for instructional simulations, however, there appears to be reasonable doubt as to its feasibility as a general CAI language. In the experiences at FSU, little instructional programming with APL was performed other than simulation packages.

Natural Language Processing

One of the initial dreams for research in CAI was the possibility of nearly natural communication between student and computer for the purpose of instruction. Over the past few years this research has become actuality based on the concept of semantic processing and semantic nets. With natural language processing systems and appropriate semantic-oriented data bases, full preplanning of stimuli and responses is not necessary, and, in fact, the flexibility of the system may be more powerful and realistic for learning.

FSU Dialogue

The thrust of FSU natural language research has been not so much on the technical aspects of computing that must be solved for such a system, but rather on the pedagogical considerations for specifying and planning the desired type of instructional dialogue. To accomplish this, a systematic approach was developed which utilized the typically stated steps for instructional development, oriented toward natural language instructional dialogues. More specifically, the analysis of instruction was based on determining a semantic network of information which the student was expected to have learned by the end of the dialogue. On the basis of this semantic network, a data base and questions to the student can be specified as performance objectives and so programmed. While this particular type of system is limited in its power for developing semantic networks, particularly for syntactic analysis of student input, the project was nevertheless a success as a prototype development. A complete dialogue was developed for a humanities course, and students using the dialogue in this course did generally acquire the semantic content as specified in the systematic approach to the dialogue development. A more extensive research program would be required to fully research and evaluate the technique used.

Future

It is anticipated that further exploration to the area of interactive systems is very bright. Present language capabilities will continue to be expanded, while more interactive dialogue and natural languages will be developed.

Instructional Management Systems

Instructional Management Systems consists of the computing software and hardware necessary for control and monitoring of the instructional process. Operationally, it is convenient to talk of the instructional data base as the associated files within the data base as well as the manipulation of those data for control and monitor functions. It is a prime tenet of computer systems analyses that the specification, design, and utility of instructional systems data bases are tied to appropriate identification and integration to the educational functions. The rest of the FSU approach has been development and dissemination of data base software appropriate to educational users in both service and research.

141

APL File System Package

One of the prime limitations of the APL/1500 system, and indeed most APL systems, was the lack of a file establishment and manipulation capability. To overcome this limitation, the APL/1500 File-Access Subroutine Package (SM10) was developed. The package permits offline access to data generated through instructional and research applications of the system. It was found that needs of users which must be filled by the system are: (a) the capability to access data for analysis by other computer systems, (b) the capability to access data for acquiring hard copy in a quicker mode than is available on an IBM 1500 system, (c) the capability to build input data to APL files, and (d) the capability to extend data base sizes. It should be noted that the file access subroutine package was built as a direct extension onto the file system capability which already had extended the APL data base functions (SM8). For example, these capabilities allowed a major project of instructional usage in information retrieval systems for the School of Library Science. The School was able to develop a system of automated abstracting and retrieval on the APL file system. The system also provided instruction for graduate library science students in the areas of automated library retrieval systems. Experience with this system indicates that any system of computers in education must provide the capability for a well-defined file system with variable structuring and flexible manipulation.

Data Base Manipulation on the Coursewriter System

Specific requirements were found for manipulation of large files on a regular basis. Because of the volumes of data collected in CAI research, highly efficient programming was needed to allow maximization of program execution times and therefore operations. One of the major problems in all computer systems, not only in education systems, is the bottleneck of input and output functions. That is, program execution is no faster than the time it takes to pass data through it, the "throughput" time. However, throughput is a function of the time for input and output, also. Throughput improvements were accelerated by programming internal execution speeds so that programs approached the I/O boundary conditions while still maximizing execution efficiency.

Sort and Merge

An internal, sequence-sensitive, bi-directional sort was developed to take advantage of the fact that CAI records and data are not randomly ordered, but are rather more often slightly out of sequence. This occurs because data are recorded for students within specific courses at approximately the same time and dates. The bi-directional sort locates the correct sequence position of a currently encountered, out-of-sequence record in no more than eight comparisons for any 100 response records. The software management allows blocking of records in groups of 100. In addition to the fast location finding of the sort, no data are immediately swapped because a table of locations is kept and accessed for addressing the individual records. That is, intermediate data swaps have been eliminated by indirect data examinations via a bi-directional linked-index listing procedure.

In addition to the high speed sort, it was also necessary to develop specialized merging programs which allowed the ordering of data by specific request. For example, it might be desirable to have records only for a given course, records for a given course within a specific time period, or records only for a segment of a course. For computational efficacy, it is expedient to block these specific records together and eliminate other. The merge and sort programs, when specifically oriented toward the type of semiordered data accumulated in CAI, fulfill these requirements most efficiently.

Instructional Support System (ISS)

A major software development project undertaken at FSU was the redesign of the FSU data management system and IBM CAI system such that they operated under one complete support and operating system. That is, either system could be controlled under one set of operating procedures. This integration of the two programming systems allowed greater optimization of computing hardware utilization, and a significant improvement in computer operations.

Management Operational Procedures

Prime sources of maximizing the utility of any instructional management system are the operations procedures and scheduling. FSU has made a major effort to ensure that the human component of the instructional management system is well integrated with the software and hardware components. Software programs which allow editing and preparation of data for data analysis were developed, along with complete user documentation. For researchers, the special need for manipulating data for use in statistical software packages was taken into account. Given the variety of data which may be collected on a sophisticated CAI or CMI system and the varieties of research designs for analysis requirements, flexible and powerful control of data must be available for researchers.

Future

In the future, investigations should key in on the development of new technologies for recording vast amounts of data during computer-aided and computer-managed instruction activities. As instruction becomes more individualized and personalized, managing and monitoring systems must be expanded.

Data Analysis Systems

The business of all instructional research is analysis and interpretation of data gathered. In order for the data to be useful, however, the CAI/CMI system must be well integrated with data analysis systems. The thrust of the FSU effort with concern to data analysis has been in the direction of providing new user capabilities for analysis of data.

Online versus Offline Systems

Many CAI researchers have suggested the need for data reduction and presentation in an online mode, with data output to the researcher as students proceed through instructional treatments on display devices. The offline mode allows gathering of data on intermediate storage media which are accessible at later times for data reduction and presentation. The offline mode has been primarily emphasized at FSU. The advantages of offline data recording are in ease of operations and flexibility with which raw data can then be transmitted to data analysis systems. Many manual operations necessary for online data gathering are bypassed with offline functions.

Report Generation

Both the EDIT and DATA PREPARATION programs provide punched output of data collected during CAI coursewriter activities for use on various computer system statistical packages. In addition, two programs were developed at FSU which provide summaries in the form of printed output reports of CAI data. The ITEM ANALYSIS SUMMARY program provides summary statistics such as the percentage of students who answered an item correctly and the average latency time for the item. The DETAILED PRINT program prints a comprehensive detailed description of a student or subject's record. Information such as course name, data, EPID, MID, student response, response latency and value of counters and switches is provided. This program has a great deal of flexibility through the use of 32 options for output specification to select or suppress specific information elements.

Future

If, in the future, the trend continues toward more powerful general purpose and algorithmic-type languages for CAI, then more general and powerful report generation systems will have to be developed with some loss in execution optimization for the gain of power and flexibility.

143

A MODEL FOR THE USE OF ACHIEVEMENT DATA

IN AN INSTRUCTIONAL SYSTEM[1,2]

Robert L. Brennan
Department of Education
SUNY at Stony Brook

INTRODUCTION

Any attempt to discuss practical aspects or evaluation in instructional environments is apt to suffer from either one of two shortcomings: the discussion may be so general that it fails to provide much guidance to the evaluator in the decision-making process, or the discussion may be so specifically related to a particular mode of instruction that it lacks generalizability to other modes of instruction. While recognizing these two pitfalls, we nevertheless subscribe to the belief that few things are more practical than a good theoretical model provided that the model has a reasonably broad range of applicability.

Thus, in this paper, we propose a definition of an instructional system which, although not all-inclusive, does encompass many frequently used modes of instruction. Also, we specify a model for considering the kinds of achievement data and time data that should be collected, why such data should be collected, and how they should be used. In short, this paper presents an integration of some useful theoretical concepts with a consideration of many practical problems of decision-making in the context of an instructional system.

As indicated in the title, we restrict ourselves here to a consideration of achievement data and time data for evaluating the cognitive aspects of an instructional system. Given the current state-of-the-art, one might argue that achievement data and time data often provide the most useful and interpretable information with regard to decision-making in an instructional system.

DEFINITION OF AN INSTRUCTIONAL SYSTEM

Let us define an instructional system as a deliberate, systematic, and replicable organization of a set of resources for the principal purpose of effecting student achievement of clearly stated instructional objectives.

This definition is somewhat restrictive in that not all learning occurs as a result of deliberate instruction, not all instruction is replicable, and not all instruction is principally intended to produce specific goals. For example, most discussions, lectures, and seminars are not replicable, even though specific instructional goals may be stated. Thus such modes of instruction would not usually qualify as an instructional system, given the above definition.

Nevertheless, the above definition is general enough to encompass most applications of group-paced, self-paced, and individualized non-traditional instruction including, for example, most instruction of a computer-assisted, programmed, or multi-media nature. Note especially that an instructional system, as defined here, may or may not be individualized. Note also that the term "replicable" is not synonymous with "inflexible"; indeed, these two terms in the context of most instructional systems are incompatible. We argue that an instructional system should be replicable in order to provide a basis for implementing objective procedures for improving the system, but improvement implies the necessity for some kind of change, not inflexibility. Finally, note that

[1] Paper presented at the Annual Meeting of the American Educational Research Association, New Orleans, February 1973. This paper was originally entitled: "The Use of Test Data in Non-Traditional Instruction."

[2] The research reported herein was partially supported by grants from the United States Office of Education, OEG-2-2-2B118, and the Research Foundation of the State University of New York, No. 0477-03-031-71.

students are an important component of an instructional system. In fact, we propose here that students be considered as much a part of an instructional system as the instruction used to teach them and the test items used to evaluate them. Thus, the process of evaluating an instructional system involves making decisions about test items, instruction, *and* students.

OBJECTIVE-RELATED MODULES

One reason that so much of the literature on evaluating particular instructional systems lacks generalizability to other instructional systems is that the unit of analysis for the purpose of collecting data and making decisions is apt to vary considerably from system to system; and, often enough, the unit of analysis varies even within the same system.

In some systems the unit of analysis is merely the amount of instruction that occurs in some specified time period; in other systems the unit of analysis corresponds with the instruction for some group of objectives which are taught together in some sequence for pedagogical reasons. In both of these cases, the unit of analysis corresponds with obvious physical characteristics of the system, and, therefore, the unit of analysis typically involves a number of different instructional objectives. However, the kinds of decisions that must be made in evaluating and revising an instructional system necessitate a consideration of all of the data and instruction relating to each separate objective, no matter when the data are collected or where the instruction occurs within the system.

In short, the basic unit of analysis in an instructional system should be the objective. In order to emphasize this fact and facilitate the collection and analysis of data for decision-making, it is theoretically and practically useful to view an instructional system as consisting of a discrete number of *objective-related modules.* As employed here, the phrase "objective-related module" refers to all of those factors in an instructional system that are directly related to a particular instructional objective. Note especially that the term "module" is not used here as a descriptive characteristic of the physical layout of an instructional system. The central aspects of an objective-related module are the objective itself and the instruction intended to teach the objective. In addition, an objective-related module contains all of the data directly relevant to the particular objective.

At first this conception of an instructional system in terms of objective-related modules may appear too theoretical or too trivial. Yet, for purposes of evaluation, the concept of an objective-related modular has several advantages over many other ways to outline or describe an instructional system. First, and most importantly, this concept directly implies that the objective is the basic unit of analysis in an instructional system. Second, the objective-related module concept emphasizes the relationship between the objective, instruction, and data. Third, any instructional system can be described in terms of objective-related modules, regardless of how the instruction is sequenced or packaged. Fourth, the objective-related module concept greatly facilitates an understanding of many of the issues and problems surrounding the collection and use of data in instructional systems.

A TAXONOMY OF TEST DATA AND TIME DATA
FOR EVALUATING ACHIEVEMENT IN AN INSTRUCTIONAL SYSTEM

Any discussion of data immediately raises two questions: for what purpose should such data be collected and what kind of data should be collected? Here we restrict the scope of these two questions to the domain of evaluating cognitive achievement in an instructional system.

Purposes of Data Collection

In general, of course, one can say that data is collected in the environment of an instructional system for the purpose of evaluation, where, according to Stufflebeam (1971) "evaluation is the process of delineating, obtaining, and providing useful information for judging decision alternatives (p.267)."

More specifically, one could say that data should be collected for the purpose of diagnostic, formative, and summative evaluation (Bloom, Hastings, and Madaus, 1971). If one considers evaluation as a decision-making process, then the diagnostic-formative-summative trichotomy refers primarily to decision-making functions of evaluation. However, we prefer to emphasize that the purpose of collecting data in the environment of an instructional system is to make decisions with regard to specific aspects of the instructional system, namely: (a) instruction, (b) students, and (c) test items. That is, we prefer to emphasize the object of the decision-making process seems to identify more clearly the specific nature of the decisions that typically need to be made in an ongoing instructional system.

Decisions about instruction are usually of primary importance; i.e., one wants to assess the effects of instruction especially for the purpose of identifying instruction that requires revision. Such decisions are often viewed as part of the process of formative evaluation. In order to make decisions concerning whether or not instruction should be revised, we will argue here that data should be obtained which can be used to determine instructional effectiveness, efficiency, and retention.

Decisions about students typically include decisions concerning student placement and certification. Such decisions are often viewed as part of the processes of diagnostic and summative evaluation, respectively.

Decisions concerning test items also need to be made in instructional systems. Specifically, one needs to determine the reliability and validity of tests used as part of the instructional system.

Types of Data

In order to make the kinds of decisions indicated above, two general types of data are useful: achievement test data and time data: instructional time and retention time. Also, we will consider two general types of achievement tests: criterion-referenced tests and norm-referenced tests. As Glaser (1963) notes:

> The scores obtained from an achievement test provide primarily two kinds of information. One is the degree to which the student has attained criterion performance, for example, whether he can satisfactorily prepare an experimental report, or solve certain kinds of work problems in arithmetic. The second kind of information that an achievement test score provides is the relative ordering of individuals with respect to their test performance, for example, whether student A can solve his problems more quickly than student B. The principal difference between these two kinds of information lies in the standard used as a reference. What can be called criterion-referenced measures depend upon absolute standards (p. 2).

In other words, the results of an achievement test can be used to rank students along a relative continuum of capability with respect of a specified group of persons (norm-referencing) or along an absolute continuum of proficiency with respect to a specified behavioral criterion (criterion-referencing). As Nitko (1970) indicates, one can make a distinction between a criterion-referenced test as defined by Glaser and Klaus (1962), Glaser (1963), and Glaser and Nitko (1971) and a mastery test as defined by Bloom (1968). Here we will not make any distinction between these two tests since, in the model we will discuss, any such distinction seems to have little practical significance.

In particular, we will argue here that one can identify eight different types of data for an objective-related module that provide meaningful sources of information for decision-making. These types of data, listed in the order in which they would usually be obtained, are as follows:

(a)   Prerequisite test data, which indicates whether or not a student has the background characteristics (attainment of previous objectives, aptitude, etc.) thought to be necessary in order to achieve the objective for the module;

146

(b) Pretest data, which measures a student's performance on the objective prior to instruction;

(c) Instructional time, which is the length of time a student spends undergoing instruction for the objective;

(d) Criterion-referenced posttest data, which measures a student's performance on the objective immediately after instruction;

(e) Norm-referenced posttest data, which is collected immediately following instruction and measures student performance relative to the performance of other similar students;

(f) Retention time, which is the length of time intervening between the posttest (usually criterion-referenced) and a subsequent retention test (usually criterion-referenced);

(g) Criterion-referenced retention test data, which is collected some time after instruction and measures student performance on the objective for the module; and

(h) Norm-referenced retention test data, which is collected some time after instruction and measures student performance relative to the performance of other similar students.

It is often assumed that only criterion-referenced or mastery test data provide meaningful information for evaluation decisions with regard to instructional systems. We agree that criterion-referenced data is more important than norm-referenced data in the context of an instructional system; however, we argue below that norm-referenced data sometimes provide useful additional information for decision-making.

A Table for Relating Data Type and Use

These data for an objective-related module are displayed in Table 1 which, in addition, indicates those types of data that are of primary importance for making particular kinds of decisions with regard to instruction, students, and test items. In essence, Table 1 provides a kind of taxonomy of achievement and time data that are useful in evaluating instructional systems.

TABLE 1

Taxonomy of Achievement Data and Time Data for Decision-Making in an Instructional System

DATA USED TO MAKE DECISIONS WITH REGARD TO:	PRE-REQ. TEST	DATA FROM AN OBJECTIVE-RELATED MODULE[1]						
		PRE-TEST	INST. TIME	C.R.[2] POST-TEST	N.R.[3] POST-TEST	RET. TIME	C.R.[4] RET. TEST	N.R.[5] RET. TEST
Instruction:								
Short-term effectiveness		*		*				
Long-term effectiveness		*					*	
Efficiency		*	*	*				
Retention				*		*	*	
Students:								
Placement	*	*		*			*	
Certification								
Mastery		*		*			*	
Grading				*	*		*	*
Tests:								
Validity					*			*
Reliability	*	*		*	*		*	*

[1] The data are listed from left to right in the chronological order that they would usually be collected. Asterisks indicate the principal kinds of data appropriate for particular decisions.

[2] Criterion-referenced posttest.

[3] Norm-referenced posttest.

[4] Criterion-referenced retention test.

[5] Norm-referenced retention test.

147

It is, of course, quite possible that a particular objective-related module may not contain all of the data indicated in Table 1. It is also quite likely that, in a particular objective-related module, a test may, in fact, consist of only one item. These and other possibilities and their implications will be treated later. For the present time, let us assume that, for a particular objective-related module, all the indicated data are collected and each of the tests contain a number of equivalent items for measuring the same objective. In the following sections of this paper we will consider in more detail, the nature of these data, why they should be collected, and how they might be used. First we consider, in some detail, the use of data for evaluating instruction and subsequently we provide a less extensive consideration of the use of data for evaluating students and test items.

EVALUATING INSTRUCTION

As Cronbach (1963) indicated, when evaluation is performed in order to effect the improvement of an instructional system, the chief aim is to ascertain changes the system produces in students in order to identify elements of the instructional system that require revision.

One of the most theoretically appealing procedures for identifying instruction that requires revision involves determining departures of attained results for the ideal. That is, the process of evaluating instruction may be viewed as the process of comparing the actual effects of instruction with the effects that would be produced in an ideal instructional system as one which would result in students achieving a maximum level of performance on all objectives in the shortest possible time and moreover, students should maintain this level of performance for as long as necessary.

A Rationale for Decision-Making

In a sense, the characteristics of an ideal instructional system provided an upper bound for the observed measures of effectiveness, efficiency, and retention. In a similar fashion, one can identify the characteristics of a *minimally acceptable instructional system* and, thus, provide a kind of lower bond or base line for these measures. If the observed measures fall within these two boundaries, then the evaluator will not usually suggest the need for revision; if not, revision is required.

The above rationale is quite simple to state, however, there are two major problems in implementing the procedure. First, one must specify the cut-offs that define the lower bound or base line for the minimally acceptable instructional system. Second, if revision is indicated, then one must determine what needs to be revised and how such revision should be accomplished. These two problems have been addressed to some extent by Emrick (1971) and Brennan and Stolurow (1971), respectively. However, the solution to both problems, given the current state-of-the-art, must rely primarily upon the combined subjective judgment of the evaluator and the subject matter expert.

Decisions concerning cut-off are especially complicated. To the extent that an instructional system is not ideal, there then exists the possibility for improvement and perhaps, the necessity for revision. Whether or not revision is actually appropriate depends upon the cut-off values for instructional effectiveness, efficiency, and retention. The cut-off values, in turn, depend upon the evaluator's and subject matter specialists' combined judgment with regard to cost factors, revision time considerations, and a number of other more subjective utilities. In addition, these factors often imply the need for different cut-off values for different objective-related modules.

Yet even with these problems, the above rationale does provide a very useful framework for identifying those aspects of an instructional system that require revision. In addition, once cut-offs are specified, the revision required/no revision required decision is essentially straightforward.

Finally, even the problems discussed above have one redeeming feature—they emphasize the necessity for a close working relationship between the evaluator and the subject matter expert.

Instructional Effectiveness

Table 1 indicates that instructional effectiveness implies a comparison of proficiency measured at two points in time—prior to instruction and at some time following instruction. One can identify either short-term or long-term effectiveness depending upon whether one obtains data from a posttest administered immediately after instruction or from a retention test administered at some future time.

The necessity for determining short-term instructional effectiveness is readily recognized; however, the need to determine long-term instructional effectiveness is easily overlooked. Consider the situation in which a student fails to achieve an objective as a result of experiencing instruction for that specific objective — the student can however, eventually achieve the objective as a result of subsequent instruction. In this case, the learning that occurred will be reflected in long-term instructional effectiveness but not in short-term instructional effectiveness.

It is important to note that effectiveness cannot be determined from a measurement taken at one point in time unless one can validly assume the complete absence of proficiency prior to instruction. This assumption should not be taken lightly. It is often (perhaps usually) the case that at least some students, prior to instruction, have a level of proficiency greater than zero. If this fact is overlooked, estimates of instructional effectiveness will be inflated.

It is also important to note that in any comparison of pretest and posttest, or pretest and retention test, performance is meaningless unless the two tests measure the same objective at the same level of difficulty. One common violation of this rule occurs when the pretest is an easier test than the posttest or retention test. This is a circumstance that will result in a deflated estimate of instructional effectiveness.

Instructional Efficiency and Retention

Instructional efficiency and retention involve a consideration of both test data and time data. As indicated in the definition of an ideal instructional system, data with regard to instructional time and retention time are very important in assessing the extent to which a given instructional system deviates from the ideal.

Table 1 emphasized that instructional efficiency involves a joint consideration of short-term instructional effectiveness and instructional time. Instructional time for a given objective may be constant for all students, if instruction is group-paced; or, instructional time may vary for each student, if instructional effectiveness and instructional efficiency are functionally related, differing only by a constant time factor for all students. In the latter case, instructional effectiveness and efficiency may provide very different information. For example, instruction may be relatively effective for an entire group of students, but some of the students may spend so much time in instruction that instructional efficiency for them is exceedingly low. One might even theoretically argue that a high level of instructional effectiveness can be guaranteed if efficiency is of no importance (see Carroll, 1963). It should be noted, however, that neglecting to consider efficiency makes little sense unless one places a very low premium on student time. For most instructional systems, student time is a very valuable commodity that one cannot afford to squander; hence, instructional efficiency assumes considerable importance, especially in a self-paced or individualized instructional system.

Efficiency, as described above, is, more precisely, short-term instructional efficiency. One might argue for consideration of the analogous concept, long-term instructional efficiency; however, to do so would involve confusing instructional time with retention time.

In this context, retention time may be defined as the time intervening between a criterion-referenced posttest and a subsequent criterion-referenced retention test. Also, recall that in our terminology, these two tests are tests of a single objective since they are part of an objective-related module. Thus, as indicated in Table 1, retention indicates the extent to which proficiency (on an objective tested immediately following instruction) is maintained for a particular period of time. In short, retention takes into account three factors: posttest performance, retention test performance, and retention time.

Note that, when viewed in the context of an objective-related module, it is clear that retention time may vary for each objective; and, moreover, in a self-paced or individualized instructional system retention time for each objective may vary for each student. These variations in retention time are often overlooked when a single retention test is used as a measure of performance for several objectives, each of which was taught at a different point in time. This is one practical reason for collecting and analyzing data in the context of objective-related modules.

The Measurement of Change or Gain

Thus far, we have been careful to refer to instruction effectiveness, efficiency, and retention only in terms of the data and concepts that provide a basis for defining these terms. From these considerations, it seems clear that any actual measure of effectiveness will be, in essence, a measure of change or gain and any actual measure of efficiency or retention will incorporate a measure of change or gain along with a consideration of instructional time or retention time, respectively.

Many measures of change or gain have been reported in the literature. (See, for example, Harris, 1963; DuBois, 1962; and Tucker, Damarin, and Messick, 1966.) Recently, Cronbach and Furby (1970) have argued that "investigators who ask questions regarding gain scores would ordinarily be better advised to ask their questions in other ways (p.80)." Unfortunately, this statement has been indiscriminately interpreted by many as a blanket indictment of the measurement of change in educational and psychological research; yet, Cronbach (1963), himself, pointed out ten years ago that "when evaluation is carried out in the service of course improvement, the chief aim is to ascertain what effects the course has — that is what *changes* it produces in pupils (italics ours, p. 675)."

The two statements by Cronbach in the previous paragraph are not necessarily contradictory. Most measures of change reported in the literature have arisen out of a correlational model that assumes an interval scale of measurement; yet, in practice, traditional psychometric measures fail to produce an interval scale. This is a principal reason why Cronbach and Furby (1970) argue that the usual measures of change are often suspect. However, this objection ceases to exist when one has an absolute measurement scale that measures interval scale units of some entity (Carver, 1971). Now, one can strongly argue that the criterion-referenced tests used to evaluate instruction, as described above, should, in fact result in absolute measurement scales, since each test consists of equivalent items for measuring performance on a single objective. Thus, in order to assess instructional effectiveness, efficiency, and retention, one change is discussed in the literature. In our opinion, however, many of these measures of change have limited utility for evaluating instruction in the sense that they usually fail to provide the evaluator and subject matter specialist with the kind of easily interpretable information that facilitates the identification of instruction that requires revision.

Also, in some cases, measures of change reported in the literature are closely related to hypothesis testing in the context of classical inferential statistics. As Lumsdaine (1965) points out:

> A weakness of the statistical habits associated with before-after and gain experiments is that the statistical tests employed are addressed to hypothesis testing rather than to estimation. . . It is true that in determining the effects (of an instructional system) one wants to rule out the null hypothesis that observed gains can be dismissed as chance results; i.e., one wants to show that effects produced were statistically reliable. However, what is obviously of more interest is a good estimate of the *size* of the gain. . . (p. 299).

Merely showing reliable evidence for some gain is of little practical importance in evaluating instruction, because the existence of some unspecified amount of gain does not provide a meaningful basis for deciding whether or not revision is required.

Descriptive Statistics and Visual Displays of Data

Another limitation of many classical statistical techniques in evaluating instruction is the frequent assumption that students be randomly sampled from some specified population. Often enough, students in an instructional system do not constitute a random sample; at best, they constitute a representative sample of the kinds of students for whom the instructional system is judged to be appropriate.

In short, in theory and in practice, many classical inferential statistical techniques fail to provide the kind of interpretable information an evaluator needs in order to identify aspects of an instructional system that require revision. Thus evaluators often rely heavily upon descriptive statistics such as difficulty levels, error rates, percentage of maximum possible gain (McGuigan and Peters, 1965; Brennan, 1970), etc.[3] Such statistics provide a method for aggregating raw data into measures that have relatively straightforward interpretations. As such, descriptive statistics, when used prudently, provide very useful information to the evaluator and the subject matter specialist. Frequently, the use of descriptive statistics is criticized because they fail to provide an objectively defined basis for inference to a specified population; however, as statisticians continually emphasize, it is, at best, misleading and sometimes meaningless to employ inferential statistics when the underlying assumptions are not fulfilled or when the resulting information is not interpretable in the decision-making process.

Thus, in our opinion, the utility of descriptive statistics, when interpreted prudently, cannot be denied. However, it is often difficult to interpret simultaneously several different, numerically reported descriptive statistics for a particular objective-related module. One useful way to approach this problem is to employ graphical and tabular presentations of data such as those indicated in Figures 1a-1d and Table 2, respectively.

Figures 1a-1d are examples of graphical technique that can be used for either of two purposes: (a) to present descriptive statistics for one student when pretest, posttest, and retention test consist of a number of items, or (b) to present the average descriptive statistics for a number of students even when any or all tests consist of only one item. In the former case, the vertical axis represents performance in terms of percent of items correct; in the latter case, the vertical axis represents the average performance for students. The horizontal axis represents the observed instructional time and retention time. The solid line, depicting base line data, provides a kind of operational definition of the effectiveness aspects of a minimally acceptable instructional system. That is, the base line pretest score represents the chance level of performance if students respond blindly; and the base line posttest and retention test scores represent cut-offs assigned by the evaluator.

In Figure 1a, both short-term and long-term effectiveness are ideal. In general, no revision is required on the basis of these two measures so long as all points on the observed data line fall above the base data line. However, even in the case represented by Figure 1a, revision might be required on the basis of efficiency if the two-hour instructional time were judged to be inordinately long. Furthermore, one cannot claim that retention is ideal unless the indicated eight-week retention time period is appropriate.

In Figures 1b-d revision is required on the basis of short-term effectiveness and/or long-term effectiveness. Figure 1b indicates a case in which instruction has no observable cognitive effect. In Figure 1c, revision is required on the basis of long-term effectiveness. Figure 1d indicated that instruction for the objective results in a reversal of learning which is corrected by subsequent instruction that is not directly related to the objective.

Another descriptive technique for visually displaying effectiveness data is given in Table 2. Once an evaluator specifies pass/fail cut-offs[4] for the pretest, posttest, and retention test, then each student falls into one and only one of eight mutually exclusive categories. As indicated in Table 2, for students in Category I (fail pretest, pass posttest, pass retention test) instruction has both long- and short-term effectiveness; thus, Category I represents the

---

[3] See Brennan (1969) for a review of the literature relating to descriptive statistics that have been proposed for use in instructional systems.

[4] If the test consists of a single item, then pass/fail is simply translated as correct/wrong.

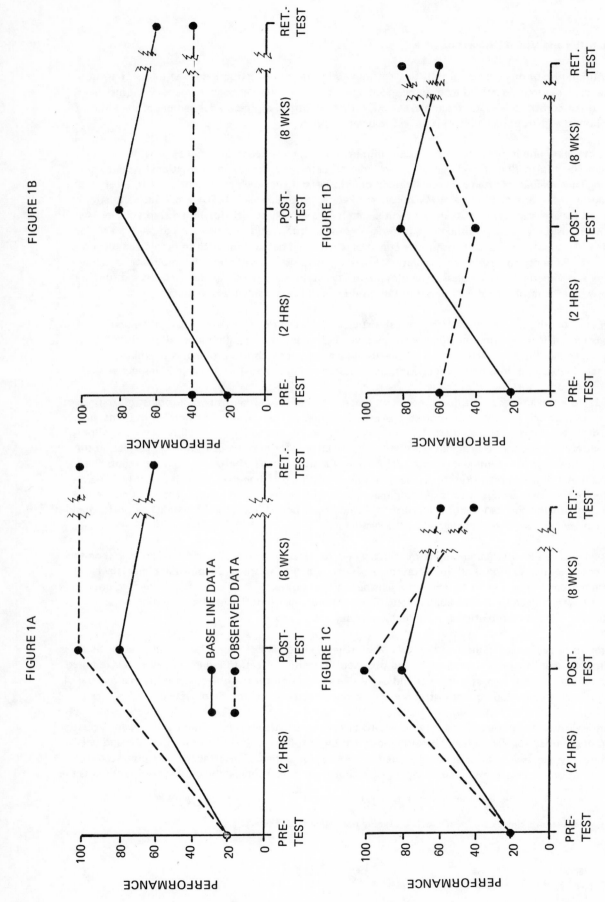

FIGURE 1A

FIGURE 1B

FIGURE 1C

FIGURE 1D

● BASE LINE DATA

● OBSERVED DATA

PERFORMANCE

PRE-TEST   (2 HRS)   POST-TEST   (8 WKS)   RET.-TEST

FIGURES 1a-1d. Examples of a graphical technique to display data for evaluating instruction. Usually it is not feasible to construct the horizontal (time) axis such that distances are proportional to time. Therefore, it is necessary to indicate the actual instructional time and retention time below the axis. In all figures, the data displayed are synthetic data used for illustrative purposes.

152

ideal. Each of the other categories indicates varying degrees of lack of short-term and/or long-term effectiveness. Category III (pass pretest, pass posttest, pass retention test) is especially interesting in that it provides an example of the difference between evaluating instruction and evaluating students. Students who fall in Category III would usually be evaluated positively for the purposes of placement and certification. However, for students who fall in Category III, instruction has not been effective; these students had attained the objective prior to instruction.

TABLE 2

A Tabular Display of Criterion-Referenced Data

for Assessing the Effectiveness of an Instructional System

| | SHORT-TERM EFFECTIVENESS | | | |
| | EFFECTIVE | NOT EFFECTIVE | | REVERSAL IN EFFECTIVENESS |
	FAIL PRETEST PASS POSTTEST	FAIL PRETEST FAIL POSTTEST	PASS PRETEST PASS POSTTEST	PASS PRETEST FAIL POSTTEST
Pass retention test	Category I	Category II	Category III	Category IV
Fail retention test	Category V	Category VI	Category VII	Category VIII

Note — Entries in the cells of this table refer to the number of students in each category. Categories are mutually exclusive and exhaustive; i.e., each student falls into one and only one category.

Comments on Data for Evaluating Instruction

The curtailment of data. In Table 1 we considered eight different kinds of data that serve various functions in the evaluation of an instructional system. In a particular instructional system it may not be feasible to collect all of these data for all objective-related modules. In such cases, the evaluator will not be able to assess at least one of the four measures discussed above. This problem is perhaps inevitable, but it need not be too serious provided that: (a) the evaluator plans the data collection activities beforehand so that the maximum amount of data is collected for the most critical objective-related modules, and (b) the instructional system undergoes a continual process of replication, evaluation, and revision. This is one reason for our insistence that an instructional system be replicable. Even when the amount of data collected is somewhat curtailed, the continual process of replication, evaluation, and revision should result in a constantly improving instructional system.

Prerequisite test data. As noted in Table 1, prerequisite test data does not provide direct evidence of the effects of instruction; however, once instruction is identified as requiring revision, student performance on prerequisite tests can provide valuable information in pinpointing the nature of specific difficulties. For this reason, the nature of prerequisite tests and their relation to specific objectives should be given careful consideration.

Testing additional objectives. Cronbach (1963) claims that evaluation whose purpose is to effect the improvement of an instructional system should ideally include: "measures of all the types of proficiency that might reasonably be desired in the area in question, not just the selected outcomes to which the curriculum directs substantial attention (p. 679)."

Essentially this is an argument for the inclusion of tests measuring objectives that have varying degrees of relationship to the actual objectives of the instructional system. Cronbach argues that such tests are necessary to assess the extent to which a particular instructional system is appropriate for users who have somewhat different educational goals. We agree, but it should be understood that student performance on such additional objectives provides evidence primarily for assessing the external validity of the instructional system, not its internal validity. Thus, student performance on such additional objectives does not provide very useful evidence for revising the existing aspects of an instructional system, although this evidence may provide a basis for adding objectives to and/or deleting objectives from the system.

Use of norm-referenced measures. Unfortunately, it is often difficult to find or construct a criterion-referenced test to measure all the types of proficiency that might reasonably be desired, as Cronbach (1963) suggests. However, it is often relatively easy to obtain or construct a norm-referenced test that can serve as a reasonably good measure of student performance on objectives similar to that in the instructional system, provided that one analyzes the data very carefully. In particular, the content standard test score techniques suggested by Ebel (1962) may be used with norm-referenced measures and may provide useful additional information regarding the instructional system. Such data, for example, may provide some basis for considering the appropriateness of the objectives in the instructional system. After all, there is no *a priori* reason for assuming that the objectives in a particular instructional system are the best objectives that could be chosen. In fact, as Ebel (1970) suggests, there is a danger that such objectives and their associated criterion-referenced test items, may be idiosyncratic. Criterion-referenced measurement must certainly carry the principal burden of evaluating instruction; however, to dismiss categorically the use of norm-referenced measures seems to be imprudent.

EVALUATING STUDENTS

As indicated previously, the student is an important component of any instructional system, and, therefore, decisions about students are intimately connected with the evaluation of the system. In fact, much of the literature that purports to treat the evaluation of instruction, and the use of criterion-referenced tests in instruction, concentrates primarily upon the evaluation of students. Here, we prefer to make a clear distinction between the evaluation of instruction and the evaluation of students. We note that decisions concerning instruction are based upon an assessment of changes, over time, in student performance effected by the instructional system. On the other hand, decisions concerning students typically involve questions of student proficiency at a given point in time, as opposed to a comparison of proficiency at two points in time. In particular, two principal kinds of decisions usually must be made when evaluating students: placement and certification.

Decisions Concerning Placement

As indicated in Table 1, any one or any subset of the criterion-referenced tests in an objective-related module might be used as a basis for different kinds of placement decisions. For example, the prerequisite test and pretest are typically used as a basis for placement decisions with regard to the instruction in an objective-related module. However, these two tests usually play different roles in the placement process. The prerequisite test is used to decide whether or not a student has the knowledge and other background characteristics thought to be necessary for attainment of the instructional objective; that is, the prerequisite test is used to identify students who will be allowed to experience instruction. On the other hand, the pretest, when employed for placement decisions, is used to identify students who will be allowed to skip instruction; that is, if a student achieves a sufficiently high level of performance on the pretest, the student is certified as having achieved the instructional objective and the student proceeds with instruction for some other objective.

154

Also, the criterion-referenced posttest and, less frequently, the criterion-referenced retention test may be used for placement decisions. The posttest often provides a basis for placing a student in remedial instruction for the objective in a particular objective-related module, or advancing the student to instruction for some other objective. On occasion the retention test may serve the same placement function as the posttest, but more frequently the retention test, when used for placement decisions provides a basis for placing students in other instructional systems.

Decisions Concerning Certification

From a practical point of view, decisions on certification of student performance are often of two kinds: mastery or the certification of minimally acceptable student performance and for want of a better term, grading.

Mastery. As noted above, the pretest may serve as a basis for certifying mastery or more precisely, determining minimal acceptable student performance. Similarly, the criterion-referenced posttest or retention test may serve the same function. Any of these tests, therefore, may serve as the basis for mastery of a particular objective. Clearly, of course, the critical issue is: What constitutes minimally acceptable student performance for the test(s) employed? In order to answer this question, the evaluator must decide, first of all, which test or tests will be used as the instrument(s) for certifying mastery. Sometimes the posttest (or pretest) alone may be used; perhaps more frequently, the retention test alone, or the retention test and the posttest (or pretest), will be used. Once this decision is made, the evaluator must specify a cutting score (or scores) for the mastery decision. It should be noted that, for the most part, the specification of cutting scores for certifying students can be made only on the basis of judgment on the part of the evaluator and the subject matter specialist. However, once such cutting scores are specified, decision-theoretic techniques are available for determining whether a student's true score is above or below the cutting score (see Hambleton and Novick, 1972).

Grading. It is not our purpose here to either condone or condemn the use of grades and grading procedures. We merely observe that grades are often demanded by particular institutions, by parents, and by students. To the extent that grades must be reported, we argue that the procedure for arriving at such grades should be reasonable and fair. Furthermore, we argue that the criteria for assigning grades should be consonant with the use to which grades will be put.

Few will argue that one way grades are used is to provide a rough estimate of whether or not a student has attained some particular level of knowledge or proficiency. An instructional system, with its use of criterion-referenced tests, provides an excellent means for assessing such performance. It is also true, we believe, that grades are often used as a basis for rank ordering students along a relative continuum of proficiency; that is, grades are often used to reflect an individual's performance with respect to the performance of other individuals in some specified group. Essentially, this use of grades implies a need for norm-referenced measurement. Now, as Nitko (1970) and others have pointed out, criterion-referenced tests may be used to provide norm-referenced kinds of information. However, criterion-referenced tests usually result in negatively skewed distributions of student scores that have little variability, and such distributions are not maximally useful for rank ordering students. Therefore, a test or tests specifically constructed to provide discriminations among students, i.e., a norm-referenced test, may often be desirable.

Thus, to the extent that grades are used to indicate two different kinds of student performance, it seems reasonable to argue that both criterion-referenced tests and norm-referenced tests are appropriate for determining grades. Ideally, for grading purposes, criterion-referenced information and norm-referenced information should be reported separately. However, if one grade must be reported, we believe that criterion-referenced information should be the more important determiner of such a grade.

A By-product of Evaluating Students

As Sorenson (1971) notes, practically any instructional system will work for some students and not for others. In order to take this fact into account, one of the developmental tasks in defining an instructional system involves the specification of students for whom the instruction is intended. Even so, when one evaluates student performance, it is often possible to identify the characteristics of students for whom the instructional system is not working. This information may provide a basis for revising the system or, in some cases, this information may be used as a basis for respecifying the types of students for whom the instruction is appropriate.

EVALUATING TESTS

Recall that in the context of an objective-related module, a test is an instrument for measuring performance on a single objective. Such a test ideally consists of many items but could consist of only one item. Therefore, on occasion, the issue of evaluating a test may resolve into the issue of evaluating a test item. In either case, however, the evaluation of a test (or a test item) involves making decisions concerning validity and reliability.

It is not our purpose here to thoroughly review the literature on measuring reliability and validity. For norm-referenced tests, procedures for measuring validity and reliability are well-known (see, for example, Lord and Novick, 1968). For criterion-referenced tests, the measurement of validity is relatively straightforward; however, at this time, few, if any, procedures have the status of generally accepted solutions to problems surrounding the measurement of reliability. (See, for example, Popham and Husek, 1969; Edmonston and Randall, 1972; and Hambleton and Novick, 1972.) Thus, rather than review the literature, we consider below certain important issues concerning reliability and validity, especially as these topics relate to the use of criterion-referenced tests in instructional systems.

Validity

In most cases, there is no reasonable external criterion for a criterion-referenced test. Usually, the only criterion under consideration is an internal criterion, namely, the instructional objective that serves as a basis for test construction. Consequently, for a criterion-referenced test in an instructional system, the issue of validity is generally an issue of content validity. The extent to which a test has content validity is usually a matter of judgment on the part of the subject matter specialist. However, in some cases, the relationship between the objective and the items in a criterion-referenced test is so close that judgments concerning the content validity of the test are hardly necessary provided one accepts the validity of the objectives. For example, procedures developed by Bormuth (1970) and Hively, Patterson, and Page (1968) produce criterion-referenced test items that are virtually isomorphic with the objective.

This preeminent concern with content validity is the reason why Table 1 indicates that achievement data do not provide the principal kind of information for judging the validity of a criterion-referenced test. It should be noted, however, that such data are sometimes used to calculate particular kinds of discrimination indices for criterion-referenced tests (see, for example, Cox and Vargas, 1966). Such indices purport to provide an additional kind of information concerning criterion-referenced test validity; however, the interpretability of such indices is a topic of some concern (Popham and Husek, 1969; Brennan, 1972b).

Reliability

The determination of reliability for a criterion-referenced test in an instructional system is complicated by several factors. First, it is generally recognized that classical procedures for estimating reliability are seldom appropriate for criterion-referenced tests. Second, we usually need to establish *both* the stability of each test and the equivalence of the several tests measuring the same objective. Third, many of these tests are used for two purposes: to measure student performance at one point in time and to measure changes in student performance over time. This dual function of many criterion-referenced tests necessitates the determination of two different estimates of reliability.

The absence of established procedures for estimating the reliability of criterion-referenced tests obviously complicates the task of evaluating not only the test but also instruction and students. In essence, the evaluator has three choices: (a) use classical procedures for estimating reliability, (b) use one or more of the newly developed techniques, or (c) use some combination of classical procedures and newly developed techniques. Probably, the last alternative is the most prudent, but in any case, the evaluator must exercise considerable caution in interpreting results.

Ideally, the reliability of tests should be determined before such tests are used in an instructional system. After all, it is difficult to justify decisions made concerning instruction and students unless one can argue that the instruments used for decision-making are reliable. However, especially for criterion-referenced tests, from a practical point of view it is often impossible to estimate reliability without using data collected in the environment of the instructional system. This is one principal reason why it is desirable to field-test an instructional system prior to its full implementation (see Lumsdaine, 1965).

CONCLUSION

We subscribe to the view that evaluation is a fundamental part of curriculum development, not merely an appendage added on after the fact. Thus, decisions concerning the collection and use of data should be made before an instructional system is put into operation. We have treated here a model for considering such decisions as they relate to achievement data and time data. This model is generalizable to many modes of instruction characterized as instructional systems and involving clearly stated objectives. Furthermore, many adaptations of this model are possible. For example, in order to avoid complication, we have tacitly assumed throughout that cutting scores for decisions concerning instructional effectiveness, instructional efficiency, mastery, etc., are the same for all students. Yet, the ideas presented here, can be generalized to instructional systems having different cutting scores for different students.

Almost invariably the task of evaluating an instructional system is a very large data collection and analysis activity ideally consisting of repeated measurement of objectives at several points in time. This task can be greatly facilitated by the use of computers. In particular, it has been demonstrated that time-shared computers provide a basis for efficient administration of achievement tests and collection of data from such tests. Brennan (1972a) provides a review of the literature in this area.

Most of the literature currently available concerning the evaluation of instructional systems treats the analysis of data primarily from the point of view of classical descriptive and inferential statistics. It is our belief that, in the future, Bayesian statistics and decision theoretic techniques such as those discussed by Hambleton and Novick (1972) and Cronbach and Gleser (1965) will play an increasingly important role in the evaluation of instructional systems. These statistical procedures are particularly appealing because they provide the potential for directly incorporating many kinds of prior information and subjective judgment into the decision-making process.

REFERENCES

1. Bloom, B.S. Learning for mastery. In *Evaluation Comment,* 1 (2). Los Angeles: University of California Center for the Study of Evaluation of Instructional Programs, May 1968.

2. Bloom, B. S., Hastings, J. T., & Madaus, G. F. *Handbook of formative and summative evaluation.* New York: McGraw-Hill, 1971.

3. Bormuth, J. R., *On the theory of achievement test items.* Chicago: University of Chicago Press, 1970.

4. Brennan, R. L., Techniques for evaluating instructional programs. Unpublished special qualifying paper, Harvard Graduate School of Education, 1969.

5. Brennan, R. L., *Some statistical problems in the evaluation of self-instructional programs.* (Doctoral dissertation, Harvard University) Ann Arbor, Michigan: University Microfilms, 1970. No. 70-23080.

6. Brennan, R. L. A generalized upper-lower item discrimination index. *Educational and Psychological Measurement,* 1972, 32, 289-303. (a)

7. Brennan, R. L., Computer-assisted achievement testing in instruction. Paper presented at Lehysysteme 72, West Berlin, Germany, April, 1972. (b)

8. Brennan, R. L., & Stolurow, L. M. An empirical decision process for formative evaluation. Paper presented at the Annual Meeting of the American Educational Research Association, New York, February, 1971. (ERIC, ED 048 343).

9. Carroll, J. A model of school learning. *Teachers College Record,* 1963, 64, 723-733.

10. Carver, R. P. Implications of an empirical study of four approaches to measuring gain. Paper presented at the Annual Meeting of the American Psychological Association, Washington, D. C., September, 1971.

11. Cox, R. C., & Vargas, J. S. A comparison of item selection techniques for norm-referenced and criterion-referenced tests. Paper presented at the Annual Meeting of the National Council on Measurement in Education, Chicago, February 1966.

12. Cronbach, L. J. Course improvement through evaluation. *Teachers College Record,* 1963, 64, 672-683.

13. Cronbach, L. J., & Furby, L. How should we measure change — or should we? *Psychological Bulletin,* 1970, 74, 68-80.

14. Cronbach, L. J., & Gleser, G. C. *Psychological tests and personnel decisions.* (2nd ed.) Urbana, Illinois: University of Illinois Press, 1965.

15. DuBois, P.H. The design of correlational studies in training. In R. Glaser (Ed.), *Training Research and Education.* Pittsburgh: University of Pittsburgh Press, 1962, pp.63-86.

16. Ebel, R. L. Content standard test scores. *Educational and Psychological Measurement,* 1962, 22, 15-25.

17. Ebel, R. L. Some limitations of criterion-referenced measurement. Paper presented at the Annual Meeting of the American Educational Research Association, Minneapolis, March 1970.

18. Edmonston, L. P., & Randall, R. S. A model for estimating the reliability and validity of criterion-referenced measures. Paper presented at the Annual Meeting of the American Educational Research Association, Chicago, April 1972.

19. Emrick, J. A. An evaluation model for mastery testing. *Journal of Educational Measurement,* 1971, 8, 321-326.

20. Glaser, R. Instructional technology and the measurement of learning outcomes: some questions. Paper presented at the Annual Meeting of the American Educational Research Association, Chicago, February, 1963. Also in *American Psychologist,* 1963, 18, 519-521.

21. Glaser, R., & Klaus, D. J. Proficiency measurement: Assessing human performance. In R. Gagne (Ed.), *Psychological principles in system development.* New York: Holt, Rinehart, and Winston, 1962.

22. Glaser, R., & Nitko, A. J. Measurement in learning and instruction. In E. Thorndike (Ed.), *Educational measurement.* Washington, D. C.: National Council of Education, 1971.

23. Hambleton, R.K., & Novick, M.R. Toward an integration of theory and method for criterion-referenced tests. Paper presented at the Annual Meeting of the National Council on Measurement in Education, Chicago, 1972.

24. Harris, C. W. (Ed.) *Problems in measuring change.* Madison, Wisc.: University of Wisconsin Press, 1963.

25. Hively, W., Patterson, H. L., & Page, S. H. A "universe-defined" system of arithmetic achievement tests. *Journal of Educational Measurement,* 1968, 5, 275-290.

26. Lord, F. M., & Novick, M. R. Statistical theories of mental test scores. Reading, Mass.: Addison-Wesley, 1968.

27. Lumsdaine, A. A. Assessing the effectiveness of instructional programs. In R. Glaser (Ed.), *Teaching machines and programmed learning — data and directions.* Washington, D. C.: National Education Association, 1965.

28. McGuigan, F. J., & Peters, J. Assessing the effectiveness of programmed texts — methodology — some findings. *Journal of Programmed Instruction,* 1965, 3(1), 23-34.

29. Nitko, A. J. Criterion-referenced testing in the context of instruction. Paper presented at the Thirty-Fifth Annual Conference of the Educational Records Bureau, October, 1970.

30. Popham, W. J., & Husek, T. R. Implications of criterion-referenced measurement. *Journal of Educational Measurement,* 1969, 6, 1-9.

31. Sorenson, G. Evaluation for the improvement of instructional programs: some practical steps. *Evaluation Comment,* 1971, 2(4), 13-17. Los Angeles: University of California Center for the Study of Evaluation of Instructional Programs.

32. Stufflebeam, D. L. The use of experimental design in educational evaluation. *Journal of Educational Measurement,* 1971, 8, 267-274.

33. Tucker, L. R., Damarin, F., & Messick, S. A base-free measure of change. *Psychometrika,* 1966, 31, 457-473.

A PREVIEW OF THE EVALUATION OF PLATO AND TICCIT

Ernest Anastasio
Assistant Director
Office of Data Analysis Research, Educational Testing Service
Princeton, N.J.

I do not intend to make a formal presentation now. I would just like to make some comments about what we have seen this morning and about some of the dialogue. As Larry just indicated, I am charged with evaluating the impact of the TICCIT program and the PLATO program. That impact would be assessed in large part as a function of how each of these systems performed in the targeted participating schools of the community colleges for TICCIT and in the case of PLATO also an elementary component of their program. Perhaps this afternoon I will have a chance to talk a little bit about the evaluation plan. It is rather comprehensive, and I would be happy to share it with anyone who might be interested. It is in written form, and it could be appropriated from me.

Let me start by saying that we have not had an opportunity to collect a lot of data, and I do not intend today to make any statements of an evaluative nature about the potential of either one of these systems. It seems to me that it is reasonable to conclude on the basis of what we have seen and heard this morning that both of these projects have very admirable goals. I think in large part reasonable goals, and it is clear that there is a substantial amount of intellectual leadership in both projects. It seems to me that the educational research community stands to gain a lot from both of them. It is also clear, that PLATO and TICCIT are philosophically and conceptually very different. One proposes to use a mini-computer to present pretty much a main-line structured instructional approach; the other proposes to develop a large computer utility with a super-computer. I think the decisions that have been made to date reflect in a large part the experiences of the developers and reflect their judgment about what should be done with computer-based education. I hope that it is clear to everyone in the room that the judgments that get made about these projects will *not* come out being significantly determined by the hardware decisions made either by MITRE or the University of Illinois. Therefore, I prefer not to talk about CPUs and hardware.

Instead, I would like to raise some issues that I think are at the other end of the continuum, the educational end. In our evaluation, we are prepared to take a very critical look at the cost question, which is clearly important. We also are prepared to take a very hard look at the technical performance question, which is obviously very important. But, we also are prepared to take a very heavy look at the educational component to collect as many measures as we can of the educational efficacy and impact of each of these programs. Without being supercritical, I would like to raise some issues that I think reflect some of the sentiments I heard this morning, some early comments that were made and some questions that Joe Lipson raised. Let me just list them, and then we can talk about them.

It is implicit certainly, and in some cases explicit, from what we have heard this morning that PLATO and TICCIT promise to tend to what I consider to be two very important areas of inquiry for accomplishment in the educational sector. Those issues can be labeled as the cognitive and affective domains. There are some cognitive issues that relate to mastery and certification. There are some affective issues that relate to acceptance, approach responsibility; some of the things that Vic talked to us about. I think it is clear in the accomplishments to date that both laboratories have kept these issues in mind. It is even clear to me that they have thought rather hard about some of the audiences they have to serve. I would like to push the discussion one step forward in that direction.

It seems to me that PLATO and TICCIT have to be accountable to some audiences whom I consider to be very important. *The primary audience is perhaps students.* Each of the presenters this morning used the word students several times, but neither one of them made students an important part of their presentation. A critical part is the question of direct impact on students. Another issue is instructors and users. Vic confessed earlier in his presentation that his slides had been prepared for a different talk and that in recent months he has become much more sensitive to the question of faculty acceptance and the like. I would like to suggest that the audience deserves much more attention than it got this morning. A third audience is administrators, the guys that have to make the decisions about whether or not these systems can really live in a school environment. We have a bad habit in research, and I am not accusing either one of these projects of setting up rather sterile environments for developmental programs, of collecting under rather constrained conditions data that the psychologists and evaluators tell us we should collect; and we run it through a regression analysis and make a decision, and then the program sits. So it seems to me, another group to whom the projects have to demonstrate a little more accountability is the administrator. A fourth group that is no less important is the professional community that is reflected by many of the people in the room here.

I guess the question that I would like to put to each of the projects with respect to the four audiences that I have just mentioned is, "Are PLATO and TICCIT in their development to be responsive as to what professionals consider to be the implicit needs of each of those four audiences?" A lot of issues were suggested this morning. There is, as I have said earlier, a kind of mainline structure approach of TICCIT versus the more adjunctive supplemental approach proposed by the PLATO people. Underlying each of those approaches are lots of very important questions about certified, controlled authoring techniques versus a less controlled target of opportunity approach that Jim was suggesting. I think that we have got to look very carefully at both and collect some data to help us make decisions about them. I am not sure we learned enough this morning to begin to even formulate some judgments. It would be unfair to require each of the presenters to explain to this group all of the components of his program, but, nevertheless, I want to caution people against drawing too many conclusions on the basis of what we saw this morning. We saw some examples of course material. In at least one case, an elementary example that Jim showed us, I think it is safe to say that the material was entertaining. I would say that neither in Vic's math presentation nor in the physics material that Jim showed us, did we see enough to allow us to formulate a judgment about whether that material was pedagogically sound. We did not see enough to let us judge whether or not that material has the potential to live in an educational environment. I guess what I am getting to is that I think these projects are certainly very complex.

I think that what we saw this morning was just a couple of facets of what is really an enormous and, in many ways, very grotesque iceberg. The tip of the iceberg is what these projects are all about, and that is what they have been funded to deliver; namely, high quality instruction to community college sectors in the United States--in only some areas of the United States. In a couple of key areas, in the case of the TICCIT project they are to deliver English and math instruction. In the case of PLATO the areas are community college accounting, biology, chemistry, English, and math, and also in the case of PLATO, an elementary program in reading and arithmetic. I would suggest that this is a very important charge.

What I'd like to suggest is that each of the projects, in considering its responsibilities to the professionals and to themselves, begin to share information and ideas with this community (the present audience) and with other interested people. Especially important is the sharing of more details about the plans for implementing and *integrating* these programs into schools. It seems to me, and I think that this morning both Duncan and Joe raised some questions about this, as did other people here, there are questions about their schedules, and the like. We know from preliminary contacts that, in both projects, faculty acceptance is clearly going to be a piece of the action. There are problems of courseware development and coordination and integration that are nontrivial. Vic mentioned that the B.Y.U. attempts to identify a structure for English programs had met with some problems, and I don't think that's particularly surprising. What I think would be particularly helpful would be if B.Y.U. and similarly if Illinois would share with us some of the specific procedures that they have implemented to overcome some of these problems. There is an enormous need for careful orientation and training programs for some of the detailed procedures on site management, and on the physical integration of these systems at the participating sites. I think we would all do well to consider some of the strategies for explicating and accommodating the capabilities that exist in the participating schools. Instructors and students can be a very rich resource in program development. They can also be a very hostile and violent resource if not treated properly. I think both projects have to formulate plans for themselves, and, as I said, share with us some of their ideas for doing that. I know from two years of experience with the evaluation of "Sesame Street" and a year with the "Electric Company" that the tenor in schools today is not to stand back and politely applaud when hardware is brought into a class-room or a learning center. Instructors are demanding that more attention be given to their roles in these developments. This is something that both projects recognize. I think that the faculty can reasonably demand help in implementing these programs; so I am suggesting that we need new procedures to assist instructors in *integrating* and coordinating these technologies into their classrooms. I think we need more information on the kind of feedback that is going to be provided to instructors. Certainly, in the case of the PLATO program in which supplemental, adjunctive kinds of uses are proposed, the burden is on the shoulders of the developers to provide the "hooks" and the "links" for the instructors and materials. We haven't learned about that yet. I think several people, including Bob, this morning mentioned the need for a formal public plan to perform formative evaluation. The question of quality control came up; I don't agree with Jim that it is an issue which a laboratory can duck. I think that the implementation of PLATO at the University of Illinois has been highly idiosyncratic and in many ways a success. I don't think that model is going to hold in the community colleges or the elementary schools. In fact, as Jim has indicated to you, they have implemented a more formal procedure for elementary course development in their own environment. In any event, I don't think it relieves the project of the responsibility to provide plans and milestones for the review and validation of course material and information about how the quality of lessons will be controlled. I think some empirical evidence is required; it ought to be demanded to support some of the directions that are being implemented in each of the very different strategies we have heard about this morning. The educational community can justifiably demand evidence of the efficacy or the appropriateness of some of the courseware development approaches that were described this morning. Finally, I think that it is time to pressure each project to release operational schedules for the transition of all aspects of this program to the schools. It is now almost October 1, and these projects are supposed to be delivering instruction by September of 1974, and lots of things need to be done. To insure that the projects don't slide backwards into the schools and to insure that neither one runs the risk of being judged a failure for the wrong reasons, I think it is important to move on to some of the stages that I have just begun to suggest. I guess what I'd like to say just by way of conclusion is that I think that both projects have gone a long way to date. I think there is a long way to go. I just want to remind everyone, since it wasn't a big part of the presentations this morning, that TICCIT and PLATO have a very strong obligation, I believe, to a community of users; and the two primary groups in that community are students and instructors. I think that we would all do well to pursue some of the things that I have been suggesting.

Q.   Ernie, could you say a couple of things about your own plans for the evaluation study? In other words, how it shapes up with what is projected ahead? What are your plans, and what steps lie ahead?

A.   Yes, I can say some words. The evaluation plan that I recently proposed to the National Science Foundation did not in any significant way get at, or propose to get at, any of the issues that I brought up this morning. We didn't know what we were getting into originally. We didn't know what PLATO and TICCIT were like. Doing this evaluation is a lot like poking a marshmallow. You know, you poke it and it is warm and it seems to conform to the poke and you take your finger away and it just pops back to where it was before. If you poke too hard, you do irreparable damage. Then people say you are the evaluator. You are not supposed to structure the project. You are imposing yourself too much. You are being too heavy-handed. In any event, we are willing to strike a balance, and what we learn through our regular contacts with the participating schools is that there are whole classes of social-institutional variables that are really critical to whether or not TICCIT or PLATO are ever going to become market-able commodities in the educational field. To be sure, there are issues of achievement, master certification, and placement that are important. This requires some kind of formal data collection instrumentation, a lot like the things that ETS has used in the past; also lots of new instrumentation—topical tests and criterion-referenced tests mentioned earlier, and the like. But, we are finding, to use the analogy I used before, that it is just the tip of the ice-berg. What really seems to count in the schools are the issues that relate to the role of the instructor, the way in which this specific technology is going to augment, replace, supplement, or whatever, his role. The evaluation design is becoming, we think, much more responsive, in the sense that we have implemented techniques for regularly interviewing participants and we have got a series of questionnaires on instructor activities, and that kind of thing. But what we need is to stay in regular contact with instructors who we can identify as participants in this program and with department chairmen. To protect us against creating an artificial society of "have" and "have-nots," we can generalize this aspect of the evaluation so that we get to lots of people in participating schools who haven't been earmarked or identified as participants. So the courseware development in both projects still has a long way to go. We haven't gone very far in terms of developing any criterion-referenced, or topical tests.

Q.   Are you looking at the process itself? The point came up earlier regarding the number of hours required to develop one student hour of material. Jim mentioned 26 hours, I believe, as a requirement for development. That is obviously an average, at best. If one looks at the spectrum of authors and types of materials needed, the differences in development time are some of the figures we need. Are there some on-site data about the processes used and plans to get data so that they are being collected now?

A.   Yes, we are very interested in process. While I'll comment, I am not willing to tell you what I think the authoring requirements on PLATO are. For anyone that is interested, if I can use your phone line, I have a program written with the help of some ETS people and some help from the Laboratory at Illinois called "off data." We are looking daily at the activities of 44 authors on this system. We are getting a very good handle on the amount of time they spend at the terminal doing different kinds of activities like editing and running in student mode, and the like. We have a lot of data being collected on a continuing basis. That is why I am not willing to give you an estimate. I think the estimate Jim gave you is certainly true for certain kinds of authoring activities. I would suggest on the basis of my activities that 26 hours of authoring per hour of terminal time is something that you cannot reasonably expect from many Tutor programmers. The people who have been around the lab for many years and have become Tutor experts can, I am sure, get half an hour of material or forty-five minutes of material in twenty-six hours. I think what we are finding, and this is in fact documented in a PLATO evaluation report which is available from Al Abner in the Illinois laboratory, is that it takes about three months of half-time programming for a new Tutor programmer to write his first lesson. It takes three months of half-time programming for an author to write his first lesson—probably a similar amount of time before he refines and augments and debugs, and whatever, in a lesson to the point where he is ready to say this, "It is something I am willing to put up to be used by a class of people." This is certainly more extreme than Jim's 26 hours.

Regarding funding, I guess PLATO is getting a total of $10,000,000. from NSF. A development like this, which moves the industry ahead of the theory that is available, would cost hundreds of millions of dollars if *not* done at a university. If you look at the figures for the development cost of the LP record or colored TV, they would be much greater. Whatever we develop in technology is expensive.

Development projects place a tremendous pressure on the people involved. I know the TICCIT group is working day and night, and they and the PLATO group are the best in the business. There seems to be no way to hurry these developments beyond a certain rate. I guess I would argue with Bob Davis that in developing some systems, the increases in pressure, after a certain point, do not make performance go up. The pressure that exists comes from interaction with professional peers. So far the pressure, in the case of PLATO, has produced what some people feel is a technological success, and perhaps it is. Now, I think it is time to demonstrate that the system can also become an educational and instructional success. There are several milestones ahead which these two projects have to reach if they are to develop systems that work in the schools.

COMMENTS ON THE PRESENTATION BY DUNCAN HANSEN

Robert J. Seidel
Human Resources Research Organization
Instructional Technology Group

1.   As I noted relevant to any computer usage in instruction, the use of task analysis, statement of objectives in achievement terms, criterion-referenced testing, etc., all have led to improvements in courses of instruction. In most instances it is unclear that the computer has played a significant role. And indeed in Dr. Hansen's presentation he cites this point.

2.   This, in turn, highlights the problem of the *situationally specific findings* which therefore require the replication and extension of results gotten in one environment in another instructional environment. The example I used at the conference was that of Hurst's successful outcomes with audio/tutorial as opposed to the failures indicated by Dr. Braun and others. The point here is that unless and until explicit instructional strategies are determined, the definition of innovative techniques by potential users is often mistakenly restricted to the superficial materials or media as opposed to the pedagogy behind those technologies.

3.   Extreme care must be taken therefore in documenting the conditions and the strategies for administering the innovations in each environment.

4.   I found myself in general agreement with Dr. Hansen's assertion that CMI if equivalent to CAI tutorial in effectiveness should be used because of its lower costs to develop and to implement as a system for instruction. However, my caveat is that the specific instance of obtaining such an equivalence may well be the result of a lack of development of a clever adaptive model of the tutor in the CAI format.

5.   In general, I agree with the stated need for adequate file structures and inquiry computing systems and take no issue with the presentation of the software portion of the paper by Dr. Hansen.

The following points illustrate with concrete examples some of the limitations of Dr. Hansen's sweeping general assertions. I refer specifically to three Florida State University documents cited as supportive by Dr. Hansen. However, I find them ambiguous at best and in some instances contradictory with his conclusions. Therefore, I disagree with the broad generalizations from the research done at the FSU laboratory. Some of these points I indicated during my presentation at the conference. Again, as I noted, it is impossible to deal with the vast numbers of studies conducted at FSU and referred to briefly in Dr. Hansen's paper. However, I will simply comment on a few points in detail to illustrate the over-generalizations which I feel are part of the Hansen presentation. Most of the research that has led to the very broad generalizations presented in Hansen's paper involved short instructional sequences on the order of anywhere between 45 minutes to an hour and a half worth of instruction. It is not at all clear that the material dealt with the hierarchically organized and rich materials of the usual instructional environment.

1.   In the discussion of anxiety in learning, Hansen states the following: "The important results indicated a consistent inverse relationship between state anxiety and learning, differential effects of trait anxiety. . ." Contrary to Hansen's assertion, the TR which he cites as support reveals that state anxiety and learning are positively

related in some instances and negatively related in others. (See especially pages 29 and 30 of the Lee Rivers *Tech. Report,* TR-27.) In addition, in that study in all cases where trait anxiety was significantly related to the criterion scores of learning, the relationship was positive. In other words, the findings are not nearly as consistent as the generalization made by Dr. Hansen would seem to indicate. Another study related to the relationship between curiosity and anxiety also was cited in Hansen's presentation (FSU *Tech. Memo.* No.34). The relationship is not at all as convincing or clear-cut as the Hansen presentation indicates. For example, on page 25 of the aforenoted *Tech. Memo.,* correlations between a state curiosity scale, a sensation seeking scale, and an anxiety state scale are presented with no significant correlational finding between the state curiosity scale (SCS) and either the sensation seeking scale (SSS) or the A-state scale (A-S). However, the interpretation is given as follows: "As expected the SCS was not found to correlate significantly with the SSS. The expected inverse relationship between A-state and the SCS was found, although this correlation did not approach significance." The sad thing about this misinterpretation is that in addition to lacking statistical meaning, the numerical value of the SCS and SSS correlation is $+.17$ whereas the numerical value of the SCS and A-state scale is smaller, $-.12$.

2.   In some instances, such as in FSU *Tech. Report* No. 12, where no differences occurred between learner control versus system control sequencing of materials, it is not at all clear that the conditions of measurement were such as to reveal important student-materials interactions which might have led to different conclusions from the no significant difference findings that occurred. In particular, I see no path analyses in the data. Yet these are essential to determine if students who have a self-selection treatment took the prescribed tasks in any different order from the tasks which were sequenced for a second group. In addition, the *nature* of the interactions between student and materials as indicated above is also ambiguous with respect to the experimental treatment conditions.

3.   In Hansen's presentation, the *Tech. Report* by Lee Rivers is cited as a major study of adaptive modeling at FSU. The results are generalized on page 20 of the Hansen presentation as follows: "The order of outcomes in terms of superiority were adaptive model strategy, remediation for all strategy, a learner choice strategy, and a no-remediation strategy." Yet if one looks at the TR in detail, we find that the results are not at all as general or clear as are implied by this statement. For example, it should be noted that there were two levels of materials presented for instruction. The first four concepts were Part 1 of the instruction, and this part was the simpler material and more familiar to the students. Part 2 was considered to be more technical material and more difficult for the student and less familiar. There were 9 concepts taught in all, four in the first part and five in the second. Only in Part 1 did the adaptive model group show significantly higher performance. However, as the author notes, these results did not hold in exactly that way for the second part of the instruction.   Within Part 2, the regression model group and the all-remediation group performed significantly better. . ., but there was no significant difference within the two sets of groups." (p. 42, Rivers, 1972) So in the more difficult part of the task, the all-remediation group was as effective as the adaptive model group. Furthermore, the mean time for the all-remediation group exceeded the adaptive model group by only 5 minutes. Therefore, the question of the practical significance to the outcome, vis-a-vis using an adaptive model strategy, is questionable. For example, how much time did it take to develop an adaptive model as opposed to simply using all the remediational capability available in the system? Moreover, the rest of the results indicated that the learning task itself showed a deterioration in performance in Part 2 of the study to the point where it is of questionable utility to talk about the task as a representative instructional task by the time concept 9 was reached.

If I were to sum up the results of the study in terms of the order of outcome, contrary to Hansen's interpretation, I would note that concept-by-concept analyses revealed that in four out of the 9 concepts there were no differences amongst the treatment conditions and in one of the other remaining 5, the all-remediation group was superior and the superiority of the adaptive model was principally restricted to the more familiar, introductory material of the instruction. Finally, I note again that the author describes the task as lasting roughly an hour and a half in length.

MINI-COMPUTERS IN EDUCATION

Ludwig Braun
Professor of Electrical Sciences
SUNY at Stony Brook

The presentations at this meeting describing the Dartmouth Computer System and the PLATO and TICCIT systems are very impressive demonstrations of the power which computers can bring to bear on the educational process. I have asked for an opportunity to comment briefly on the role of the mini-computer in education because I believe that the proceedings of this meeting would be incomplete without some recognition of this role.

Clearly, there are many computing jobs for which the mini-computer is not adequate. The enormous social-science data files which the Dartmouth student has available can not be implemented on a mini-computer. Certain kinds of very complex computations and certain very desirable languages can not be implemented on a mini-computer. Nonetheless, there is a great deal which can be done in the classroom with mini-computers.

There are two reasons why I feel that the mini-computer is becoming an important component in the educational arsenal. First, mini-computer manufacturers and soft-ware houses have developed and are continuing to develop very efficient and very user-oriented soft-ware, so that the mini is much easier to use than was the case as recently as five years ago. Second, the cost of mini-computers has decreased dramatically over the last decade. The price of the Digital Equipment PDP-8, for example, had decreased by a factor of 2 every three years, on the average, during that period. Once large-scale integration hits the mini-computer, the prices should again drop dramatically.

In the Huntington Computer Project, we have had experience for about six years with mini-computers in high schools. In 1967, when we were formulating the purposes of the Huntington Computer Project, Arthur Melmed suggested rather strongly that we should explore the use of the mini-computer in the classroom, as well as the use of time-shared terminals into a larger computer. One of our major accomplishments, in fact, has been the demonstration of the value of the mini-computer in the high school. The two high schools which started with a PDP-8 six years ago still have them and swear by them. They insist that they would not have time-sharing, because of the communication problems which can arise. In both cases, additional memory and additional peripherals have been added to the system so that the systems now are much more powerful than they were in 1968. This indeed is one of the attractions of the mini-computer. For less than $20,000 a school can have a complete eight-terminal time-sharing mini-computer. Certainly the class of problems which can be handled in such a configuration is not very large; however, significant learning activities can be run with such a machine in mathematics classes, for example. Further, for just a few thousand dollars a year, additional components may be added to increase the capability, which will satisfy almost any high school teacher or student.

I should like to relate also my experience with the use of a mini-computer in undergraduate courses in system dynamics. We have a PDP-8 with only an 8K core and a simulation language called ISL (developed by Inter-active Mini-systems, Inc. in Kennewick, Washington). With this simple system (which can be replicated for under $10,000 including soft-ware costs) we can simulate dynamic systems of up to 80th order and containing time-varying and nonlinear components. On bench mark tests comparing our PDP-8 plus ISL with a 360/50 using CSMP, we have obtained comparable accuracy and have obtained solutions with comparable amounts of CPU time. At Stony Brook, we currently are using this machine in an undergraduate course in bio-engineering. The students are studying the dynamics of the respiratory system, and of the transmission of heat from the core to the skin under various environmental circumstances. I can visualize the time (in the not-too-distant future) when the teacher of Physiology or Biology or Engineering, e.g., will wheel a mini into his classroom, and, using a language like ISL, will explore with his students the dynamics of systems which are far more complex, and far more realistic, than is the case in most classrooms today.

One other aspect of mini-computing which is important in education is the advent of the mini-time-sharing computer. Hewlett-Packard with its 2000 and 3000 series machines and Digital Equipment Corporation with its TSS-8 and PDP-11/45 systems already have had a dramatic impact on high school-level computing. Probably the best example of this exists at the TIES Project in Minneapolis, although similar activities exist in Colorado, Northern New Jersey, and Massachusetts, to name just a few.

In conclusion, I should like to say that mini-computers have a potentially very important role to play in education because:

1. Their low price can bring computing power into even the poorest school system.

2. The computing power of the mini-computer is increasing dramatically because of both hardware and software improvements.

3. Already the capability is entirely adequate for many educational purposes at the college level, as well as at the pre-college level.

4. Their size and flexibility (comparable to the flexibility of a portable 16 mm sound projector) make them very attractive to the educator.

5. Their lack of dependence on communication systems (compared to the dependence of time-shared systems on communication) is very attractive partly because communication systems are responsible for a sometimes unacceptable deterioration of system reliability, and also because communication costs frequently are comparable to computing costs, and can even exceed the cost of the computing.

Part Four

PERSONALIZED, OPEN

LEARNING ENVIRONMENTS

CHICAGO'S TV COLLEGE: A TELEVISION-BASED OPEN LEARNING MODEL

James J. Zigerell
Dean of TV College

It is a common fault of educators—as well as of critics of the arts—to evaluate a project without regard to the objectives the project's planners and managers set for themselves, and without regard to the limitations under which the managers must work. Nowadays, for example, in the world of instructional television it is only to be expected that the critic will condemn an instructional TV project, or express misgivings about it, if it does not employ the expensive production techniques of the television commercial, even though the project has goals quite different from those of the advertiser, is aiming at a narrow target audience with specialized needs—and operates with a budget far below the six million dollars of *Sesame Street.*

True, there is waiting to be served a vast pre-school audience, weaned on frenetic TV advertising, possessing the limited attention span of the child, and often suffering from the cultural deprivation that comes from impoverished home and family experience. The attention of this audience cannot be captured and held without a massive multi-sensory stimulation. But each instructional broadcast effort must be judged on its own terms: the audience it selects as its target; the nature of the educational service it provides this audience; the factors that operate to make it "cost effective"; the instructional "void" that would result if it were not operable.

TV College—the operation described in this paper—is a long established project. It is best approached, as it has been in several published studies during the eighteen years of its history, as *one*—by no means the *only*—model of an open broadcast-based educational extension. As a model, it has been consistently effective—as effectiveness is measured by the instruments familiar to educators—in a large metropolitan area, containing some six and a half million population. Every school year there are enough viewers who take advantage of TV College instructional services to make the costs of open television production and broadcast manageable and "effective."

Before I describe the elements that have enabled Chicago's TV College to survive, while similar projects in other parts of the nation have proved to be short lived, an important disclaimer must be made a part of the record. TV College administrators and production personnel do not claim to have exploited the resources of the television medium itself to reshape instruction or change learning styles, although over the past few years they have made serious attempts to improve overall production quality and add the entertainment values to instruction needed to recruit and hold new kinds of audiences.

Now let us look at the elements that have given TV College its distinctive shape as an instructional service, discuss the overall management of instruction, and describe the measurement techniques which supply information about and help control student performance and costs of operation. In particular, we shall be looking at 1) the objectives of the project as they have evolved over an eighteen-year period; 2) the instructional system and its overall design; 3) the TV College target audiences, their needs and their performance; 4) the cost factor.

TV College is an extension of the City Colleges of Chicago, a two-year public community college. It is now part of a unit tentatively called the Learning Resources Laboratory, a recently established unit that, when fully developed, will provide a staff of learning specialists and variety of instructional materials for the seven colleges making up the City Colleges of Chicago. In short, the purpose of the Learning Resources Laboratory is to further innovation in teaching and learning at the community college level.

Open color telecasts are presented via the city's public television outlets: VHF Channel 11 and UHF Channel 20. Weekday daytime and Sunday morning broadcasts are carried by Channel 11; evening broadcasts are carried by Channel 20. For the 1973-74 school year, however, the schedule on Channel 20 will be suspended, since the station's signal strength and range are unsatisfactory. It is hoped that within the next eighteen months the Channel 20 antenna will be moved to a better location and its transmitter replaced.

TV College telecourses are also available to Chicago area residents in videocassette (SONY U-MATIC, ¾'') recordings in certain Chicago Public Libraries, as part of a recently inaugurated project called *Study Unlimited*, which is funded by a grant from the Illinois Board of Higher Education. Students can view telecasts at regularly scheduled times in groups, or can arrange to view cassettes on an individual basis. The latter option will enable a student to complete a course in less than the conventionally prescribed time.

It is also possible that within the next two years TV College materials will also be distributed to the colleges of the City College system, as well as to health care institutions, government offices, and industrial sites, via the four channels of an ITFS system. The University of Illinois—Chicago Circle Campus has indicated its intention to make use of the system for professional in-service training if and when it is in operation. The license will be applied for by the City Colleges of Chicago.

Administrative direction of the Learning Resources Laboratory and TV College operations and planning is entrusted to an Executive Dean. He works under the direction of the City Colleges' Vice Chancellor for Faculty and Instruction.

It is fitting, of course, that TV College be an extension of a community college, since the community college by its very nature is committed to instructional innovation and services to citizens of all ages and backgrounds.

Instructional Objectives

A valuable UNESCO monograph, *The New Media: Memo to Educational Planners* (1967), was organized around the five educational needs that can best be served by ITV. Although the compilers of this publication were concerned primarily with attacking urgent educational programs in the world's developing nations, the needs they identified are ones demanding careful attention in the developed nations as well. They are as follows:

1. the need for improving instruction in the classroom;

2. the need to teach those who are and will be teachers of the young and old;

3. the need to increase and spread literacy and the skills of living in an urban, technological society;

4. the need to provide continuing education for adults;

5. the need to provide extramural extensions of the school and college.

Since its beginning, TV College has been greatly concerned with all but one of these needs. As yet, unfortunately, it has done little to offer training in literacy and the skills of urban living. Nor has each of the needs been served well. As for the one need hardly served at all, I shall indicate how TV College hopes to reach out to those whose needs are not for formal adult or higher education, but for basic educational skills.

Adults who complete all, or part, of the first two years of college by watching television at home are no longer news in Chicago. What started in September 1956 as a bold new departure in extending educational opportunity, a three-year project underwritten in part by the Fund for the Advancement of Education of the

Ford Foundation, has long since blended into the educational landscape of the Chicago metropolitan area. In the words of an earlier published TV College report, the trial years from 1956 to 1961 "showed that a junior college program can be offered effectively on open-circuit TV" — without any sacrifice of instructional quality. Accrediting agencies, professional associations, colleges and universities throughout the Midwest accept credit earned through TV College without question.

It also quickly became apparent that the Chicago area, served by educational VHF and UHF channels, contains a virtually inexhaustible audience of mature, highly motivated people capable of completing college courses by studying on their own. Once the Ford Foundation grant had been exhausted in 1960, the General Superintendent of Chicago's Public Schools, who was then the chief administrative officer of Chicago's junior college system, recommended that the instructional television program be continued and supported in its entirety by taxpayers' funds. Since 1966, when the City Colleges of Chicago came under the control of its own Board of Trustees, the instructional television service has received only the warmest support from the central administration.

Over the past twelve or thirteen years, TV College has regularly polled viewers' opinions of its instructional service. An overwhelming majority report that they like their TV courses and, even more important, that they enjoy studying on TV. The results of one questionnaire distributed to TV College students who had gone on to conventional study in four-year colleges deserve mention. Most of the three hundred respondents stated that they learned just as much by TV as they did in the conventional classroom. They stated further that the grades they made in their conventional courses in four-year colleges were about the same as their TV grades, not appreciably lower. Further—and this is not surprising, since Chicago's TV College courses are produced for open-circuit broadcast—they all judged their television courses to be better organized and more effectively presented than the conventionally taught courses they had taken in the college to which they had transferred.

The first three years proved that a metropolitan area the size of Chicago, with a potential viewing audience of some six to six and a half million people, contains a virtually inexhaustible audience of mature, able, and highly motivated students eager to enroll as credit students in college-level television courses.

The record speaks for itself:

- —Over 150,000 individuals have enrolled in televised courses, with most taking no more than one course;

- —Of this total, some 80,000 students were enrolled officially in the college for credit;

- —Another 70,000 students have enrolled unofficially as non-credit students;

- —An average of 10,000 viewers watch every TV College program;

- —TV College is on the air an average of 25 hours weekly;

- —The student retention percentage (that is, number of students who complete a semester's work) averages between 70-75%.

Here are a few other highlights:

- —To date, approximately 2,150 students graduated from the City Colleges of Chicago took one semester of their work by TV;

- —A sizable proportion of TV College students also take conventional courses on campus;

- —Approximately 40% of TV students plan to teach.

173

The Instructional System

Curriculum   Until recently, what was produced and telecast was largely predetermined by the original TV College objective, namely, enabling a student to complete the entire two-year college program leading to the Associate in Arts (A.A.) certificate without leaving his home, by combining television viewing and correspondence study. General education courses—e.g., Natural Science, Humanities, Social Sciences—required of all students who are graduated from the City Colleges of Chicago have been rotated at regular intervals, so that a viewer taking all his college courses on TV can complete the two-year program leading to the Associate's degree within three years or so. Two general courses are offered during each semester of the academic year. But, as already indicated, most students complete only four or five courses on TV. Very few complete an entire two-year program.

·Other offerings are "electives," made up of courses not required of all students seeking the Associates certificate. The preferences and academic goals of TV College credit students—as made known by their responses to questionnaires as well as by other surveys—have remained fairly constant over the past twelve years. Elective courses are scheduled in clusters of "bands," e.g., mathematics and sciences, business and secretarial skills, general cultural subjects.

Since the early days, 40% of TV College credit students have regularly expressed a desire to enter teacher-training curricula. Accordingly, courses related to their interests have been scheduled each year—for example, introductory courses in education (e.g., philosophy of education, history of education) and psychology. These courses, especially when presented over a short eight-week summer term, also attract teachers looking for in-service training opportunities. For example, a Summer 1968 survey disclosed that of the 455 students enrolled in courses in Philosophy of Education and Educational Measurement and Evaluation, 77 already held bachelor's degrees and 10 held master's degrees; 6 held regular public school certificates, 26 provisional certificates; 47 had taught during the preceding year in Chicago-area public and private schools; 82 had enrolled in one or both courses to fulfill requirements for regular public school certification.

It is noteworthy that TV College experience in this respect forecast initial Open University experience in England. A sizable portion of the first-year's Open University enrollment was comprised of teachers seeking fuller certification and technicians seeking higher credentialing. It is also noteworthy that there is now a surplus of teachers in the Chicago area, a factor to be considered in future TV College programming.

Only recently TV College has begun to shift its curricula emphases, prompted by a number of factors. First, the State of Illinois requires that the public community college devote a large portion of its total curriculum to technical-occupational programs. Second, the TV College staff, always uncomfortable about its programming holding appeal only for the relatively narrow audience capable of completing college and university courses, is eager to present series which hold appeal and value for viewers whose interests and capacities are not academic. What this means, in short, is that more introductory courses of vocational nature are now being produced for open broadcast. If and when an ITFS system is available—and if and when CATV systems are installed within the Chicago metropolitan area—vocational courses of highly specialized nature, aimed at groups much too small to be served by open VHF or UHF broadcast, can also be presented.

There have been noticeable shifts in audience preferences within the past several years. Some of these shifts reflect changing student tastes of conventional campuses—for example, the decline of interest in foreign language study.

Audience interest is persisting in cultural subjects. Viewers still enroll in large numbers in art, music theory and appreciation, philosophy, and history courses. This is not surprising in a major urban area in which are concentrated large numbers of people who display the traits of what the studies identify as the ETV audience.

In recent years, too, more programming has been devoted to "adult education." Usually these ventures are supported by funding from outside sources. Special series have been done in areas like Real Estate and Art

Appreciation. As yet, with the exception of a series in consumerism, little has been done in basic "coping" skills—literacy, etc. It is expected—once an ITFS system is a reality—that offerings in a variety of entry-level occupational skills can be presented.

In summary, seventeen years of experience, and a steady flow of information derived from student questionnaires, are guides in selecting and scheduling courses. By rotating courses carefully and not repeating them at too frequent intervals, a high level of credit and not-for-credit enrollments has been maintained.

As has already been indicated, TV College is now seeking to broaden its goals and cultivate audiences with needs different from those of students seeking the A.A. degree. As a result, the years to come will see more programming with an unmistakably occupational and community service emphasis.

Reuses of Courses   Courses proved to be effective in achieving their objectives are replayed as often as three or four times over a period of five or six years. No course, however, is replayed until it has been thoroughly reviewed and edited by its teacher, with a view to improving and updating. Usually the teacher will remake one or two of the programs in their entirety and remake portions of other programs.

One thing should be noted with respect to replays of courses: they must be scheduled with sufficient time between showings so as to maintain the level of credit enrollment necessary to keep costs favorable. The level of audience for economical operation is not constant. Usually a credit course cannot be offered more than once every other year.

Some TV College courses are released for reuses outside Chicago. Since 1966, the Great Plains National Instructional Television Library of the University of Nebraska in Lincoln, Nebraska, has handled rentals of courses. Courses are available in videotape or videocassette. Community colleges outside Chicago, but within the Channel 11 signal area, are also free to accept enrollments in courses as they are broadcast, provided they supply local coordination. Beginning in Fall 1973, TV College courses will be made available to all Illinois public community colleges without rental charges.

Interinstitutional use of courses has been slow to develop in the U.S.A., despite much talk about it. Only within the past year have there been signs that shared use is on the increase. No doubt the new emphasis on open learning systems, prompted by the success of Britain's Open University, has had something to do with this. On the whole, however, faculty resistance, deeply rooted feelings about institutional autonomy, and the generally unimaginative production quality of much instructional television have impeded both interinstitutional uses of televised materials and interinstitutional planning and development.

The Components   Anyone administering an instructional television service soon learns that a telecast, no matter how well structured or imaginatively produced, cannot carry the entire teaching burden. Printed materials and appropriate face-to-face activities are also essential if a high level of student interest is to be maintained and student success insured.

Every TV College course is accompanied by a syllabus called a Study Guide, the content and scope of which varies with the nature of course and the preference of the television teacher. Every guide, however, does contain a statement of course objectives, a detailed course outline, and precise instructions as to readings and written projects.

Over the years the TV College staff has discovered that the judicious employment of self-scoring and programed learning materials, based on either linear or branching methods, reduces passivity on the part of the student, and, in fact, increases the percentage of students completing courses. When editing series prior to replays, teachers are encouraged to prepare such materials. Studies have shown that these materials improve the rate of student retention.

The regularly enrolled student earns his credit through one of the colleges of the City College system, not through TV College. He reports to a TV College campus center for three examinations. The first two—or "midterm"—are each one hour long. The third—or "final"— is two hours long. Face-to-face conferences with students are scheduled several times each term. The teacher or coordinator of a television course schedules himself for telephone conferences every week. In certain courses—e.g., shorthand, typing, foreign language—the television student is required to attend on-campus class sessions as many as seven or eight times a term.

Most courses, too, entail a significant correspondence component—that is, students mail written work to television instructors or other teachers (called "Section Teachers"). The objectives and nature of the projects are specified in the Study Guide.

The Faculty   Most teachers come to TV College from classrooms of the City Colleges of Chicago. It can be argued that this has been one of the shortcomings of the program. The Ford Foundation consultants, when TV College planning was barely underway in 1956, suggested that celebrated scholars and academic personalities from Midwestern universities be recruited to present courses.

On several occasions, professors from outside the college have been recruited to teach courses—in Astronomy and American History, for example. The experience has been somewhat disappointing. The only time the employment of an outside teacher has been successful is when his own institution made the television course in question one of their own offerings and enrolled students on their own campuses. This is not meant to imply that outstanding professional talent should not be recruited wherever it is found. Certainly, colleges undertaking the production of courses on regional or cooperative bases will want to recruit, if possible, scholars and teachers with reputations that go beyond their home campuses.

TV College has only seldom employed instructional teams to assist the television instructor prepare his series. An important reason for this was the early commitment to produce a telecast that is essentially a visually enhanced, carefully rehearsed classroom performance, a commitment dictated—and still dictated in part—by limited funding and the necessity of presenting a range of courses each term. The instructional team approach, if it is to be effective, must have a television producer-member with strong academic credentials—a commodity not readily available on this side of the Atlantic. Carried to its logical outcome, it would seem to lead to the employment of professional actors or broadcasters, rather than teachers, as course presenters—a procedure which, desirable though it may be under certain circumstances, is beyond the means of a single institution.

TV College lacks, it need hardly be said, the resources of money and personnel required for thoroughly "mediated" instruction. But even if resources were available, it is questionable that televised instruction intended to impart cognitive learning and complex skills can be divorced entirely from the teacher "figure." There is a still unexamined premise which has taken root in the educational broadcast world—and parts of the academic community—which holds that the fastmoving, high-visual production techniques effective in inducing the non-critical frame of mind needed for the willing reception of the advertising message—or capable of commandeering the attention of the pre-school and juvenile mind—can be adopted wholesale by college and university broadcasters. It is conceivable that close analysis and orderly step-by-step presentation require subdued and unobtrusive production methods—a tailoring of means to ends. All this, of course, is a task for the researchers.

It is true, of course, that the talent pool in most institutions, especially in two-year colleges, is relatively small. But by careful recruiting and maintenance of favorable working conditions—e.g., adequate time for preparation and studio presentation, a full Summer for preliminary preparation and organization of study materials, and a full semester with no duties other than studio recording—TV College has managed to recruit a roster of instructors from City Colleges of Chicago campuses who have learned to teach effectively on television.

TV College Students and Their Performance

TV College classifies credit students as follows: a) Homeviewers; b) TV Concurrent students; c) TV-in-class students; d) Not-for-credit students.

Homeviewers are credit students who watch classes at home or off campus and have no regular contact with campus activities. They make up 75 to 80% of the total credit enrollment every term.

TV Concurrents are students who take courses in the classroom while enrolled in TV courses. They may watch open telecasts at home, or on campus on videotape or videocassette closed circuit. They make up 20 to 25% of the total enrollment every term.

TV-in-class viewers are students of normal college age who view telecasts in groups in the classroom. In the past, they watched courses as they were broadcast on the air. Nowadays it is more common for them to watch on closed-circuit broadcast, with programs transferred to one-inch videotape modes or videocassettes. These students meet with a classroom teacher, who may or may not be the television teacher, once a week for additional instruction. This kind of instruction has never flourished on campuses. As indicated below, research shows conclusively, however, that unselected students taking TV courses in the classroom must have supplemental classroom instruction if they are to match the performance of adult homeviewers.

Not-for-credit students do not take examinations, nor do they submit written work. For a nominal registration fee ($1.00) they are sent course study guides. No official records are kept on them.

As might be expected, the students who enroll as non-credit viewers possess a relatively high level of educational background. Many have university degrees. They are the people one would expect to be watchers of educational TV. They read books and serious magazines, follow community affairs, attend concerts and the theater.

Student Activities Visitors to TV College always ask about the mechanics of planning and controlling activities for thousands of students within a seventy-five mile area. The present system, it goes without saying, was developed only after much trial and error.

Since most students are removed from City Colleges campuses, folders listing courses to be offered, the topics of programs, textbooks required, the broadcast schedules, and the places and times of registration, must be mailed out each term. Some 40 to 50 thousand copies are mailed out each term, and about 10,000 are distributed to public libraries, schools and public agencies.

Students enroll in all seven colleges of the City Colleges of Chicago. Physically handicapped students may register by mail, as well as students who have completed several courses on television. A hundred to two hundred students are enrolled in penal institutions.

When students register, they elect a TV College Center to which they report for examinations and conferences. The four centers are located so that students living in all parts of the city and its suburbs can reach them easily.

All credit students are given a copy of what is called a Credit Bulletin at the time of enrollment. This bulletin contains the dates and times of examinations, the telephone number of television teachers and times when they can be reached, as well as other necessary information.

As already indicated, students take three examinations in each course: two while the course is in progress and one at the end. The Credit Bulletin indicates the dates and times of examinations. Most examinations are of the objective, multiple-choice variety which can be scored by a machine. All these examinations are "item-analyzed," that is, analyzed with a view to determining what percentages of students give correct responses to items. These analyses are sent to teachers to help them improve examinations. (It should be noted, too, that some teachers require essays as part of examinations.)

As indicated earlier, teachers schedule themselves for two hour-long telephone conferences each week, during which times students may telephone to seek help or make comments. They also schedule open conferences at which time they meet with their students.

TV College makes special provision for handicapped students. Students confined to their homes or hospitals by illness and physical defects are administered examinations by proctors—clergymen, nurses, or social workers. Students who are inmates of the three penal institutions TV College serves are administered examinations by members of the prison educational staff.

Over the past dozen years, Chicago's TV College has conducted careful studies of student performance and shared its experiences in several published reports. Early interim reports, *Final Report of a Three Year Experiment* and *Chicago's TV College,* summarized TV activities from 1956 through 1959.

The first-named report, aimed at researchers and specialists, presented detailed statistical analyses of the performance of students taking courses on open-circuit television. During the first year of the trial, experimental attention was directed to comparing the achievement of junior college students viewing TV and studying at home with that of students taking the same courses in conventional classrooms. The performance of students watching TV lessons on campus and receiving follow-up classroom instruction was also studied. During the second year, careful studies were made of the performance of the "TV-at-home" student and that of the evening students of comparable age and motivation taking the same courses in conventional classes. To control the teacher variable, whenever possible, the TV teacher was assigned to the on-campus control group. The third year saw experimental activity centering around the use of TV series as direct instruction for unselected junior college students of normal college age. Comparisons were made between "TV-in-class" and conventionally taught courses.

The authors of the *Final Report* came to the following general conclusion:

> When evaluated by the techniques of measurement and analysis used in this experiment, television instruction is a thoroughly effective means of extending college opportunities to at-home students in all subject areas explored in the project (p. 66).

Among more specific conclusions of interest were the following: 1) the at-home TV student, typically a highly motivated mature adult, tends to outperform his counterpart taking evening courses on campus, and 2) unselected students of normal college age watching a TV course in class will not perform satisfactorily unless they are provided follow-up classroom instruction.

The consistently high level of performance of the TV at-home student does not signal any superiority inhering in televised instruction. We must look at the student. A homeviewing student selected at random would probably be a 30-year-old woman—75% of the credit audience is female. The chances are excellent that she is married, with a home and children to look after. Her high school record was good. She probably finished in the upperhalf of her class. Since she is kept busy as housewife and mother of small children, she can take only one or two courses at a time. Probably she had no opportunity to go to college before marriage, or if she did, was able to complete no more than a year. She is interested in making a career for herself outside the home—either to experience a sense of personal fulfillment or to add to the family income. TV College courses start her on her journey. Later on, when circumstances are right, she will transfer her credits earned via TV to another college and enroll in conventional courses.

Data have been gathered on TV College students over the years. Several thorough studies were made in the mid 1960's, including a Ph.D. dissertation. These studies tended to confirm the view of the TV College credit student as possessing a composite of lower middle class traits—with a strong drive for upward mobility, interest in learning for the sake of personal advancement, etc. Most TV College credit students have been clustered in lower middle class and middle class communities of the metropolitan area. The greatest incidence of failure in TV College performance comes in students who live in inner city and disadvantaged areas of the city. For that matter, enrollments from these areas make up little more than 5% of total enrollment.

Within the past few years, however, population movement out of the city has accelerated. Credit enrollments from suburban areas have been reduced sharply because suburban areas now supporting public community colleges are no longer required to pay tuition charges of residents who enroll in the Chicago system. (As indicated, TV College is tuition free only for Chicago residents.) TV College itself is now attempting to reach the disadvantaged segments of the city's population.

There is a real need presently for information about the new kinds of TV College students. Some of the data can be gathered through the new *Study Unlimited* project. As part of this activity, videocassettes of TV College courses are stored in Chicago Public Library study centers. Several graduate students in Educational Measurement and Evaluation assigned to TV College and the Learning Resources Laboratory are now preparing an instrument to be distributed to *Study Unlimited* students who enroll in these courses. Its purpose, besides gathering data as to age, educational background, etc., is to determine what elements make for failure in off-campus independent study.

Costs

Anyone acquainted with open-circuit television production knows that it does not come at cut-rate prices. Inquiries about cost take several forms: e.g., how much does it cost to produce a single course? How do TV College costs per student compare with on-campus costs per student? What are the categories of cost?

Overall TV College costs cannot be discussed until the factors entering into the calculations are identified. Significant costs include those for 1) studio production and transmission as established by an annual contract with the television studio; 2) teacher, production, administrative and clerical salaries; 3) reference and research activities, graphic work, on-site filming; 4) preparation and printing of study guides, promotional materials, and examinations; 5) supportive instructional activities—follow-up classroom instruction, conferences, counseling, etc.; 6) indirect instructional services, such as examination proctoring, special registration activities, etc. Not included are costs for on-campus library services, regular registration services, heating and lighting of classrooms and laboratories used by TV College students—services available from 8:00 a.m. until 10:00 p.m. on City Colleges campuses whether TV students are present to use them or not.

Since about 1966, the total annual amount budgeted for TV College activities—exclusive of foundation or federal and state grants earmarked for special projects—has been between $800,000 and $900,000. Each year some $330,000 goes for studio operations, about $275,000 for teacher and indirect instructional salaries, and another $250,000 for staff salaries, videotape and equipment purchase, and overhead.

The cost of producing a thirty-program (45-minute) series is currently some $60,000, of which $35,000 goes into studio production and purchase of videotape stock; $15 to $16,000, on an average, for teacher's salary; about $7,500 for the services of a producer's assistant, graphic artist, and scene designer; and another $2,500 for administrative and clerical support. Transmission costs for twice repeated on-the-air broadcast of an entire series add up to another $7,000. Added to this are the expenses of printing several thousand course study guides and examinations— another $1,800 to $2,000. Thus the total outlay for initial production and on-the-air presentation is some $70,000. It must be borne in mind that an effective course can be presented on open circuit, with only minor editing and updating, as many as four or five times over a six- or seven-year span.

A crucial question, however, is the cost of TV College instruction on the basis of student credit hours generated. Put more simply, how do TV College costs per credit hour compare with those of conventional instruction? The average cost per-credit-hour of instruction in the City Colleges of Chicago is $50.00. (A full-time student earns fifteen credit hours in a semester.) By enrolling the equivalent of 500 to 525 full-time students each semester (about 2000 individuals) and presenting seven courses, of which only three are being presented for the first time, TV College can keep its per-credit-hour cost at about forty-five dollars. Thousands of non-credit viewers are also served.

CONCLUSION

The foregoing remarks have presented in outline what are the features that characterize a television-based open-learning system with, perhaps, the longest history of continuous operation in the nation. The model is one that does not lend itself to duplication everywhere. It has always been fortunate in having enthusiastic and unwavering administrative support. It has also been fortunate in having an extensive broadcast schedule on a major public television channel. Above all, it could not remain effective on a cost basis were it not for the large urban population it reaches.

To continue to provide meaningful service, it must stay abreast of change in its community and seek out new audiences.

REFERENCES

1. Bretz, Rudy, "Case Study: Chicago's *TV College*," in *Three Models for Home-Based Instructional Systems Using Television,* Santa Monica, California: Rand Corporation, 1972.

2. Erickson, C. and H. Chausow, *Chicago's TV College: Final Report of a Three Year Experiment,* Chicago: Chicago Public Schools, 1960.

3. Erickson, C., H. Chausow, and J. Zigerell, *Eight Years of TV College: A Fourth Report,* Chicago: Chicago City Colleges, 1964.

4. McCombs, Maxwell, "Chicago's Television College," in *The New Media: Memo to Educational Planners*, Paris: UNESCO: International Institute for Educational Planning, 1967.

5. Reid, J. Christopher and Donald MacLennan, *Research in Instructional Television and Film,* Washington, D.C.: U. S. Government Printing Office, 1967, pp. 61-65.

6. Zigerell, J., "Chicago's TV College," AAUP *Bulletin,* March, 1967, 49-54.

7. _____ "Chicago's TV College," in *Television and Education,* Munich: International Institute for Educational Television, 1968.

8. _____ "Television Instruction: Where Do We Go From Here?," *Educational Technology,* September, 1969, 72-76.

9. _____ "Universities Without Walls With No Illusions," *Educational Television,* October, 1971, 17 pp.

10. "Chicago's TV College," in *Universita e Televisione,* ed., Pietro Prini, Rome, Italy: RAI-Radio Televisione Italiana, 1972.

VIDEOTAPE APPLICATIONS IN ENGINEERING EDUCATION

Lionel V. Baldwin
Dean, College of Engineering
Colorado State University

OFF-CAMPUS GRADUATE PROGRAMS

The rapid pace of today's technology and its industrial application has had a great impact on engineering education in the United States. Prior to 1950, the four-year bachelor's degree was the degree of choice for 90 percent of the graduates in engineering.* Today, we graduate essentially the same total class size, but over a third of the students receive graduate degrees. The additional study and specialization which the M.S. degree in engineering offers has lead some educational leaders to argue that professional practice in the near future will require it as a prerequisite.

Approximately half of the M.S. degrees awarded in engineering today are earned by part-time students. At least seventeen colleges of engineering in the U.S. now use television to extend high quality, advance degree education to students employed at locations remote from established campuses. These are on-going, diverse learning systems which I estimate reach over 15,000 students annually in at least 700 separate course study groups.[1] Each year several additional colleges of engineering bring similar programs on line.

Employers of Engineers are generally responsive, occasionally enthusiastic, in making available the in-plant facilities for video instruction. My experience in managing and enlarging the Colorado State University program parallels the findings reported in a 1969 National Science Foundation report on "Continuing Education for R & D Careers." The employers typically view the new video-based program as an addition to their existing tuition refund program and, unfortunately, they tend to manage the new learning situation as an additional fringe benefit for their professional staff. There are few serious professional development programs, but on the other hand, most engineers do feel encouraged to participate. Only about one-third of the participants are oriented toward degree work; these tend to be the younger staff members. The majority of the participants prefer the university credit courses for in-depth learning of the fundamentals of a subject as they seek job-related diversification of their education rather than a degree. It's worth nothing that the 1969 N.S.F. survey of 17 large R & D facilities found that the university credit course was the preferred mode by employees for continuing their education. The professor's lecture was more popular learning situation than employer-sponsored non-credit courses, short intensive courses off-site, professional meetings and in-plant seminars. Some media experts are inclined to argue that this preference is due to many years of conditioning. Nonetheless, this preference does assist the video programming in this special educational context. The non-participants in the video-based systems are generally older; this important issue will be discussed later.

Video delivery is now enabling mature, well motivated groups of practicing engineers and other professionals to participate in graduate credit courses at their place of work. These courses are regularly scheduled offerings on campus attended by full-time students. The classes are held in specially equipped studio-classrooms so that not only the lectures but also the student questions and discussions are transmitted. Appendix A details the facilities used at Colorado State University which are typical of the classroom settings employed in all programs of this type.

---

*These estimates are crude, order-of-magnitude numbers given here to give some idea of scale. The first national survey of these programs is now underway under the guidance of a special task committee on "The Cost Effectiveness of Continuing Engineering Studies by Television" of the American Society of Engineering Education, Continuing Engineering Studies Division. The survey chairman, Mr. Albert J. Morris of Genesys Systems, Inc., has promised a fall 1973 report.

Although the studio-classroom situations are similar, there are a variety of signal delivery systems employed to link the industrial facilities to the campus. The first major system (1964) at the University of Florida employed two-way, point-to-point microwave which was leased from the telephone company, to link the main campus to several extension centers in central Florida (3). In 1969, Stanford University began serving in-plant classrooms in the San Francisco Bay Area with a four channel ITFS (Instructional Television Fixed Service) system which featured FM-talkback capability (4). Project Colorado SURGE (State University Resources for Graduate Education) was the first (1967) to employ courier carrier videotape as a delivery system (5). Some of the newer systems, such as the Oklahoma System (6), now employ interconnected combinations of point-to-point microwave for long hops, ITFS for distribution in population centers and videotape for remote areas and make-up of missed broadcasts. A list of the engineering college programs and the primary delivery systems now operating is included as Table I. Active debates concerning the relative merit of these transmission schemes once raged on the importance of interactive talkback during the class between the remote student and the professor, versus the great scheduling flexibility of videotape systems. This has subsided and discussions now center on a rational analysis of population groupings in a given region and economic analysis of how to serve then with various proven technologies. I want to come back to this point later.

TABLE I

Engineering Graduate Programs Offered Off-Campus by Television*

PROGRAM	DELIVERY MODE
GENESYS — University of Florida	Pt-to-Pt Microwave (leased)
TAGER — Southern Methodist	Pt-to-Pt Microwave (owned)
SURGE — Colorado State University	Videotape
Stanford University	ITFS and FM Talkback
University of Tennessee	Videotape
Iowa State University	Videotape
University of Colorado	Videotape
University of Minnesota	ITFS
University of Michigan	Pt-to-Pt Microwave (leased) and ITFS
University of Southern California	ITFS
Oklahoma I.T.V. Network	Pt-toPt Microwave and ITFS
University of California at Davis	Pt-to-Pt Microwave
University of Pennsylvania	ITFS
Case-Western Reserve University	ITFS
SUNY — Buffalo	ITFS
University of Arizona	Videotape
Cornell University	Videotape

*There may be a few omissions or new programs which were missed but this represents the author's best knowledge. List is approximately chronological.

A brief description of the SURGE program will illustrate many features common to these outreach programs. The course work is delivered to industries in the form of videotaped class sessions with supporting written materials, produced for classes on the CSU campus. Every course in this program is a regularly scheduled offering on campus attended by full-time students. The SURGE classes are held in specially equipped studio-classrooms so that not only the lectures but also the student questions and discussions are recorded on videotape. After the tapes are made, they are packaged with class materials, assignments and examinations and carried by a commercial delivery service to each of the industrial and government locations. The class sessions are viewed on a regularly scheduled basis by the off-campus students. The off-campus classes usually view class presentation two days following the on-campus class; over 80 percent of these off-campus sessions are during regular working hours. Tapes, however, may be retained by the industry so that any person missing a class session may see the tape at some later time. After being viewed at the off-campus location, the tapes are returned to the campus, erased, then reused to record other class sessions.

The SURGE students are required to complete the same assignments, reports and examinations as the on-campus students. Laboratory work is frequently required in electrical engineering courses; the SURGE students use the laboratory facilities of their employer to perform these studies. The students of many courses need computer facilities to complete assignments. Here again, the industrial computer facilities are utilized. To minimize the inconvenience of limited library facilities, the faculty frequently send a single Xerox copy of reference articles to each off-campus section.

In the 1972-73 academic year, 34 industrial and government facilities participated in the SURGE program. These are listed in Table II.

TABLE II

Industrial Firms and Agencies Participating in SURGE Program

Academic Year 1972-73

COMPANY OR AGENCY	LOCATION
Adolph Coors Brewery	Golden, Colorado
*Ball Brothers Corporation	Boulder, Colorado
Bell Telephone Laboratories	Denver, Colorado
Canal Zone Society of Professional Engineers	Balboa Heights, Canal Zone
C. F. & I. Steel Corporation	Pueblo, Colorado
Cobe Laboratories	Lakewood, Colorado
Colorado Department of Health	Denver, Colorado
Colorado State Penitentiary	Canon City, Colorado
*Dow Chemical Company	Golden, Colorado
Eastman Kodak Company	Windsor, Colorado
First National Bank of Denver	Denver, Colorado
Hewlett-Packard Company	Colorado Springs, Colorado
*Hewlett-Packard Company	Loveland, Colorado
*Honeywell, Inc., Test Instrument Division	Denver, Colorado
*I.B.M. Corporation	Boulder, Colorado
Lamar Community College	Lamar, Colorado
Lowry Air Force Base	Denver, Colorado
Marathon Oil Company	Littleton, Colorado
*Martin-Marietta Corporation	Denver, Colorado
Mesa College	Grand Junction, Colorado
M & I Incorporated	Fort Collins, Colorado
Mountain States Bell Telephone	Denver, Colorado
*National Center for Atmospheric Research	Boulder, Colorado
Nelson, Haley, Patterson & Quirk Inc.	Greeley, Colorado
Northeastern Junior College	Sterling, Colorado
Stearns-Roger Company	Denver, Colorado
U.S. Air Force Academy	Colorado Springs, Colorado
U.S. Bureau of Reclamation	Denver, Colorado
U.S. Bureau of Reclamation	Billings, Montana

Table II. Industrial Firms and Agencies Participating in SURGE Program (Cont'd.)

COMPANY OR AGENCY	LOCATION
U.S. Geological Survey	Denver, Colorado
U.S. Geological Survey	Cheyenne, Wyoming
White Sands Missile Range	White Sands Missile Range, New Mexico
Woodward Governor	Fort Collins, Colorado
Wyoming Highway Department	Cheyenne, Wyoming

*Original locations for initiation of program, Fall 1967.

Table III is a summary of the number of courses and locations, and student enrollments, both on-campus and off-campus, for the six-year history of the program. The important features of this tabulation are the great diversity of the offerings and the number of small, dispersed study groups. The SURGE average of reaching 3.40 students/section* and 3.78 sections/course is in sharp contrast to classical ETV style. An average of 12.9 SURGE students (3.40 x 3.78) is added to an on-campus enrollment average of 15.6 students. Thus, faculty productivity is almost doubled by the addition of the off-campus learners. This added production is obtained at a reasonable marginal cost as shown in Appendix B.

TABLE III

Colorado State University

SURGE Enrollment Summary

1967 — 1973

QUARTER	NUMBER OF COURSES	LOCATIONS	NUMBER OF STUDENTS ON-CAMPUS	NUMBER OF STUDENTS OFF-CAMPUS	TOTAL/YR. OFF-CAMPUS
Fall, 1967	4	7	105	189	
Winter, 1967	9	9	132	249	
Spring, 1968	8	9	100	206	644
Fall, 1968	12	13	283	341	
Winter, 1969	15	14	305	320	
Spring, 1969	13	15	314	288	949
Fall, 1969	15	14	209	336	
Winter, 1970	14	14	262	295	
Spring, 1970	14	14	162	165	796
Fall, 1970	17	15	232	403	
Winter, 1971	20	19	289	316	
Spring, 1971	18	16	235	202	
Summer, 1971	6	6	67	51	972
Fall, 1971	22	23	410	351	
Winter, 1972	24	22	353	284	
Spring, 1972	23	20	331	253	
Summer, 1972	7	10	79	93	976

*A "section" is a group of students enrolled in a given course at one location. Each section receives an original tape.

Table III. Colorado State University SURGE Enrollment Summary (Cont'd)

Fall, 1972	32	24	527	426	
Winter, 1973	30	28	750	426	
Spring, 1973	31	29	367	275	
Summer, 1973	17	16	96	150	1,277

Students in the SURGE program are enrolled as graduate students of CSU and are charged the regular resident, part-time tuition rate which is currently $25 per quarter hour. The participating industries and government agencies provide playback equipment, classroom facilities and administrative support of the program. No other charge is made by the university. The SURGE students receive academic credit on official CSU transcripts. No notation is made to distinguish on-campus and off-campus students in the records.

While there is no prescribed pattern, each faculty member teaching on SURGE is encouraged to make at least two visits per quarter to each industrial location for direct contact with each of his students in a class. Additional live interaction between faculty and students occurs in occasional telephone calls and, more rarely, by student visits to the campus. During the first three years of SURGE, the CSU Human Factors Research Laboratory conducted an educational evaluation of the program (7). These studies consistently indicated that the students in the remote classes were attaining levels of achievement equal to that of the on-campus students. Later surveys showed off-campus students' attitudes toward the videotape method of instruction were more favorable than to other options available to them. The faculty and on-campus students generally have favorable attitudes as well.

Advantages realized in the videotaping of upper division and graduate courses for engineers and scientists in SURGE are (8):

1. Videotape allows complete freedom of scheduling of courses at each industrial location on a two-day delayed, regular sequence.

2. Videotapes may be retained for those individuals who would otherwise miss a class because of illness or travel.

3. Students both off-campus as well as on-campus may use the tapes to review lectures.

4. Courses may be taught at locations beyond the bounds of a feasible live ITV system (there is no ITV system operating in Colorado at this time).

5. The capital cost of the videotaping operation is significantly less than a live TV system capable of providing the same opportunities.

6. Faculty may review classroom presentation for self-evaluation.

During the first six years of the SURGE program, over 50 engineers of participating companies have been awarded M.S. degrees completely through the videotape program. Over 16,000 quarter hours of university credit have been earned by other professionals without leaving their place of employment. Other benefits accrue directly to the faculty who have profited from the interaction with top practitioners in their area of interest. Much of the viability of the programs stems directly from this stimulation.

To complete this discussion of off-campus graduate programs in engineering, let me return to the problem of selecting the most cost-effective delivery system. In a recent review of the program costs reported for the Stanford ITFS, University of California at Davis, and SURGE program, Loomis and Brandt (9) point out that the dominant cost in all three systems is administrative "overhead." In fact, between $20-$30 per TV classroom lecture hour must be assigned for production and program management. This is the dominant factor in total television system cost of between $30 and $50 per TV classroom lecture hour for these three systems. Furthermore, another $4 to $7 per TV classroom lecture hour is required to outfit the TV classroom regardless of type of delivery mode. Thus, choice of delivery hardware is not as big a cost issue as one might assume at the outset and control of support staff cost requires relatively more attention. The decision process on a delivery system in a given setting might proceed by first examining the educational issues and data (if any have seen only opinions so far) concerning live audio talkback. Audio talkback can be surprisingly expensive, perhaps $1 to $7 per TV classroom lecture hour. If

> the decision is made to employ a system without talkback, the decision as to whether to use point-to-point microwave, ITFS or videotape delivery systems, depends primarily on relative cost. In general, widely scattered small class sections tend to favor a videotape operation; geographically concentrated small classes tend to favor ITFS broadcast; and concentrated large sections over potentially larger distances than the ITFS system tend to favor point-to-point microwave. (9)

On-Campus Undergraduate Programs

The use of television to reach additional, well-qualified students off-campus is a natural and non-threatening application. However, the aspirations of and live options available to full-time campus students, as well as problems with faculty attitude, has limited the applications of video technology in engineering education on-campus. On my campus, many other disciplines make far more imaginative use of video for instruction than the College of Engineering. Two interesting pilot programs, however, may be of interest. The descriptions will be brief and anecdotal, not the "hard stuff" now in vogue in educational technology circles. These programs are personal favorites of mine, though, so I will risk the hubris usually reserved for a dean's pet project.

Undergraduate study opportunities in engineering during the summer session on my campus have long been a disaster area. We cancel more courses than we teach due to poor enrollments and the courses which are taught operate at the same cost as a regular session but with a third the enrollment. This past summer session, however, we confidently announced we would offer eight required freshman and sophomore courses and we did teach all eight at less than half our usual summer session unit cost. At the suggestion of several enterprising faculty members, all eight courses were taped in a SURGE classroom as the course was taught during either the winter or spring quarter. Copies of all class handouts, notes and problem solutions were filed for use with the videotaped lectures during the summer session. A faculty member met each class for a two- to three-hour problem session each week. One of the professors experimented with a modified Keller plan (10) in which the student could view the tape on his own time schedule, follow a supplemental printed lesson plan and have open access to an undergraduate tutor. An extensive evaluation of the program pointed to numerous areas in need of improvement, but on the whole, the students understood that the videotape was a necessary ingredient to assure the diversity of the offerings. They reacted much more favorably to this experiment than they did to some of our earlier, ill-fated attempts of several years ago which occurred during the academic year.

This coming academic year one of the faculty members plans to offer a lower division elective course in this modified Keller method on "Introduction to Experimentation," packaged by Dr. Ernest Kabinowicz of the M.I.T. Center for Advanced Engineering Study. Later in the year, he will offer an upper division elective course based on video course materials we are requesting from the Bell Telephone Laboratories. Perhaps this enriching mode of introduction will encourage the use of quality video packages leased from others so they will find an appropriate niche in the regular campus offerings.

My other pet project is a freshman engineering program which has proven very popular over a six-year span of development (11). The key factor is a strong personal association which the students develop with their engineering professor-advisor during the year. A specific group of 25-30 freshman are instructed for the entire year in an integrated three quarter credit course by the same engineering professor, who also serves as their academic advisor. The subject matter ranges over computer programming, graphics, report writing and project design. That's right: electrical engineering professors teach graphs as a personal sacrifice to encourage the student-faculty relationship. The average number of office consultations which the students made last fall quarter was 3.4. Figure 1 demonstrates the strongly favorable response which this professor-advisor scheme receives on an independently run, anonymous evaluation.

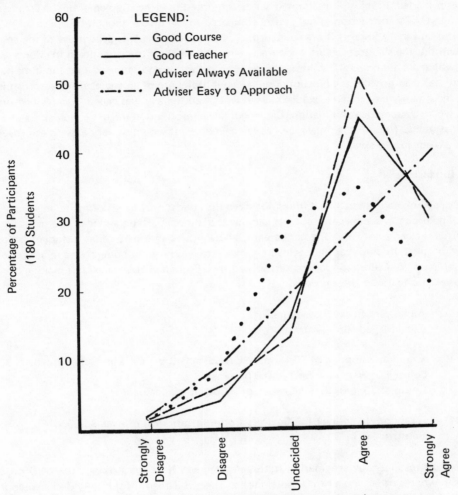

Figure 1. Satisfaction survey results for freshman engineering course.

The educational technology component of this program is an outgrowth of increased engineering faculty awareness of the problems incurred by freshmen. Following serious complaints that the residence halls were noisy (e.g., "My roommate who is studying X never studies."), we had one wing (of four) of a co-educational dormitory complex closest to the Engineering Building reserved for engineering applicants. A lounge area was outfitted with blackboards, electronic calculators, reference books, and manned regularly by undergraduate tutors chosen on the basis of high academic ability and good personality. Another room housed a Computer Managed Learning System terminal (12) which offered instruction on the slide rule and a computer card punch.

Each room in the residence hall has an outlet to two CATV systems, one of the area commercial and ETV broadcast stations and the other channel operated by the College of Engineering as an ITV program to supplement classroom credit offerings. Three channels were regularly operated on weekly offerings. Three channels were regularly operated on week days from about 10 a.m. to 10 p.m. last academic year. One channel continuously presented the day's schedule and special announcements concerning campus events, seminars, student society meetings. The other two channels repetitively presented coordinated programs on college algebra, calculus, study skills and FORTRAN. To increase viewing, the graduate student in meteorology presented a local weather report three times a week. Fifteen engineering orientation films obtained from various technical societies, government agencies and other universities were shown regularly throughout the year. At the end of fall quarter, 97% agreed (67% strongly) that "a special dorm for engineering students is a good idea." A total of 85% agreed that good use was made of the special facilities provided. Frankly, I was somewhat disappointed that the supplemental CATV instruction did not receive better use. CATV instruction faired poorly compared to the tutors, though I suspect CATV did quite well compared to the university library! But to our surprise, the students made excellent use of the engineering orientation films without the slightest faculty encouragement. Over 68% of the students in the dorm watched the orientation films (which are a mixed lot!) voluntarily, on their own time and reported that the films helped them. Please bear in mind that traditionally the most unpopular event in the life of an engineering freshman is to be required to watch these same films in large lecture halls in what traditionally was called "Dean's Lectures." I believe this hint is worth systematic examination. Career guidance information might be welcomed on community and campus CATV systems. The surveys I have seen convince me that it would be very easy to improve on the traditional faculty advisor in this area.

Some Challenging Extensions

The SURGE program, and others like it, does not serve the educational needs of many engineers where the TV signal reaches. The program assumes that the off-campus students can attend and learn in the usual campus graduate courses. This is clearly not true. The mathematical background in use by today's student far surpasses the original training of most 40-plus year old engineers. This point was brought home to me in a recent survey which we conducted in one of Colorado's largest aerospace firms. From a professional staff mailing list of over 3,000, we mailed a questionnaire to three groups:

> Group A — All current SURGE students.
> Total Mailed: 65. Returns: 45, or 69.2%

> Group B — A random sampling of 70 former SURGE students, men who had enrolled
> before but were no longer in the program.
> Returns: 20, plus 9 undelivered, or 28.6% usable returns.

> Group C — A random sampling of 250 names from the entire list of over 3,000.
> Returns: 76, or 30.4%.

Table IV summarizes the responses by age, marital status, and degrees. Note the striking skew of Groups B and C to older employees in what is otherwise a similar total group. There is a need for specially designed courseware for the older engineers which the graduate curriculum does not satisfy. The problem here is largely an economic one, because the universities do not have on-going campus instruction to add these potential students to. If you add the usual direct cost of instruction, say $100 lecture hour, to the video system costs of $30-$50 TV lecture hour, the funding problem gets tough. Yet, these employees do need an opportunity to revitalize their education at mid-career, because the social costs of not doing so are great indeed. Perhaps the federal government should examine this problem and identify an appropriate role for its involvement. The problem is of a "software cost" nature, not delivery hardware or methodology.

A second opportunity is in the area of career guidance. The orientation films now available are generally marginal at best. We need honest, timely presentations not the heroic propaganda of yesteryear. The opportunity to inform young people about the career options open to them through the use of guidance films on CATV is a real one. It is information that young people seek which can be supplied via a medium which fits their life style. Quality films are needed.

TABLE IV

Survey of Engineers at a Major Colorado Aerospace Firm

	PERCENT RESPONSE		
AGE	**GROUP A**	**GROUP B**	**GROUP C**
20-25	20	10	3
26-30	38	25	20
31-35	27	5	22
36-40	9	15	13
41-45	2	25	20
46-50	0	15	16
51-55	2	0	4
56-60	0	0	3
61-up	0	0	0
No Response	2	5	0
MARITAL STATUS			
Married	89	85	80
Single	9	10	16
No Response	2	5	4
DEGREES			
Partial	0	0	3
AB or AS	2	0	3
BS	78	70	57
MS	16	15	18
BA	0	10	4
MA	2	0	1
PhD	0	0	4
Other	2	15	4
No Response	2	0	6

Some have several unrelated degrees.

The open learning concept is receiving a great deal of attention now. The structures are beginning to take shape in parts of the United States. I have yet to hear of an open learning system which would employ the open door or TV studio-classroom technique already proven economical and educationally sound in engineering graduate programs. Why not add students to campus classes as we do in SURGE and reach these people in their homes via CATV or in study groups at their place of employment? I have heard much about the shortcomings of "the face of the tube," but I have yet to see a plan which would increase higher educational productivity in a more natural fashion. The obvious advantage of the SURGE methodology is its low cost and great diversity of courseware. Many of our U.S. universities have the traditions and ability to explore this simple form of extending classroom learning situations to nearby locations. Shouldn't it at least be tried as a part of our general exploration of the open learning concept?

The public policy and administrative issues associated with the introduction of educational technology are complex. But as a middle level manager in higher education, I am more concerned with old budget practices which preclude a fair hearing of technically based instructional options. The total lack of consideration which is given to capital outlay amortization in budget preparation can no longer be tolerated. In a growing system, physical plant construction may be financed over several years by bonds. But rarely do public officials make a decision from alternatives which recognize that most technically based options are capital intensive and will not survive a budget exercise which focuses on minimum expenditure *that year.* State officials strive increasingly to control annual expenditures and rightfully so, but "tight budgets" are wedded to fixed labor costs and perpetuate the spiraling costs of a labor intensive system. I believe that officials managing federal programs must recognize that innovational diffusion is greatly inhibited by our inability in education to plan capital expenditures properly.

REFERENCES

1. American Society for Engineering Education, "Final Report: Goals of Engineering Education," *J. of Engineering Education,* 58 (Jan., 1968).

2. Social Research, "Continuing Education for R & D Careers," Prepared for the National Science Foundation, NSF 69-20 (1969).

3. Nattress, John A., "Genesys—Past, Present and Future," unpublished report, College of Engineering, University of Florida.

4. School of Engineering, Stanford University, "Report on the Stanford Instructional Television Network," (April 1969-August 1971), Stanford, California (Aug., 1971).

5. Baldwin, Lionel V., "In-plant Graduate Courses on Videotape: Project Colorado SURGE," *J. of Engineering Education,* 1055-1058 (May, 1969).

6. Kriegel, M. W., "Application of Technology in Continuing Education," paper presented at 1972 FEAM/UNESCO Seminar on Continuing Education of Engineers, Helsinki, Finland (Aug. 21-24, 1972).

7. Baldwin, Lionel V. and C. O. Neidt. "Use of Video Tape for Teaching In-Plant Graduate Engineering Courses," *Adult Education,* Vol. XX, No. 3, pp. 154-167 (1970).

8. Davis, Preston, "Engineers Run the Show at CSU," *Education Screen and Audio Visual Guide* (May, 1969).

9. Loomis, H.H., Jr., and Brandt, H., "Television as a Tool in Engineering Education," Special issue of *I.E.E.E. Transactions on Education, E6,* Issue 2, pp. 101-109 (May, 1973).

10. Stice, James E. (editor), "The Personalized System of Instruction (PSI), The Keller Plan Applied in Engineering Education," Bureau of Engineering Teaching, University of Texas at Austin, Bulletin No. 4 (Dec., 1971).

11. Britton, C.C. and Schweizer, H.H., "Freshman Engineering Program at Colorado State University," paper submitted for publication to *J. of Engineering Education* (1973).

12. Hayman, R.W. and W. Lord, "A Technology-Based Educational System Using Computer Management," *Educational Technology* (December, 1972) Vol. XXII, No. 12, pp. 43-52.

13. Baldwin, L.V., Davis, P., and L.M. Maxwell. "Innovative, Off-Campus Programs of Colorado State University," Special report to the President's Science Advisory Committee Panel on Educational Research and Development, Colorado State University (April, 1972).

14. C.S.U. Principal Investigators, "Innovative Educational Programs of Colorado State University," Special report to Advisory Committee for Science Education of the National Science Foundation, Colorado State University (July, 1973).

APPENDIX A

SURGE FACILITIES

Studio Classrooms — One of the four CSU studio classrooms is illustrated in Figure 2. Each classroom is equipped with at least three cameras. A camera over the instructor's desk allows him to display written or illustrative materials. The instructor controls the overhead camera for functions such as zooming, focusing and composing. A monitor at the instructor's desk displays the picture being generated by the overhead camera. Another camera at the back of the room is mounted on a pan-tilt head; this camera is controlled by a technician in the central record facility. The technician may remotely pan-tilt zoom and focus the rear camera. If the instructor goes to the three-panel chalkboard or walks around the room, the technician follows his movements. A wide angle, fixed camera at the front of the room is located to pick up a segment of the student class. By means of switches at the instructor's desk, the instructor selects the camera which is to be recorded. Two rooms have split-screen capability which allows the instructor to show two pictures on a single screen. Two monitors are located at the front of the room to allow students in the class to see all material presented via the overhead camera. A button is located in front of each student to activate an overhead microphone, which picks up the questions and other dialogue between the professor and students. Because students sometimes fail to push the microphone button, a similar button is located at the instructor's desk and the console at the recording head-quarters.

Two of the studio classrooms are identical to that shown in Figure 2. These rooms each seat 30 students. A third studio-classroom was tailored for the needs of the highly interactive instructional methods which are common in the College of Business. This seminar room accommodates 16 students around a large oval table. The TV camera arrangement is similar to that outlined above. A fourth studio-classroom seats 125 students in a small, wedge-shaped auditorium.

Control Console — Each classroom has an individual console at the recording facilities where a technician (frequently a work-study undergraduate student) is employed whenever an instructor is in the classroom. Figure 3 is a view of this area. The technician operates the back camera electronically from this location. He has tele-phone communications to the professor and can override the audio gain. Courses are not rehearsed, thus, the technician listens to the class presentation and takes verbal cues so as to display the best picture possible on videotape.

Record Area—The record facility shown in Figure 4 consists of thirty-two videotape recorders and monitors on which tapes are made for the remote locations. An original videotape record is made as the class is conducted on-campus for each off-campus section. A switcher designed by the television staff is used to program the needed number of recorders for any given course. The number of tapes needed for each classroom varies from hour to hour.

Tape Delivery—Each videotape in the inventory is given a number. A card catalogue is maintained on all tapes recording the location of each videotape within the system. Tapes are packaged in fiber shipping cases and addressed for the proper destination. Each evening the tapes are picked up by commercial courier (United Parcel Service) for delivery the next day at each remote location. Approximately 400 tapes are shipped to the remote locations weekly.

In-Plant Classroom — At most in-plant locations, a multi-purpose conference room serves as the regularly scheduled SURGE classroom. One or two 23-inch TV monitors and a videorecorder are the only special equipment.

Figure 2. Studio Classroom Instructor's Console

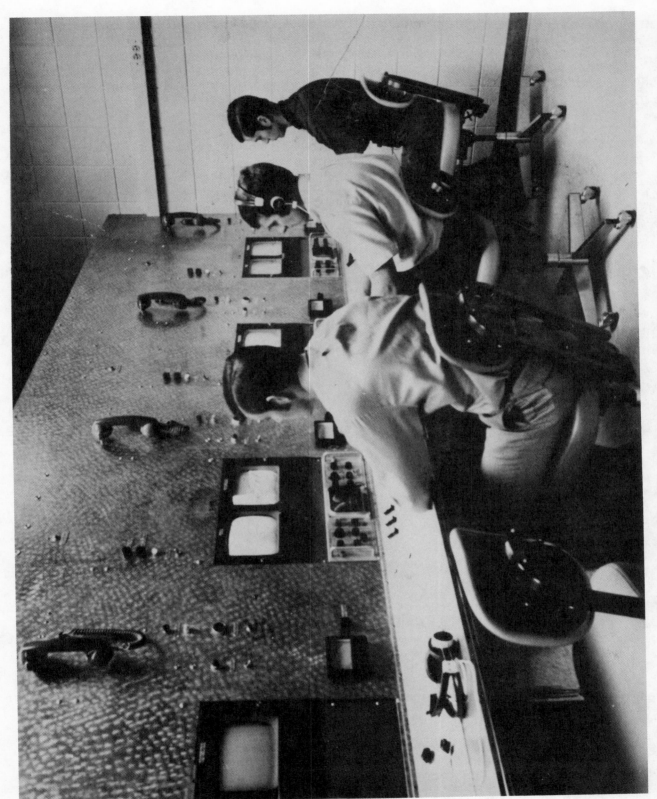

Figure 3. Central Recording Control Console

193

Figure 4. Central Recording Facility

194

In 1967, Ampex one-inch tape machines were employed solely, but less than half of the locations now rely on this machine. The most popular machine in use today is the half-inch EIAS machine, but it is losing favor to the three-quarter-inch Cassette recorder. CSU supplies all three tape formats.

APPENDIX B*

COST ANALYSIS OF SURGE PROGRAM

The institutional setting can greatly affect the costs of any program. In order to properly qualify the information to be presented concerning costs of the off-campus programs, a brief statement concerning the Colorado State University setting is in order.

Colorado State University in 1967 did not have a history of either off-campus general extension of evening courses offered on-campus for part-time students. Consequently, the university had no administrative superstructure to manage general extension. Faculty were not accustomed to extra pay for off-campus or evening instruction. When the SURGE program was initiated by the College of Engineering, the Dean of Engineering chose to integrate the activity into the resident graduate programs of the departments. The Dean of the Graduate School obtained approval from the faculty committees and faculty government for the changes of traditional rules necessary to accomplish this integration. The faculty, therefore, added the part-time students to regular classes with the full expectation that traditional standards of graduate student attainment would be met. It was also possible to obtain the full impact of increased faculty productivity without the burden of a new administrative structure.

On the other hand, the University had taken steps in 1965 to organize media support within the Office of Educational Media as a central service organization. The function of this organization is to provide University-wide media support through its five operating units: Audio-visual, Graphics, Motion Picture, Photographic and Television Services. The total level of expenditure of the Office of Educational Media for staff and expenses in 1972-73 was approximately $500,000.

When television was implemented on campus at Colorado State University in 1965, a television policy was adopted by the governing board which placed the responsibility within the Office of Educational Media for: general supervision of all TV programs, purchase, inventory and maintenance of all equipment, all operating funds for the production and distribution of televised materials for resident instruction. Professional staff were employed for the television operation. Moreover, staff of the Office of Educational Media had demonstrated a strong willingness and ability to deliver. Thus, the placement of this responsibility was not a function of authority but rather a means of obtaining a coordinated, well-managed program with an avoidance of splintering and duplication.

Projects such as SURGE, CO-TIE, HI-TIE and others have been smoothly integrated into an active campus program. There are several advantages to this procedure. Much test apparatus and other equipment needed for the on-campus program is available to be used for the new off-campus program. One highly qualified television engineer is able to design the off-campus program components as well as the growing campus system of TV. Videotape, recorders, and related items are bid in University-wide quantities, thus reducing cost. Technical standards and equipment compatibility is maintained and improved utilization of both facilities and staff is realized. As the off-campus programs at Colorado State University expand into many disciplines, the inclusion of such efforts under a single service organization continues to be advantageous. Of course, all academic decisions remain the responsibility of the academic departments and colleges involved.

The cost of instruction for the SURGE program which serves practicing engineers and professionals in industry can be estimated with precision, because the program has completed six years of operation and attained

---

*This material has appeared in two previous unpublished CSU reports (refs. 13 and 14).

a relatively stable level of activity. The following discussion concentrates on this program although much of the information on the cost of operation is applicable generally to all regularly scheduled courses videotaped for use off-campus.

Faculty productivity measured in terms of student-credit hours, increased significantly in SURGE courses. The five-year average enrollment of students per course is 16.2 on-campus and 18.2 off-campus. There has been no adjustment in faculty teaching schedules due to this additional load. Rather, grading and graduate assistant help has been supplied to accommodate the increased enrollment.

The "direct cost of instruction" on-campus in the traditional mode is defined here as the instruction cost (faculty salaries) divided by the total number of student quarter credit hours associated with that instruction. This index is frequently cited as a measure useful for comparing regional variations between similar schools and between various disciplines. Clearly, although a dominant cost in most instruction, this factor does not represent the total cost of instruction. The direct cost of instruction on-campus in the CSU College of Engineering averaged over all levels of instruction in 1972-73 is $37.45 per quarter student credit hour (qt. cr.). Comparable data gathered by Dr. F.E. Terman and averaged over seventy-one engineering colleges yields $49/qt. cr. (*J. Engr. Ed., 59,* pp. 510-514 (1969); a six per cent annual increase was assumed to update these data). It is widely recognized that graduate level instruction is appreciably more costly than undergraduate and that wide variations in this index are usually found between the physical sciences and social sciences. For the M.S. level SURGE courses, which are predominantly in engineering and mathematics, the CSU direct cost of instruction on-campus has been estimated to be $65./qt. cr. This figure is viewed as a conservative estimate for graduate instruction, which averages 16 students per course. Any effective, non traditional instructional system would generally be expected to compete with $65./qt. cr. if introduced on-campus. We apply such a comparison directly to the off-campus instruction of the SURGE program.

The cost of the SURGE program can be divided into three broad categories: (1) amortization of equipment, recording space and tape, (2) operating cost of production, delivery and program administration, and (3) incremental direct instructional cost of adding off-campus students to existing classes. We discuss these cost categories in the following paragraphs in a manner which makes the scaling laws of the program clear. That is, we will focus on the cost of recording a class hour in a studio classroom plus the cost of making and delivering tape copies with instructional support.

Equipment, Recording Space and Tape — The cost per hour of recording is dominated by the amortization of the $25,000 for the remodeling and equipping of a studio classroom and control console. Table B-1 gives the details. Assuming five-year amortization with six per cent interest and 1000 hours per year of utilization, we calculate $6./hr. Note that only the cost of the TV facility is considered, because a regular on-campus class must be held in a classroom, and we are interested only in the direct cost of adding off-campus students via video tape.

A video recorder and monitor ($800) was amortized over three years assuming 1000 hours/year of use and six per cent interest. The resultant cost is $0.30/hr.

An hour reel of 1/2-inch videotape purchased in large lots costs $20. An average life of 100 uses yields $0.20/hr. The videotape original copy which is costed here is not distributed to off-campus students, but rather serves as a redundant or spare copy to insure system reliability.

The central recording facility space which houses the control console and a single recording unit is 300 sq. ft. This space was valued at $30/sq. ft. and amortized over 40 years with interest. This cost increment is $60/hr.

The total cost in this category for recording an hour's class time is the sum of the above or $7.10/hr.

Each additional tape copy requires $0.30/tape for recorders and monitors and $0.20/tape for the tape inventory. That is, the incremental cost in this category for each additional tape is $0.50/tape.

TABLE B1

Studio Classroom and Master Control Station

Capital Outlay

(For Black and White TV Equipment)

3 TV Cameras @ 1,000	$ 3,000
1 Sync generator	1,000
1 Pan tilt control unit	1,100
5 TV monitors @ 160	800
2 Zoom lenses @ 1,100	2,200
Instruction desk with control unit, split screen generator, and back pack play back recorder	4,000
Electronic control, amplifiers, cables special room wiring	2,300
Master control panel with TV monitors, switching unit	5,600
Studio classroom air conditioning and necessary remodeling	5,000
Total Cost	$25,000

Operating Cost of Office of Educational Media — The basic operating budget for production and program management at CSU for the current level of activity (80 courses/year) is $60,300. This budget includes fractional time of an administrator, a program coordinator and a TV engineer plus two full time TV technicians and a secretary. Other direct costs include student labor, supplies and spare parts, travel and telephone, and program correspondence. At the level of 80 courses per year or 2400 recording hours, this base operating budget is $25.25/ recording hour. Details are given in Table B-2.

A recent survey of both the CSU videotape system, the ITFS broadcast system of Stanford University and the microwave link of the University of California at Davis and the A.E.C. facility at Livermore showed these "overhead costs" to be dominant in all systems (ref. 9).

Each tape copy of an hour's length requires an additional $0.50 for tape handling and $2.50 for round-trip delivery by commercial courier. The incremental cost in this category for each delivered tape is $3.00/tape.

Operating Cost of Instruction — The faculty does not receive any additional pay or work load allowance for teaching a regular campus classs in the studio-classroom. So there is no instructional cost for the recording hour. Rather it is the instructional support of the off-campus students which must be estimated here. The marginal cost of adding 15 students to a 3 quarter credit course is assumed to be 10 hours/week of graduate teaching assistance to help the professor with all aspects of the instruction. This allowance amounts to $1.00 for each off-campus student who views an hour length tape, or if we let S be the average off-campus enrollment in a SURGE location, $1.00 S/tape. To this incremental direct cost we add an allowance for secretarial support, supplies and telephone of $0.30 for each off-campus student who views a tape, or $0.30 S/tape. A travel allowance of the direct cost of faculty visits to the SURGE locations is $1.25/tape, independent of the number of students in a location but directionally proportional to the number of locations (or tape copies made each recording session).

The total cost of instructional operating expenses can be expressed in formula fashion as: $.75 + $1.30S$/tape, where S is the average student enrollment in each off-campus section.

Total Cost of SURGE Instruction — The factors outlined above are summarized in the following table in 1971-72 dollars:

TABLE B2

Base Operating Costs

			PRESENT LEVEL	EXPANDED LEVEL
Administrator	$24,000.	1/10 time 1/10 time	$ 2,400.	$ 2,400.
Coordinator	$16,000.	½ time ¾ time	8,000.	12,000.
TV Engineer	$15,000.	1/5 time 1/5 time	3,000.	3,000.
TV Technicians	$10,800.	2 full time 3 full time	21,600.	32,200.
Secretary	$ 5,300.	1 full time 1½ full time	5,300.	8,000.
Student Labor	@ $2/hr	3000 hrs. 6000 hrs.	6,000.	12,000.
Travel and Telephone			3,000.	3,000.
Supplies and Spare Parts			8,000.	11,700.
Printing and Mailing Announcements			3,000.	3,800.
			$60,300.	$88,100.

Allocated to each master recording on an hourly basis, these cost factors are:

$$\frac{60,300}{2,400} = $25.12/hr.$$ Current operation of 80 courses annually.

or

$$\frac{89,100}{4,800} = $18.56/hr.$$ Expanded operation of 160 courses annually.

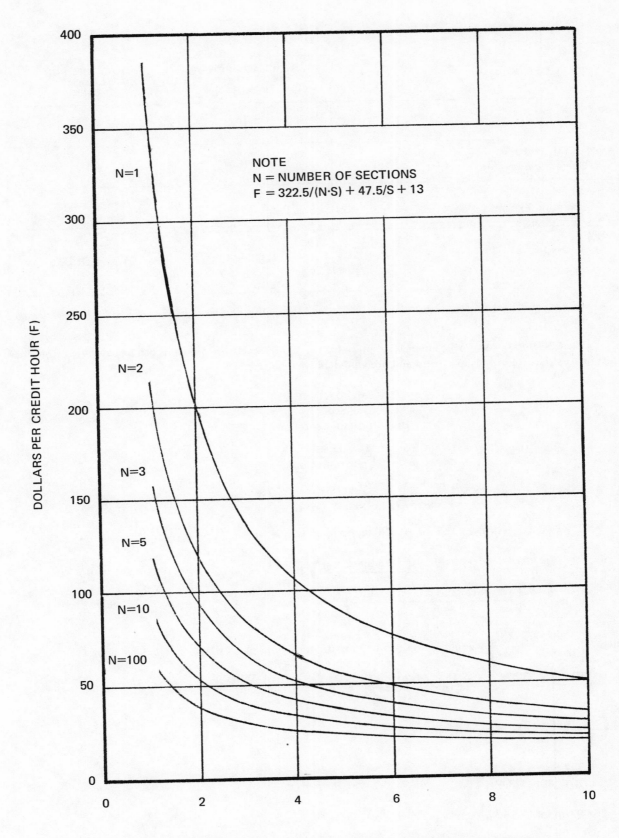

Figure B-1. *CSU Off-Campus TV Cost Analysis.*

199

	DOLLARS PER RECORDING HOUR	DOLLARS PER DELIVERED TAPE
Equipment, Space and Tape	7.10	0.50
Office of Ed. Media Operating Expenses	25.15*	3.00
Instructional Operating Expenses	−	1.25 + 1.30 S
Total	$32.25	$4.75 + $1.30 S

*Based on ability to operate at current CSU level of 80 courses/year. This value becomes about $18.56 for an enlarged program of 160 courses/year.

The CSU unit costs of off-campus instruction for the 1971-72 SURGE programs can be computed from these cost factors. The following enrollment and program data are required:

$$\text{Total Courses} = 69$$
$$\text{Total Sections} = 261$$
$$\text{Total off-campus enrollment} = 883$$

Therefore, $N = \dfrac{261}{69} = 3.78 \left(\dfrac{\text{sections}}{\text{course}}\right)$ or $\left(\dfrac{\text{tapes}}{\text{recording hour}}\right)$

$S = \dfrac{883}{261} = 3.40 \left(\dfrac{\text{students}}{\text{section}}\right)$

and let C = 1.00 qt. credits granted for 10 contact hours of course work.

$$F = \dfrac{\left(\dfrac{\text{recording hours}}{\text{course}}\right)\left(\dfrac{\text{dollars}}{\text{recording hour}}\right)}{\left(\dfrac{\text{av. off-campus student credits}}{\text{course}}\right)}$$

where $\left(\dfrac{\text{dollars}}{\text{recording hour}}\right)$ is subdivided into fixed cost/course hour plus variable costs/course hour.

$$F = \dfrac{(10C) \cdot \left(\dfrac{\$32.25 + [\$4.75 \cdot \$1.30] N}{N \cdot S \cdot C}\right)}{}$$

$$F = \left(\dfrac{322.5}{NS}\right) + \left(\dfrac{47.5}{S}\right) + 13.$$

$$F = \dfrac{322.5}{(3.78)(3.40)} + \dfrac{47.5}{3.40} + 13.$$

F = $51.97/qt. cr. ≈ $52./qt. cr.

Recall that the on-campus instruction in these courses has a direct instructional cost of $65./qt. cr. for an average course enrollment in 1971-72 of 15.6 students. The average cost of instruction for *both* on-campus and off-campus instruction is:

$$F_{ave} = \frac{15.6\ (65.)\ +\ 12.9(52.)}{15.6\quad 12.9} = \$59/\text{qt. cr.}$$

Clearly, the program lowers the instructional cost from the point of view of the university and also increases faculty productivity. But it should be stressed that this is a very narrow view of the cost of this instruction. If the part-time student had commuted to campus during his regular work hours, the opportunity cost which is neglected here would have been large indeed—perhaps, $300./qt. cr.! Furthermore, the university may have been required to add campus classroom space and parking. Even more important, the cumulative cost of technical obsolescence to the national economy should be estimated because advanced engineering and management training frequently does not occur unless programs like SURGE are initiated.

A convenient graphical presentation of the SURGE program cost analysis is given in Figure B-1. The marginal cost per quarter credit hour produced (F) is shown as a function of the average number of students per section (s) with the total number of sections per course (N) shown as a parameter. In the CSU example detailed above, S = 3.40 students/section and N = 3.78 sections/course which yields F = $59/quarter credit. It is worth noting that video based programs for practicing engineers such as SURGE are far removed from the classical ETV model. That is, rather than $50,000/hour of production costs spread over millions of viewers, the televised engineering programs must operate at near zero production cost because the potential audience is small. In fact, the TAGER system of SMU in Dallas will televise a course for a total of 4 students, the Iowa State University videotape system sets a total enrollment minimum of 5, and the CSU record in this regard shows instances of taping for 2-3 total off-campus students.

The cost factors tabulated above are realistic and may be useful more generally than simply estimating the cost of a specific program in Colorado. For example, the decision whether to install a videotape system or an ITFS broadcast system, is a trade-off study between subtracting $3.50 N (the cost of making and delivering tapes) and adding the amortized cost of the ITFS hardware on a course hour basis to the base value of $7.10. For example, see "Technical and Economic Factors in University ITV Systems," by C.A. Martin Vegue, Jr., A.J. Morris, J.M. Rosenberg, and S.E. Tallmadge, Proceedings of the IEE, Vol. 59, No. 6, pp. 946-953 (June 1971).

THE BRITISH OPEN UNIVERSITY: CONCEPTS AND REALITIES

Brian Lewis
The Open University
Institute of Educational Technology
Buckinghamshire, England

PART I — TEACHING AT THE OPEN UNIVERSITY

Introductory Remarks

The Open University was established (by Royal Charter) in 1969, with a permit to start teaching in January 1971. This may not sound too difficult. However, no conventional British University had ever been set up so quickly. And the Open University was certainly *not* conventional.

The Open University is an ambitious project. Its declared aim is to bring higher education within the reach of many thousands of adults who are able to study only on a part-time basis, and in their own homes. Moreover, it is striving to do this for adults who have *none* of the usual entry qualifications. And it is relying for its success on the novel deployment of a wide range of educational and mass media resources.

In short, the Open University is the first attempt, in Britain, to set up a full-scale home-based, multi-media system for higher education. As the original government committee put it:

> The objects of the Open University are to provide opportunities, at both undergraduate and postgraduate level, of higher education to all those who for any reason have been or are being precluded from achieving their aims through an existing institution of higher education. This does not imply competition with existing institutions, but rather an attempt on a national scale to complement their efforts; an attempt which may well increase the demands upon existing institutions, as students, stimulated by the experience of part-time study, increasingly come to want the opportunity for full-time study.

At the time of its conception, the (proposed) Open University had no close precedents anywhere in the world. Nobody had any clear idea of how many students might want to enroll, or what they would be like, or what their abilities might be. The one attempt to forecast possible demand came from a survey carried out by the National Institute of Adult Education. This came up with a forecast ranging from 34,000 to 150,000 in respect of those people who said, "I will certainly be one of the first students."

For financial and administrative reasons, it was necessary to restrict the size of the first intake of students — with the result that 24,000 students were provisionally registered (in 1970) and 20,000 of these actually paid their fees and started work in January 1971. By the close of the year as many as 80% had stayed the course, and 75% of these passed their examinations. This pattern of success was repeated in 1972, and the public image of the Open University is now gratifyingly high. At the time of writing this overview (September 1973), the Open University has just held its first graduation ceremony in respect of 900 graduates. The current student population stands at around 40,000. And over 35,000 applications have already been received in respect of courses due to commence in January 1974. The prevailing mood within the Open University is one of cautious self-congratulation. Everybody recognizes that the system is far from perfect. But the political decision to give it a chance seems to have been well vindicated.

202

The Main Teaching Arrangements

As already indicated, the Open University is primarily a home-based study facility. The primary teaching resources are:

1. Postal packages of home study materials

2. Nationwide television and radio programs

3. Local study centers

4. Short residential summer schools

The home study materials and the television and radio programs convey the "core" content of the courses. The local study centers provide opportunities for students to study and to discuss their problems either (a) among themselves, or (b) with visiting tutors or counsellors. The short residential summer schools, which are usually held in host universities, enable students to get together in large numbers and for more ambitious purposes. A variety of additional teaching aids — such as home experimental kits, computer terminals, self-administered comprehension tests, homework and fieldwork assignments, tutor-marked and computer-marked feedback on homework, and assorted audio-visual aids — all help the student to consolidate his learning and to monitor his progress in an accurate way.

To obtain a degree at the Open University (OU), a student must accumulate 6 "course credits" for an ordinary degree, and 8 "course credits" for an honors degree. To do this, the student must successfully complete 6-8 courses of study, at a rate of not more than 2 courses per year. Each course calls for about 12 hours of home study per week, sustained over a period of about 9 months of the year. So all students are able to accumulate the required number of credits in their spare time, if they so desire.

In its first year of teaching (1971), the OU initiated "foundation" (first year) courses in the Arts, Social Sciences, Mathematics and Science. In its second year of teaching, a first year foundation course was also started in Technology, along with second level courses in Arts, Social Science, Mathematics, Science and Educational Studies. Six course credits secure a general (B.A.) degree, and *eight* course credits secure an honors (B.A.) degree. In certain cases, students can be granted exemption from 1-3 of the lower-level courses, and this reduces the time needed to qualify. It therefore takes about 3-5 years for most students to obtain a degree, although every effort is being made to allow slower students to complete their degrees at a slower rate (e.g., one course per year) if they so desire.

Professional training and "up-dating" courses are also being run—e.g., in Education, Computing, and in various branches of Technology. The first of these have already been started, and later ones will be determined by public demand and available resources. They will be of shorter duration (requiring, say, the accumulation of only 1-3 course credits), and will lead to the award of certificates or diplomas. A postgraduate program, leading to the award of higher degrees, has also been launched. In all cases, the OU aims to use essentially the same kind of "teaching at a distance" multi-media approach.

It is worth adding that the Open University's courses are in general designed to have practical application in the real world. They are seeking to meet genuine social and economic needs, and they should therefore be of practical value both to the student and to potential employers.

Who the Students Are

As already indicated, the OU is first and foremost a University for adults. In the years to come, it may become both possible and desirable to accept ordinary school leavers in (say) the 18-21 age range. However, the initial decision was to admit nobody under 21, unless there were exceptional circumstances (e.g. of physical disability) which would prevent a person under 21 from gaining acceptance elsewhere. At the request of the Department of

Education and Science, the University is currently planning to accept 500 18-year olds as a pilot experiment in 1974. 250 of these will be technically qualified for University entry, and 250 will not.

In its efforts to offer higher education to as many adults as possible, the OU has waived many of the traditional entry requirements. It therefore caters to a large number of people who would otherwise have been prevented from pursuing degree courses. These include adults in full-time employment, housewives who find it hard to leave their homes, persons who do not have the usually mandatory educational qualifications, persons who are physically handicapped, and persons who live too far away from already-existing colleges of higher education. Among the fully employed part-time students, there is already a significant number of adults who are looking to the Open University (a) to provide qualifications for an alternative career, or (b) to provide the kinds of specialist up-dating and retraining courses that have already been mentioned.

The implications of such a radical "open door" policy should not be overlooked. It gives rise to a highly heterogeneous population of students — of varying age levels and interests and backgrounds — and adds greatly to the complications of teaching effectively at a distance. By way of example, diagram 1 gives some summary background data in respect of the 6,790 students who studied the first year foundation course in science during 1971.

What the Study Materials Look Like

Study materials are sent through the post to the student, at intervals of about 4-6 weeks. Each package contains a sequence of correspondence materials, accompanied by study notes, exercises and experiments, and self-administered comprehension tests which the student can take to help satisfy himself that he has understood the main teaching points. Also included is a set of written homework assignments which the student is expected to return, within a specified time period, for marking, some of these assignments are marked directly by the OU computer, and others are marked by specially appointed part-time correspondence tutors.

The "core" correspondence materials are (usually) specially written by members of the OU's central academic staff. The remaining materials consist of carefully chosen extracts and offprints, taken from standard textbooks and other professional literature. Each package also contains discussion notes (which the students are invited to discuss among themselves), and recommendations concerning suitable follow-up reading. Additional materials in the form of audio tapes, long-playing records, and transparencies are included in some study packages.

Most study materials make a special point of giving the student a variety of things to *do*. Tasks are set which can take the form of pencil-and-paper tests and exercises, scheduled observations, group discussions, home experiments, local fieldwork, and the like. The aim of such tasks is to create experiences in the student which help to confirm and consolidate the expositions contained in the printed texts. In particular, all science and technology students receive a comprehensive home experimental kit which requires controlled and systematic use and reportage.

So far as is possible, each study package is a self-contained entity. It provides the student with everything that he needs, in order to advance his studies for a further 4-6 weeks. In some courses, it has been found necessary to refer the student to "set books" that he is expected to buy or borrow from his library. But the study packages constitute in general, the core materials of the course.

The Role of the British Broadcasting Corporation —
an Educational Partnership

To reinforce and supplement the packaged study materials, the University works in collaboration with the B.B.C. to produce a regular series of radio and television programs. At the present time, facilities exist for the transmission of one radio and one television program per week, in respect of almost every main course that the OU is planning to run. Transmissions occur mostly at off-peak listening and viewing times. Each program is

Summary data on occupation, educational background, and age of the total intake of 6,790 students who studied first-year Science in 1971.

Occupation	%
Housewives	4.8
Armed Forces	2.3
Admin. and managers	5.0
Education	26.5
Professional and arts	7.2
Scientists and engs.	11.6
Technical personnel	23.6
Skilled trades	2.5
Other manual	1.6
Communic'n and transport	0.9
Clerical and office	3.9
Shop and personal serv.	3.2
Retired/Not working	1.1

Educational level attained	%
No formal quals.	6.6
CSE—RSA Cert.	1.6
GCE "O" level, 1—4 Subj.	6.9
GCE "O" level, 5+ Subj.	11.3
GCE A level, 1 Subj.	3.5
GCE A level, 2+ Subj.	9.7
ONC or OND	6.8
HNC or HND	19.3
Teacher's Certificate	18.7
University Diploma	6.2
University Degree	4.5

Date of birth	%
Post 1945	10.8
1936-1945	44.4
1926-1935	30.0
1916-1925	12.2
1906-1915	2.1
Pre 1906	0.4

Diagram 1

broadcast twice — once in the early evening of a weekday, and once on a week-end morning. So every student has two opportunities to listen and view. This is a substantial undertaking which greatly enhances the effectiveness of the written study materials. However, it will not be possible to repeat programs in future years unless more radio and television channels become available. And plans are already under way for "dawn" listening and viewing.

Radio is used in a variety of ways—to orientate the student toward studies that he is just about to commence, to discuss subjects that are inadequately dealt with in the correspondence materials, to recapitulate or summarize materials that have already been studied, and so on. Radio is also used to communicate with students at short notice — e.g. to clear up recurring points of difficulty, or to make announcements of interest to certain sections of the student population. Occasionally, arrangements have been made for nation-wide hook-ups between central administrative and academic staff, regional staff, and volunteer student spokesmen.

Television can also have a valuable orientating function, especially at the beginning of a course when the student is struggling to make sense of unfamiliar concepts. However, it is most commonly used, at the present time, to convey information that requires special visual effects. Lectures and demonstrations which involve the use of special (e.g. scientific) equipment, small group discussions on matters of controversy, visual accounts of the Arts and Sciences, of developing technology, of political and economic and educational systems, of unfamiliar countries and societies and civilizations, of our own (and other people's) historical and cultural heritage—these are just a few of the subject matter areas to which television has usefully been applied. Some quite distinguished and highly motivating "evocative" programs have also been made. Television, like radio, has the capacity to bring education right into the student's own home. Correctly used, these media can do much to add a dynamic and personal flavor to the tuition, and they help to foster a sense of participation and involvement in a major national venture.

Tutors, Counsellors and Study Centers

To provide more personal support for those who feel the need for it, the OU has set up nearly 300 study centers throughout the country. These typically consist of a small number of rooms that sympathetic authorities (local colleges of education, for instance) have hired out to the University for purposes of study and discussion. All centers are equipped with radio and television receivers. Many of them also contain tape recorders, projectors, a library of the broadcast material in recorded form, and computer terminals for the use of mathematics students. Each center is regularly visited by specially-appointed Course Tutors and Counsellors. These are professionally qualified people (lecturers from nearby colleges, for example) who are appointed on a part-time basis to hold seminars and discussion groups, and to advise on the various problems—both academic and personal—that individual students might be encountering. Every effort is made to keep study centers open at times (throughout the evening, for example) which are most convenient to all concerned. Discussion groups and the like are also held at these times. The whole study center operation is co-ordinated and monitored by Senior Tutors and Senior Counsellors who are full-time members of the Open University Staff. These senior staff are based on Regional Offices but they tend to travel around a great deal and hence provide critical links between the local part-time staff and the central staff at the University's main headquarters.

The number of part-time staff associated with any one study center is *not*, of course, large. But every student has several chances every month to discuss his problems—either individually, or in small group discussion— with the appropriate part-time member of staff. If a student is unable for some reason to attend a study center special arrangements can be made to visit that student (albeit infrequently) in his own home. Part-time staff therefore operate rather like doctors. They have a caseload of students. At certain times of the week they are out visiting "emergency" cases. At other times of the week they are available for consultation at a study center.

Attendance at a study center is advisable, but not compulsory. At the present time, study centers are located mainly in well populated areas, so that the majority of students are always within a few miles of such a center. As indicated above, many study centers consist of rooms hired in some nearby college of higher or further education. This incidentally brings OU students into contact with other student bodies; and it may eventually lead to an extension of study center facilities. If the demand arises and if resources permit, efforts will be made to enrich the OU's study centers—e.g., by adding library books, laboratory equipment, and other learning resources. Additions of this kind will be easier to make if the study centers are already housed within educational centers that sympathize with the OU's general aims and objectives.

Residential Summer Schools

The educational resources so far described (correspondence materials, home kits, radio and television programs, and study center discussions) are intended to be sufficient, by themselves, to promote effective learning. Even so, a case can be made for getting students together in much larger groups (a) to convey something of the traditional "university experience," and (b) to achieve certain additional objectives that might otherwise be neglected. The OU has accordingly devised a system of one-week residential summer schools, which are held at host Universities in different parts of the country. Summer schools are compulsory and they are currently being arranged to take place during the summer vacation of the host Universities involved. Since the OU's academic year runs from January to early October, summer schools therefore occur about two-thirds of the way through each student's course.

Each one-week summer school caters for several hundred students drawn from different parts of the country. Although the period of residence is short, several noteworthy objectives can be achieved. For example, OU students have the chance to use and savor the host University's facilities—fully-equipped laboratories and demonstration rooms, large-scale lecture halls, reference libraries, and the like. Central academic staff also have an opportunity to meet students *en masse* and individually, and this can provide useful additional feedback on student attitudes and progress.

Summer schools can serve a variety of useful purposes. They can provide opportunities for intensive laboratory work, using a full range of standard equipment. They can provide opportunities for special project work in (for example) the Social Sciences. They enable large-scale exhibitions to be set up and visits to be arranged to places of cultural or scientific interest. They provide a forum for mass discussion on matters of difficulty or dissension. They enable distinguished visitors to give invited addresses. They provide opportunities for setting and discussing and evaluating special homework assignments. They provide opportunities to re-run radio and television programs that students may have missed. And they provide additional opportunities for members of staff to engage in diagnostic and remedial teaching.

Above all, courses of this kind enable students to get to know each other, and to exchange views and experiences. This can have a strong motivational and integrative effect on the student population as a whole. And it can help to counteract any tendencies (induced, perhaps, by the study centers) for the student population to fractionate into small inward-looking groups. Similar comments apply, of course, to the numerous members of staff — academic and administrative, full-time and part-time central and regional — who attend the various schools that are run. These members of staff are able to meet each other, and to meet a wide cross section of the student population, all at first hand.

Evidence from other countries suggests that attendance at a summer school, even for a short period of time, can have a notable educative effect. It can also boost student morale (even if the students spend most of their spare time gossiping and grumbling), and it can help to promote a sense of corporate identity. Home study is, at the best of times, hard going. The rallying effect of a well-run summer school should not be underestimated.

Students as Teaching Resources

No account of the University's teaching resources would be complete without some reference to the students themselves. Most students tend to be regarded solely as learners — often as passive and inadequate learners who ideally need to be carefully nurtured by expert teachers and great minds. In reality, students are a potent and much-neglected *teaching* resource. If a University's formal teaching resources (its lectures, set books, and the like) are in any way defective, and if no teacher is around, students are obliged to do the teacher's job for him. They must acquire the skill of extracting information from books and journals and from each other, and they must use each other as sounding boards for their own developing opinions and expertise.

The most successful students all tend to pick up these self-help skills at a fairly early stage. At the OU, study centers undoubtedly help to foster the development of such skills. By means of small-group discussions, students are more able to discover and question hitherto unrecognized assumptions in the subject matter they are studying, and to uncover gaps and limitations in their own knowledge. They also have the chance to pursue lines of enquiry which are of special interest to them, but which are dealt with only lightly in the main study materials.

One of the best ways of learning about a new subject is to try teaching it to other people. There are, of course, some obvious dangers in the method. If nobody in the group knows what he is talking about, group discussion will merely produce a sort of "pooled ignorance." On the other hand, carefully prepared study materials, duly backed up with annotated discussion notes and easily-accessible follow-up reading, can enable students to hold profitable small-group discussions even when no tutor or counsellor is present. Students are a teaching resource in the sense that they (a) compensate for deficiencies in the resources provided by the University, and (b) help other students to extend and apply their newly-acquired knowledge in accordance with the needs and interests and abilities of those students. Considerable effort is being made to ensure that the study centers provide a suitable environment for the conduct of such activities. Failing this, students are being encouraged to set up self-help groups in their homes or at other suitable venues.

Organizational Structure of the University

The headquarters of the Open University are being developed in a rural setting, some 50 miles north-west of London. The exact site is on the outskirts of the designated area of the new city of Milton Keynes, in North Buckinghamshire. It is close to the M1 (London-Scotland) motorway, about 4 miles north-east of Bletchley.

Modern buildings, which have all been specially erected, are currently housing several hundred academic and administrative staff — together with a large-sized data processing and record-keeping system, and extensive facilities for the design and production and packaging and dispatch of the University's study materials. Also nearing completion are research laboratories (for academic members of the staff), a much enlarged lending and reference library, a lecture hall, canteens, and so on. There are no undergraduates on site, but room is currently being found for a small number of postgraduate students.

To control and monitor a nation-wide home study system, a rather elaborate organizational structure is required. For this reason, the University has divided the country into 13 semiautonomous regions. Each region has its own Regional Head Office, staffed by a Regional Director and other senior administrative and academic personnel (in particular, the senior tutors and senior counsellors mentioned earlier). Each Regional Office maintains detailed records of all students coming within that region, and the Regional Office staff are responsible for coordinating all the University's activities (tutorial, counselling, study center, summer school, etc.) that go on in that region. The overall organizational scheme is partly captured in diagrams 2 and 3.

The formal structure of the Open University is therefore hierarchical. Part-time tutors and counsellors are responsible to the Regional Office staff who are in turn responsible to the University's headquarters at Milton Keynes. In practice, of course, the real day-by-day structure is heterarchical. Control over the University's affairs fluctuates around the system and, ideally, always tends to reside with the person (or group of persons) best qualified to act.

The Assessment of Student Performance

The OU has departed from the traditional practice (in British Universities) of relying almost exclusively on formal end-of-year examinations. It has also tried to recognize some of the many limitations of traditional numerical marking schemes. And it has taken account of the needs of adults who are struggling to study at home

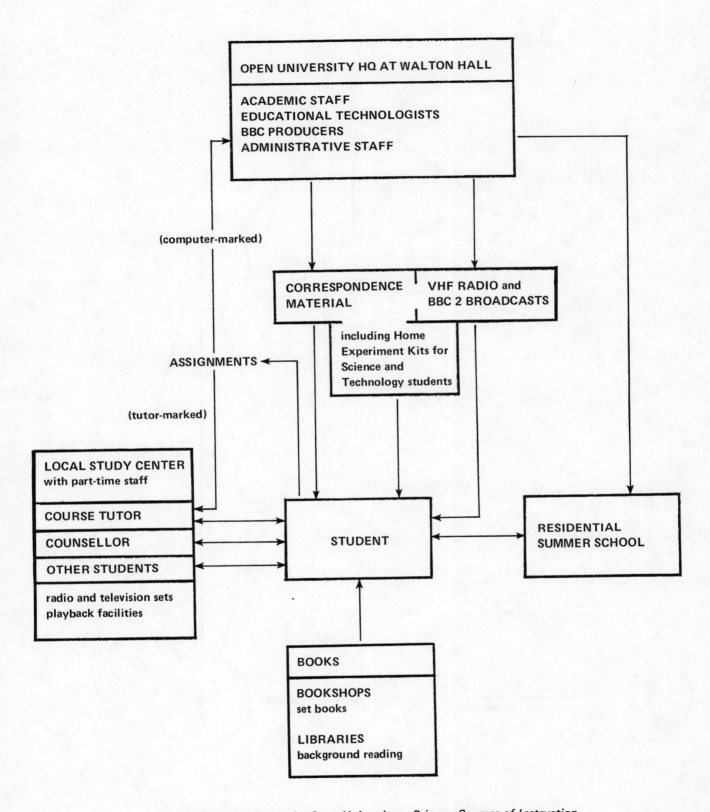

Diagram 2: Studying at the Open University — Primary Sources of Instruction.

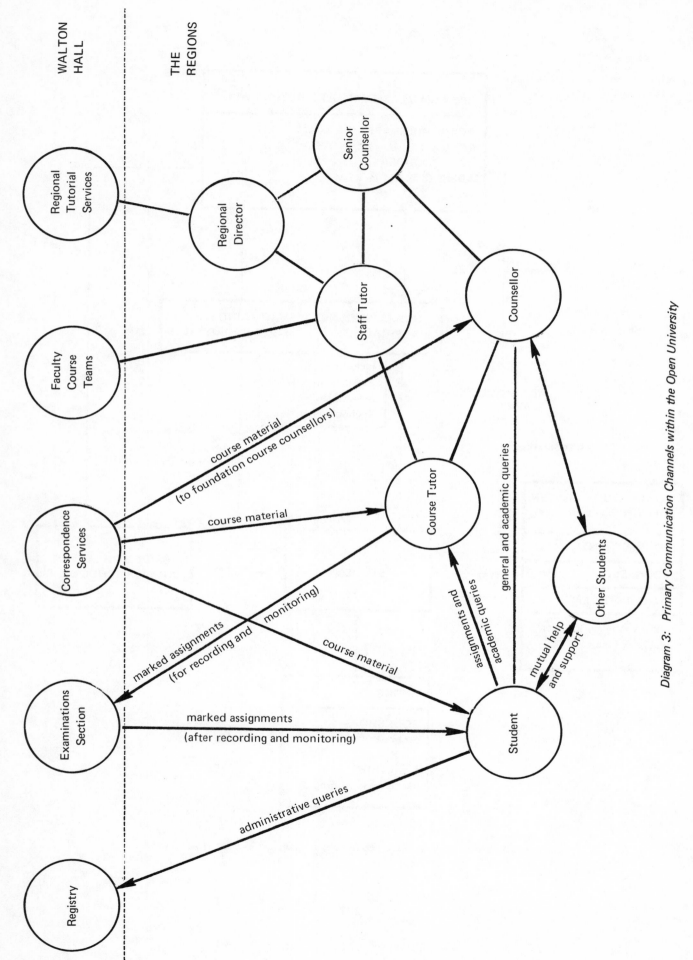

WALTON HALL

THE REGIONS

Regional Tutorial Services

Regional Director

Senior Counsellor

Faculty Course Teams

Staff Tutor

Counsellor

Correspondence Services

course material
(to foundation course counsellors)

course material

Course Tutor

marked assignments
(for recording and monitoring)

course material

assignments and
academic queries

general and academic queries

mutual help
and support

Other Students

Examinations Section

marked assignments
(after recording and monitoring)

Student

Registry

administrative queries

Diagram 3: Primary Communication Channels within the Open University

210

in their spare time, and who therefore feel the need for regular feedback on their progress. In the light of these considerations, the OU has chosen initially to operate a "continuous assessment" procedure, using (in most cases) *grades* rather than numerical marks.

As already indicated, all study packages contain homework assignments which students are expected to return, duly completed and within specified time limits, for marking. Some of these assignments are in computer-markable form, and students are requested to post these directly to the OU's headquarters at Milton Keynes. The remaining assignments are sent to the special group of part-time staff mentioned earlier — namely, the local correspondence tutors.

Performance on homework assignments is recorded, for each student separately, on computerized student record files. If a student has undertaken any special work assignments (e.g., at study centers, or summer schools), then the marks obtained for these special assignments are likewise recorded individually. At the end of each study course, all students are required to attend an Examination Center to take a short examination (of about 2-3 hours duration) under properly supervised conditions. Marks obtained at this examination are then compared and combined with all the other marks that the student has accumulated, over the year. Finally, a weighted composite mark is calculated to decide whether a course credit should be awarded, and, if so, whether it should be awarded "with distinction."

It is worth bearing in mind that the continuous assessment procedure, together with the week-by-week flow of essential radio and television programs, can have a powerful and sometimes oppressive *pacing effect* on the student population. The imposing of time limits on homework, and the study sequence of synchronized B.B.C. broadcasts, constitute a strong inducement to students to keep up to date with their studies. In recognition of the fact that some students may fall behind with their work for reasons that are beyond their control, all students are allowed to skip a small number of assignments if they so desire. In effect, this means that the award of the overall continuous assessment grading is based on (say) the best half-dozen assignments that each student sends in. For an elaboration of the implications of this arrangement, see Lewis (1972).

The Handling of Assessment Data

Computer marked assignments consist of multiple choice (and similar) questions that can be answered simply by making a series of marks on specially designed answer sheets. Students post these answer sheets, duly completed, to the University's headquarters. They are then decoded by an automatic document reader, and evaluated by computer.

Tutor marked assignments consist of essay questions and short answer questions which, by their very nature, cannot be marked by computer. Students must therefore post these assignments to designated correspondence tutors, who are responsible for marking them in accordance with pre-arranged guidelines laid down by the University's central academic staff.

For each homework assignment that is received, the computer generates a detailed statement of how well the student has done (a) on individual questions, and (b) on the assignment as a whole. At the present time, the OU computer has only limited facilities for interpreting the homework data that it receives. However, a variety of computer programs are currently being developed to enable student progress to be evaluated with greater sensitivity—e.g., by showing which questions, and which groups of questions, cause the most difficulty to which kinds of student. At the level of the individual student, *cumulative* indices of success and failure are also being devised to show how well each student is doing (in comparison with other students, and in comparison with his own past performance) at each stage of the course. It will then be easier to detect those sections of the course on which the student does best (or worst), and also to detect any sudden improvements or deteriorations in individual performance. If successive course units tend to vary unevenly in content or level of difficulty, this should also be more easily detectable.

From time to time, the computer generates summary statements—both to Regional Offices and to the students themselves—showing how each student is progressing. If any student shows evidence of sudden and severe deterioration, emergency signals are sent to the Regional Office, so that the student in question can be contacted and offered help.

Similar initiatives can be taken by the correspondence tutors, and by all other part-time members of staff. As a matter of routine, the correspondence tutor posts the student's homework back to him, duly marked and annotated, as quickly as possible. At the same time, he sends a record of his marking (and any further comments) both to the OU's headquarters and to the Regional Office. The tutors who attend study centers, and the counsellors who also attend study centers, can likewise report back on the progress of individual students. It follows that both the Regional Office and the OU's headquarters can accumulate a large amount of information about student progress — information which flows in from a variety of sources, and which needs to be sorted and interpreted by the kind of software now under development.

The OU as a Self-improving System

When students return their homework assignments, they are periodically invited to register their opinions on such matters as the intelligibility, difficulty, and interest of the assignments they have completed. They are also invited to say whether, and to what extent, they have made use of the OU's study center facilities. At the same time, the part-time members of staff—the correspondence tutors, the tutors who attend study centers, and the counsellors — are asked to comment on the students that come under their care, and on the study course as a whole. In particular, part-time members of staff encourage students to talk about their academic and personal study problems, so that the OU can build up a more accurate picture of student needs and interests.

To induce feedback of this kind and to secure more specific types of information, the University has established a Survey Research Department which regularly sends questionnaires to representative samples of students. Eventually, it is hoped to set up consultative panels of students, and to have fully-trained interviewers and social workers circulating around the system. There is, in fact, already provision in the Royal Charter for the convening of Regional Assemblies and consultative committees and for student representation on the Senate. Arrangements have also been recently completed for the starting of student magazines and newsletters.

By way of summary, diagram 4 records the main assessment and evaluation procedures currently in use at the Open University. As can be seen, the data collected from computer marked assignments (CMAs) and from tutor marked assignments (TMAs) and from various additional sources (end-of-course examinations, questionnaires, letters, telephone calls, etc.) can serve several different purposes. For example, the data can:

(a) provide the main basis for a formal assessment of student achievement, and

(b) enable relevant feedback to be given to individual students while the course is actually in progress, and

(c) facilitate the revising of those parts of the course that appear to be teaching less effectively than was originally hoped.

With regard to (c), it is worth remarking that each course that the OU runs is carefully monitored, during the first year or two of its existence, by a specially-appointed "maintenance team" of academics. This team is responsible for modifying parts of the course in the light of the total assessment and evaluation data it receives. Unfortunately, the current budget for revision is severely limited, and the revision process itself is largely a judgmental one. (In other words, it is not guided by any cogent theoretical model.) Diagram 5 depicts the main channels of communication involved and, collectively, they seem to be more than sufficient to guarantee that all *major* defects are picked up during the first year of each course's presentation.

Although the student population is scattered across the whole country, the numerous communication channels shown in diagrams 2, 3 and 5, make it comparatively easy to gather a great deal of information on

A summary of assessment and evaluation procedures

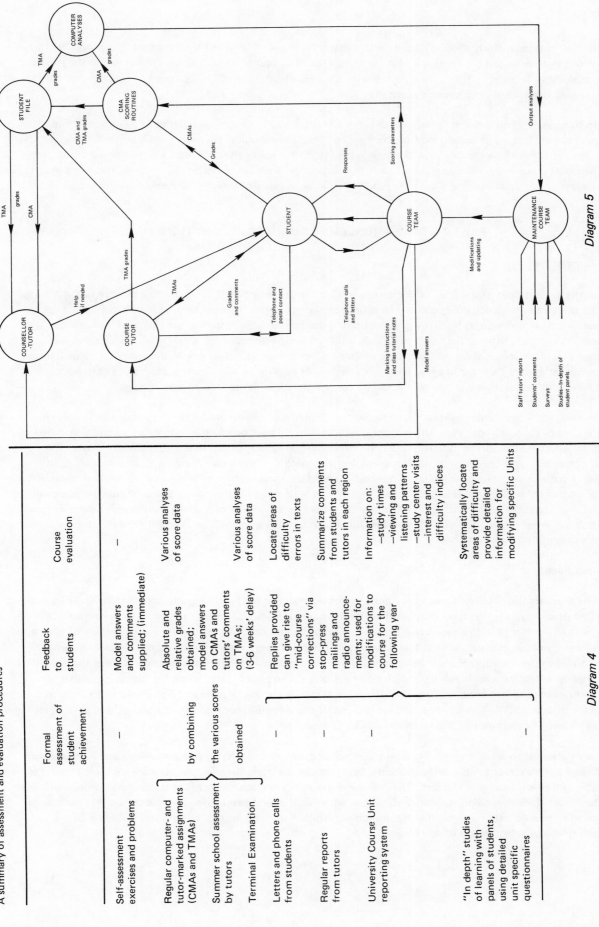

	Formal assessment of student achievement	Feedback to students	Course evaluation
Self-assessment exercises and problems	—	Model answers and comments supplied; (immediate)	—
Regular computer- and tutor-marked assignments (CMAs and TMAs)	by combining	Absolute and relative grades obtained; model answers on CMAs and tutors' comments on TMAs; (3-6 weeks' delay)	Various analyses of score data
Summer school assessment by tutors	the various scores obtained		Various analyses of score data
Terminal Examination			
Letters and phone calls from students	—	Replies provided can give rise to "mid-course corrections" via stop-press mailings and radio announce-ments; used for modifications to course for the following year	Locate areas of difficulty errors in texts
Regular reports from tutors	—		Summarize comments from students and tutors in each region
University Course Unit reporting system	—		Information on: —study times —viewing and listening patterns —study center visits —interest and difficulty indices
"In depth" studies of learning with panels of students, using detailed unit specific questionnaires	—		Systematically locate areas of difficulty and provide detailed information for modifying specific Units

Diagram 4

Diagram 5

213

academic and personal study problems, and on the strengths and weaknesses of the study materials, on the effectiveness of the tutorial and counselling and study center facilities, and on the conditions under which the students are most likely to succeed or fail. Data obtained in this way are helping the OU to strengthen its instructional system slowly but surely, from year to year.

In this connection, it is worth noticing that the OU has many of the characteristics of a Direct Action Research Project. Instead of opting for time-consuming "feasibility studies" on multi-media systems of higher education, the British Government took the imaginative step of actually allowing such a system to be set up and run. The result was a high-risk undertaking in which mistakes were bound to occur and to go on occurring. But, in the long run, this could well be the quickest and most effective way of solving the many intricate problems involved.

PART 2 — SOME PROBLEMS OF COURSE PRODUCTION

Initial Conceptions

In the earliest days of the OU, before course production actually began, most academics were fairly optimistic about the ease with which courses could be produced. For example, it was widely believed that, during the first year of course production (1970), a group of 8 or 9 academics — along with a handful of expert advisers and assistants—would have little difficulty in producing a full 36-week Foundation Course. It was recognized that a great deal of written material would have to be produced. But there was a tendency to perceive this particular task as requiring little more than the imaginative brightening up of already existing lecture notes and professional papers. The whole operation was one that could be contemplated, in advance, with equanimity.

Indeed, many academics confidently expected the business of course production to occupy not more than 100-200 days of each calendar year. Universities characteristically have both a teaching function and a knowledge extending function. The former is concerned with introducing students to knowledge that already exists. The latter is concerned with challenging and deepening and enriching (and even transforming) such knowledge. In accordance with this dual image of what a University should be, most academics took up their appointments on the explicit understanding that they would have time for at least some of the more significant knowledge-extending activities — postgraduate supervision, private research, professional writing, consulting, conference attending, and the like. In other words, the OU was to be a *real* University, not just a production house for the development and dissemination of undergraduate course materials.

The Harsh Reality

These expectations seemed reasonable enough at the time. But they were rapidly shown to be sadly inaccurate. In the first place, nobody had fully thought through the numerous implications of requiring academic members of staff to work together in large cooperative teams. Secondly, no-one had fully pursued the implications of having to teach a heterogeneous population of students who were mostly trying to study in their spare time (and perhaps for the first time) in the isolation of their own homes. To cut a long story short, it soon became obvious that in order (a) to produce effective teaching-at-a-distance materials, and (b) to have time to spare for the various other activities in which academics normally engage, the overall staffing of the OU would ideally have to be increased by a factor of at least 3-4. This kind of increase was out of the question, because the OU budget would not permit it. So a number of compromises and sacrifices had to be made.

In an attempt to establish high teaching standards with too little staff, both the academic and non-academic staff proved to be extraordinarily self-sacrificing. Many academics have, for example, forgone substantial periods of holiday and study leave due to them. They have cut their private research activities to the barest minimum, in order to devote themselves almost exclusively to the business of course production. At the same time, the rate of production of new courses has been slightly diminished, so that the courses that *are* produced stand a better chance of doing an effective job of teaching.

214

As a result of taking these steps, the production of quality courses is now merely difficult, rather than impossible. But the conditions of service for OU academics (and for many of the supporting staff) must be among the worst in the country. There is still an exhausting rush against time to produce high quality materials. And the pressure may well continue for at least 5-10 years — because this is the time that it will take to establish a solid stock of well-validated courses.

The Size of the Problem

It is difficult for an outsider to appreciate just how abnormal are the problems that confront OU academics and administrative staff. The planning and production of correspondence materials, home experimental kits, student activities, multiple-choice tests, radio and television programs, and the like, make demands on staff which are unlike anything they have ever experienced before. For example, special care must be taken to ensure that each correspondence unit is a sound and coherent and memorable piece of exposition. The main teaching points must be fully explained. Misleading statements and irrelevant scholastic displays must be eliminated. There must be no mistakes, nonsequiturs, gaps, or other defects in the argument. All written materials must in fact be well structured and self-explanatory and pitched at the right level of difficulty.

The whole operation is extremely time-consuming. If an academic wants to write a really effective piece of exposition — one that will either stand on its own or serve as essential supplementary reading to a prescribed textbook — it could easily take him as much as 2-3 weeks to produce an adequate first draft. His first draft would then need to be tried out, along with some appropriate evaluative tests, on a representative sample of potential students, to see whether it achieves what the author wanted it to achieve. Feedback data from these students can then be used as a basis for revising the original draft, and for polishing it up into more final form. Ideally, the revised draft should *also* be tested (preferably on a different representative group of volunteer students) to make sure that the revision process has been effective, and has not inadvertently introduced further defects and obscurities. In fact, the test-revise-retest cycle should be repeated as many times as is necessary to satisfy the author (and his colleagues) that the correspondence unit really does teach. However, each new cycle can add at least 3 weeks to the overall production time. It need hardly be said that the OU does *not* have either the time or the resources to put its instructional materials through the optimal number of (3-4) cycles. However, it is not at all uncommon to find 50-100 hours of academic effort being invested in each single hour of student study time.

In addition to writing the basic correspondence unit, the author must devise appropriate homework assignments. If the homework is to be marked by computer, he must specify *exactly* the marking scheme that the computer must use. At the very least, he must say how many marks must be added for each correct answer, and how many deducted for each wrong answer. In addition, he may call for the award of bonus marks for special combinations of correct answers. And he may request the computer to provide him with some detailed information on differential patterns of right and wrong answers.

If the homework is to be marked by correspondence tutors, the author must provide these tutors with appropriate guidelines and checklists. And he must tell the computer how to handle the marks or grades that these tutors eventually award. Since correspondence tutors may often be called upon to explain points of difficulty, the author must also circulate adequate briefings on the overall aims and objectives of his units. In some cases, he may wish to provide the study center tutors with special discussion materials. And he may want the students to perform experiments, or engage in certain kinds of group activity or field work. All of these activities greatly add to the total production time. And all of them ideally need to be put through the test-revise-retest cycle to make sure that they are (a) unambiguously clear, and (b) likely to have the effects intended.

The preparation of concomitant radio and television programs is no less arduous. Administrative and economic constraints make it difficult to put these programs through a test-revise-retest cycle, so even greater efforts must be made to ensure that they are right the first time. Experience has shown that even the simplest looking program can take several weeks to plan and produce—especially if it has to be carefully integrated with the correspondence materials, or if anything out of the ordinary (e.g., a special sequence of visual effects) is required.

Some Organizational Difficulties

To obtain a first insight into the practical difficulties of course production, let us consider a situation in which 8 academic members of staff (call them $A_1, A_2, \ldots A_8$) agree to collaborate on the production of a 32-unit course. To simplify the discussion, we shall focus solely on the problem of producing 32 *correspondence* units. And we shall suppose that each academic agrees to write just 4 of the 32 units. As a further simplification, we shall assume that A_1 agrees to write units 1-4 and A_2 agrees to write units 5-8, and A_3 agrees to write units 9-12, and so on.

After several weeks of joint discussion on the aims and objectives and content of the course, the academics go away and start writing. If we accept the kinds of time estimates mentioned earlier, and if we assume that each academic writes his units in numerical order, it follows that after a lapse of a few weeks the first *in extenso* drafts of units, 1, 5, 9. . .will be nearing completion. Unfortunately, this natural-looking arrangement rules out the possibility of testing the draft units, in a systematic manner, on volunteer students. Unit 1 can, of course be tested. But unit 5 can be meaningfully tested only on students who have worked through units 1-4. And units 2-4 have not yet been written.

This is a very considerable difficulty. If the academic members of staff are trying to achieve good continuity from one unit to the next, A_2 will have written his unit 5 as a follow-on to what he *expects* to appear in units 1-4, For example, A_1 might have said that his units 1-4 will introduce some basic concepts in statistical analysis. In preparing unit 5, A_2 will therefore feel free to build upon the statistical knowledge that he believes A_1 will impart in units 1-4. Insofar as A_2 takes this statistical knowledge for granted, his unit 5 will be largely unintelligible to the volunteer student who has previously seen only unit 1. Difficulties of this kind tend to increase over successive units. A_8, who has bravely agreed to do units 29-32, is engaging in a tremendous act of faith if his unit 29 tries to build upon or summarize material that 7 different colleagues have not yet written.

Should A_2 send off his completed unit 5 to the Media Production Department, with the request that it be set up and printed? If A_2 does this, he will place A_1 under a strong moral obligation to work into his remaining units (2-4) all the knowledge that unit 5 has taken for granted. If A_1 now refuses to co-operate (claiming, for example, that A_2 misunderstood what he, A_1, had undertaken to do), then unit 5 will be partly unintelligible unless expensive alterations are made at the galley proof stage. And A_2 is likely to feel that A_1 has let him down. At the same time A_2 will have only 3 units left (namely 6-8) in which to accommodate to the demands of A_3 and other colleagues. Instead of arranging for units 1, 5, 9. . . to be printed without further delay, it is tempting to stack them away on a shelf so that they can be altered, if necessary, at a later date. As more units come off the assembly line, everyone gets a clearer idea of what his colleagues are trying to say. Earlier units can then be taken off the shelf (so the argument goes) and adjusted to harmonize with the later ones.

However, it is a mistake to suppose that the mutual adjustment of units becomes easier as more and more units are produced. Moreover, the retention of units leaves the Media Production Department with almost nothing to do at the beginning of the writing year, and with almost everything to do at the end of the year. To provide the Media Production Department with a steady flow of work, each academic may have to finalize his first unit before he has even started to write detailed *in extenso* drafts of his follow-up units.

In practice, the situation often seems to be less serious than it really is. For example, it is open to each academic to dash off rough outline drafts (of 1,000 words or so) of all 4 units, and to circulate these among his 7 colleagues. This can be a somewhat unnerving procedure, because it requires everyone to display materials which, because of their rough and ready form, would not normally be allowed to see the light of day. It is, moreover, difficult to respond to such material in a constructive way. There tends to be rather a lot of it. And, because of its tentative nature harsh or detailed criticism always seems to be out of place. There is patently nothing "final" about the rough outlines produced—and everyone tends to think that, when the time comes, he will have very little difficulty in accommodating to the wishes of his colleagues. Unfortunately, these hopes are rarely justified. When the time comes, it may be very difficult indeed to adjust to one's colleagues in a satisfactory way. In some cases, an academic may even cite his first outline draft as "evidence" that certain proposed adjustments are unreasonable. "If you wanted me to incorporate that sort of material into my unit, you should have made your requirements clearer weeks ago. . . ."

This kind of comment is made in perfectly good faith. At the root of all these difficulties is the failure to communicate intentions and requirements. However wellmeaning and co-operative the 8 academics might be, they habitually fail to see, in the first instance, the force of the points that their colleagues are urging. For example, A_1 might fondly imagine that he can meet the requirements of A_2 by adding a sentence here, a footnote there, and a paragraph somewhere else. In reality, the knowledge that has been pre-supposed in unit 5 might, if taken seriously call for a radical restructuring of units 1-4. By the time A_1 realizes this, it is too late to do anything about it. And unit 5 will therefore be building on skimpy and inadequate foundations.

Instead of using outline drafts as a first basis for communicating intentions and requirements, it might be thought that longer drafts (e.g. of 5,000 words or so) would be more appropriate. This is not the case. Longish drafts, when produced in a hurry, tend to be discursive tours around the kinds of topics that the writer is *hoping* to cover, just as soon as he gets down to the business of writing seriously. When the serious writing begins, the inadequacies of each person's first thoughts will become apparent. Certain topics will be dropped, others will be introduced, and just a few may be selected for treatment in greater depth. Alterations may also be made to improve the structure and format of the initial rough drafts. It follows that the drafts are likely to undergo considerable change and, in consequence, do not deserve to be taken too seriously.

If long drafts are produced, there is in fact a very real danger that chaos will ensue. Accusations will be made that certain colleagues are planning to pack too much material into their units. Predictions will be made that styles will clash, and that units will lack continuity. Suggestions will be made that the whole course needs to be "re-thought," and that the order of presentation of certain units should be changed. A deeper problem arises if some academic members of staff fail to understand each other's subject matter. If A_3 and A_2 come from different disciplines, A_3 may do his best to make helpful suggestions to A_2 — but his comments may nevertheless strike A_2 as being naive and irrelevant.

In general, the production of hurriedly written long drafts is not a good idea. It is irksome to have to read so much material especially if everyone believes (a) that it is going to be radically changed, and (b) that it fails to do justice to the potential abilities of the writers. It can also provoke endless worries and arguments. And any attempt to alleviate such worries (e.g. by the production of hurriedly written amendments) may well have the opposite effect of hardening resistance and/or generating yet another crop of anxieties. In this respect, the breathless activity of writing, circulating, and re-writing does *not* lead to a rapid convergence of opinion. The procedure is not self-correcting.

Constraints of Time and Money

It might be thought that all the main difficulties and stresses and strains could be avoided by means of appropriate forward planning techniques. As might be expected, careful planning can greatly facilitate the production of correspondence and other materials. But it is important to realize that the nature of the operation, and the time pressure under which everyone is working, are such that planning cannot possibly solve (or even foresee) all the problems that can arise.

Suppose, for example, that the academic members of staff decide to strengthen their course by the addition of prescribed background reading materials. The most economic way of getting such materials to the students is to arrange to have them published, on the open market, as a "Reader" in paperback form. However, it takes time to negotiate with publishers. And it takes time to select the contents of the Reader, and to secure copyright clearances, and to agree to editorial changes with the original author and publisher, and to insert editorial comments and summaries, and to arrange for the whole volume to be set up, proof read, printed and distributed. The entire venture is impossible, in fact, unless arrangements to publish are put in hand in the very first quarter of the writing year. It follows that the academic members of staff cannot have their Reader unless they are prepared to finalize its contents well before most of their correspondence units have actually been written. This is a frustrating situation which no amount of forward planning can satisfactorily resolve. In the course of writing a unit, it often becomes clear that the ancillary reading material, which was chosen in all good faith at the course planning stage, is not after all the most suitable choice. But there is no possibility of substituting a better selection because, by the time the mistake has been discovered, plans for the Reader are irreversibly advanced.

In addition to having to work under acute time pressure, the Open University is also laboring under severe *economic* constraints. This is a further source of frustration. If money were less of a problem, academic members of staff could afford, for example, to drop the idea of hurriedly concocting a one-volume Reader. They could arrange, instead, for the last-minute inclusion (in the student's correspondence package) of carefully selected off-prints. Such an arrangement would give them more time to select the best possible background reading material. But the *cost* would be very much higher. Because of the financial restrictions under which the University is operating, academic members of staff are obliged (at some risk to their professional reputations) to dash off a one-volume Reader which, for the reasons given above, might well prove to be far from optimal.

Even now, we have touched on only a few of the many background pressures and irritations that academic members of staff encounter from day to day. Moreover, our discussion has been grossly oversimplified. In practice, academics do not normally agree to write just 4 successive units. Instead, they want to be involved in the entire course — writing one or two units here, and a few more there. Quite often, they want to write more than they have time to write — and each may feel that his ration of the course is too small to enable him to do a worthwhile job.

Another fact of life is that different academics have different working methods, and different views of the educational enterprise in which they are involved. One member of staff might be enthusiastic about computer-marked objective tests, whereas another might deplore them. One academic might prefer to write in a friendly and egalitarian manner, whereas others might adopt an impersonal approach. There are literally dozens of ways in which differences of approach and opinion can arise. If the differences happen to reflect strong underlying convictions, then the possibility of open conflict is never far away.

Organizational Aids to Efficiency

The foregoing account is probably a minimal statement of the main difficulties and pitfalls associated with the production of OU course materials. There are many additional difficulties of a more specialized and less obtrusive kind, some of which are described in a series of papers appearing in the British Journal of Educational Technology. See Lewis (1971, 1972). An important point to bear in mind is that almost every decision that is made can have hidden and unexpected implications. Because of the constraints under which the OU is operating, there is neither the time nor the money to indulge in trial and error experimentation. If the right decisions are not made at the right times, production plans may be held up and the quality of the course materials will suffer.

One way of easing the burden is to employ a variety of judiciously chosen assistants. It is helpful, for example, to have assistants who can engage in literature searches — e.g. to locate background reading materials, and suitable illustrations for proposed correspondence units. There is also a need for people who can handle copyright problems, and who can help to co-ordinate the diverse activities in which different members of staff are likely to be engaged at any given time. In addition, there is a need for more specialized assistance in the form of editors and designers and artists—people who proof read, and advise on problems of format and layout, and create special-purpose illustrations, and so on. Finally, there is an all-pervasive need for professional advice on the overall strategy and tactics of the whole operation. Within its limits of resources, the OU has in fact secured a modest number of assistants and advisers of the kind required. It has also established its own Institute of Educational Technology to advise on the design and evaluation of the teaching materials that are produced, and to make recommendations that will help the University to become a rapidly self-improving system.

What else can be done to facilitate the planning and production process? Well, there are some rather obvious precautionary measures that production teams can take. For example, most teams find it convenient to organize themselves, at an early stage, into *small working groups* of 3-4 members. Within each working group, one member has primary responsibility for writing a particular set of correspondence materials (or for preparing a particular set of broadcast materials), and the other members have mainly an advisory or watching role. As a further safeguard, the working groups overlap in their membership — so that everyone can function as the main author in some groups, and as an adviser or observer in other groups. It follows that each academic can remain in close contact with those colleagues (those writing adjacent units, for example) whom he is most likely to have to accommodate. In this way, incompatibilities of approach have a good chance of being picked up at an early stage.

There are, however, quite severe limits to what this kind of arrangement can achieve. It is easier to detect disparities of approach than to decide what should be done about them. (Imagine, for example, the difficulties that can arise if three scientists, in overlapping working groups, all start to write in different ways about "theories and models"). The setting up of overlapping groups also tends to produce only localized, rather than extended, continuity. There is still a danger of conceptual drift occurring from one sequence of units to the next. To secure some sort of macro-control over the whole 32 units, it helps to have an overall chairman and arbiter who is a generalist — in the sense of being able to span the various disciplines of his colleagues — and who also has the knowledge and vision and charisma to keep everyone moving in the same direction. Needless to say, this is easier said than done.

Some Recent Developments

In recognition of the very real difficulties that arise when teams of a dozen or more experts collectively try to produce a full course of up to 9 months' duration, several attempts have been made in recent months to simplify matters. One popular strategy has been to abandon the quest for close-knit overall integration, and to divide courses into several self-contained "blocks" of 4-8 units each. This enables everyone to work in much smaller groups, and to worry much less about what their colleagues are producing in *their* blocks. A similar ploy consists in producing ½-courses and 1/3-courses (and even one-sixth courses) of not more than 18 or 12 (or 6) weeks' duration each. In addition, the original aim of generating 36 weeks' work (in respect of each full course) has been widely modified to a less gruelling 30-32 weeks' work. This reduces the work load on the course teams, and gives the student a very welcome week off, here and there, in which to catch up or revise or just rest.

Several other simplifying strategies exist. There is, for example, an increasing tendency to rely more heavily on already-existing texts — instead of trying always to create special new materials from scratch. In view of the clash of viewpoints and styles that can arise when different academics contribute to a common course, some academics have also agreed to hand over the main writing chores to just one or two like-minded colleagues. This means that, for one course, just one or two academics will take responsibility for the bulk of writing, the remaining academics acting as their assistants throughout. In subsequent courses, the roles will be reversed. It is too early to pass judgment on the efficacy of these and other strategies. The division of courses into loosely related "blocks," for instance, might well disturb the insecure student who wants well-integrated materials. But it might well appeal to the kind of student who wants to think for himself. The limiting case would occur if every course team author decided to "do his own thing" in polite disregard of the contributions of his colleagues. We would then have the sort of teaching that goes on in almost every conventional university.

Activity Networks and Schedules

In order to plan and produce a complete course, it turns out that several hundred quite complicated decisions have to be routinely taken and acted upon. As additional aids to efficient action, special charts are needed to enumerate, as exhaustively as possible, what these decisions are, and who should take them, and why and when, etc. Supporting tables are also required to point up the major implications (financial, organizational, psychological, etc.) that particular decisions are likely to have—both in the short term and in the longer term.

There are numerous ways of depicting the production process in diagrammatic form. Each diagram that is drawn inevitably highlights some features of course production at the expense of others. And no single diagram can possibly do justice to the full complexity and variability of the production process as a whole.

Diagram 6 has a certain historical interest. It represents the very first attempt (in May 1969) to give a brief characterization of the overall production process. The diagram partitions the process into 3 stages. Stage 1 is concerned with the progressive clarification of course team *intentions* — starting with vague ideas about the nature and ethos of the course as a whole, and finishing with clear-cut ideas about the proposed content and rationale of every component of the course. Stage 2 is concerned with the progressive implementation of course team intentions. And Stage 3 is concerned with the purely technical (but difficult) business of final *production.*

Diagram 7 is a later characterization. The terminology is different. There is a stronger hint of the need for certain activities to go on concurrently. And there is a more explicit recognition of the need to re-cycle (e.g., to revise aims and objectives and initial drafts of units, in the light of ongoing experience). Diagrams 6-7 are, however, essentially compatible, Underlying each diagram is the recognition that effective course production calls for the kind of rational planning which enables initially hazy ideas to be firmed up and tried out (e.g. in the form of tentative drafts of correspondence materials) and subjected to critical discussion and revised again, so that — in the space of not more than a year — a polished and well-integrated course can emerge.

Diagrams 6 and 7 have a useful *orientating* function. They capture the most important and most commonly recurring features of course production, and thus provide the outsider with a helpful overview. But they were never intended to be used as practical guides to action — for the simple reason that they do not contain nearly enough *detail.* In order to see this, it is worth looking at diagram 8, which gives a fairly comprehensive list of the "products" which course teams may be called upon to generate.

As diagram 8 shows, the main products—the primary and secondary course materials, home experimental kits, homework assignments, radio and television programs, and the like—are devised for the direct benefit of the student. In addition, a considerable amount of explanatory material has to be prepared and despatched to other quarters — e.g. to regional staff, study center staff, correspondence tutors, summer school staff, examiners and moderators, data processing staff, and the publicity department. It would be a big mistake to underestimate either the difficulty or the importance of producing this ancillary (supporting) material. Time expended on providing explanatory notes for study center tutors is time well spent. So also is the time devoted to thinking about summer schools, and to drawing up sensitive marking schemes for homework assignments. Any production scheme that failed to stress the need for such items would be seriously defective as a practical guide to action.

To comprehend course production at *this* level of detail, some rather large charts are required. One such chart — described as an activity network because it depicts a large interlocking network of essential course team activities—covers 6 pages of a paper by the present writer (Lewis, 1971b). It is unfortunately too large to be reproduced in this chapter. By way of compromise, diagram 9 accordingly shows just one small segment of a rather simpler network that is actually being used by one OU course team.

Networks of the kind illustrated in diagram 9 can be embellished in various ways. For example, they can be annotated to show the approximate time (in days or half-days) that each activity is likely to take on average. They can also be annotated to indicate who ought to have primary responsibility, etc., for each of the activities shown. However, it is important to note that each course has its own distinctive characteristics and requirements, so *no* network can ever serve as anything more than an overall general guide. In particular, time estimates can be notoriously misleading. Certain activities can take anything from a few hours to a few weeks, depending on how much time and effort the course team members care to lavish upon them. See Lewis (1971 c).

What, then, is the value of such networks? Well, their main value is to act as memory joggers—to draw attention to what needs to be done and to suggest one or two good ways of doing it. In addition, of course, it is necessary to have a fairly firm set of *schedules.* In the last analysis, the clock cannot be ignored. So it is necessary for course teams to realize that extra time spent on one activity means less time spent on another.

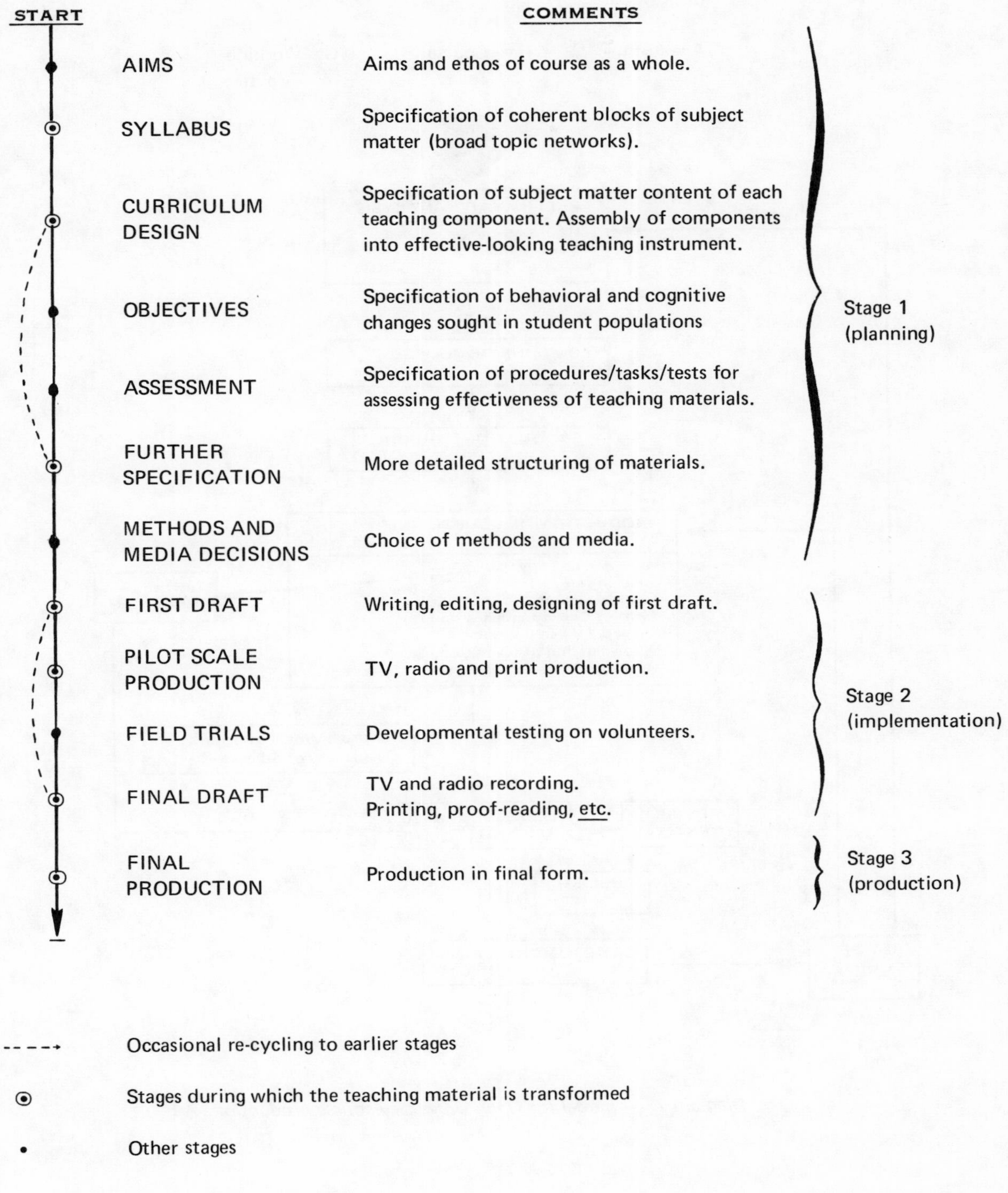

START		COMMENTS	

AIMS — Aims and ethos of course as a whole.

SYLLABUS — Specification of coherent blocks of subject matter (broad topic networks).

CURRICULUM DESIGN — Specification of subject matter content of each teaching component. Assembly of components into effective-looking teaching instrument.

OBJECTIVES — Specification of behavioral and cognitive changes sought in student populations

ASSESSMENT — Specification of procedures/tasks/tests for assessing effectiveness of teaching materials.

FURTHER SPECIFICATION — More detailed structuring of materials.

METHODS AND MEDIA DECISIONS — Choice of methods and media.

Stage 1 (planning)

FIRST DRAFT — Writing, editing, designing of first draft.

PILOT SCALE PRODUCTION — TV, radio and print production.

FIELD TRIALS — Developmental testing on volunteers.

FINAL DRAFT — TV and radio recording. Printing, proof-reading, etc.

Stage 2 (implementation)

FINAL PRODUCTION — Production in final form.

Stage 3 (production)

- - - →   Occasional re-cycling to earlier stages

⊙   Stages during which the teaching material is transformed

•   Other stages

Diagram 6: *An early characterization of the activities involved in OU course production* (after ISA Consultants, May 1969).

The initials show where lies the chief responsibility for decisions at each stage:

A = Author   CT = Course   WG = Working
                          Team   Group

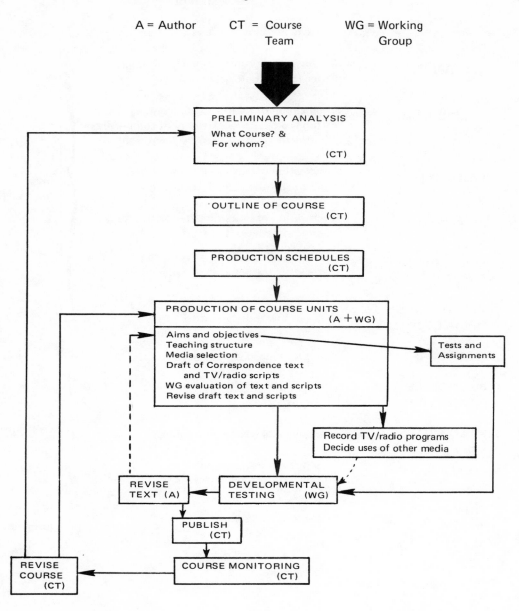

Diagram 7: A model for Open University course production.

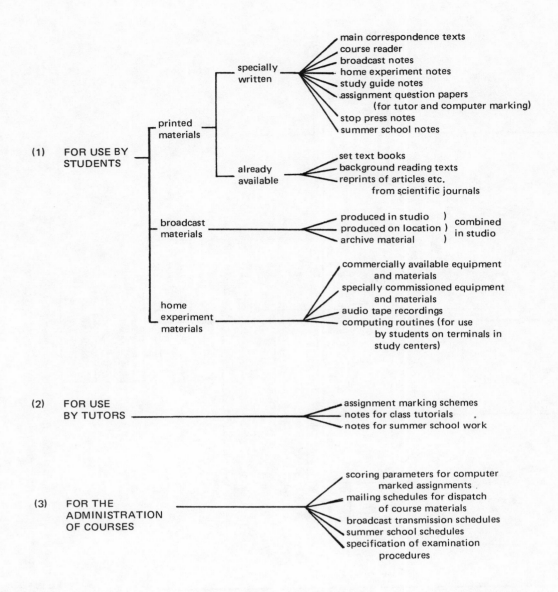

(1) FOR USE BY STUDENTS

printed materials
- specially written
  - main correspondence texts
  - course reader
  - broadcast notes
  - home experiment notes
  - study guide notes
  - assignment question papers (for tutor and computer marking)
  - stop press notes
  - summer school notes
- already available
  - set text books
  - background reading texts
  - reprints of articles etc. from scientific journals

broadcast materials
- produced in studio)
- produced on location) combined in studio
- archive material)

home experiment materials
- commercially available equipment and materials
- specially commissioned equipment and materials
- audio tape recordings
- computing routines (for use by students on terminals in study centers)

(2) FOR USE BY TUTORS
- assignment marking schemes
- notes for class tutorials
- notes for summer school work

(3) FOR THE ADMINISTRATION OF COURSES
- scoring parameters for computer marked assignments
- mailing schedules for dispatch of course materials
- broadcast transmission schedules
- summer school schedules
- specification of examination procedures

Abbreviated list of items in home experimental kit sent to students taking a first year course in Science

Instruments and apparatus: Spectroscope, plotting compass, flowmeter, stopwatch, stereoviewer, slide viewer, McArthur microscope, chemical balance, colorimeter, pump for SO_2 in air determination, laboratory burner, thermometer, tuning forks.

Glassware: Various (including test-tubes, syringes, microscope, slides, etc.): also retort stand equipment.

Chemicals: 69 different chemicals.

Miscellaneous: Atom models, litmus paper, carbon electrodes, magnet, graph paper, logarithm tables, etc.

Diagram 8: Summary of main components of a typical OU course.

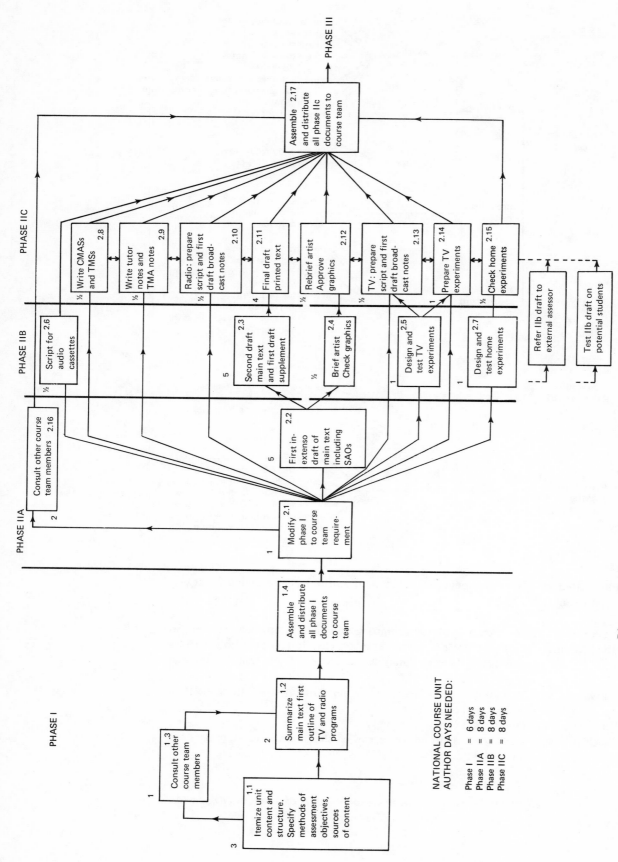

Diagram 9: *Extract from a simplified activity network, designed to guide the production of course materials in a science-orientated course.*

224

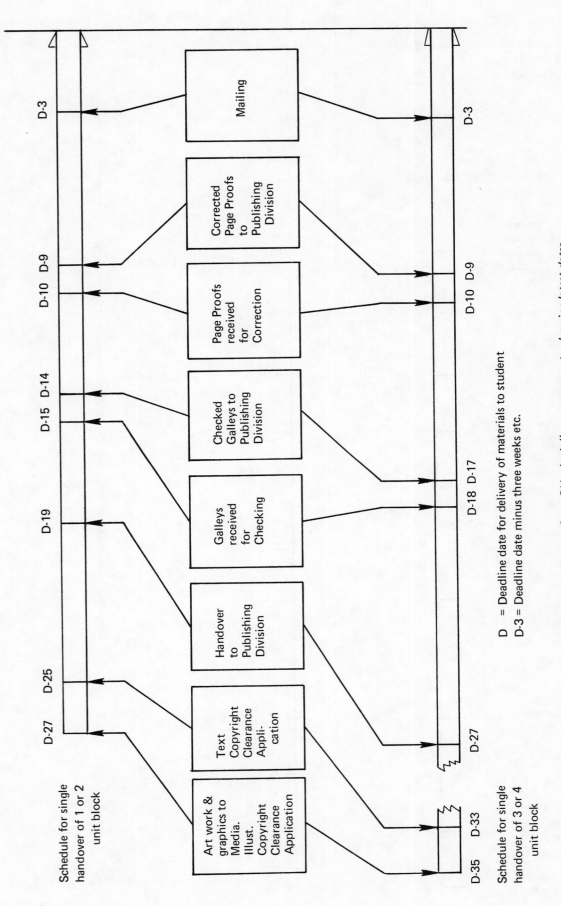

D = Deadline date for delivery of materials to student

D-3 = Deadline date minus three weeks etc.

Diagram 10: Extract from OU scheduling arrangements, showing latest dates for completion of certain key stages in course production process.

225

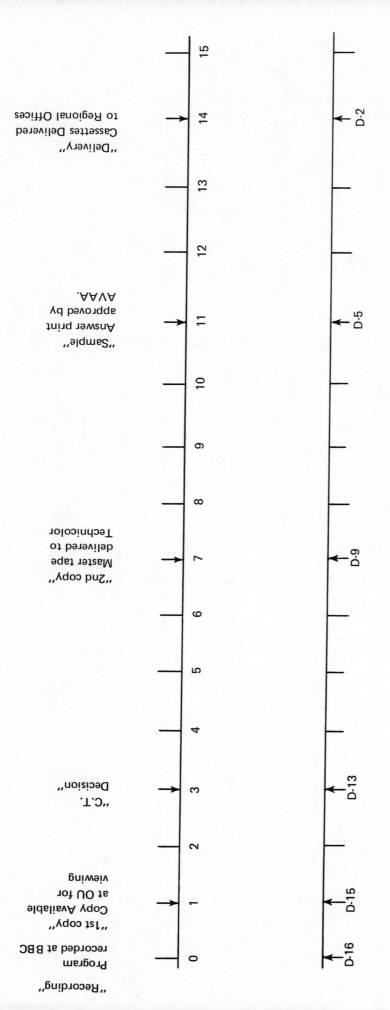

"Recording"

Program
recorded at BBC

"1st copy"

Copy Available
at OU for
viewing

"C.T.
Decision"

"2nd copy"

Master tape
delivered to
Technicolor

"Sample"

Answer print
approved by
AVAA.

"Delivery"

Cassettes Delivered
to Regional Offices

0   1   2   3   4   5   6   7   8   9   10   11   12   13   14   15

D-16 D-15   D-13   D-9   D-5   D-2

Diagram 11: Schedule for the preparation of television cassettes (latest dates).

226

Each course team accordingly operates a number of backward-running schedules of the kind shown in diagrams 10 and 11. These schedules are backward-running in the sense that absolute deadlines are determined (e.g. the latest time for settling copyright problems, or handing over graphics, or completing final draft of correspondence text), and the work is then spread as evenly as possible over the weeks leading up to the deadlines in question. This typically leads to the production of a large matrix in which a separate column is assigned to each key activity, and a separate row is assigned to each week of the year. In each cell of the matrix it is possible to record the stage that a certain activity should have reached by a certain week. It is also possible to record the name of the person(s) responsible for handling that stage of the activity.

As a further safeguard, the Vice-Chancellor's office operates a general monitoring system over course production as a whole. In this way, it is possible to predict the kinds of demands that are likely to be made on the Media Production Department and on other parts of the Open University's system, and to co-ordinate the flow of material from the individual course teams through the production and despatch system, and on to the student. Arrangements of the kind just described are by no means optimal, but they have so far enabled the OU to avoid serious crisis.

Further Reading

A continuing series of papers, by the present writer, is appearing in the *British Journal of Educational Technology*. The first 5 in the series are:

1.   Lewis, B.N., Course Production at the Open University I: some basic problems. *Br.J.Ed.Tech.* Vol.2, No. 1, 1971a.

2.   Lewis, B.N., Course Production at the Open University II: Activities and Activity Networks. *Br.J.Ed.Tech.* Vol.2, No.2, 1971b.

3.   Lewis, B.N. Course Production at the Open University III: planning and scheduling. *Br.J.Ed.Tech.* Vol.2, No.3, 1971c.

4.   Lewis, B.N. Course Production at the Open University IV: the problem of assessment. *Br.J.Ed.Tech.* Vol.3, No.2, 1972.

5.   Lewis, B.N., Educational Technology at the Open University: Indices of quality. *Br.J.Ed.Tech.* (In press), 1973.

JUDGING PRODUCTIVITY POTENTIAL OF AN INSTRUCTIONAL SYSTEM:

A REACTION TO PAPERS BY BALDWIN AND LEWIS

Stephen Yelon
Professor of Educational Psychology
Michigan State University

An educator often has to judge the productivity potential of an instructional system, a proposed instructional system or one in practice. He can do so by checking to see if a project director uses procedures which are likely to create an instructional design which in turn is likely to result in increased learning, quicker learning, less expensive learning, and more acceptable learning.

A project director can find procedures leading to productive design by abstracting from the procedures used to form proven productive instructional systems. He can combine what he finds in exceptional systems with what he knows about models and theories of instruction. The purpose of this paper is to give a check list of procedures to project directors.

There are five basic procedures that must be included in a potentially productive instructional system. A proposal should include procedures relating to (1) The measurement of productivity, (2) The derivation of goals, (3) An account of resources and limitations, (4) An application of social science, and (5) An evaluation for improvement.

Measurement Procedures

Let us look at each procedure; the first procedure results in the creation and use of measures. One asks, "Does the proposal include plans to have an objective agency measure many aspects of the productivity?"

To be more productive, a project director must know how well his system is doing in all possible respects. To measure many aspects of productivity one must go beyond using credit hours or courses listed. Productivity may mean any of the following things:

> More students achieve important objectives.
> More students apply what they have learned in the real world.
> More students remember what they have been taught for a longer period of time.
> More objectives have been achieved in a given time.
> The achievement takes less time for planning and for learning.
> The achievement takes less money.
> The achievement takes less work.
> Students, faculty, and people in the community are more satisfied with the results.
> More students demand the course work.

Measuring varied aspects of productivity is imperative in an open setting where a project director is never sure what results he is going to get because of the experimental techniques often used.

An objective agency should be used to evaluate productivity because it is often difficult for one to see his own errors beyond his experience. The objective agency should be called in to measure the productivity of the system both as it is being developed and when a prototype is complete.

Although Baldwin did measure some aspects of productivity he certainly did not measure all and left out some important productivity measures. He talked of many offerings for less money, added enrollment, less work for more course offerings, freeing of schedules and making learning more acceptable to students. He did not, however, mention students applying what they had learned in the world, or achieving more objectives. He did not mention anything about an objective agency doing the measurement.

Lewis spoke of 900 graduates and 40,000 students enrolled, a low dropout rate, and other measures of acceptability to the students and to the community, but he did not talk about productivity in terms of student learning.

Goal Derivation Procedures

The second important procedure to create productive instructional design is the derivation of meaningful goals. One asks, "Does the proposal include procedures to derive meaningful goals?" To be productive a project must meet student needs. Therefore, a project director must assess student needs and then set goals which meet those needs.

The assessment of a community's status to determine prerequisite achievement, attitude, belief, skill, and interest is crucial in an open system where students have little direct contact with staff and where students are quite different from those attending traditional colleges and universities. Goals must be stated to communicate instructional intent to students and staff. The goals must be communicable, comprehensive, and reality based.

By creating goals based on audience assessment, a project director can make learning much more meaningful to the students; and therefore, increase the completion rate, increase student satisfaction, increase enrollment, and increase the number of objectives that students will learn because he has accounted for their pre-requisites. When a project director states goals clearly, students may select courses more accurately and are likely to achieve a certain amount of satisfaction by recognizing the results of their labors. The faculty are likely to plan and implement their teaching with greater efficiency and are likely to be satisfied when seeing concrete results. By eliminating irrelevant objectives and adding important ones, a better use will be made of project money.

Baldwin alluded to some assessment of the needs of older engineers, but it seems that this assessment did not come before setting course goals. Course goals were not stated in the paper. Lewis reported on assessing student needs and stated that staff continue to survey student needs, interests, and progress. Course writers assume students do not have any prerequisites for a given course and let the students take exemptions to find their proper placement. Practical goals are used by staff for writing course units.

Procedures for Accounting for Resources

The third procedure used to create productive instructional design calls for making the best use of the resources and limitations present in the system. One asks, "Does the proposal include procedures which will create a design to take into account the resources such as time, media, staff, students, community, money, space, and course content?" The general strategy a project director should follow is to maximize the usefulness of the resources and work around or reduce the limitations.

In an open system a great deal of time and money may be spent on expensive media to reach students in remote areas. This time, money and media are three resources that must be used very well.

A project director can use time well by carefully planning production strategies. He could generate a proto-type early to test his planning procedures, his teaching procedures, and his testing procedures. He can use materials similar to those he will generate. He could create a program with the barest essentials of content and then, as empirical evidence is collected, he could add necessities to the program. He could plan to keep all of the units in draft form except for the first one. The lessons learned from testing the first unit could be applied to the second, then the second unit could be tested. He could plan for his planning; he could assign responsibilities and set dead-lines. In practice he could test students and materials frequently so that any remedies would be small enough to be handled quickly and inexpensively. He could create instructional products which are self-contained, tested, and re-usable.

Baldwin saved time by producing instructional products, and saved the instructors from repeating things that they had already done. To save time these products were used during working hours and for remedial work. No other strategies to save time were mentioned. Lewis saved time in many ways; he provided student exemptions of courses, by having faculty work groups analyze rough outline drafts, by using objectives and conceptual dia-grams to get the students to learn more quickly, by trying to work around the problem of sequencing of instruc-tion, by using activity schedules to set deadlines and assign responsibilities, by using existing texts and by getting the system out and ready for testing.

Fred Allen, the noted radio comedian, once said, "The reason they call radio a medium is that nothing on it is ever well done." All project directors are told to use media appropriately; however, there are very few people who know what the appropriate use might be for different forms of media. Baldwin used television to extend place; whether he used television appropriately, we cannot tell. But Baldwin seems to be wedded to videotape, and may have eliminated other kinds of media development which may be considerably less expensive and, perhaps, in some cases more appropriate. Lewis uses all forms of media, each with a particular rationale.

In an open system where the maximum amount of students have to be reached, the staff must be used well. To do so an administrator must employ strategies such as division of labor, team work, and work schedules including deadlines and responsibilities. He must work at increasing the staff's motivation to do a good job by using participative management, by providing concrete and direct rewards to the faculty, by employing com-munications systems so that the staff can work well together, by training faculty in learning system design, in the psychology of learning, in the exact nature of their system, in the ability to work together as a team and in the ability to use resources. He may even go so far as to be sure that the values of the staff members coincide with the goals of the system.

In all of these ways a project director can increase the satisfaction of the staff by giving them control. He can increase the probability of learning by finding good suggestions through participative management.

Baldwin used staff to create the videotapes and occasionally to visit the students. Lewis used staff by employing methods of division of labor and teamwork, by setting up a system for communicating criticism to each other, by dividing groups into writers and observers, by choosing people of similar views to write rather than to fight it out, and by using tutors to do the job of human contact and immediate feedback.

In an open university system staff cannot possibly do all of the teaching and cover all of the remote areas in which students will be placed; thus, the students, the most neglected resource in any instructional system, must be used well. They must be taught to tutor each other and to benefit from the system. Baldwin did not mention anything related to the use of students for peer teaching. Lewis took the students into account by easing the pace of assignments and by planning to teach students to teach each other.

To use money well, an accurate assessment of the costs must be made. A project director must learn how to estimate costs accurately and learn how to amortize the costs over time. He must take into account the import of the goal for which he is spending money, he must ask how much money is it worth to reach a given goal. Few instructional developers, including Baldwin and Lewis, speak of the question of money related to goals. Baldwin, however, uses money well by making an accurate assessment and being able to amortize the costs of course work over time. This ability comes from years of experience of producing videotapes. Lewis uses money well by not spending any more than budgeted, by requiring staff to put in more time, and by not wasting money by producing special books and extra costly, unnecessary media.

Procedures for Applying Social Science

The fourth procedure for creating productive instructional design is the application of principles. One asks "Does the proposal include procedures for applying social science principles, those that include the psychology of learning, motivation, and attention, and the principles of sociology and anthropology?" If a project is to be productive, new materials must work the first time to reduce additional cost and time for revision. A project director must use what he knows from sociology to assess and take into account the characteristics of certain groups. In open systems this is important; it is also important to apply general principles of learning, motivation, attention, communication and perception.

Baldwin describes practice, assignments, and visits, but I cannot be sure, in reading his paper, whether there was a concerted effort to introduce psychological principles into the creation of the system. Lewis, however, provides clear evidence of the use of psychological principles dealing with practice, feedback, interaction, progressive testing, repetition, use of objectives, use of knowledge structures, and so on.

Formative Evaluation Procedures

The fifth procedure for creating productive instructional design is formative evaluation.* One asks, "Does the proposal include procedures for self-improvement through data collection?" To be productive a project director has to be committed to improvement. To improve a project, a director must collect evidence to find areas of success and areas of failure. Even if all other procedures are put into effect errors will be made because of the presence of new audiences and new techniques. Evidence must be collected in order to eliminate those errors. Baldwin describes some research done to improve one of his pet projects. Lewis states that the formative evaluation process is built in: students, tutors and survey researchers are always collecting data to find out where the system can be improved; tests are analyzed for this purpose as well.

The presence of these five procedures does not guarantee productivity because there are many problems and many issues related to each procedure. In general, however, if these five procedures are included to plan an instructional system, the chances are that the system would be productive. I believe that if in the long run the instructional systems described by Baldwin and Lewis are productive it is because they planned using procedures like those described to design their systems.

---

*As yet techniques are not well formulated but I have completed a draft manuscript of a text on formative evaluation, which will soon be available.

A REACTION TO "CHICAGO'S TV COLLEGE:

A TELEVISION-BASED OPEN LEARNING MODEL"

G. R. Klare
Ohio University

The success of Chicago's TV College, as described by Dean Zigerell, is most impressive. Let me comment briefly on the major indices of success now and come back to them again later.

1. *Program duration.* The TV College has been in existence for 17 years—many times longer than most instructional television, or ITV, efforts.

2. *Enrollment.* The number of students reached during the College's existence is over 150,000, with more than half taking courses for credit. This makes the TV College by itself as large as a state university in terms of students taught.

3. *Satisfaction.* The satisfaction registered concerning the TV instruction compares favorably to that for conventional college courses, in fact exceeds it in some regards. This is surprising in view of the less positive results of most early ITV research covering the same kind of instruction.

4. *Cost.* The cost per student-credit-hour is very close to that for conventional courses, in fact, slightly less. This is in many ways the most impressive of all indices.

Rather than say more about the indices of success now, it would be more profitable, I think, to look instead at the probable reasons for success. The most impressive area of success has been with the largest segment of the audience—the homeviewers, who make up 75% to 80% of the credit enrollment at the present time. Let me, therefore, concentrate on the probable reasons for success with the homeviewing audience.

The logical place to look first is at what the literature in ITV says, to see if the Chicago TV College's experience bears it out. Two related points are frequently cited in the literature.

1. *Manner of presentation.* This is frequently given as critical to viewer acceptance of ITV.

2. *Use of specialists.* This is often described as necessary for effective use of television as a medium for instruction.

Did the Chicago TV College follow these dicta? Let's look, beginning with manner of presentation of programs.

It seems almost axiomatic now in ITV that one does not present a so-called "Talking Head" or "Talking Face"—unless, perhaps, they happen to belong to someone like Bill Cosby. The message seems to be, that a regular instructor should not stand in front of the camera as he would in talking to his class, at least not for as long as a quarter or semester. As we found in our large introductory psychology classes of 2,000 some years ago, students seem to prefer a live human being even if they can only see him with field glasses.

Yet, Chicago's TV College does not seem to have been too concerned with this matter of manner of presentation. As Dean Zigerell says, the TV courses are basically ". . . a visually enhanced, carefully rehearsed classroom performance." He also says that the College does not use "fast-moving, high-visual production techniques."

Next, let's look at the matter of use of specialists. Here, again, the TV College does not seem to have followed the "game plan." As Dean Zigerell says, "instructional teams have seldom been employed," and "TV College lacks . . . the resources of money and personnel for thoroughly 'mediated' instruction."

Why, then, has Chicago's TV College been so successful? Dean Zigerell has, I think, provided the clues in his address. But I would like to emphasize them, so that it is possible to suggest ways for others to profit from his experiences. He says, at one point, that the Chicago metropolitan area contains a "virtually inexhaustible audience of mature, able, highly motivated students eager to enroll as credit students in college-level television courses."

I'm sure Dean Zigerell chose his adjectives carefully:

a. "highly motivated,"

b. "able,"

c. "mature;" and as he added later in his paper,

d. "largely female."

And just in case some additional characteristics should be needed, I'll leave a place for "Other."

As an instructor, I can't help remarking, that highly motivated, able, mature women students are likely to learn under any teaching method or any instructional conditions, no matter how good or poor. As most of us know, it would be pretty difficult to keep such students from learning. Apparently the only things that did, in the case of the Chicago TV College audience, was the lack of accessibility to education and/or tuition funds.

Given such a situation, I think certain implications follow from the Chicago TV College's experiences when others—or even Dean Zigerell and his group—wish to serve different audiences with the same success as his current homeviewing audience. I think it can be instructive to look at these implications as a help to others now, but also to suggest some needed research as Chicago's own audience changes. Since Dean Zigerell says that an attempt is being made to reach the disadvantaged segments of Chicago's population, we might look at the implications with that kind of changed audience in mind. And again, use the applicable indices of success that I mentioned earlier.

Implication One. The most interesting and important implication is that the characteristics of presentation will probably need to be changed for a new audience, at least if enrollment is not to suffer. What *kinds* and *degrees* of changes will be needed? That is a question for research—or trial-and-error—of course. But some hypotheses are suggested by the TV College's experiences. Note that four likely candidates for changed presentation are the amount offered of:

a. fast-moving, high-visual production techniques;

b. self-scoring and programmed materials;

c. face-to-face and telephone conferences; and

d. vocational orientation in courses.

Again, I have added an "other" category to cover other possible characteristics not listed. Given subjects who are highly motivated, high in ability, highly mature and in large proportion women, only relatively small amounts of the four program characteristics are needed. *But,* given subjects who are, in some combination, less highly

233

motivated, less able, less mature and/or are in smaller proportion women, which of the program characteristics will need to be changed? Only time can tell—and I hope it *will* tell. That is, I hope that as the prime audience for Chicago's TV College changes, an attempt will be made to relate the changes in people characteristics to those in program characteristics.

Other program characteristics not listed may, of course, need to be changed also. I would like to suggest one myself, in fact. I believe that the instructional material used, particularly the written material, will probably have to be made more "readable," i.e., easier to understand and more efficient to read. As motivation and ability go down, the need for improved readability goes up, if materials are to remain effective. (For a brief discussion of readability and its effect upon reader behavior, see the attached paper, "Readability and the Behavior of Readers.")

In summary, keeping enrollment up with a less easily taught audience will not be easy. Such a change has other implications for the indices of success mentioned earlier.

Implication Two. The second implication is that the satisfaction expressed by the student viewers is likely to decrease. At least in the early stages, student comments are likely to move in the direction more typically found in evaluation of the type of presentation used in Chicago. This is likely to show up in something of a drop in the high current numbers who:

a. say they enjoy studying on TV, or who say they like their TV courses;

b. say they feel they learn as much from TV as from conventional classes, as is now the case;

c. say they find their TV courses better organized and presented than conventional classes.

It is hard to say how grades in the TV courses will compare to those in conventional courses, since grading tends to be so subjective and thus subject to other pressures. It would seem desirable to compare actual grades rather than, as in the study reported, to ask students how their grades compared. Human memory being what it is, I usually find self-reports of grades somewhat higher than actual grades.

Implication Three. The cost of ITV instruction is likely to increase. It will be interesting to see whether the cost per-student-credit-hour can be held as low as for conventional instruction. This is not meant to be a criticism of ITV: I hope it *can* be kept as low. What really concerns me is whether Dean Zigerell and his group will be able to get extra money to vary their presentation if this is needed. I hope, especially, that some research money will become available to study the characteristics of the new audience and to try various changes in presentation in order to maintain the success currently being achieved.

In summarizing, let me make several points. My comments were not meant, as I've indicated, to detract from or disparage the success of the Chicago TV College. As Dean Zigerell has said, an ITV presentation must be evaluated in terms of what it sets out to do and for whom. What I hope, is that it will be possible to document the ways the current approach must be changed to deal successfully with a changed audience.

This will take research time and money. But it could be very worthwhile for any other ITV programs in the planning—or even operational—stages. With the current growth of the open-learning and open-university models, this could help many states—and perhaps also some countries—to move faster along the road to effectiveness.

READABILITY AND THE BEHAVIOR OF READERS

G. R. Klare
Ohio University

One of the best ways to tell people what "readability" is, I've found, is to start by showing them what it isn't. I happen to have here what I think is a particularly good—or bad—example from the *Federal Register.*

> The maximum price for a primary fish shipper sale of fresh fish or sea-food (except shrimp, salmon or halibut) to a retailer or purveyor of meals where the sale is negotiated or made at a branch warehouse as herein defined and where the fish or sea-food is sold and delivered from the stock of a primary fish shipper wholesalers branch warehouse which is remote from his main place of doing business, and at which warehouse the primary shipper employs two or more full time employees who are stationed at and engaged in making sales and performing services solely for the primary fish shipper from such warehouse, is the price listed in Table D in 22 plus the allowance provided in 6 for a service and delivery sale where such sale is made, plus the transportation allowance in 9 plus the appropriate container allowance in 21.

After reading this passage, I think you can see one of the reasons that price controls may be unpopular with those who have to apply them. The passage illustrates one extreme of the most common dictionary definition of readability: relative ease of understanding or comprehension due to the style of writing. This definition contains the two points most commonly agreed upon concerning readability:

(a) the emphasis upon "understanding" or "comprehension," and

(b) the emphasis upon "style in writing" rather than content, i.e., upon *how* something is said rather than upon *what* it is said.

These two points will come up again at different places in my discussion, which concerns the relationship of readability to reader behavior, with special attention to reader persistence.

In order to establish a relationship, of course, a measure of the variables involved is needed. Let me begin with readability. The most common measure of readability is the socalled "readability formula." Well over 100 such formulas have been published (my count to date is 141); 33 were developed by one research worker alone, in recent years. The large number is partly a reflection of the many different purposes and materials to which formulas may be applied. But it is also partly a reflection of the convenience of computers in manipulating and analyzing the data needed for formula development and for formula application. At least 29 computer programs currently exist for applying readability formulas to large bodies of data.

I do not want to get deeply into the topic of readability formulas and their variety and diversity. That is another topic for another day. Instead, let me simply provide a capsule description of formulas. Fortunately, this can be done quickly as follows.

1. The variables in readability formulas usually consist of counts of language, or style, elements which have been found to correlate highly with comprehension scores on a wide range of passages.

2. The variables are usually chosen so that, in addition to their predictiveness, they are objective, quick, and easy to apply.

3. The most commonly used variables are some measure of word difficulty, such as familiarity or length, and some measure of sentence difficulty, such as complexity or length.

4. The variables are usually combined in a regression equation.

5. The formula is usually applied to samples of written material, especially when the material is lengthy.

6. The formula provides scores which serve as an index of the readability, i.e., the reading difficulty, of the written material. Sometimes grade-level scores are used, and sometimes a different scale is used. But the interpretation of the scores, at least, usually involves grade levels because their meaning is easy to grasp and apply in an educational situation.

Let me show you a typical readability formula. It is the Flesch "Reading Ease" formula, with a table beneath it that is commonly used to interpret the scores it provides.

Table 1. Interpretation Table For Flesch Reading Ease Scores

Formula: R.E. = 206.84 − .85wl − 1.015sl

R. E. SCORE	DESCRIPTION OF STYLE	TYPICAL SYLLABLE LENGTH (100 WORDS)	TYPICAL SENTENCE LENGTH	TYPICAL MAGAZINE	POTENTIAL AUDIENCE SCHOOL GRADE COMPLETED
0-30	Very difficult	192 or more	29 or more	Scientific	College
30-50	Difficult	167	25	Academic	H.S. or some College
50-60	Fairly difficult	155	21	Quality	Some H.S.
60-70	Standard	147	17	Digests	7-8 Grade
70-80	Fairly Easy	139	14	Slick-fiction	6 Grade
80-90	Easy	131	11	Pulp-fiction	5 Grade
90-100	Very Easy	123 or less	8 or less	Comics	4 Grade

The formula, R.E.=2−6.84−.85wl−1.015sl, is at the top. R.E.="Reading Ease," which usually varies from 0 (which is practically unreadable) up to 100 (which is easy reading for any literate person); wl=the variable word length in syllables per 100 words (with its regression weight of .85); sl=the variable of average sentence length in words (with its regression weight of 1.015); 206.84=a constant which adjusts most readability scores to the scale from 0 to 100.

Actually, the constant doesn't manage to put *all* writing on the 0 − 100 scale. The *Federal Register* passage I showed you earlier yields a score of −71, which you can see is way off the scale. It has values of 233 syllables per 100 words, and 154 words per sentence. That's pretty unusual, but I could actually have done even better. I spared you a sentence of 495 words long that I found in a study of correspondence materials I completed recently, and that I will be referring to again. I think you can see, at any rate, why such material goes somewhat beyond the interpretation table's highest descriptors:

a. "very difficult" in style,

b. "scientific" in magazine level, and

c. "college" in reading level.

Since readability formulas provide convenient indices of reading difficulty, they have been very widely used in all areas of education, mass communication, publishing, industry, and the military services. A number of validity studies have also been done in order to relate readability scores to reader behavior, particularly comprehension of written material. These studies are of two kinds.

1. Correlational—where readability scores have been related to comprehension scores on large numbers of passages of diverse content. An example would be passages from a standardized reading test.

2. Experimental—where a particular passage (or set of passages) has been rewritten at one or several new levels of readability, to see what effect this has upon comprehension.

Rather surprisingly, the relationship between readability scores and comprehension has been far from perfect. Many reasons for this are possible, of course: inadequate measure of comprehension, poor testing conditions, etc. But in an on-going review of the literature, I have found that two other factors are frequently responsible for the lack of relationship, or a low relationship.

The first of these is failure to consider level of reader competence. By this I mean such things as reading skills, verbal ability, specific background for the material, etc. To give you a quick illustration, let me provide two passages.

Adjustment of each of these transformers requires loosening the knurled nuts on the diametrically opposite screws which travel in helical slots in the cylindrical housing, and moving them along the slots with the fingers. If a tight fit makes this operation difficult, the desired result is facilitated by oscillatory rotation to the limits permitted by the oscillatory rotation to the limits permitted by the width of the slots, accompanied by axial pressure in the direction of the required axial movement.

The relative contribution of motivational and cognitive factors is difficult to ascertain since there is always a covariation of these variables in the humor stimulus. It should, however, be possible to arrange a large set of humor stimuli so that cognitive and motivational aspects of these stimuli are orthogonally represented (if such independence is not possible to create, that would be interesting too).

The first passage, with a score of 23 on Flesch's Scale, is intended for technicians in the Bell System. Most of the technicians are high school graduates; few have any more education than that. The second passage, with a score of 11, is intended for fellow psychologists by a psychologist writing about humor.

This second passage may not, as one reader said, be funny. But it is probably easier for its intended audience of psychologists than the first passage is for its audience of technicians. It seems safe to say, furthermore, that technicians would have more trouble reading the humor passage than psychologists would have reading the transformer passage. My point is simply this: when a passage is said to be readable, the statement should also say for *whom* it is readable.

The importance of this factor, reader competence, is easy enough to see, and the relationship is a logical one, at least within broad limits. The less competent the reader, the greater will be the effect of improved readability upon reader comprehension and reader persistence. This is the case for reading skill, background, etc.

There is another factor, however, that is not so easily spotted in validity studies. Let me explain, using as an example a study I made recently of the readability levels of correspondence materials.

The United States Armed Forces Institute, or USAFI, as you may know, is the chief "correspondence school" for the Armed Forces. It provides correspondence materials in academic subjects at primary, secondary, and college levels, plus vocational materials at roughly high school level. USAFI asked me to analyze the readability level of 30 sets of their high school and beginning college materials (a set consists of one or more books plus a study guide). I analyzed a rather extensive sample of materials—over 150,000 words—using a computer version of the Flesch Reading Ease formula developed by several colleagues, one of whom was Larry Stolurow.

USAFI research personnel Clay Brittain and Kim Smart then related the readability scores to the probability that students would send in all of their lessons, which is usually not the case. Sufficient course completion data were available on 17 courses for such an analysis (there were insufficient data on 13 new courses). A rank order correlation of .87 ($p. < .001$) was found, holding length of course (a critical variable) constant. The product moment correlation coefficient on these same data yielded a value of .75 ($p. < .01$).

Here we can see that level of readability is so clearly related to the reader behavior of persistence. In a sense, of course, there must be a relationship to reader comprehension also, since the amount comprehended would go up if only because more material is read when readability is improved. The next step, ideally, is to be sure that the results of this correlational study can be followed up successfully with an experimental study. I have provided USAFI with versions of standard lesson materials in which the readability has been increased (i.e., improved), but with the content held constant. This experimental study of the relationship of comprehension and persistence to readability has not been carried out as yet. But even at this stage, the USAFI study shows that, under the typical learning conditions in correspondence instruction, readability can play a significant role in reader persistence.

Now let me generalize briefly from these results. It seems probable that the chief underlying factor here is reader motivation. That is, the less highly motivated the reader is, within certain limitations or extremes, the more important readability is. I believe, therefore, that reader motivation as well as reader competence must be considered when evaluating the relationship of readability to reader behavior. Here is a picture of the proposed relationship.

A Model for the Relationship of Readability
to the Behavior of Readers

THE READER'S LEVEL OF PERFORMANCE	IS A	THE READER'S LEVEL OF COMPETENCE	INTERACTING WITH
(e.g., his comprehension, speed of reading, depth of reading, etc.)		(e.g., his reading skills, verbal ability, specific background, etc.)	
THE READER'S LEVEL OF MOTIVATION	INTERACTING WITH	THE READABILITY LEVEL OF MATERIAL	
(e.g., his reading purpose— from "reading to learn" to "reading to forget," set, "stakes" etc.)		(e.g., the reading grade level, word difficulty, sentence difficulty, etc.)	

Why hasn't the effect of a factor as obvious as reader motivation been accounted for in validity studies? I think I know one answer, at least. Subjects in experiments, especially if there are desirable rewards, tend to be rather highly motivated. Or, if they aren't already, most experimenters try to raise the level of subjects' motivation. After all, an old dictum states that subjects should be highly motivated during experimental testing in order to get stable scores.

Yet, looked at in the way I am suggesting, it appears that experimenters might actually be *reducing* the likelihood of a significant relationship between readability and comprehension. My on-going review of validity studies suggests exactly this. Most of my work involves the reading of microfilmed dissertations. Though they are hard on the eyes, they are a lot more illuminating than journal articles, which seldom provide critical details because of space restrictions.

What I have noticed is that a combination of two sets of conditions commonly found in experimentation usually seems to reduce the likelihood of a significant relationship between readability and comprehension. One set of variables consists of motivation-raising conditions, such as:

a. having as the experimenter the subjects' regular instructor; and/or

b. carrying out the experiment during a regular class period; and/or

c. stating, or at least implying, that the study is of considerable importance (i.e., will contribute to course grade, or help to determine the need for remedial work, etc.).

The second set of variables consists of provision for increased motivation to have an effect upon performance, such as:

a. providing generous reading time; and/or

b. allowing more than one reading of experimental passages; and/or

c. permitting referral to the experimental passages during the testing period.

Given, then, a combination of conditions which increase motivation, plus the opportunity for increased motivation to affect reading behavior, the likelihood of a significant relationship between readability and comprehension level appeared to decrease.

We now have a dissertation being completed at Ohio University by Carl Denbow that appears to demonstrate the motivation factor in another way. Two passages were rewritten so that for each there were two levels of readability: easy (approximately grade 5-6) and hard (approximately 13-15 grade level, or college). Subjects read a version of a passage, rated the content for interest to them, then took a "close" (deletion) comprehension test on the passage. One passage, which was on gun control, was rated significantly more interesting than the other, which was on wheat prices. The overall effect of readability was significant, but readability also had a significantly greater effect upon the comprehension of the non-preferred than the preferred passage.

What are some implications of my little model of readability and reader performance for instructional materials? I can think of several.

1. The readability level of materials is especially important to the persistence and comprehension of readers of low competence or low motivation or both. Put conversely, readability is of relatively much less importance to readers of high competence and motivation. In fact, readability is not even very important to a reader of moderate competence if his level of motivation is high enough, as many average citizens demonstrate every April 15 or thereabouts.

2. Tests of validity should be made under typical learning conditions, particularly as far as motivation is concerned. This may frequently call for a field type of test, when a laboratory-type of test is instead often carried out. It is entirely possible that the potential value of readability in correspondence

instruction might not have become apparent in a laboratory study as it did in the course completion study. It is similarly possible that *other* potentially valuable instructional variables may be falsely abandoned as non-significant because the conditions under which testing occurs do not represent well the conditions under which learning typically occurs.

3. Finally (and less clearly), it is possible that certain variables in written instruction may be more effective under conditions of low motivation. What the variables most effective under the condition of relatively high motivation might be is not clear to me. Perhaps organizing or thematic factors or test-like events (questions) might be candidates. But it is at least becoming clearer that readability is most effective under the condition of relatively low motivation.

And that condition, as in our correspondence study, is far more often typical during learning than we would like to think it is.

SUMMARY AND IMPLICATIONS FOR DAY THREE

Personalized and Open Learning Environments

Lawrence M. Stolurow
Professor of Education
SUNY at Stony Brook

I will try to come to grips with important issues arising, in my opinion, from today's presentations. We have heard a number of excellent papers and Professor Yelon has already reacted to them in a very interesting and stimulating way. Consequently, I will try to develop some of the ideas which were suggested to me by the papers and discussions rather than retrace steps. Later we will prepare a more thorough and careful treatment of the findings, problems and their implications. Professor Harrison and I plan to summarize by identifying points raised by symposium papers and their implications to suggest some possible directions which NIE might program in its development of educational technology.

It is clear to all of you, as it is to me, that many useful contributions were made here today and that there is a great deal of food for thought in the papers presented. Today's presentations considered in the background of the previous two days make it clear that the technology used in higher education has worked, is working and can be made to work even more efficiently, extensively and acceptably to both students and faculty.

It also is clear that it is not appropriate to talk about *a* technology any longer. We have heard about several viable educational technologies each of which, while developed as a separate effort, appears to be capable of coexisting, with advantage, in a single institution along with the others. The integrated use of the several technologies would represent the next logical step in the evolutionary process traced by the three days. It would permit students to select from a wider range of possible pedagogies according to their preferences and demonstrated value along the general lines suggested by Professor Lumsden's "free pedagogical economy."

It also is apparent that each of the technologies is dealing effectively with a set of problems and students. What is not always apparent is that the most difficult problems with which they deal are those that have plagued education throughout its history; these are the problems of teaching in efficient ways so as to produce learning and the desire to learn. An important historical difference between old and new approaches and one that has given impetus to the search for new and more efficient ways of teaching is the growth in the numbers of students to be accommodated by an educational system. In the more recent past, increases in numbers meant a search for ways in which the system could deal with larger and larger groups. Some of the technologies are designed to do this in relatively simple ways such as voice amplification to permit a teacher to reach a larger number of students. Other technologies, however, for example computer-aided instruction, are designed to increase the numbers of student related to, while also personalizing their experience in the learning environment.

One thing that the new technologies have done that was not done earlier is to make the basic problems of education more apparent to us. While this is a very useful contribution, it does not come without cost. The cost is that the problems are thought to be those of the technology, produced by the technology and peculiar to it. The fact is that they are problems which are indigenous to education and basic to the process of education itself whether, or not, technology is used.

One reason why educational technology has illuminated the basic problems of teaching and learning is that it minimizes the human factor in the delivery process. In order to minimize or eliminate the human component in delivery it is necessary to make very explicit just what is necessary and sufficient to achieve a set of instructional objectives. Everything has to be carefully planned in detail prior to the delivery of the instruction to the student. Things can not be left to the teacher's imagination and improvisation on the spot because there is no one present at the time to imagine and improvise. In educational technology what you see in development is what you get in delivery.

When it is possible to teach without a teacher the failures of the process to produce learning or the resulting inefficiencies are clearly those of the process of delivery that is used. On the other hand, when a teacher is the source of delivery, it is *not* clear where the problems are. The method, or strategy, used in the teaching program may be good, but it may not have been properly employed and other things may have been added inadvertently by the teacher that alter or reduce the effect it has. One major area of interest in this regard which is, as yet, unresolved, is the contribution of the teacher's personality to the effectiveness of the instructional experience. With the capacity to deliver instruction without the presence of the teacher, research on the relative effectiveness of instructional methods and strategies becomes possible in a way that allows for the presence and absence of a teacher and of teachers with different personality characteristics. The technology permits the introduction of a set of comparative conditions not previously available to the educational researcher.

The interdependence of the developmental process by means of which instructional materials and delivery plans are designed and developed differ among human and technological systems. In human systems the interdependence is so great that they can not be separated without great effort and this limits the degree of scientific inquiry that is possible. There is no way one can determine the relative contribution of the design from the delivery of instruction unless the capacity to deliver one design in a variety of ways and by a variety of means that can be specified and replicated exists. While it was always possible for a human teacher to separately plan an instructional interaction in detail sufficient to permit someone else to carry it out with comparable conditions prevailing and critical conditions maintained, this has not been seriously considered for a number of important reasons. As a result the developmental technology for instruction has not emerged prior to the development of viable delivery systems. With traditional approaches, reliance is, and has been, placed upon knowledge of subject matter and the intuition of the teacher. Educational technology in all of its forms of delivery, as revealed in this symposium, has formulated and used a developmental technology of some kind. Generally this has meant that technical specialists are involved so that the developmental process is more involved with respect to personnel as well as techniques than it is when accomplished by conventional means.

There is no doubt that delivery technology has captured the imagination and interest of a larger group than has developmental technology. There are a number of reasons for this. One is that the delivery technology for instruction is shared by the entertainment, business, and scientific communities. This sharing has had its good and bad sides for all of the educational technologies. The technology for development, on the other hand, is unique to the instructional process, although that has not been as clearly recognized as it might be. A strong and self-validating technology is required for the development of instructional systems and materials. Brian Lewis has provided us with some interesting and useful guidance here.

The technology of development was probably most developed in the presentation by Brian Lewis and it was elaborated upon by Professor Yelon. These two excellent presentations indicate that this technology is the application of the behavioral and social science theory and findings to the design of learning environments, and not an isolated development. When properly practiced it is a carefully planned activity requiring a variety of specialists and its own technological capabilities all of which are different from those required for delivery. Professor Klare's presentation also brought out, although it did not delve deeply into the point, that there is a need and an emerging response to that need. It is the need for new tools and methods for materials development. A fairly technical area is emerging to meet this need. It is designed to provide authors and instructional-materials designers with computer capabilities that can make the process of original materials development and their redesign more cost effective,

242

reliable, and valid. The computer is being developed as an information processor, not as a number cruncher. This area of technology could be described as applied educational psycholinguistics. It could become a substantial area of specialization in the near future if properly guided and sufficiently funded.

The area of applied educational psycholinguistics will require a whole array of computer software capabilities in an integrated environment tailored for the author, instructional-materials-and-systems designers, and the educational researcher specializing in instructional pragmatic and in the theory of instruction. In addition to the many existing editorial and text processing capabilities and the ability of computers to set type, a variety of analytical software is being developed, and it will be expanded upon as authors and instructional designers learn their trade and define new requirements. Readability analyzers, synonym banks, parsers with targeted areas of application, key word in context analyzers, disambiguation systems and indexing software all represent bits and pieces of a computer-based system needed to serve the educational industry. Furthermore, it could be developed at this time to serve with advantage the needs of instructional systems designers and authors for all of the technologies.

Professor Hanson referred to computer-managed instruction (CMI). This conception of a management system that provides a user with rapid and convenient access to bits and pieces of information or processing capabilities so that they interrelate with one another is an important concept with respect to the use of computers in personalized and open learning environments. This conception was not developed for either the delivery or the development processes faced by the institutions such as the Chicago TV College, the Open University and the others reported in today's session. It, if applied to these environments, could be an enriching and facilitating addition to what they have and doing so would represent the next stage of their evolution as alluded to earlier.

Related to the CMI conception is its counterpart for the developmental technology of instructional materials and systems. I refer to this counter-part notion as computer-managed authoring, or CMA. CMA could turn out to be one of the most significant developments of the seventies, and if it is not, then the other technologies will not grow at the rate and to the level of efficiency that is possible and essential for the rapid spread of educational technology, and the realization of its economic benefits. A well designed authoring system with appropriate capabilities would be able to assist an author or instructional materials or systems designer in the development of a wide variety of different forms of pedagogy and delivery. It would assist in the reforming of informational data bases to identify objectives and to relate the statements of objectives to forms of assessment. It would assist in putting together a Scenario for TV, a script for an audiotape or film. It would generate graphics and permit their rotation and perturbation for selection of displays in support of information and concepts in instructional dialogues, simulations or in the preparation of slides for use offline as well as online. Not only would the CMA software support the manipulation and generating capabilities by aiding authors in the production of materials for instruction, it also would provide a capability for storing units, tagging them and later retrieving them so they could be recombined into a variety of relationships with other materials to form whole new sets of instructional materials to meet unanticipated needs.

We do not hear as much about the development and use of computer-based systems today as we might have thought. The personalization of instruction in an unbounded learning environment is an ideal set of conditions for the realization of the potential of CAI, broadly conceived and developed. Furthermore, with CAI the level of detail required in planning and the range of variation possible in instructional interactions is greater than it is for any of the other forms of instructional technology. However, I feel that many are not ready, nor do they feel the time is ripe, to make the leap. They may be right, but someone has to be working within the existing centers in which technology is being successfully employed to develop the computer capabilities that will move the entire enterprise to its next level.

CAI is an interesting technology to pursue at this time since it bears a very supportive relationship to all the other delivery technologies, and to CMI and CMA. It might be useful to look at some aspects of the relationships. In the area of development of materials CAI is probably the most demanding on the author or materials development team because of the level of instructional detail it requires, particularly if the full range of delivery modes is used as appropriate for the accomplishment of a variety of specific objectives over the long haul. To a greater extent TV, films and even audio-tutorial technology allow greater freedom to the developer of materials than does

CAI. This has both its good and bad sides. On the good side it is important to point out that the rigor and detail required for CAI materials development could make a substantial contribution to the other technologies by defining and specifying variables and conditions that should be attended to under other conditions of delivery as well. The requirement for objectivity and explicitness in planning an instructional experience or a learning environment produces documentation that can serve as a model which is either shared or used as a point of departure in the development of materials for other technologies. Thus both the diffusion of information and the validation of concepts and techniques for both design and delivery become better and more effectively realized. While not appreciated widely, the cost of developing an hour of CAI is less than it is for an hour of most of the other technologies and significantly lower than that for TV or film. Not only that, but also the cost curves differ. The developmental cost for CAI has been coming down while that for the other technologies has been rising over the same period of time. On the bad side, CAI delivery costs are greater than they are for the other technologies, especially film and TV. We need to consider the total system when we deal with the question of productivity.

Since CAI materials require greater detail and more complete analysis than is the case for the other technologies and since this could be turned to an advantage for the educational industry by providing guidance to the design and delivery forms used by all the instructional technologies, it would seem that CAI has a special place in the set of technologies we have been dealing with. This point is supported further by the fact that CAI systems generate more specific effectiveness data than do the other technologies. CAI is an interactive technology that records interactions in detail, and in a form that is retrievable and processable by computers—facilitating the formative and summative evaluation processes. It is important, for these reasons alone, to consider CAI in terms of a long-, as well as a short-term investment. As an investment within the set of technologies it has many more facets of potential significance and value to the improvement of instruction and learning environments in general, than the others. It not only produces instruction in the short term and with a degree of effectiveness comparable to the others, if not superior under some conditions, it also can be used in ways that are supportive of the other technologies and their growth. It has the further advantage of costing less to produce. When it exists at least two other important things also become more feasible. One is the development of information about developmental technology for instructional materials and systems in general. Another is research findings which increases our understanding of the process of instruction, the design of learning environments and the research methodology required to further these ends.

Many feel that the level of detail required to develop CAI materials and systems is not warranted by the level of existing knowledge. This seems to be circular argument based upon a short-sighted view of the state of instructional research and the scientific process. New tools for scientific inquiry have always opened up new areas of discovery and deepened our understanding of the natural phenomena studied. Instructional systems are now available that permit detailed control of learning environments and allow for the manipulation of personalized conditions for the purpose of studying interesting and useful statistical interaction effects with methods and strategies of instruction. The fact that previous research has identified little that vigorously supports a theoretical position like that proposed in my idiographic model, for example, does not dissuade me from the position that research on statistical interaction effects involving personal characteristics of the learner and the specific nature of programs of instruction are a useful and appropriate area of research which justify the development and use of CAI systems. Without the computer to manage the conditions and the independent variables it is difficult to do research in this important area so basic to the personalization of learning environments. Thus the fact that there is so little existing data does not seem surprising nor should it be unexpected.

The basic problems facing educational technology are the very problems that face education generally. These are the problems of learning and instruction. Personalization of instruction if it is to be realized and cultivated requires research and the level and scale of the research has to be different from that with which we are familiar. Also the capabilities of CAI systems are unique so one needs a system to study their implications. Consequently, the investment into educational research has to be reassessed. Many feel that the educational industry seems to have experienced too little too late in the sixties. I am not convinced of that at all, and feel that neither should you since the things we have heard about today and on the previous days are the fruits of those investments. In this light the problems with diffusion and perception seem to me to be more with the expectations than with the results. The frustration with lack of progress and discouragement in the lack of support which many claim to feel, seems to be the result more of what was expected than the realities of what was delivered. If we consider what could have been delivered with the limited knowledge base, the newness of every one of the technologies, and the scarcity of top quality personnel, the result has been very good indeed. In my opinion, the reports we have heard are most encouraging and speak very well of the fruits of a meager investment relative to the size of the problem and the short time available to cultivate educational technology when it is just coming of age.

The decades of the fifties and the sixties have produced educational technologies that not only deliver at competitive levels with the traditional modes in many areas of higher education, and especially in professional education, they also provide larger numbers, if not new groups, with quality instruction. New segments of the adult population are being reached by television in this country and abroad. These students are presenting new and equally interesting problems to institutions. The established institutions are being challenged by this student group much as the returning veterans challenged the colleges and universities in the fifties. In retrospect many of the academics who complained at the time that the veterans were in colleges are now looking with nostalgia at the time when the student veteran was on campus as an eager and dedicated student. The reports by professors Zigerell and Lewis have suggested that this may happen again with another population of students. From the research point of view the returning adult, who after several years decides to get an education or to complete a degree program represents a segment of the student population about which we have very little data. We therefore have to proceed cautiously in extending the knowledge we now have which is so heavily based upon the typical college freshman or sophomore. This new group represents an important research area for an NIE program.

The basic problems of teaching and learning have to be considered whenever an educational institution relates to students. The nature of the student population can be an important factor in determining the results obtained from particular approaches and conditions of learning. The different technologies provide the educational researcher with different capabilities in dealing with basic issues about learning and instruction; not only do they contribute in a scientific manner to this end, but also they permit research *in vivo*. Scientifically they provide a way of stabilizing the conditions of learning to make them more replicable, and they permit the manipulation of variables. Furthermore, they aid in the collection of data in "real time" — while the student is learning — rather than restricting research to the collection of data after the fact.

Unfortunately we do not have much of the data needed to make valid decisions about the nature of the optimum conditions for a learning environment to be used with different students. We do not have many of the methods and tools for identifying critical student characteristics to study a number of research questions relating to personalization. We know much less than we would like about how to get different kinds of students to learn efficiently and how to get them to like learning. To a great extent the lack of available tools is at the bottom of these problems. With conventional approaches to instruction, the collection of data represents a substantial additional undertaking with its cost add-ons. While it is still a significant undertaking when instructional technology is available, it is nevertheless true that with CAI at least the additional cost of producing research data is not proportionally as great nor the task as difficult. The reason is that the basic investment in the development of materials and systems automatically produces the data needed as a byproduct if the CAI system is properly put together in the first place. The additional input that is most required no matter what context is involved is in the research design and the implications it has for the numbers of students required. Computer technology does not help here. This discussion is intended to underscore the point previously made that the educational technologies are not just instruments for delivery and development, they also are tools useful in the production of new knowledge about teaching and learning. They are *in vivo* research tools.

An important question, not addressed directly by the papers presented today, but one to which we all should be sensitive is how we make each technology more of a hand-maiden, a better tool and eventually a well honed instrument for research on the instructional process. In dealing with this set of problems we are not just dealing with formative evaluation which was so nicely developed by Professor Yelon but also with summative evaluation and the approaches to it provided by quasi-experimental designs as well as more rigorous experimental designs.

Ideally the technology when used for research as well as for delivery of instruction should not intrude on the process of instruction itself, but rather serve as an aid in the solution of instructional problems. An important difference in our present viewpoint from that which we held in the past when teachers were the only available source of instruction is that the system of delivery should be a catalyst, facilitating the learning process without entering into the process itself. In this symposium we have not talked about obtrusive and unobtrusive technology. I think it is correct to say, however, that all of us are interested in seeing that the new instructional technology be as unobtrusive as possible. One way to do this is by making the content and the process of information and perceptual experience more apparent than the delivery system itself. The delivery system technology, whether it is TV, AV, AT or computer mediated interactions, should blend into the background of the learning environment; it should not compete for the student's attention with what it is that the student should be learning. Neither should its demand for learning new skills be excessive.

There are many different ways to look at the perceptions of educational technology as it relates to an educational institution. The purpose in doing this is to develop a perspective that permits us to make a decision about the alternatives in a consistent frame of reference. The papers presented today indicate that there is a considerable range of variation in the capital investment required, the types of resources needed, and in the expertise necessary. Videotape technology and the mailing of cassettes represents a lower level of investment in facilities than does the use of broadcast television with electronic delivery. Professor Baldwin has kindly shared with us some cost data of videocassettes and Brian Lewis, Professor Zigerell, information about television. In spite of significant differences, it was quite clear that each technology can become an effective and impressive approach either within an existing institution, or in a separately developed institution. The costs involved differ not only with the mode of delivery and the capital investment but also with the kinds of personnel required.

While each technology can become standard practice in an institution, the question of effective transfer to new institutions remains an unsolved problem. Not dealt with here is the question of how an institution that wants to emulate an established pattern actually gets started. The documentation provided could be helpful in the early stages. The successful institutional efforts about which we heard are not themselves equipped to assist others to get started in any substantial way if they want to establish a comparable capability. This problem should be faced by funding agencies.

The widespread use of educational technologies in other institutions raises several questions which in the context of this symposium on productivity in higher education are significant. First, it is important to point out that the cost of each of these examples does not necessarily have to be justified on the basis of transfer to other institutions. The cost of developing each of these centers probably can be justified on the basis of its use in the institution in which it has grown and developed. It is interesting, as Professor Yellon has pointed out, that the number of students related to by television technology represents a growth curve that can not be matched by a university with walls.

This point raises another interesting question regarding the cost analysis that can be made of educational systems. It is the question of the cost of adding additional students. Audiotapes, television and CAI all can add large numbers of additional students without incurring a major step-function in their cost curves, whereas a university with walls does incur a step-function with relatively small amounts of growth. While the average cost per student may not differ when alternative approaches are compared over a particular range in the size of the student population they serve, it is still possible that the alternatives could differ significantly in the periodicity and magnitude of the additional capital investment to accommodate growth in student population.

Another aspect of the cost problem is the inequity in the burden of proof. The new approach is in a defensive posture. Each of the presentations we heard today has had to be more cost conscious and more defensive about its costs than the conventional institutional arrangement which it replaces or happens to be compared to. It frequently, though inappropriately, is assumed that what is now being done is cost effective and the best that can be done with existing resources. Any discussion of alternatives to the established practice often elicits a defensive posture rather than a willingness to study and explore the alternatives in their terms and in relation to questions of productivity or relative benefits. This defensive posture often is manifest as an offensive posture and the attack is frequently focused on the very questions which are hardest to answer by the conventional system itself, namely, how effective is it. Often this argument is made on the basis of information relating to the input and not on the basis of the output (effects on students). Certainly the input analysis as described by Brian Lewis leaves little doubt about the care and detail of the information analysis engaged in when materials are developed for use in the British Open University. Few conventional systems, if any, can provide the equivalent information and documentation regarding the input to its courses. When we can not measure the output or when we can only measure some small aspect of it, we rely on the care and the type of procedure used to produce learning effects. If a conventional system hires teachers with the right credentials and uses the right textbooks it is assumed that it is doing a good job whether or not there is any objective data on the performance of its students. When different procedures are used and when videotapes or computers are employed to deliver the instruction, for example, then output measures are required, but they still may be held suspect by the established institutions. If some of the measures of student effects are new, then there is a long process of credentialing of the instruments and procedures that has to be engaged in. They have to be validated, their reliability has to be established and the academic peer group has to be convinced that the instruments are, in fact, producing useful and meaningful information. There is an additional problem, however. It is that the comparison with the conventional system is difficult, or impossible to make for any one, or more, of a large number of reasons. This puts things into limbo with respect to adoption and use of the new approach and the staying power is on the side of the conventional system since it is already funded and has its sources of funds rather well established and the mechanisms for obtaining them well developed.

Still another manifestation of the inequity in the burden of proof comes when the data are available from a summative evaluation in which two or more, instructional systems are compared. We experienced some discussions during the symposium regarding the studies producing "no statistically significant difference." Many, if not most, studies comparing conventional and a new alternative have produced results indicating no significant difference in the performance of the students. This finding should be viewed in perspective, but it usually is not. These studies compare a new technology which is relatively young and not well developed with an established alternative that has reached its plateau of growth. Proper perspective can be achieved when we view the new technology in relation to its growth cycle to determine where it is at the time the comparison was made. Since the technological approach is typically at an early point in its developmental cycle and the conventional approach is typically at maturity, the comparison is like that of a child to an adult in getting a task done where maturity plays an important part. When viewed in this way the "no significant difference" result is, in fact, encouraging, not a disappointment.

Consider the two kinds of error we can make in making inferences based upon data relating to variables presumably affecting the instructional environment. One kind is to reject hypotheses that are useful; the other is to accept hypotheses that are not useful. The selection of the minimum confidence level and the statistical test used affect the relative likelihood of these two kinds of error. It would seem appropriate to develop guidelines for this research problem. At this point in time and given the nature of the information base and the status of instructional theory, it would seem that the better strategy to use would be to use practices that may result in our accepting more false hypotheses than we reject useful ones. One reason is that when research is done *in vivo* the cost is not as great as it is when research is conducted separately. Therefore the cost of further testing would not be as great. Most of the cost of research on instruction conducted in vivo would be appropriately assigned to the cost of instruction itself since students would, in fact, be taught anyway. The argument is bolstered further by the fact that in conventional instruction there is a wide range of variation from instructor to instructor anyway and even from time to time for a single instructor. Therefore the testing of hypotheses that are well conceived and carefully introduced would be likely to generate no more variation in the conditions of education than now occurs. Furthermore, the hypotheses tested would be generated to improve the level of effectiveness of the learning environment so the spirit with which the variations would be produced would have the same kinds of expectations as any teacher who was trying to improve a learning environment based upon his, or her, intuition.

The data processing models used in collecting and evaluating data to make decisions about alternatives in the redesign of learning environments can make an important difference in the growth and development of a field. Most of the research conducted thus far has relied on descriptive and inferential statistical models in which comparisons of central tendencies or variables are involved. The problems requiring decision however involve more information. Important are the data on utilities and costs. It would seem appropriate, therefore, to develop a project that fostered the use of decision-theoretic models and the development of methods and instruments to produce data relating to utilities and costs. This should be a high priority effort within NIE. It could benefit from the applications of these models in other sectors of public interest such as the environmental area where subjective utilities are being used. Consistent with this orientation is the use of newly developed testing models to determine the student's confidence in his own information relative to a set of problems he is given to solve. This is sometimes called confidence testing. As a set of conditions this approach to evaluation increases the reliability of a test rather substantially. It also has the advantage of providing more information for both formative evaluation and student evaluation. Professor Lumsden's recommendation that education be restructured so as to provide students with pedagogical options would if implemented produce data on student preferences for optional routes to an educational goal. This is consistent with what is being proposed here. I would go further and suggest that the system be designed to allow for the collection of data on the preferences of others as well. We need to know what the teachers prefer to work with, what the parent and taxpayer prefers, and what the administrators and managers prefer. It is conceivable that these might differ. If so then there is a problem to be faced in attempting to optimize the situation for the set of individuals involved in making the system work. It would not be useful to set our sights on the maximization of the student's preferences if it resulted in a minimization of all the other preferences involved.

The fact that there has not been a more extensive use of decision theoretic models is not an oversight or accident. In part it is historically determined since these are relatively recent developments, but possibly more important is the fact that the instruments and procedures have not been developed to produce the kinds of data needed to use these models. A difficult problem is the design of situations so that preferences can be measured. Another is the collection of subjective utilities; a third is cost in financial terms. None of the accounting systems has been developed to the level that permits these models to be used with maximum effectiveness. However, this should not be used as an excuse to ignore their potential contribution. On the contrary the models, if we are convinced of their ultimate value, should be used to determine the nature and priority of a methodological research and development effort to provide the techniques and tools.

A further complication worth noting is the fact that costs and utilities vary over time. It is necessary therefore to plan the development of procedures that are cumulative and historical. We need to develop cost curves and utility curves and relate these to other conditions and variables. Decisions made at any point in time take a while to become effective. We need to know what the conditions are likely to be when they become an actuality. The actual costs and today's estimates of utility may not be an accurate index of what they will be when a new technology is introduced in the future. To use decision models with cost data it is important to develop the data base for use in forecasting. Comparison of labor intensive approaches with technological alternatives requires attention to the curves. The cost of labor is going up and the cost of hardware is going down. But the costs are not just the direct costs or current expenditures. They also, in the case of labor, include continuing costs associated with benefits, especially pensions. The recently publicized budget of the city of New York, for example, produced considerable comment relating to the item on retirement pay. It is quite clear that we need to consider the use of personnel resources in terms of the percentage of the total costs and in relation to their need to achieve educational goals. We must define need in a different manner than in the past since there are obvious technical solutions to the delivery and development problems which did not exist before. We have to include in the definition of need the preferences and subjective utilities of the students and the other parties in the educational system. The student population to be considered in planning and operating an educational system is becoming quite different and the trends in the nature of the student population are already clearly different from the recent past when the student population in higher education came predominantly from the graduating high-school student group. As technology of the kind we have heard about today increases in its development and availability the kinds of students and the numbers of students to be related to will change dramatically. This also means that either new institutions are to be formed to accommodate the different educational needs or the present ones will have to modify their programs and procedures to accommodate a wider range of students and student needs. Probably both will happen if we judge on the basis of what we have heard here at the symposium.

It is paradoxical that we seem to be at a new frontier in education just at a time when the financial resources are proportionally drying up. This means that we are faced with an economic condition that is going to force change but that we will have to proceed with care and a great deal of planning to conserve the scarce resources available to try and to explore alternative solutions. It would seem that the technology can relate to this mix of conditions in a useful way. It can, for example, permit the modeling and simulation of alternatives. As a method of planning this may provide the needed guidance as well as cost benefits.

Part Five

GENERAL SUMMARY AND

RECOMMENDATIONS

EDUCATIONAL TECHNOLOGIES: RECOMMENDATIONS FOR RESEARCH AND DEVELOPMENT

Lawrence M. Stolurow
and
Shelley A. Harrison

The Symposium Format

This symposium was planned to explore, in some depth, the potential and implications of using new and advanced communications technology-based systems for improving the organizational effectiveness and operational efficiency of higher educational institutions. To accomplish this, speakers were invited and their papers commissioned. Each one was asked to present information about the technological area with which they were most familiar and in which they were currently active.

The seminar, consisting of an evening session on Sunday and three full days and two evenings, examined a range of alternatives for increasing the productivity of higher educational institutions with respect to instructional technology. It seems to the planners that the heart of the problem and the most critical function of institutions of higher education is instruction. For this reason that process was the primary focus of attention.

The invited experts were free to either present their prepared paper or to depend upon the group to have read the paper in which case they could spend the scheduled time to elaborate or further develop and editorialize. Discussants were identified to comment upon the papers and to provide a critique as well as to develop implications and useful elaborations. In some cases problems were identified and difficulties pointed out. In addition, the assembled group were given opportunities to discuss and develop points relating to the presentations.

In planning the symposium a matrix representation was developed and used. We rejected rather early a set of rubrics that related to media and to types of systems. Our rationale was simply that the real problems were those that could be referred to as the design and development of learning environments for students in higher education. Media and systems were to be considered as tools and not as the defining condition. The three-by-four matrix gave structure, focus and operational guidance both to the symposium itself and to this report. We found that the participants when invited and introduced to the conception responded positively. There was no argument or negative feeling expressed so we are led to believe that while unconventional, the structure did not inhibit or distort the analyses we sought and the constructive developments we were after.

Following the keynote paper on Sunday night, a three-day opportunity to meet was cast into an operational plan that was represented by assigning each day to a type of learning environment. On each of the three days, the plan was to look at four characteristics of every exemplary model presented that day. On each day, for each model, we considered four topics: media, methods, management, and measurement. Since each day represented a class of learning environments, it was necessary to have a few models presented on a day so as to represent both the breadth and focus of technological applications under the specified conditions. The interesting outcome is the fact that on each day, or in other words for each type of learning environment, the range of different and successful technologies in use is broad, and certainly no single technology stands out as the best one to use, either overall or in any particular learning environment, nor does it seem that any technology is automatically excluded from use in any of the learning environments. Since all of the technologies are possible within each type of learning environment, it seems that decisions regarding which one to use must be based on other considerations.

The set of three days was conceived not only as a continuum or evolutionary progression, but also as one that was multi-dimensional in nature. Two intuitively obvious parameters were used to characterize each day and to convey this developmental sequence of days dealing with environments beginning with, but departing from, convention as the symposium moved from the first to the third days. The first day was devoted to a consideration of what might be called Conventional Instruction—"ground zero" in the sequence. During this day the participants were busy looking into the use of technologies in support of conventional learning environments; we identified these as "grouped and bounded." The second day dealt with "individualized and bounded" learning environments. The third day dealt with "personalized and unbounded" learning environments. It became quite clear that technology can be a useful tool no matter which type of environment is available for learning. The lower bound is simply that some technology can be used in all learning environments. The upper bound problem, however, is more difficult to specify: namely, what is the maximum use possible in each type of learning environment. At this time we do not have data to suggest what the upper bound would be for each type of technology in each kind of learning environment. Related is the optimization problem, what is the best mix of existing technology to achieve a cost-effective solution to the learning and satisfaction produced.

Productivity, Problems and a Proposal

The keynote paper presented Sunday night was commissioned from Professor Keith Lumsden, an economist from Stanford University. His paper was titled "Technological Innovation in a Hostile Environment: Problems of Increasing Productivity in Higher Education." Lumsden argues, from the perspective of an economist, that a number of controlling conditions have had a subtle, but pervasive, effect on the operation of academia. Professor Lumsden identifies the main ones and related them to the problem of producing changes in the practices that could be accomplished at least in part, with technology or technological aid which is available and could alter productivity in the academy. He also argues that the incentive system, within the university for both students and faculty, requires a "massive research effort" if significant increases in educational productivity, regardless of how they are measured, are to be realized through the use of technological innovations. His paper is divided into four parts. The first discusses possible functions of the university and problems encountered whenever differences in perceived function cause conflict. The second discusses major obstacles to change. The third indicates the inadequacies of much of the previously conducted research on the economics of higher education. Finally, he proposed a research effort to examine pedagogies while content was kept constant. Each pedagogy would provide an alternative set of learning conditions while maintaining a set of educational objectives. The study should be designed with the purpose of determining the relative costs and effectiveness of the alternative pedagogies. As a general form of research to produce data in many areas this is seen as a national priority; it is to provide data not now available regarding student preferences.

Professor Lumsden's paper discusses obstacles to change and includes several intriguing notions about overcoming them. One that makes sound economic sense and an interesting psychological condition with respect to the student and his opportunities to use learning resources is, in effect like providing the student with a book of tickets such as one gets to see Disneyland. The total can be spent anyway one likes. Within a uniform tuition system this would be possible based upon the known costs of a four year bachelor's experience. Students would have to pay for their instruction in terms of the cost of the resources they want to use (the alternative pedagogies) to achieve a level of competence, self satisfaction, or both, in pursuit of their academic goals. Students who chose to learn something by means of an audio or video cassette which might cost less than a human tutor or even a seminar, could spend less by making this choice and could then use the savings in other ways.

In order to make this type of experiment possible a number of conditions have to be met. The options would have to be available. This means that the instructional materials have to exist and be in alternative forms for delivery or capable of being encoded in some alternative forms. Ideally, the alternative pedagogies should have some established validity—possibly data showing that there exists a student for whom each alternative has been found to produce the competencies involved. Some may argue that this minimal condition is not sufficient, but that is another matter. The administration of the institution involved has to make the decision to allocate the resources needed to make a set of options available. Data should exist for the student to permit him (or her) to process it to decide on one of the alternatives. In order to do this research has to be done to produce the data and the student has to have had prior educational opportunities of a similar sort by means of which he (or she) would be prepared to make the type of decision required. A set of previous research projects has to be completed which relate to the points mentioned and which included representative samples so the range of human variation which is likely to be involved will have been studied.

Fundamental to Lumsden's proposal is the assumption that the student (a consumer) will get what he (she) pays for, and that the more one pays, the greater the cost to the institution to develop, or provide what you get. This means careful economic analyses are needed so the pricing of alternatives is realistic.

In order to get the data that do not exist and to get the ultimate project funded, Lumsden argues that the research should be supported by the Federal Government. His position is that the research is a public good and no group could benefit from doing the studies in an unselfish way. Data are needed on costs, probability of successful completion of the objectives for different types of students. Lumsden assumes the position that different kinds of students will respond differently, and/or simply prefer one pedagogy to another. While the evidence for this type of thinking does not exist in the published research to the degree one would like, it seems that there are data which do suggest the potential validity of the "interaction hypothesis" along the lines of the "idiographic model" for CAI, for example. The problem is to identify the characteristics of students that should be known so the data can be employed in making differential decisions both initially with respect to the teaching program used, and during the course of learning as has been modeled for adaptive CAI.

One question raised by Lumsden's paper was the strategy and criteria to be used in making the decision to conduct the study along the general lines suggested. Lumsden suggests that we wait until reliable data exist on both cost and effectiveness. The course of history does not argue that this has to be the basis for taking the next step. The best next step can be taken and if reasonably successful it can attract the necessary funding. This was what happened in aviation once the first heavier-than-air craft flew. Once the possibility was actually demonstrated, then interest in the problem developed and the scientific basis for further development takes place. Involved would be the development of the instruments and methods for determining costs and benefits. One could argue that the requirement for the existence of reliable cost benefit data as a precondition to the large-scale research is a strategy that turns out to be overly conservative. The reason is that it could throttle down efforts to get the job done in the name of rationality, while producing a negative social benefit.

The whole question of research and especially educational research was raised by Lumsden's paper. Most of the participants clearly have been persuaded of its value, but they were not persuaded that educational research is sufficiently accepted by the academic community as a whole. Research on instruction does not seem to add the legitimacy to the result that is comparable to the value added by research in the social sciences, let alone the physical, the natural sciences, or medicine. Here is another problem lurking in the background that impinges upon the accomplishment of the effort suggested by Lumsden. It seems that it is necessary to get basic educational research itself honored and appreciated. Even scientists who in their own substantive area (e.g. physics) are convinced of the value of research shift standards when they consider the procedures for solving problems relating to the teaching of their own science. This is a serious problem. There is a real "credibility gap" for the faculty. The students, on the other hand, seem quite willing to accept and use educational research data when it is provided them. But another question complicates the situation. This is the question of priority with respect to our needs at this time. Lumsden seems to assume that we have the materials for the major experimental effort he proposed. Many others feel that we do not; they assert that we should be doing research on production and not on testing alternatives. To what extent the belief that there is an insufficient amount of material available is related to the point previously made about the credibility of the data that exist concerning materials is not known. These perceptions and beliefs are obviously related, however.

In order to obtain critical data such as student preferences and the cost of the alternatives for achieving a particular objective, a sizable research effort is clearly needed. Just how large a project should be mounted to answer the questions raised by Professor Lumsden remains to be determined. That question and the nature of the research design to be used in the study should be the purpose of a research effort that is the initial phase of a longer-range program in educational technology.

Let us indicate some of the more obvious aspects of such a study. It would have to be planned on a national scale to include the variety of educational elements representative of the different pedagogies, learning environments, physical facilities, faculties and different student populations. The research design, collection and analysis of data and the coordination requires a centralized effort so the program would best be managed by one group, but, of necessity, it would involve many colleges and universities.

Also required is a project designed to develop a list of the critical parameters for use in a national survey of educational programs and institutions. To begin with, a preliminary list would have to be derived from an analytical study of available research and from theory. The process by means of which the instrument used in making the survey is developed, must, of necessity, be iterative so it provides the required information by successive approximations. This means the study will extend over a period of years. It also has to be a rather comprehensive study since information is needed about the characteristics of the students as well as their achievement levels following different learning experiences under different conditions.

Unlike previous large-scale studies, the design would be generated at least in part, by the hypothesis that there are statistical interaction effects rather than that there is a linear correlation among the variables. Assumptions about the structure of the data base to be assembled are critical determiners of the design used in collecting the data to be analyzed. If it is assumed that there are statistical interactions between variables representing student characteristics, on the one hand, and variables representing the learning environment, on the other hand, then the instruments used as well as the sampling, and the collection of the data should take these hypotheses into account.

Evidence of statistical interaction effects between variables representing students, on the one hand, and instructional programs, conditions and learning environments, on the other hand, are needed for differential diagnosis and selective prescription of instructional experiences. Since the number of variables to be considered is potentially very large and the amount of existent information relatively small, careful planning of research is indicated. Large samples of students are required. Selected sociological, anthropological, and psychological data, for example, would have to be collected for each student. Each variable representing a student characteristic would be related to one or more dependent variables relating various kinds of student performance to rate of learning, to achievement level, and to various measures in the affective domain. In order to answer the cost-benefit questions, it would also be necessary to include data relating to the costs incurred in achieving learning effects and the different affective reactions.

To obtain all of the kinds of data required, it is clear that some new instruments and procedures would have to be developed. For example, colleges and universities do not routinely collect data relating to such student characteristics as their personality characteristics and level of anxiety. Standardized tests of student achievement are not usually given both at the beginning and end of each course or every academic year, yet this is necessary for the measurement of learning gains. Colleges and universities often do not give final examinations but even these are given more often than are pre-tests. Information about what students already know is critical for the assessment of what they have learned, and for making instructional decisions about what to teach individual students. The large unanswered question about the efficiency of academic programs is: "How much time is spent by the faculty teaching things students already know?" The only way to answer this question is to collect information before the students are presented with a new learning experience. The mechanics of doing this can vary. For example, the data for the next course can be collected at the end of the last learning experience at the same time as the final, or post-test, is given. The one testing experience can be both a pre-test and a post-test. However, such practices have not yet become a regular part of college or university plan. As a result, it is unlikely that the critical data needed to make the survey of existing data for use in planning more definitive studies of alternative pedagogies will be available. Therefore, while the need for a survey exists at this time, it should be planned with this knowledge in mind so as to maximize its payoff. To do this its planning should include the collection of data from the administration and the faculty to determine their willingness to change their practices so as to collect the required data. It also should include questions dealing with the ability of the institution to meet these requirements. This part of the study should reveal possible deterrents to the collection of such data so they can be dealt with in any subsequent planning.

Cost data do not exist in colleges and universities in the detailed form required for cost-benefit analysis of instruction. Most colleges and universities do not budget or analyze the cost of individual courses of instruction or even programs of instruction. The cost unit is usually the department, and a department may deliver instruction to a variety of different programs, therefore, its costs have to be analyzed in detail. With the present accounting systems in colleges and universities it would be difficult, if possible at all, to specify the costs of even the more obvious items such as the physical plant improvements and new construction. These facilities frequently are shared in their use by a number of different programs. The amortization of their costs and the distribution of their costs are problems that must be dealt with in a comprehensive economic research project aimed at the problems of cost-benefit analysis within higher education. Space, supplies, materials and personnel costs, all have to be identified at the level of the working unit for which a cost-benefit analysis is being made. All of the contributing components have to be included in the analysis no matter what group provides the service or the facility. The complexity of the problem and its relative novelty indicate that there is a significant research and development requirement to produce the models and methods needed to permit institutions of higher education to participate in a realistic way in a cost-benefit analysis of their educational efforts.

The economic models and the accounting and budgeting procedures required for a cost-benefits analysis also have to be developed. In fact, this is a necessary first step, but one that could run concurrently with the research and development work involved in generating the student performance data required to determine the benefits (e.g., learning gains, satisfaction) from particular programs. Only if similar accounting procedures are used by different institutions can a multi-institutional research study deal with the question of cost-effectiveness in any meaningful and satisfying way.

It is clear that we can expect differences in the basic costs relating to education simply because of differences relating to the part of the country in which schooling is provided. Salary and materials costs vary over the country and taxes also show great variations. Tuition varies for the private and public institutions and the newer ones are amortizing building and other facilities acquired at much greater cost than the older and more established institutions.

From this brief analysis of some of the many problems that confront a cost-benefit analysis, it seems that a definitive answer is not likely to be forthcoming in the very near future. The point that needs to be made at this time, it seems, is that the education industry is being placed on the alert; it has to become *cost conscious* and develop methods and procedures for good cost accounting. The cost-benefits analysis is a one edged sword; it only cuts out and down. It is especially sharp in relation to educational technology, and yet labor intensity is so characteristic of education that it is hard to believe that technology can not, over the long haul, produce savings. We need to ask why education is the last stronghold of the cottage industry. We also need to ask whether we can continue to afford it as a cottage industry.

If we proceed to examine this very important set of problems in a serious and methodical way, in the manner it clearly deserves, there are a number of positive things that can be done. Data of the kind suggested in this seminar could be collected both from the input and the output side. Models could be developed. Simulations prepared and run. Empirical studies could be conducted to test the simulations and to validate their predictions. The information from the empirical studies could then be used to improve the models. The models could provide the basis for redesigning operating systems.

At this point we see a critical need for a set of organized research and development activities which could be derived from the papers presented and the growing literature in the field. Its form would embrace the study described by Lumsden with the additional implications included along the lines just described here and later on. Each project, however, would have to be developed and related to the whole set so as to provide a program of research all of which should be conducted within a systems framework. Not only its management, but also its continued review and systematic modification should be centralized to achieve maximum efficiency. This program of research and development could be the defining activity of NIE in the next several years. The collection of data on a national basis to provide a data base for the wide range of educational decisions to be made is an important national need. In fact it is a critical need at this time. Educational technology, as said before, is making this need apparent and, in addition it is casting the problem into an operational form that makes the approaches to its solution clearer. Technology, especially computer technology, could be an important tool to get the job done. NIE could consider a division within its administrative aegis that operates like the Bureau of Labor Statistics, for example. By starting with that model in mind, but at a lower level of support, this division of NIE could provide higher education with many very badly needed services.

Professor Lumsden's paper and some of the implications drawn from it might raise the specter of standardization, control, and restriction of educational practices in the minds of many educators. It seems to us that this is clearly unfounded, and appears to be a set of fears which reflect lack of knowledge and faith in the knowledge of individual differences among people and institutions, not to mention ethnic and sub-cultural groups. The psychological variations among students are certainly as complex as the variations in physical size, preferences for food, clothing, housing and all the other physical artifacts of our society. Why then should it not be the case that variety will also prevail in education. In fact, it would seem reasonable to assume that the variety might even be greater in its range of variation than it is for any of the physical characteristics.

When we consider the question of optimization, we are thinking not only of the most efficient learning environment for an individual, given his, or her, peculiarities, but also his, or her, preferences which includes attitudinal data relating to the preferences the student might have for a particular type of experience. Also, if we accept Lumsden's recommendation then different individuals will probably pay more for certain experiences and less for other educational experiences just as they do for the different entertainment, food or other consumer goods, options. Even in what appear to be more highly controlled economic units such as manufacturing of competitive consumer products, a wide variety of companies (organizational systems) and production plans co-exist in a free economy. There is little to suggest that the educational industry will move to a consistent pattern or anything approaching uniformity as more and better information becomes available to guide decision-making and as the technology improves. The problem will more likely be one of getting the industry to use the available data at all let alone in interesting ways.

We may have to move in education the way the country did in agriculture. We may have to establish, at various campuses, or centers, the counterpart of the agricultural experimental station. These units might be called *Educational Experimental Stations.* They would have professional expertise in technology and the information that could be applied in efforts to improve the different institutions and help them make use of available information to solve the problems indigenous to their instructional and educational objectives, their student body, faculty, alumni and local conditions.

Through a national network of *Educational Experimental Stations* the use of technology might become more widespread and the available information more efficiently utilized. Models for such activities are needed. There is every reason to assume that if interesting and viable models were developed they would serve more than just the institutions of higher education. However, by starting with these institutions the investment in their development would be less and the payoff greater. The diffusion of their effects throughout the country could be facilitated by university and professional societies. Furthermore, the limited personnel available for such an undertaking, at this time, could be concentrated, if there is a smaller number of centers. This would permit the assembly of a "critical mass" of personnel sufficient to get the job done.

No institutions of higher education are currently training the types of personnel needed to provide the varieties of expertise needed for the staff of an Educational Experimental Station. Some institutions are beginning to train some of the specialists that would be needed in a team effort. There is a curricular problem. The field needs a comprehensive program, especially the graduate training of professional educational technologists. It not only needs specialists, but also generalists with the mixture of knowledge and skills required to deal with many of the complex problems in education which are not now being faced by properly trained personnel, nor are questions being dealt with by research and development in a scientific manner. They are being treated as philosophical and intuitive issues.

RECOMMENDATIONS

Professor Lumsden's argument that public funding is essential is sound and convincing. For this reason we recommend that NIE develop a program in educational technology with the following areas:

Recommendation 1: Study grants be provided to develop one, or more, plans, with cost estimates and time projections so as to make explicit the dimensions of the "massive" research effort proposed by Professor Lumsden.

The study grants would have to deal with a set of related questions. One is the question of feasibility. This would entail a survey of the available materials that could meet the requirement of having alternative pedagogies available from which students could select the one they preferred. The number of different alternatives that is made available to a group of students to produce preference data also is important. One reason is that students have to learn how to make the decisions required by this condition and to do this they need to have the opportunity to learn what the alternatives mean to them. The cost and effectiveness of the alternative pedagogies with different kinds of students also has to be determined. Sampling is an important consideration since students from a variety of backgrounds and studying in a variety of institutions each of which provided them with a set of options would be needed. To collect the required data on student preferences for pedagogies as suggested necessitates a "free" economy, one in which the alternatives can compete with each other for students in a particular college or university setting. The research design should *not only* allow students to learn with pedagogies of their choice but also should assign some students to nonpreferred pedagogies. This would make it possible to determine what effect, if any, preferential matching has upon the outcomes for cognitive, affective, and skill learning. Some learning models for example, would predict that not having the use of the preferred pedagogy would produce less learning because of reduced motivation.

Recommendation 2: Development projects should be funded to design models for measuring input and output and to evaluate measuring instruments and procedures for educational systems using each model.

Models as well as appropriate measuring instruments and procedures are needed to provide a rationale for the development of instruments and to validate them. The measuring instruments and procedures would have to be developed for both input and output parameters and should cover a variety of indices.

Recommendation 3: Development projects should be funded to create and test models of student and faculty incentive and reward systems based upon both psychological and economic data and theory.

These models and their implications would be based upon available data and theory. They would be designed to permit an institution of higher education to make available pedagogical alternatives in ways that allow the alternatives to compete with one another. They also would reveal the critical conditions for empirical study.

Recommendation 4: Research projects should be funded to collect data on student preferences for pedagogical alternatives and to study statistical interaction effects between (or among) student characteristics and pedagogies.

The research would have to be designed to look at the question of preferences in many, but selected, institutions. The pedagogies would be related to the dimensions of a research design, and the conditions would have to provide the needed measures and allow for the analysis. The results of the projects established under the first three recommendations should be related to the planning and conduct of this research.

Grouped and Bounded Learning Environments

A visit to a college or university campus reveals that the academic rooms almost always are used for a lecture, less often for a seminar or a laboratory demonstration or experiment. It is in this sense that these spaces can be said to house grouped and bounded (in both length of time and in scheduled time, as well as in topic) learning environments. They are referred to here as the "conventional," or traditional, ones used in higher education because they dominate the scene today and are being built for use in the educational institutions of tomorrow! In them students are "taught" as a group, and the instruction takes place in a specific number of predetermined slots of time for all who enroll. The students are expected to enter the room at one time, to take a course together, and to be minimally responsive and reactive to what goes on. Being "together" seldom means that the students interact with each other in the classroom to either relearn or learn. The set of conditions characterizing Grouped and Bounded Learning Environments can be represented as a point on a continuum that also contains the other two learning environments included in the symposium.

One of the most widely discussed and frequently adopted changes in programs of instruction is the time allowed. Carroll's learning model equates time with aptitude for the type of learning involved. Many schools are shifting to a three-year rather than a four-year curriculum for a bachelor's degree. But, this is not a manipulation of time in the sense that Dr. Carroll uses it as equivalent to aptitude. In Medicine, where competencies are a primary concern, the changes in curricula consist more in time changes and in shifts in sequence than they do in pedagogy changes. However, while competency is a more valid benchmark than the time available for learning in an academic program, learning environments have tended to be bounded by time. This has the significant effect of making aptitude the determiner of successful completion if other factors are equal and if we accept Dr. Carroll's theory. If we liken education to the process of aging wines, then simply keeping the student in the collegiate bottle for the right length of time is all that is necessary to produce a finished product, according to these simplistic manipulations of the time allowed. The processes in making wine go on in a closed and stable environment and depend more on the nature of the raw materials put into the environment than upon the characteristics of the environment. With students in a learning environment the situation is different. We do not think that most academics really believe in the wine model for students; however, many critics appear to act as if they do. Many administrators also get trapped as indicated by their predilection to adjust programs in terms of time rather than in terms of what the student is to learn to do. Time should be a dependent variable, a result derived from an academic plan, and not an independent variable.

Alternative pedagogies are the means by which a fixed set of objectives relating to knowledge, skills, and values are to be achieved by the educational system. Pedagogies that are truly alternatives are designed to develop the same competencies. While admittedly it is much more difficult to enumerate competencies than to adjust the time allowed for study, and even more difficult to get academic and professional groups to agree on those competencies which they feel are a minimal set for a person completing a degree, it is nevertheless true that that is the task which the academic community should be working on. It is probably necessary to work in stages until it has achieved an acceptable approximation of what the group would accept since this is not an established and accepted way of defining their task.

Toward the end of defining educational objectives, whether it is for conventional instruction or more personalized environments, there is an evolving educational technology. It is a development of the fifties and sixties. Relative to the age of the university system it is very young, but it seems to be growing rapidly. This is a technology that involves ideas and methodology, not just hardware. To some extent its growth has been stimulated by support from the larger external environment in which we live. Thus the clamoring for an accountable educational system. You have to know what it is you expect to produce by the system in order to hold it accountable. If there are no agreed upon objectives, then anything that is produced has to be accepted as a useful outcome. Those of us who have worked with teachers and professors to develop statements of objectives for the purpose of defining the focus of an educational program know full well how difficult that task is and how much it is resisted in its accomplishment by those more used to other, older ways allowing them more freedom and the illusion of success no matter what they do. Some of this resistance may be due to the technique and the technology itself which is used by the programs attempting to accomplish a technological solution to their problems. Undoubtedly their techniques can be improved upon, but in addition, there seems to be an inherent problem in the technology of developing objectives which is difficult for a faculty to do. This fact raises questions. One of them is the question of how to identify objectives. Another is how to get agreement on objectives by the faculty involved. Any research plan using alternative pedagogies depends critically on the use of a single set of objectives for all of the alternatives.

Probably related to the problem of getting agreement is the fact that one of the most difficult concepts to get across to faculty is that the list of objectives is a specification of the *minimum* level that many students will achieve just as they do now. One result of better established and organized learning produced through the use of technology and the time saved for the learner with high aptitude is the opportunity to achieve even more.

The reports we have heard indicate that in spite of the difficulties, it is possible to get agreement on objectives and to develop sets of them that are acceptable to groups. The accomplishment of this step often is underrated in its contribution to the entire effort. It is a step which when accomplished in a non-trivial way results in a great deal of re-thinking of courses and curricula typically with greater sensitivity to the psychological, typically the learning problems of the students, but also to the organizational questions and the priorities involved in presenting information, concepts and principles to students. It is interesting to relate this step of getting agreement on objectives to what happens conventionally. In the conventional situation agreement on objectives is achieved "after the fact" rather than "before the fact." In this older mode of doing business, the book is written and published. Then agreement, at least to an extent, is achieved when other instructors choose it as their text.

It is apparent that significant innovations can and are taking place within the grouped and bounded learning environments. Where this is the case, the institution, in general, carries on business as usual in most other areas and it accommodates the changes. Stice and Hereford report this initial phase of their efforts at Austin as did Hurst for Purdue and Miller for the many institutions using technological aids. Not all of the technologies have the same potential impact on the institution, nor do they all serve as catalyst for change or as instruments in their own right, but most do. It is important to consider the implications of the change agent function of the technologies. Also this function should be considered in relation to each institution's long-range plans for change, since some technologies will be more acceptable initially than others and since each does result in review and deep analysis of instruction in both its content and process dimensions if it is done correctly and seriously. Once started, changes do take place in the way the faculty and the institution do business, in the attitude toward teaching and in the long-range planning of curricula to keep it consistent with changes in areas of study, particularly in the professions. In this sense technology is not just an episodic change agent, it is one that integrates changes and blends them into a larger more coherent conception with its own potential for growth and development. Through the use of many of the technologies themselves the organizing and evolving process itself can be facilitated. Which technology is used first and what technologies are used in particular combinations seem to be questions which, at this point in time, are less critical than the simple questions about the process of getting started and of gaining some experience in the use of one or more of them. A pluralism of technologies is certainly indicated for larger segments of instruction such as courses. Options should not be closed out, priority is to be given to change for the improvement of learning not to a particular technology just because it is inexpensive or simple.

Professor Arthur Luehrmann, from Dartmouth, correctly takes the position that we should not expect that computers will only reduce the manpower requirements for managing instruction (CMI) and for delivering instruction (CAI). While he acknowledges these goals and their value to the educational industry, he quickly points out a much more profound effect of the computer on students which education must recognize and make maximum use of. This unique contribution of computers is the way in which the student's knowledge of computing can affect the content and intellectual structure of his whole education and determine in profound ways the manner and mode with which he relates to problems. Luehrmann's thesis is "...that computing is a new and fundamental resource in the same sense that reading, writing, and mathematics are fundamental resources." With respect to the way institutions relate to computers, Luehrmann proposes that the model be the university library. The library is a "cost center," not a "profit-and-loss center." It is justified on the value of the service it provides. Using this model, Dartmouth provides computing services to all—faculty and students alike— and operates its time-sharing system (DTSS) with Basic as its programming language. Not only does it serve the campus, but also thirty other institutions. Of the 300, or more, terminals that can access the system from the campus, about 130 can be processed simultaneously. Both funded and unfunded users are served and the bills of the unfunded accounts are paid for in the end by transferring general funds of the college into them. The total computer center budget is about $1.2 million for Dartmouth usage. With 4,000 students, the average cost is about $300. per student per year, or approximately 9% of their annual tuition fee.

261

Project COMPUTe is an effort to develop and distribute course materials dealing with computer use. It is at Dartmouth, funded by NSF, and available to faculty members at any institution. Its goal is to publish and disseminate approximately 20 textbooks or monographs. Awards are made to individuals whose publications relate to new and interesting uses of the computer in education. This project is designed to fill the gap or shortage of good materials for use in courses where the use of a computer makes sense.

Recommendation 5: That funds be provided to selected university centers meeting a set of criteria with respect to educational technology and scholarship. Each would serve as an Educational Experimental Station. And among its functions it would support projects like COMPUTe. This would mean both support to the authors of texts that use computers, of CAI materials and of CMI programs and assistance in making these materials and programs useful to the educational industry.

Professor Robert N. Hurst, Department of Biological Sciences at Purdue University, described a very successful use of technology, the Audio-Tutorial system of instruction (A-T). It too is a child of the sixties, a teenaged technology. Beginning with the caveat that you cannot legislate change in Education and get a viable effort, Hurst quotes the Carnegie Commission's *Fourth Revolution* on the criteria that should be used to determine whether technology should be employed in an instructional program..." the learning task to be performed should be essential to the course of instruction, and...the task should be performed better with the use of technology." He reports that Dr. Postlethwait began the A-T system at Purdue out of frustration with the lecture methods for heterogeneous groups of students, therefore it is important to distinguish between a lecture on tape and a tutorial on tape. The latter is a concept which itself is a technological development. The tapes are prepared using a plan that begins with a task analysis and moves from it to objectives. This set of steps is common to almost all of the technologies. In addition, the tapes require the student to do things. Audio tapes were used because they were available, durable and inexpensive to produce and use reliably. Professor Hurst reports that A-T is a "now" technology. Critical to the design and use of A-T is the procedure by which the tape leads students, logically, from one experience to another. They systematically get the student to the desired performance level as specified in statements of objectives. The tape serves as the integrating vehicle. The presentation is conversational and pacing is individualized, allowing the student to stop, back up, or to replay, as necessary. Also important is the fact that A-T frees the hands and eyes to integrate with other experiences. In practice A-T is not always audiotape; 8 mm film is also used. In 1969, the concept of learning for mastery was introduced; learning time is now the dependent variable. Students take the time they require to achieve the specified minimal level of mastery. Mini-courses are the basic element of the system. These "little" courses, each with a beginning and ending, are designed around a single topic. Upon completion of a mini-course the student is given feedback through reports of his performance on an oral and written quiz.

Since the students learn for mastery, all redundancy can be eliminated. Experience at Purdue resulted in the elimination of 25% of the redundant material that had been in two conventional courses. This illustrates the realization of the Carnegie Commission's "Less Time—More Options."

One of the problems with A-T is *management,* and experience indicates that the approach could be benefited substantially by a CMI capability.

Recommendation 6: That a research project be funded to develop a CMI system and machine independent program capable of handling A-T mini-courses, the tests and feedback to students.

Professor David Miller's presentation included a definition of educational technology; namely, that of Norman MacKinzie—"the systematic study of the means whereby educational ends are achieved." The main thrust of Professor Miller's paper is to present the wide range of low-cost technologies now available for use in higher education. Consistent with Professor Hurst, he proposes three criteria that determine the spread of usage: (1) satisfy an educational need as seen by the instructor; (2) readily available and convenient to use; (3) relatively low in cost to student, instructor and institution.

Professor Miller has developed a "large class" and an "individual study model" which can accommodate all of the low-cost technology. Each model offers a way to increase the student-to-faculty ratio. The first uses an increased class size. The order of priority of three technologies examined for manner of use, cost, convenience and availability are: (1) the overhead projector; (2) slides; and (3) film. His second model covers the variety of individual uses of technology: "the challenge of designing successful systems that provide individualized opportunities for guided self-study depend heavily on low-cost people and, when appropriate and available, low-cost technology."

Recommendation 7: That the higher education community's needs would be best met if an information service and evaluation center were funded. It could provide data, both technical specifications and cost and also serve as a clearing house for experience data provided by center studies and user reports. Institutions could be kept current on usage and on materials available as well as techniques to produce materials for low-cost devices. Ideally this function would be included in the set provided by the Educational Experimental Station.

Professor James Bess' paper "Latent Environmental Effects of Educational Technology," covered an area of study that is badly in need of research. He concerned himself with the *measurement* of effects of new or experimental instructional technology. Not only is there the obvious need to assess the changes in the learner as broadly as possible, but also in the environment in which the learner lives and works to acquire knowledge, attitudes and skills. Bess begins with a discussion of variables that might be used in studies of technology. In collecting data relating to the environment it would be desirable to have information before and after the technology was introduced. The difference could provide a measure of change, and, if sensitive enough, an index to the nature of the changes. Changes in faculty are a potentially interesting, but difficult set of data to acquire.

Professor Bess deals with the interpersonal environment of the campus and examines variables relating to the impact of teaching-learning technologies on students. He identifies conflicts between the needs of the students and the aims of the curriculum, e.g., immediate vs. future, subjective and interpersonal knowledge and skills vs. objective vocationally related information. While the two sets are related they unfortunately are often opposed to one another "...particularly in bounded, conventional systems of higher education, designers of new technologies have not adequately comprehended the synergistic nature of institutional and student needs and have concentrated on the latter." Bess argues for "A much more comprehensive conceptualization of the environmental conditions requisite to the satisfaction of both affective and cognitive learning...." While he recognizes that mastery of academic knowledge and skills can contribute significantly to one's self-perceptions and feelings of worth, he points out that the established pattern of the institution to concentrate on this is also the primary thrust of the educational technologies. To change this it is necessary for faculty to recognize that the out-of-class activity of students has a direct relationship to the in-class learning.

The nature of the relationships among the technology, the environment and student's growth and development should be explicated. "Beyond the measurement problems in evaluating the effects of new instructional technologies on students are a whole host of other environmental factors particularly those involving the faculty." He summarizes by pointing out that "...learning which affects the whole person requires careful design of the total environment in which the process takes place. In bounded conventional systems, it is unlikely that new instructional technologies will result in profound benefits without positive social system reinforcement." Measurement of the attitudes in the environment in which new instructional technologies are introduced will reveal the presence, or absence, of values which support long-lasting learning and which encourage attention to student growth and development. In our opinion this argument supports the following:

Recommendation 8: That research be supported to develop measures and experimental procedures for assessing the impact of different technologists on various institutional elements.

Recommendation 9: That research and development of a fairly extensive nature be funded to work on problems of social and attitudinal conditions in the environment surrounding technological developments — the ripple effects.

Recommendation 10: That support be provided for the development of methodology and instruments as well as studies of affective and sociological effects of technology.

Characterizations of the host environments in ways that reveal their receptivity or hostility and their ability to accommodate the changes required to make individualizing technology work well, are an important national educational priority. The interpersonal environment of both faculty innovators and student users is a significant unknown that requires substantial analysis and study.

Recommendation 11: That institutional research be supported to (a) develop ways of using new instructional technologies to produce a better relationship between the students' academic and non-academic life; and (b) support studies of the "ripple effects" of technologies within the institution.

Individualized, Bounded Learning Environments

The individualized, bounded learning environments represent the efforts, typically of one or two more enterprising, risk-taking faculty members, to change an institution's way of doing business. The changes are a matter of degree, and there is a large gray area between the things described the first day and those covered on the second.

Professor Bunderson and his colleagues at Brigham Young University represent a joining of forces in that he and some of his colleagues at the University of Texas moved to B.Y.U. in 1972 to consolidate the NSF funded TICCIT project with MITRE Corporation. This consolidation fits what has been referred to as the "critical mass" requirement for personnel in a significant educational technology effort. The project effort is a team phenomenon involving a university and a not-for-profit corporation working with federal funds. MITRE personnnel are responsible for systems engineering and the B.Y.U. faculty for the instructional design specifications for the CAI system and the courseware. Professor Bunderson acknowledges the importance of the institutional and extra-institutional attitudinal and sociological problems but does not deal with them. He also describes the immediate "context" or organization at B.Y.U. in which this project is housed.

Professor Bunderson deals with the "...disciplined design approach to the solution of educational problems and the interdisciplinary cross-fertilization between the designers and developers..." He points out a significant but not widely recognized point in this connection, namely, "It is the explicit recognition and use of human goals and values,...in a rigorous, empirically based process of design and development that provides the critical distinction between a design science and a natural science."

The paper deals with design goals, institutional level goals, effectiveness goals for individual students, and goals for educators. This is an interesting taxonomy that could have generalizable value to the emerging educational technology. Even more significant in the long run are the concepts and techniques described. This is one of the most developed presentations of educational technology as a process available. It reflects the concern and attention to the empirical and conceptual base needed to produce a vigorous educational technology.

Recommendation 12: That funds be provided to develop a handbook describing and illustrating courseware development techniques.

Recommendation 13: That funds be provided to develop management information, including role (job) descriptions for the personnel involved in instructional systems development and evaluation.

Dr. Parry demonstrated the PLATO IV system and described its operation. The system is one of a kind and is not a production item in the inventory of any company. It uses components such as Control Data Corporation Cyber-73 computer, an Owens-Illinois plasma display panel, Magnavox terminals and computer-controlled accessories developed at the University of Illinois (random access image selector, audio device, and touch sensitive surface on the screen). Remote communication has to be over either microwave or cable TV to meet projected cost figures, but the system can communicate to remote users, as was the case for the demonstration at the symposium, by normal telephone circuitry.

Lessons for use on PLATO are written by faculty in the TUTOR author language which only exists on that system but which is apparently easily learned.

This is a large computer utility dedicated to instruction. Its design was based upon an effort to minimize the cost of delivery of instruction. While the projected cost figures have not been met, the system is operational and impressive in its capabilities and in the quality of the delivery.

The primary recommendation following from this report has already been activated. NSF has already funded an evaluation project at ETS for both PLATO and TICCIT, as indicated in the paper by Dr. Anastasio.

Stice and Hereford's presentation covers what might be called a management technology for instruction. PSI, the personalized system of instruction, often referred to as the "Keller Plan," was conceived by Dr. Fred S. Keller in its most current form. A number of variations exist even on the Stony Brook campus where it is being used in Education, Physics, Psychology, and Biology, to name a few departments. Like A-T, the lecture is greatly deemphasized as a medium of information transfer. In fact, it is used as a *reward;* the professor only gives his lecture on a topic in which he is personally interested and about which he feels he has something worthwhile to say. Students who attend only do so because they *want* to.

Keller lists the following five essential features of PSI: (1) self-pacing; (2) unit-mastery for advancement; (3) the lecture as a reward; (4) written interactions between student and teacher; and (5) the use of proctors for testing (often repeatedly), immediate scoring, tutoring, and inter-personal interaction.

The University of Texas at Austin began with PSI in 1966 in Psychological Foundations of Secondary Education. Now there are thirty courses taught in fifteen departments in six colleges, and all without administrative coercion. This is not to suggest that there are no snags or problems. Stice and Hereford give a balanced report and indicate that they had problems and were led to seek funding from the outside. The Sloan Foundation, of New York City, is now underwriting the program for two years. The funds are being used to develop (or redesign) twelve PSI courses and to evaluate course data in an attempt to answer a set of questions. Both formative ("internal") and summative (comparative) research and evaluation studies are in process. An important area of interest is feedback to instructors and proctors. The variety of courses on the one campus makes it possible to study PSI across courses, departmental, and college boundaries so as to study the method itself. Even basic problems in educational research are being raised and studied since the methods that were developed for grouped and bounded learning environments do not apply to individualized and unbounded environments.

Also of interest is the study of student characteristics in relation to the effectiveness of PSI courses. This is a topic of interest to a number of the technologies because it is so fundamental to the individualization of instruction.

Recommendation 14: That funds be provided to summarize the research on individual differences so as to identify characteristics of students and working hypotheses regarding their interaction with conditions and variables in learning environments.

The cost issues were not dodged, and the pattern common to the technologies utilizing more hardware seems to be present with PSI as well. "Cost and time will be relatively high during the initial offering of a PSI course but will drop in subsequent semesters to a level comparable to that for more traditional forms of instruction."

Having developed a course and the required materials, cost benefits could result if it could be transferred to another institution.

Recommendation 15: That funds be made available to study the transfer problems associated with PSI courses and other technologies as well.

Professor Duncan Hansen's paper is not only one of the most fact-packed but also one of the more controversial papers presented in the symposium. (See Dr. Seidel's discussion.) He cites a number of interesting and relevant research studies conducted at FSU relating mainly to CMI. His position is "Using a computer-managed instructional (CMI) model to encompass computer-assisted instruction (CAI), simulation, adaptive testing, natural language dialogues, media management, scheduling, record keeping and evaluation, the potential of each of these components as training procedures becomes most enhanced." The studies he refers to were reported in technical reports to funding sources. They are organized into four catagories: learner strategies, training strategies, validation strategies, and computer system strategies.

Professor Hansen argues that the emphasis should be on a management model not on technology. For him this means the management of the entire enterprise for instruction, not just the newer technological aspects. While this is certainly a valid point, the distinction between the management technology and the delivery technology is interesting. However, it also is the case that both are educational technologies and both are necessary. Hansen's point is that the need now is for a computer-managed instructional (CMI) model that encompasses CAI and a whole host of other functions. Like Professor Lumsden, however from a different but related perspective, Professor Hansen argues for a strong and multifaceted national research effort. "The primary research need is to extend the set of available indices reflecting training." A "four strategy theme approach" is described for the work at Florida State University (FSU): learner strategies, training strategies, validation strategies, and computer system strategies.

Learner-strategy research dealt with: rule learning; behavioral-objective learning; memory; subjective organization; anxiety and curiosity; and graphics. Several interesting findings were reported. For example, "Results of research into the role of behavioral objectives in learning and into subjective organization have led investigators to feel that these are less rewarding areas." Hansen also reports that for rule learning, "1. Instruction should present general instructional objectives to inform the student as to what is expected of him. 2. Presentation of rule statement can prevent the 'discovery' of an incorrect rule. 3. Presentation of sample test items gives the student a chance for practice and immediate feedback." Probably more controversial than other data were those reported relating to the anxiety and curiosity research.

Professor Hansen recommends several lines of research for the future in each of the four areas. One of the areas he mentions that also was mentioned repeatedly in the symposium was research on the processes of revision.

Recommendation 16: That funds be provided to support the systematic study of the process and methodology of materials revision based upon empirical data.

Recommendation 17: That funds be provided to conduct research on adaptive and tailored testing, especially as it relates to student evaluation and to materials revision.

Professor Brennan presented "A Model for the Use of Achievement Data and Time Data in an Instructional System." He considered both theoretical and practical issues involving the use of these two types of data in evaluating an instructional system. The two previous recommendations also could be appropriately made as inferences from Professor Brennan's paper.

Professor Brennan presents a taxonomy of test data and time data for evaluation purposes, both students and instruction. His thesis is that evaluation is a fundamental part of curriculum development, not merely an appendage added on after the fact. It requires planning as well as technological resources, especially research design, reliable and valid instruments, and data. He presents an evaluation model which uses achievement and time data and is generalizable to many modes of instruction as well as to instructional systems, provided they have clearly stated objectives while most of the literature currently available on evaluation treats the analysis of data using classical descriptive and inferential statistics. Brennan predicts that Bayesian and decision-theoretic techniques will play an increasingly important role in the evaluation of instructional systems.

Recommendation 18: That funds be provided to develop models and methods, including computer software, for the use of Bayesian statistics and decision theoretic statistical techniques to the range of relevant problems in educational technology.

Dr. Anastasio briefly reported on the NSF funded evaluation project at the Educational Testing Service (ETS) which is just beginning. An interesting aspect of this project is that a separate agency is being supported to evaluate these two CAI projects while they themselves are evolving. This provides an opportunity seldom enjoyed in education, namely, to permit the group doing the development to receive continuous and constructive input at a time when it can be useful rather than after the fact.

*Recommendation 19 :*That funds be made available to have independent evaluation studies made of a variety of educational technologies (e.g., A-T, Keller Plan, Video systems) while they are being developed.

Dr. Seidel, Human Resources Research Organization, raised many questions not only about the papers relating to individualized and bounded environments but also about general issues. For example, he felt that "...the discussion surrounding the concept of validity (whether it was concurrent, predictive or construct validity) to be interpreted differently by the various speakers. Secondly, the concept of evaluation and the concept of technology as means versus ends in themselves were unclear with respect to education. The concept of evaluation also seemed to have different meanings for different people although nowhere explicitly stated. Finally, the questions of incentives for faculty members to use technology, incentives for administrators to push the use of technology, and the guidelines for use of technology in an educational environment all seemed to be somewhat ambiguously touched upon and nowhere clarified to anyone's satisfaction.

"Nowhere did I find that we as a group ever came to grips with the definition of the concept of productivity ....However, more than once I noted the presence of cost/effectiveness as the paramount raison d'etre for the use of technology. Also, as noted above, technology was implicitly assumed to be inextricably interwoven with statements of ends or educational purposes. (The paper by Bess touched on important issues of measurement but unfortunately added to the means-end confusion.)"

"Perhaps the latter is the place to start to try to clarify my own position with respect to the ambiguities as I saw them in that conference. From our work at HumRRO, it has become quite clear to us that there are multiple purposes for using the computer as a new technology in education and that in only one of these purposes, that is, cost/effectiveness purpose, is it appropriate to talk about fixed objectives and fixed economics for making evaluations of alternative means of instruction. (We are including this discussion in our book.) But there are other purposes for which computers are also used (as I tried to indicate at the conference): Purposes such as computing literacy, enhancing the curricula for a discipline, providing computing opportunities as a tool and finally, overall educational reform using the computer. The concepts of validity, methodology for evaluation, as well as criteria of evaluation are all different dependent upon which of the above mentioned purposes are being prescribed. Dr. Filep made a strong case for the cost/effective use of technology in education. He noted that $29.9 billion was spent for higher education in 1971 and that in 1981 the expenditures are likely to jump to $46 billion. Yet as he indicated there will be the same number of learners. Therefore, in order to cut costs, educational technology can have a very important role to play. Note, however, that this approach, this premise, or this purpose, draws one into a closed box of evaluation in that it assumes objectives do not change and that economics do not change. Therefore, the whole concept of computers or other technology providing a "value added" capability cannot be addressed. Yet education can be viewed as an open-ended process leading to new objectives and having a general transfer value for the individual and for society."

"The other purposes noted above become more salient when one asks the question, 'Is the current educational model appropriate?'. The issues arose in one presentation discussing the concept of the PSI model where the individual making the presentation felt that the old exams are not appropriate despite an orientation towards the use of behavioral objectives. His question was how do you compare the results of the PSI program to the so-called conventional mode of presentation. My answer to this is quite simple: You cannot gain consensus on a criterion for measurement until you can agree on the objectives. Moreover, if new objectives are proposed, then the evaluation has to be made in terms of (a) the acceptance or not of the new objectives, and if they are accepted, (b) the effectiveness or viability of the technology towards meeting those objectives. But in no way is it appropriate to make a comparison of cost/effectiveness between old and new since you have added something to the instructional repertoire which was not present previously. In this case it generally means that you have enhanced the curricula of the discipline."

"The methodology and the criteria for evaluation become even more difficult to conceive of in classic terms when the goal of using technology (my interest being in use of the computer) is towards the process or experience of using the computer's technological capability as a tool for student growth. This is opposed to a purpose which focusses on a product as a result of the use of the technology, that product being mastery of some specified set of behavioral objectives. And when one stretches the purpose even further towards the affective domain such as creating a more positive attitude toward, and awareness of, the value of technology and learning in general, classic psychometrics are in no way relevant nor are mastery methods relevant for evaluating the worth of the technology for education. Humanistic judgments of acceptance and long-term, broad-ranging effects on the total person become the relevant criteria. Here is where I see substantial value for Bess' measurement interest (broad social effects)."

"In short, the purposes of education and the purposes for the use of the technology within a given role of education or educational model must be clearly stipulated in order that one can speak without ambiguity of the value of technology for education. Productivity similarly must be defined in terms of the purpose for which education is being provided as opposed to a simplistic implication from our industrial society (see, for example, Hagerty, *Educational Researcher,* October, 1972) towards increasing the number of units of output per unit time spent in the production process."

"Lastly, I was very pleased to hear the group address the problem of models for implementation of new technologies in terms of the organizational structures which might provide the most viable entities in order to make the development of such technology a feasible endeavor within education. Serious questions have to be considered concerning the role of a single orthodox institution in terms of its viability as the basis for implementing technology on any continuing basis. This is especially true for the development, dissemination and use of computer-based curricula. Development complexities, different instructional orientation, specialized personnel requirements, and unique financial burdens all require an innovative approach. The Discipline Center approach described by Art Luehrmann is one interesting type of model which is worthy of further elaboration and consideration by the federal government and perhaps by regional organizations. For example, as we discussed at one evening session, the state university system in New York might well designate curriculum development and evaluation to be carried out at one center and that center would do minimal amounts of operational teaching. The responsibility for actual delivery and use would occur at other institutions within the state system, etc."

Dr. Seidel's points are important and underscore several of the previously made recommendations. His comments relating to an empirical study reported in Professor Hansen's paper, however, do suggest a new recommendation.

Recommendation 20: That funds be provided to conduct research on the relative effectiveness of the following four CAI strategies: adaptive model; remediation-for-all; learner-choice; and no-remediation.

The reported data from Rivers' study, while interesting and provocative, were not definitive. Hansen's interpretation was challenged, or, at least, qualified by Seidel. It is significant enough to justify recommendation 20.

Personalized, Open Learning Environments

Dean Baldwin reports on a program using videotapes in Engineering Education now in operation at Colorado State University. Seventeen engineering colleges have offered these programs over the past nine years. This use of ITV systems is a significant fraction of the U.S. higher education experience in providing graduate instruction, for credit, at the student's place of employment. The SURGE program at Colorado State University is one of the largest and oldest. In surveying the on-going learning systems, Dean Baldwin reports that his data "....are crude, order-of-magnitude numbers..." The first national survey of these programs is now underway under the Chairmanship of Albert J. Morris. The study is called "The Cost-Effectiveness of Continuing Engineering Studies by Television." What is needed is a comparable study of applications in other areas such as undergraduate instruction. The results could provide guidance to institutions wanting to do similar things.

Recommendation 21: That a national survey be conducted to determine the nature, extent, cost, and benefits of video-based programs in different areas of Education, both professional and nonprofessional.

It is clear that video technology in higher education is becoming a more and more interesting way of relating to the existing needs for graduate instruction in engineering. But, Dean Baldwin also reported on the use of video instruction for undergraduates on campus, including a modified Keller plan and a career guidance program on dormitory CATV. Their extension of video technology at Colorado State University has interesting implications, but the extension is not limited to undergraduates. Video technology also is being used in Continuing Education to meet the needs of older (over 40) engineers, to the career guidance of young students and the "open learning concept." Many of the same materials can be used to meet these different needs.

Since SURGE, for example, has generated tapes and associated course materials for use in off-campus centers, it became a relatively simple matter to use them for other groups as well. Dean Baldwin reported a successful new use in summer school. In fact, one faculty member combined their use for the format of a Keller plan to make the learning environment more individualized. In addition, a lower-division elective course was offered during the regular semester, in the modified Keller method. Of interest is the fact that the video tape, in this case, was prepared by a professor who is on another faculty. This is only one way of achieving a shared distribution of materials. The liberalization of attitudes about sharing materials of this kind needs to be examined to determine a variety of ways of making materials more acceptable throughout the community of professors who are the consumers. Unlike other economic systems, the ultimate consumer, the student, does not now select the materials he pays for and uses.

Dean Baldwin feels that "....old budget practices...preclude a fair hearing of technically based instructional options." The most serious problem, in his view as a middle-level manager, is "the total lack of consideration which is given to capital outlay amortization in budget preparation..." He also points out that "tight budgets" are wedded to fixed labor costs and perpetuate the spiraling costs of a labor intensive system."

Recommendation 22: That a study be conducted to determine alternative budget models and associated materials that will be useful to universities and colleges wanting to adopt the new technologies.

Dean Zigerell points up the need for a reasonableness of evaluation perspective, the use in evaluation of what the project planners set as their goals and objectives. Separate from this is the question of whether they chose wisely and well in relation to the larger society and its needs. These are separate issues. We tend to overlook the former or confuse it with the latter. The Chicago TV College, an eighteen-year old effort, is an extension of the City Colleges of Chicago, a public two-year community college. It is interesting that the TV College is now a part of a unit—the Learning Resources Laboratory—which will provide learning specialists and a variety of instructional materials for the seven colleges making up the City Colleges of Chicago. This fact should be viewed in the light of the points previously made about the sociological factors and the context in which technology must grow and develop and the recommendation made about Education Experimental Station needs. It would be interesting to note what the critical factors were that led to this shift. Also of interest would be the institutional administrative plan since these kinds of information could be useful to other groups contemplating a similar development.

The Chicago TV College also represents a multifaceted facility. It not only produces materials for television broadcast, it also produces videocassettes for the Chicago area. The latter allows for the greater personalization of instruction. Plans are being made to use four channels of an ITFS system as well. The audience potential is virtually unknown, but assumed to be "inexhaustible."

Recommendation 23: That funds be provided to study the audience needs and desires in major metropolitan areas and to study the alumni of the Chicago TV College to see what career and long-range impact their TV instruction has had.

Other previously made recommendations are also supported by Dean Zigerell's paper, especially the recommendation that the problems of transferring technology to other institutions be studied. It is particularly interesting in this regard to note that a consistent 40 percent of TV College-credit students have regularly expressed a desire to become teachers. As a result, a number of relevant courses exist for teachers and could be transferred to other locations.

Recommendation 24: That funds be made available to (a) conduct a market analysis for the teacher education TV courses to determine the demand for them in other locations, and (b) to determine the problems and cost of transferring them.

The need is for an analysis of the problems of interinstitutional transfer. Undoubtedly this is rooted in attitudes of faculty, but the problem is sufficiently serious and promises cost benefits that need to be taken advantage of.

Brian Lewis presents a fact-packed paper; a comprehensive account of the British Open University's main teaching arrangements. Also included are data based upon their experience since 1969, when it was established by Royal Charter. Teaching, however, began in 1971, but the two years were filled with activities that were new and unprecedented approaches to problems in higher education. This is the first "...full-scale home-based, multimedia system of higher education." It provides opportunities at both the undergraduate and postgraduate levels to all who are precluded from realizing their educational aims in an existing institution. In spite of these limitations in time and breadth of scope, twenty thousand students actually paid their fees and started in January, 1971. As many as 80 percent stayed in, and 75 percent passed their examinations. 1972 saw a repetition of this, and the current student population is approximately forty thousand students.

The main student location is the home, but four teaching resources are available: postal packages of home-study materials; television and radio; local study centers; and short residential summer schools. The first of these constitutes the "core" content of the courses. To get a degree, a student must successfully complete six to eight courses of study at a rate of not more than two courses per year. Each course requires twelve hours of home study per week for nine months. The students are adults over twenty-one, but plans to admit younger students exist.

The courses give students many things to do, and each study package is self-contained and sustains activity for four to six weeks. Radio and television supplement and complement the core materials. Students return the homework within specific time limits.

The constraints experienced by the "faculty" are more in the development of materials than in their delivery. Assigned work is partially processed by computers. There are tutor-marked assignments as well. For each homework assignment the computer generates a detailed statement of how well the student has done. Progress reports are made to regional offices and to students. Student opinion is routinely solicited, and questionnaires are regularly sent to representative samples of students. These kinds of feedback are processed. O.U. has its own Institute of Educational Technology which, among other activities, has primary responsibility for guiding and informing the process of self-improvement.

Dr. Lewis reported in useful detail the problems and processes in course development. Underestimation of the task and limited resources have burdened the staff members, but "...the production of quality courses is now merely difficult, rather than impossible." It takes two to three weeks to produce an adequate first draft, which then needs to be tried out or tested with a sample of appropriate students. Then revision follows, and the new draft is tested—a test-revise-retest cycle—until the author is satisfied. Each new cycle adds three to four weeks, at least. In addition, the author must devise appropriate homework. In doing this, he must specify exactly the plan for marking to be used by the computer. Patterns of staff differentiation in function have emerged and are described.

The use of "self-contained blocks" of four to eight units each, authored separately, has resulted in an effective strategy for producing courses that run thirty-six weeks' duration. Some one-half courses or one-third courses also are being developed.

Recommendation 25: That funds be provided to develop, out of the O.U. experience, for example, requirements and specifications for as yet undeveloped aids to course development, so as to increase the productivity of the course development process.

Recommendation 26: That funds be provided to plan and develop a set of courses to be used by an open university network.

This recommendation was made by Chancellor Lipson. He included in his paper a detailed proposal for such an effort. His bench mark is 300 courses, and he estimates a $60 million per year cost for a five-year period. A cooperative effort is envisioned for: (a) production of course materials; (b) systems of student access; (c) proficiency tests; and (d) evaluation of the system.

Professor Klare reported on "readability" studies of correspondence materials like the "core materials" used in the O.U. At least twenty-nine computer programs currently exist for applying readability formulas to large bodies of text. The studies indicated some interesting relationships between reading difficulty and drop out. These studies of USAFI (United States Armed Forces Institute) data are from thirty courses. A rank-order correlation of .87 was found between the readability scores and the probability that students would send in all of their lessons. Clearly readability is related to persistence.

Recommendation 27: That funds be provided to conduct experimental studies of the relationship of comprehension and persistence to readability by using materials designed to meet a single set of objectives, but written at different levels of readability.

Recommendation 28: That funds be provided to develop interactive versions of readability programs to aid authors in developing materials for targeted student users.

Professor Yelon addressed himself to the papers by Baldwin and Lewis with respect to measurement and evaluation. In his opinion Dean Baldwin did not look at all important productivity measures; he did not mention the application (transfer) of learning or the achieving of more objectives. Lewis omitted student learning in his summary of the O.U. experience.

Recommendation 29: That funds be provided to develop a comprehensive list and appropriate guides for collecting productivity data in evaluation of educational technology programs.

Yelon also raised one of the sensitive questions, procedures for applying social science to development, delivery, and evaluation. Probably the single most promising and cost-effective solution to the problems of educational technology is a good social science theory and techniques for applying it. Therefore our final recommendation based on this symposium is the following:

Recommendation 30: That funds be provided to develop social science and behavioral theories that relate to the problems of educational, and especially, instructional technology.